DATE DUE

GAYLORD			PRINTED IN U.S.A.

CRIME and CRIMINAL BEHAVIOR

CRIME and CRIMINAL BEHAVIOR

GENERAL EDITOR

William J. Chambliss

George Washington University

KEY ISSUES IN *Crime* AND PUNISHMENT

SAGE | reference

Los Angeles | London | New Delhi
Singapore | Washington DC

Los Angeles | London | New Delhi
Singapore | Washington DC

FOR INFORMATION:

SAGE Publications, Inc.
2455 Teller Road
Thousand Oaks, California 91320
E-mail: order@sagepub.com

SAGE Publications India Pvt. Ltd.
B 1/I 1 Mohan Cooperative Industrial Area
Mathura Road, New Delhi 110 044
India

SAGE Publications Ltd.
1 Oliver's Yard
55 City Road
London EC1Y 1SP
United Kingdom

SAGE Publications Asia-Pacific Pte. Ltd.
33 Pekin Street #02-01
Far East Square
Singapore 048763

Vice President and Publisher: Rolf A. Janke
Senior Editor: Jim Brace-Thompson
Project Editor: Tracy Buyan
Cover Designer: Candice Harman
Editorial Assistant: Michele Thompson
Reference Systems Manager: Leticia Gutierrez
Reference Systems Coordinator: Laura Notton

Golson Media
President and Editor: J. Geoffrey Golson
Author Manager: Lisbeth Rogers
Layout and Copy Editor: Stephanie Larson
Proofreader: Mary Le Rouge
Indexer: J S Editorial

Printed in the United States of America.

Library of Congress Cataloging-in-Publication Data

Key issues in crime and punishment / William Chambliss, general editor.

    v. cm.

    Contents: v. 1. Crime and criminal behavior — v. 2. Police and law enforcement — v. 3. Courts, law, and justice — v. 4. Corrections — 5. Juvenile crime and justice.

    Includes bibliographical references and index.

    ISBN 978-1-4129-7855-2 (v. 1 : cloth) — ISBN 978-1-4129-7859-0 (v. 2 : cloth) — ISBN 978-1-4129-7857-6 (v. 3 : cloth) — ISBN 978-1-4129-7856-9 (v. 4 : cloth) — ISBN 978-1-4129-7858-3 (v. 5 : cloth)

    1. Crime. 2. Law enforcement. 3. Criminal justice, Administration of. 4. Corrections. 5. Juvenile delinquency. I. Chambliss, William J.

    HV6025.K38 2011

    364—dc22   2010054579

11 12 13 14 15 10 9 8 7 6 5 4 3 2 1

Contents

Introduction
The Complexity of Crime and Criminal Behavior

Pick up any major daily city newspaper, or search its Website, and peruse the different sections looking for crime stories. You may be surprised at the vast array of behaviors that are incorporated under the category of crime. Of course there will be assaults, robberies, and occasionally murders and rapes reported in the main sections of the paper. But if you look further into the other sections, you will discover that a rock star has been arrested for assaulting his partner, a movie star for drunken driving or shoplifting, a businesswoman for fraud, or a student for using a fake I.D. What this exercise should alert you to are the vast array of behaviors that are defined as criminal, and are therefore incorporated into the study of crime and criminal behavior.

In this volume, authors address a variety of topics under the wide umbrella of crime and criminal behavior. The authors examine the historical contexts of each topic and present pervasive arguments for and against the ways in which legislators and courts have defined and responded to behaviors defined as criminal. While some issues seem to have very clear policy and legal responses, many of the authors are quick to point to arguments that make policy decisions much more difficult. There are noteworthy sociological characteristics connecting the wide range of topics.

Crimes with sensitive subjects, such as crimes against women, children, and minorities, have a complexity that warrants significant study. Articles dealing with sensitive subjects range from Jennifer Grimes's article on hate crimes to Wendelin Hume's analysis of child abuse to Erica Fields and Alisha Kirchoff's article on date rape. Definitions of these types of crimes vary from jurisdiction to jurisdiction, and from one time period to another. Proponents for statutory rape laws and child abuse laws cite the fact that minors are in desperate need of protection from predators due to their inability to successfully defend or care for themselves. On the other hand, criminal laws prohibiting child abuse, hate crimes, and domestic violence are often criticized due to their lack of standard legal definitions and for the negative effects these laws may have against structures like the family. Similarly, opponents of statutory rape laws believe that the law has not kept up with contemporary moral standards, where many teenagers engage in sexual relations under the legal age. In the case of hate crimes, opponents feel that these laws are redundant because they are punishing for already punishable offenses.

Also important in this volume are crimes that are carried out by groups and larger organizations or states. These types of crimes are typified in the articles on terrorism, war crimes, civil disobedience, and corporate crime. The ways in which these crimes are dealt with, such as war crimes, can create precedents that affect the functioning of the international community. For example, the Nuremberg Trial after World War II established the International Criminal Courts. These courts are defended because they can prosecute crimes that domestic courts are unable to prosecute. On the other hand, war crimes are problematic because of the anonymity of the actors and the fact that what constitutes a "war crime" often depends on which side is victorious.

Another theme present in this volume pertains to crimes that are difficult to prosecute. Internet crime, prescription drug abuse, and intellectual property crime are examples. While Internet crime leaves evidence that most Internet criminals cannot get rid of, victims of Internet crimes often do not realize that they have been subjected to criminal activity until much later, due to a lack of perceived likelihood that they will be victimized. The effort to fight prescription drug abuse has made strides in the creation of databases that help target offenders, but these databases are criticized for being potential breeches of confidentiality. Those who want to protect intellectual property are met with criticism that doing so violates free speech rights. The same problem of difficulty in enforcement applies to white collar and corporate crimes, which is why these offenses are often handled in civil rather than criminal courts.

Finally, there are crimes where there is a general disagreement on whether or not the behavior is harmful to society or the individuals involved. The chapters on euthanasia and assisted suicide, gun control, vagrancy and the homeless, prostitution, gambling, and marijuana all provide examples of these types of crimes. Typically, those in favor of laws against these activities are met with opposition demanding not only that the laws be changed, but that these behaviors be decriminalized completely. For example, those in favor of legalized gambling and marijuana use argue that criminalizing products and services in high demand leads to organized crime groups and public corruption. Proponents of legalization also see benefits in the potential for raising taxes. With respect to gambling, there is also the argument that criminalizing some forms of gambling while the state engages in other forms (lotteries, for example) is the ultimate hypocrisy.

Critics of legalizing gambling and marijuana argue, on the other hand, that legalizing these activities amounts to endorsing immorality and the social harms (e.g., gambling and drug addiction) they cause. Vagrancy laws are negatively seen as ignoring the root causes of homelessness, while offering safety to homeless individuals on the positive side. Either way, authors conclude that the current status of many of these laws leave a great deal to be discussed and potentially amended.

Crime and criminal behavior certainly encompasses a wide variety of subjects, and these authors provide many topics worthy of extensive debate within this umbrella. When examining crime and criminal behavior, it is necessary to determine what the laws are protecting, and at what cost.

William J. Chambliss
General Editor

DIFFERENT DRUMMERS

Jazz in the Culture of Nazi Germany

Michael H. Kater

New York   Oxford
OXFORD UNIVERSITY PRESS
1992

Oxford University Press

Oxford   New York   Toronto
Delhi   Bombay   Calcutta   Madras   Karachi
Petaling Jaya   Singapore   Hong Kong   Tokyo
Nairobi   Dar es Salaam   Cape Town
Melbourne   Auckland

and associated companies in
Berlin   Ibadan

Copyright © 1992 by Michael H. Kater

Published by Oxford University Press, Inc.,
200 Madison Avenue, New York, New York 10016

Oxford is a registered trademark of Oxford University Press

Library of Congress Cataloging-in-Publication Data
Kater, Michael H., 1937–
Different drummers : jazz in the culture of Nazi Germany /
Michael H. Kater.
p.   cm.   Includes bibliographical references and index.
ISBN 0-19-505009-6
1. Jazz—Germany—1931–1940—History and criticism.   2. Jazz—
Germany—1941–1950—History and criticism.   3. National socialism.
I. Title.   ML3509.G3K37   1992
781.65'0943'09043—dc20   91-17866

9 8 7 6 5 4 3 2 1

Printed in the United States of America
on acid-free paper

For my mother,
who introduced me to music

Swing is musical Hitlerism. There is a mass sense of "letting one's self go."

Professor Harry D. Gideonse, Columbia University,
quoted in the *New York Times,* 2 November 1938

A famous air ace and winner of the Knight's Cross once was asked what he would do, having returned to his quarters from an enemy mission. He replied: "I tune in to a radio station featuring dance music, lie down on my cot, and stop thinking until I get hungry."

Podium der Unterhaltungsmusik, 15 July 1943

Anything that starts with Ellington ends with an assassination attempt on the Führer!

SS-Sturmbannführer Hans Reinhardt, Gestapo
Hamburg, July 1944

Preface

It is impossible to begin this book without relating a couple of personal anecdotes, for had certain events in my life not occurred, it would probably not have been written.

In late 1959 I was a very young graduate student of history in Munich. I could not make up my mind whether to continue formal studies at the university or to go on playing vibraphone in jazz combos forever, as I had done at fraternity functions in Toronto and now was doing almost every night in the bohemian suburb of Schwabing. One evening I chanced upon a fancy club, near the university, which featured a quintet, including an excellent vibraphonist. When I asked him if I could sit in, the musician nodded in the direction of the drummer, a dapper, slender man with a dark complexion, who gracefully gave me permission to play. Having accompanied the group on a number of jazz standards, I was accorded a few words of encouragement by the drummer-bandleader when I left. His name was Freddie Brocksieper, and little did I know that decades hence I would meet him again in Munich-Schwabing, though under very different circumstances.

As it happened, I suppressed my urge to become a professional musician and instead became a historian—for better or worse. In the mid-1970s I decided to play again more seriously. I joined York University's jazz music department as a mature student and spent several years performing semiprofessionally with some of its better graduates, having changed my style from swing to post-bebop, "mainstream" jazz. Whenever research assignments led me to Germany, I would look for a chance to sit in on jazz groups. This is how I met Joe Viera, who held one of the few professorships in jazz in Europe and also led his own combo in Munich. He performed regularly at the annual international jazz festival in Burghausen (near the Austrian border), which he had cofounded, and where I joined his band once. Viera impressed me not only as a fine musician and teacher but also as a scholar. In his Schwabing house there was a huge archive, with shelves filled with material on the development of jazz in Europe. His aim, he told me, was to write the definitive history of European jazz after World War II. But what about jazz before 1945? Viera knew of only a few studies in that area, and of even fewer that covered jazz in Germany. He confessed that he was not ready to embark on such a project.

At the beginning of the 1980s, this conversation, more than any other factor, motivated me to engage in a serious study of jazz during the Third Reich. Further talks with Viera convinced me that, although this appeared to be an unlikely pairing, it would be worthwhile to analyze this relationship in some detail in order to find out more about the music as well as the nature of German fascism. This was also a period during which increasing investigations were being made into the social and cultural history of Nazi Germany; from this vantage point, a closer look at jazz might prove enlightening.

When I began my research, the problem of sources seemed insurmountable. There were no easily definable primary sources and barely a dozen treatises on the subject. Among the latter, the book by Berlin record collector Horst H. Lange, which dealt with all aspects of German jazz from its beginnings through 1960, was by far the best. However, the fact that it had been published in 1966 already rendered it dated, and it contained not a single documentary reference. At the time my hope rested with the huge collection of unpublished records of the Reich Music Chamber, housed in the Berlin Document Center, yet I was not sure how much "jazz" material I would actually encounter there.

My research started in earnest in 1986, after Viera had convinced me that I would have to talk to as many eyewitnesses as possible. Referring primarily to musicians, he provided my first leads; it soon became clear, however, that there were two overlapping groups that also had to be interviewed if I was to gain a total picture of the era: jazz fans and impresarios.

As I commenced what was to turn into an incredibly long and arduous series of interviews, I was virtually handed over from one former musician to another, from one jazz fan to his or her friend. Sometimes these people lived not only provinces or countries but continents apart, and often they were well beyond retirement age. Especially in terms of musicians, I was lucky to be able to talk to several individuals just before they passed away; in one case I could not speak to him because he already lay near death, and another died three weeks after I had seen him.

Among the six or seven people who deserve my primary gratitude I cannot fail to mention Viera, who stepped in at a point where success and failure hung in the balance. Dietrich Schulz-Köhn not only graciously granted me numerous extended interviews and supplied me with many personal documents and artifacts but also facilitated important meetings with individuals from his colorful past. Eventually I met Hans Otto Jung, a distinguished musician both of jazz and the classics and a patron of the arts in the broadest sense, whose kindness knew no limits when it came to providing me with information, mountains of private papers, and the sort of hospitality accorded only to a friend. He and his wife,

Ursula, who also spared no effort to establish necessary connections for me, must be warmly thanked. It was through them that I met Werner Daniels, a retired Düsseldorf executive, who not only left me a copy of his wartime jazz newsletters but also shared insider information about many aspects of the music business in those days, as well as specific details concerning the situation at the front, where he had served. Kurt Michaelis also repeatedly provided general and specific information; I could always rely on him to answer what must have seemed the most trivial of questions. Finally, Thorsten Müller introduced me to what was left of the onetime Hamburg Swing scene; it was through his good offices that I was able to meet with and talk to several of Benny Goodman's former fans, who endured their own, peculiarly vicious, confrontation with the Gestapo.

I must thank all those individuals listed in the appendix of this book for their cooperation; as Joe Viera had prophesied, they supplied me with more information on jazz during the Third Reich than any archive could ever have contained. Nevertheless, I owe a large debt to the directors of the Federal Archive in Koblenz and the Berlin Document Center, particularly to Daniel P. Simon, who never refused my requests to see significant portions of the Reich Music Chamber records.

Throughout the present project, as well as in the past, I received generous assistance in the form of financial grants from the Social Sciences and Humanities Research Council of Canada, based in Ottawa. York University, which granted me a Walter L. Gordon Research Fellowship for 1990–91, has unflinchingly supported my efforts in financial as well as other respects. In Germany, I was able to count on the help of the German Academic Exchange Service (DAAD), as well as the Alexander von Humboldt-Stiftung.

While this book was still in manuscript form, I had the good fortune of having parts of it examined by experts in jazz who were also scholars and friends. My colleague Robert Witmer, professor of ethnomusicology at York University and one of my former jazz instructors, was kind enough to set me straight on a number of contentious musicological issues. Stewart Marwick, whose passion for jazz music is only surpassed by his wit and sense of literary style, saved me from certain embarrassment in a number of places through judicious editing. Kristie Macrakis also made several valuable suggestions for improving my book; in her case I feel some guilt because she was in the process of writing something very important of her own.

For stimulating conversations over the years, help with sources, and suggestions of various kinds I am deeply indebted to Roy Ackerman, Gerhard Conrad, Gordon A. Craig, Eike Geisel, John Gittins, Eric J. Hobsbawm, Peter Jelavich, Klaus Krüger, Robert Jay Lifton, Rainer E. Lotz, Rainer Lübbren, Sybil Milton, Albert D. Mott, Michael Pointon, Clark Reynolds, Josef Škvorecký, and Jürgen W. Susat. Gerhard A. Ritter of Munich and Adelheid von Saldern of Hanover invited me to discuss the subject of jazz in the Third Reich and related matters with their colleagues and students, as did Robert Jay Lifton (in New York) and Kristie Macrakis (once at Harvard and again when she was a Humboldt Chancellorship Scholar at the Free University of Berlin). I profited greatly from these lively discussions.

Many an obscure source would not have surfaced had not Mary Hudecki and John Carter, of York University's interlibrary loan service, labored to ferret it out for me—sometimes from as far away as East Germany. Thanks is due them, as it is to Nancy Lane at Oxford University Press. I have benefited from her unwavering support during several critical phases of the book's gestation.

My wife, Barbara, and my two teenage daughters have been excessively patient during the researching and writing of this book—listening to many a jazz recording in the process. In the course of countless conversations I had with my wife, she forced me to analyze complex issues more thoroughly, especially in cases where psychological aspects were involved. Her uncanny sense of aesthetics also guided me. To my surprise, my writing derived inspiration whenever my daughters practiced flute or baritone horn for various school assignments, even though it wasn't exactly jazz they were playing.

As this preface was being written, I felt certain that, even with the massive amount of help I received, mistakes of fact or interpretation still remained. I accept with equanimity the fact that I alone bear responsibility for all such errors or oversights.

Contents

Abbreviations

AEF	Allied Expeditionary Forces
BA	Bundesarchiv Koblenz
BBC	British Broadcasting Corporation
BDC	Berlin Document Center
BEF	British Expeditionary Forces
DAF	Deutsche Arbeitsfront (German Labor Front)
DIA	BBC Data Inquiry Service Archive, London
DTU	Deutsches Tanz- und Unterhaltungsorchester (German Dance and Entertainment Orchestra)
Gestapo	Geheime Staatspolizei (Secret State Police)
HJ	Hitlerjugend (Hitler Youth)
IfZ	Institut für Zeitgeschichte München (Institute of Contemporary History, Munich)
Kadeko	Kabarett der Komiker (Cabaret of Comics)
NHSA	Niedersächsisches Hauptstaatsarchiv Hannover (Lower Saxon Main State Archive, Hanover)
NRV	Norddeutscher Regatta-Verein (North German Regatta League)
NSBO	Nationalsozialistische Betriebszellenorganisation (National Socialist Shop Organization)
NSDAP	Nationalsozialistische Deutsche Arbeiterpartei (National Socialist German Workers' Party)
OKW	Oberkommando der Wehrmacht (Armed Forces High Command)

PA	private archive
POW	prisoner of war
RAD	Reichsarbeitsdienst (Reich Labor Service)
RBT	Radio Berlin Tanzorchester (Radio Berlin Dance Orchestra)
RIAS	Rundfunk im Amerikanischen Sektor (Radio in the American Sector)
RKK	Reichskulturkammer (Reich Culture Chamber)
RM	Reichsmark
RMK	Reichsmusikkammer (Reich Music Chamber)
RRK	Reichsrundfunkkammer (Reich Radio Chamber)
RTK	Reichstheaterkammer (Reich Theater Chamber)
SA	Sturmabteilungen (storm troopers [Brown Shirts])
SAB	Staatsarchiv Bremen (State Archive, Bremen)
SAH	Staatsarchiv Hamburg (State Archive, Hamburg)
SAM	Staatsarchiv München (State Archive, Munich)
SS	Schutzstaffel (Black Shirts)

DIFFERENT

DRUMMERS

Introduction
The Ambiguous Culture
Jazz in the Weimar Republic

Berlin in the 1920s! In its halcyon years Germany's capital boasted on average a million and a half foreign visitors. When the American black dancer Josephine Baker arrived here from France in 1925, she found it dazzling: "The city had a jewel-like sparkle, especially at night, that didn't exist in Paris. The vast cafés reminded me of ocean liners powered by the rhythms of their orchestras. There was music everywhere."[1]

Berlin was a showcase of the new arts and talents, those that were fostered by the more liberal spirit of the post-1918 republic of Weimar. It was the new universal vortex of high culture for the elitist connoisseur, as well as of lighter offerings for an upwardly mobile, "modern" German mass consumer.

By 1927 high culture was flaunted in no less than three major opera houses, more than forty theaters, and several concert halls. Museum exhibitions and small galleries featured the art of early dadaists like George Grosz and that of expressionist painters Otto Dix and Oskar Kokoschka.

In the Romanische Café, near the Kaiser Wilhelm Memorial Church and the Kurfürstendamm in Berlin's fashionable new West End, witty newspaper columnists and sagacious critics—among them Alfred Kerr, Kurt Tucholsky, and Erich Kästner—quaffed their beers while exchanging ideas or just meditating. University students would amble into the area, perhaps entering one of the sumptuous movie palaces or the countless bars, in one of which aspiring concert pianists were known to play the classics for a few marks a night.[2]

Otto Dix, a habitué of the Romanische Café, painted the dancer Anita Berber, who represented a peculiar kind of culture that defied categorization. This bisexual daughter of a professor of classical music personified the sensuality in which Berlin was awash in those years, which the composer Friedrich Hollaender has captured in his memoirs: "Naked female flesh teases the eyes . . . in the supermarket of eroticism . . . where red little boots promise a whole arsenal of humiliations." Berber's favorite haunt was a cabaret called the White Mouse, where she would perform pornographic dance numbers and then break champagne bottles on the heads of raunchy male clients. When she died in November 1928 from a lifelong abuse of alcohol and cocaine, her funeral was attended by an array of whores, pimps, bartenders, and transvestites.[3]

In its best days republican Berlin had over twenty cabarets. By and large they offered a sophisticated fare, including biting political skits, saucy and sometimes indecent dance routines, and catchy songs. The most famous of them, founded in 1924, was the Kabarett der Komiker (Cabaret of Comics), which its clientele endearingly called the Kadeko for short. German stars of film and operetta, such as Trude Hesterberg, appeared there, as did foreign artists like Jeanette MacDonald and Josephine Baker. Among its brilliant satirists were Joachim Ringelnatz and Werner Finck. Composers writing in a lighter vein—Friedrich Hollaender, Peter Kreuder, Mischa Spoliansky—starred in its programs and were among Germany's best.[4]

Some not so well-known plays were staged in a cabaret setting, as was *The Two Cravats* in 1929, for which a neophyte actress had been signed; her name was Marlene Dietrich. It was after the Austro-American director Joseph von Sternberg had watched Marlene in this play that he decided to cast her in *The Blue Angel*. The film premiered in Berlin on 1 April 1930 and a star was born.[5] Already at that time Berliners were being enthralled by American imports from Hollywood, among which the first true talking picture, *The Singing Fool* with Al Jolson (1928), had left an indelible impression.[6]

If cabarets were intimate and intellectually somewhat demanding, variety revues were on a larger scale and were intended more for the ordinary public. There were three or four of these in Berlin, the most prominent being the Scala, which was owned and operated by the Jewish banker Jules Marx. The Scala was capable of seating three thousand persons for each show, some of which were affordable matinées. They took place in a circus atmosphere: clowns like Grock and Rivel caused storms of laughter; acrobats flung themselves through the air; wild-animals acts followed tap dancers and clairvoyants; comedians, popular singers, and personalities from film and stage competed for an awed public's attention.

The Scala's hallmark was the American-style chorus lines, whose members were selected for their natural beauty and shapely legs. These girls often married wealthy patrons.[7] Another mammoth revue was staged by Eric Charell, who for three years running hired the famous Tiller Girls direct from London. From 1914 until 1927 the pianist and composer Rudolf Nelson had a smaller revue at the Nelson-Theater, on the Kurfürstendamm, where he produced some two dozen shows.[8]

A uniquely novel institution in the Berlin entertainment scene was the five o'clock teas, which were based on the London and Paris models. They took place in the five principal hotels of the city, the Adlon and the Esplanade arguably being the most snobbish. Society dance bands—such as those led by Marek Weber, Bernard Etté, and Dajos Béla—played for mostly younger patrons; these social dancers tended to be solid middle class rather than upper crust. Perennially modish dances were the Charleston, the tango, and the fox-trot.[9] Members of the social elite and often the demimonde danced the nights away in illustrious establishments with exquisite cuisines and exotic bars, such as the Barberina and the Ambassadeurs, not far from the Kurfürstendamm. Alluring nightclubs with names like Rio Rita, Kakadu, or Königin-Bar duplicated these offerings on a smaller but even more expensive basis.[10]

Much of Berlin's light-entertainment culture was in one way or another intertwined with the new art from America, jazz. Anita Berber was known to dance in the Eldorado, a homosexual and transvestite bar, where Rudi Anhang, dancer and jazz banjoist, accompanied her. Berber's specialty was a depraved dance number entitled "Cocaine," performed to the music of Camille Saint-Saëns. She also did a piece called "Morphium," whose music Mischa Spoliansky had written. Spoliansky, who had composed the score for *The Two Cravats,* employed in the orchestra pit a jazz band comprised of American saxophonist Teddy Kline, British trumpeter Howard McFarlane, and a twenty-two-year-old German pianist by the name of Georg Haentzschel.[11]

Spoliansky and Hollaender collaborated musically at the Kabarett der Komiker, which, apart from its own jazz-inspired creations, highlighted American jazz bandleader Alex Hyde.[12] Hollaender had written the music for *The Blue Angel,* and this film briefly showed off the talents of the Weintraub Syncopators, Germany's best-known jazz combo, for whom Hollaender once played the piano. The Syncopators were a great hit at the Scala, whose director in 1929 also imported the Revellers, an American jazz-oriented vocal ensemble, among other groups.[13] In addition, Hollaender served as pianist for Rudolf Nelson's revue, and Nelson's friend Charell could take credit for the German premiere of Paul Whiteman's jazz orchestra at his Grosse Schauspielhaus.[14]

Jazz was imported to Germany at the very end of World War I, when it already had a footing in England and France. It is likely that German prisoners of war were exposed to it in French camps, and that the Allied occupying forces brought records and sheet music into the defeated country. The widely known "Tiger Rag" was marketed on a Berlin-based record label as early as January 1920.[15] Jazz was given a boost by the postwar dance craze, which served to shake off the memories of war. In 1918 the fox-trot and the tango invaded Germany, followed a year later by the one-step and the Boston. The shimmy was fashionable in 1921, the two-step in 1922, and the famous Charleston finally dominated the scene in 1925.[16] Economic turbulence and a period of inflation that lasted from 1920 to 1923 made large German orchestras performing the new jazz dances a rarity. More common were small combos consisting of a pianist, a drummer, and a violinist doubling on saxophone, that archetypal jazz instrument.[17]

After financial stability was attained in 1924, more hard currency could be spent on entertainment by an increasingly pleasure-hungry public. Hence the mid-1920s witnessed the growth of more sophisticated and larger bands. They usually accompanied social dancing in plush, big-city hotels and could do so with a jazz flair—or what passed as such—when called upon. The most prominent of these orchestras were those led by Bernard Etté, Marek Weber, and Dajos

Béla, who normally worked in Berlin but also toured important regional centers such as Leipzig, Hamburg, Frankfurt, and Munich.

Etté, originally a barber, developed his salon orchestra in 1923 out of a conventional trio. He pioneered "American" sound after sojourns in the United States in 1924 and 1927.[18] Marek Weber first introduced the afternoon tea dances in 1924 at the Adlon hotel, where he was engaged until 1928, the year he embarked on a nationwide tour.[19] Béla was Weber's friendly rival. Spoliansky played piano in this band in 1925, along with Howard McFarlane on trumpet. Toward the end of the republic this orchestra was featured in all the prominent Berlin establishments, such as the Eden or the Excelsior, from where it broadcast its music in December 1931.[20]

Two German bands that sought to highlight American jazz more than any other were Eric Borchard's small combo and Stefan Weintraub's Syncopators. Both had become legends by the late twenties. Borchard's combo was already popular in 1925, when he started appearing in prominent Berlin movie theaters; in 1927 a local guidebook listed him as "the most beloved figure of Berlin's nightlife." The bandleader was eventually destroyed by the cardinal vices of the decade: sex and drugs. While on tour in June 1931, the morphine-addicted Borchard inadvertently killed one of his lady friends in an attempt to revive her after an overdose. Borchard was put on trial and convicted; he soon vanished into obscurity.[21]

All the members of the Weintraub Syncopators—a mere amateur schoolboy band of five in 1924—mastered several instruments with amazing dexterity. Stefan Weintraub excelled on piano, drums, guitar, xylophone, vibraphone, celesta, and ukelele. They were catapulted to fame in early 1927, when Friedrich Hollaender decided to use them in his revues. For a while Hollaender himself took over the piano, whereupon Weintraub switched to drums. The band was featured all over Germany and even did club appearances in neighboring European countries.[22]

After 1923 the earliest bandleaders in Germany attempting to play jazz seriously tried to fill their ranks with as many native American, British, and Canadian musicians as possible; they knew only too well that German instrumentalists were able to copy them. The Anglo-Americans, on the other hand, were attracted by good wages, based on a stabilized mark, and they appreciated the respect given them by musicians and fans alike. Some remained only for a short while, as did the American Chicago-style drummer Dave Tough, who in 1927 crossed the Atlantic to England with his friend Danny Polo, the reed player, and then went to Germany, where he stayed for several weeks before moving on. But others, including Polo himself, liked Berlin and the touring routine and remained well into the Third Reich.[23]

Among those who stayed, American banjoist and guitarist Mike Danzi was probably the most important, not because of his jazz style, which was merely passable, but because of the length of time he remained in Germany and his influence on native German colleagues and transplanted Anglo-Americans alike. Having arrived in Hamburg in November 1924, Danzi worked briefly with the Borchard band before joining the American orchestra of Alex Hyde on tour. In the years to come, he participated in innumerable Berlin recording sessions and at one time or another played with almost all the German jazz and dance groups of note.[24]

Another foreigner, this time from England, was the saxophonist Billy Bartholomew, who differed from Danzi in that he had mastered a more erudite jazz style and was able to form his own commercially successful orchestra, which delighted fans well into the thirties. Bartholomew had played with Borchard in 1924, and in May 1928 his own band won the coveted contract to open the Berlin Delphi-Palast, a huge multimedia entertainment complex.[25] He was particularly fond of working with fellow Anglophones, such as the Americans Nick Casti and Teddy Kline, who played trumpet and reeds. These Americans would also do studio assignments while slipping in and out of German-led bands.[26] While still with Borchard back in 1924, Bartholomew had befriended Harold M. Kirchstein, a German banjoist and guitarist born in New York, who had just returned to Germany for the second time. In 1927 Kirchstein was with Béla's orchestra, on his way to a prolific composing and arranging career that was to make him famous by the early thirties.[27]

The Anglo-Americans were greatly admired by a few native followers who were too young to have had the traditional dance-band experience of the Ettés and Webers and were frankly more interested in the harmonic and melodic possibilities of New Orleans or Chicago-style jazz rather than its social-dance dimension. Chief among them were the pianists Franz Grothe and Georg Haentzschel, both Berliners born in 1907, who were to enjoy a lifelong friendship forged in the excitement of the late twenties. Grothe began in 1926 as a member of the Borchard group, when only nineteen years old. A year later he switched over to Bartholomew, and from 1928 on he was employed by the prestigious Béla orchestra. Learning his essential jazz technique from the American Danny Polo, he soon made his mark as a composer and arranger, chiefly of Bostons and fox-trots, some of which originated after his collaboration with Anglo-Americans like Howard McFarlane.[28]

If anything, Haentzschel was even more interested in jazz. He received his big break in 1928 as a pianist with Marek Weber. He then worked with Lud Gluskin, who headed an American touring band associated with the Jean Goldkette organization in Detroit. Haentzschel's piano style was influenced so lastingly by his American and English friends that in 1930–31 he did a stint with the Syncopators, whose musical standards were said to be the highest among German jazz bands.[29]

To this younger generation of German jazz musicians—there may not have been more than twenty—whose formative years paralleled the final phase of the Weimar Republic also belonged the trombonist Walter Dobschinski and the clarinetist Ernst Höllerhagen. Dobschinski started out as a pianist, but by the end of the twenties he had adopted the trombone because in fronting the band he had a better view of "numerous pretty girls one could take out after the job." In 1930 the emerging Swiss bandleader Teddy Stauffer heard him in Berlin and hired him on the spot.[30] Höllerhagen, after the mid-thirties himself a member of Stauffer's Original Teddies, was a product of the Cologne Conservatory as well as a veteran

of various silent-movie pit bands. In January 1933 this young man was performing with an obscure twelve-piece orchestra in Berlin's Café Corso, where a
critic described him as "a true phenomenon" on the clarinet.[31]

Berlin was a mecca for these jazz exploits, since only a few large German
cities imitated the capital, and on a smaller scale. Hamburg came closest, with its
international port-based entertainment industry, supported by the demimonde and
wealthy patricians alike. It possessed several venues for touring dance and jazz
musicians: the Café Heinze, where Stauffer's band liked to perform; Trocadero,
host to orchestras like Marek Weber's; and—considerably less reputable—the
dance casino Faun in the red-light district of St. Pauli.[32] In Leipzig, fun-loving
Saxons patronized the Kristall-Palast, where Josephine Baker gave a cameo
performance in January 1929 and the Weintraub Syncopators enthralled jazz
lovers eight months later.[33]

Yet compared to cosmopolitan Berlin, these cities were still too provincial
to support an indigenous jazz culture, so that sooner or later aspiring local jazz
artists had to move to the capital. This was the case with Fritz Brocksieper, born
in 1912 of a German father and a Greek mother in Constantinople. In the
metropolis of the Ottoman sultan he used to march, as a five-year-old, beside
military bands blasting Middle Eastern music, and it was the Turkish cymbals
that intrigued him most. His family having resettled in Munich in 1918, young
Fritz later took up the drums to the detriment of an engineering course; in the
early 1930s he was busily playing in mediocre local bands. Apart from an
amateur university student jazz group, there were no musical formations in which
Fritz could mature, and certainly no resident Americans. Inevitably, he relocated
in Berlin, but only after years of arduous road jobs, most of them plain dance
routines.[34]

But most German musicians had opportunities to hear major visiting bands
as their models. The first of those made its appearance in 1925, when economic
conditions improved. It was the orchestra of black pianist Sam Wooding, who
had made a mark for himself back in the United States but in the pantheon of jazz
greats was not a dominant figure. Wooding's all-black eleven-piece band accompanied the Chocolate Kiddies Negro revue, with a score by Duke Ellington,
which had been assembled especially for a European tour. After stints in London
and Paris they opened at the Berlin Admiralspalast in May 1925 to an ecstatic
audience.[35] Wooding then named his band after the revue and toured all of
Europe for several years, repeating his popular success in major German cities
like Leipzig, Hamburg, and recurrently Berlin.

The pianist always insisted that he did not want to play for dancing but for
listening, and he entertained lofty ambitions for a more respectable, "symphonic" style of jazz, which, critics feel, tended to make him less creditable as a
jazz man.[36] But for all his artistic shortcomings, Wooding had the instinct to hire
some of the top American players of his day, to whom European musicians and
audiences could only bow: Tommy Ladnier and Doc Cheatham on trumpets,
Willie Lewis and Garvin Bushell on reeds, and Herb Flemming on trombone.
Not only did Wooding persuade a host of initially indifferent listeners to accept

this music, but at least one German musician, Ernst Höllerhagen, learned from him directly when he joined his band for a short period.[37]

Sam Wooding has sometimes been called the black Paul Whiteman.[38] This is because Whiteman was the most prolific exponent of the pretentious "symphonic" jazz style through which Wooding hoped to attain legitimation as a black artist. Yet in the United States Whiteman, too, employed such jazz stars as Bix Beiderbecke (cornet), Eddie Lang (guitar), and Frankie Trumbauer (reeds), and he exerted a decisive influence on fledgling musicians like pianist Art Hodes.[39] Whiteman's "symphonic" jazz orchestra, representing diluted, refined jazz as opposed to authentic jazz, premiered with George Gershwin's *Rhapsody in Blue* in Berlin's Grosse Schauspielhaus in June 1926 and received accolades similar to Wooding's.[40] Again, as the American musicologist Gunther Schuller has put it, Whiteman's music was "designed to make people listen to music, not to dance," which, given the dance fads of the late twenties, did not fail to impress German musicians and aficionados alike.[41] The bandleader's success was heightened in 1930 by a bad American film, *The King of Jazz,* which was repeatedly shown in German movie houses, even though purists were already sneering at Whiteman for his openly commercial proclivities.[42]

The next orchestra to enthuse Germans was that of the British showman Jack Hylton. This master of the stage had a talent for selecting as his band members the finest that England had to offer, but he also employed Canadians and expatriate Americans. Hylton's German debut occurred in Berlin's Scala in January 1928, and he immediately earned the reputation of having "the best and most beloved European big band."[43] Apart from amusing acrobatics, Hylton's men excelled through their sense of rhythm and discipline as much as through the novelty of English and American hit tunes, which were still rarely heard in Germany. With his light touch, sense of humor, and the sheer precision of his style, Hylton was closer to the essence of jazz and thus effectively counteracted the pomposity of both Wooding and Whiteman. Yet he was also inclined to a "sweet" quality of sound that characterized Whiteman's music as well.[44] During several visits to Germany, Hylton managed to cultivate an exceptionally loyal audience that would throng to hear him even in midsize towns, faithfully buy his records, and listen to him on the radio.[45]

The seminal effect of these principal performers, however they may have differed in their basic attitude toward jazz, was bolstered intermittently by visits of other masters of the art, all from the United States. Thus in 1925 Josephine Baker, who indirectly acted as an ambassador for the music, was accompanied by the sterling band of Claude Hopkins, which then included the youthful clarinetist Sidney Bechet. La Baker returned to Berlin on her own in 1927, and Bechet played in the capital's Wild-West bar two years later, causing a sensation.[46] In May 1929 the multi-instrumentalist Adrian Rollini, best known for his bass-saxophone work, slipped over to Berlin from London for a few days and nonchalantly joined various local combos, mesmerizing them with his virtuosity.[47]

Thus an indigenous generation of German jazz fans was being groomed in the fascinating jazz culture created by native and Anglo-American musicians. They were usually born between 1910 and 1920 and came from middle-class homes, many in Berlin but also, because of the spread of touring bands, gramophone recordings, and radio, from other large towns and even the provinces. Invariably, as teenagers they had been exposed to the pop tunes of the day, often dance pieces of little sophistication, through their private music teachers, sympathetic parents, or school chums. The most usual musical media were the family piano, private record collections and, increasingly, radio broadcasts. But as they progressed in maturity, so also did their tastes develop; before long they found themselves listening to the arrangements of a German dance orchestra like Weber's or Béla's, with unmistakable jazz allusions.

If these were commonalities in jazz education, individual preferences and opportunities for broadening one's horizon shaped those young people in different ways. Often, interest in jazz and a certain urbanity went hand in hand. Kurt Michaelis, a nineteen-year-old dental technician's apprentice from Leipzig, traveled to London in the summer of 1932 to hear Louis Armstrong in person; Armstrong's records had been circulating within the small circle of Michaelis's friends. Young jazz fans regularly attended concerts by visiting stars, be they Wooding, Hylton, or the British ten-piece band of Bobby Hind. Like Michaelis, Gymnasium student Dietrich Schulz of Magdeburg, in neighboring Sachsen-Anhalt, bought a subscription to the English jazz journal *Melody Maker,* the most respected of its kind in Europe, which from then on kept both boys up to date with the latest in jazz news. In central Berlin, student Hans Blüthner regularly sampled live performances by the prominent German bands, but favored the much-vaunted concerts of British artists Billy Bartholomew, whom he savored at the Delphi on 8 April 1931, and Jack Hylton, who was at the Universum a year and a half later.[48] Little did these three young men know what crucial roles they would play in keeping jazz alive during the Third Reich!

Inevitably, these youthful fans would try their hand at an instrument, with varying success. Some, like Rolf Goldstein in Berlin, were able as young children to play American pop tunes by ear and found themselves improvising on the melody. Dietrich Schulz's Magdeburg classmate Fritz Schulze, too, mastered the keyboard, so that in his senior high school years he was lionized by schoolmates and teachers alike. Dietrich Schulz himself first tried violin, then drums, and finally trombone, but made no headway. Hans Otto Jung, a wealthy vintner's son from Lorch on the Rhine, was lucky enough to have the classical composer Paul Hindemith visit the parental home. On those occasions the boy first listened to classics performed by members of Hindemith's Amar Quartet and then to jam sessions, in which the celebrated composer played a "hot" fiddle, accompanied by father Jung on the string bass.[49]

The nourishment for this small but growing cell came from recordings, both domestic and imported. Marek Weber's orchestral sound had been cut in wax as early as 1921.[50] In 1924–25 Alex Hyde's visiting American band—not a memorable outfit—recorded with the Berlin firms of Vox and Deutsche Grammophon.[51] In 1926 Deutsche Grammophon created its German Brunswick label, which was licensed to represent the American Brunswick organization, market its products in Germany, and press its own discs, often on the basis of English or American masters. This resulted in an enormous boost for jazz in Germany, for now original American groups became much more widely known among the fans. Hence in 1930 Duke Ellington's "The Mooch," played by his famous Cotton Club Orchestra, was advertized in a German Brunswick record catalog. The prestigious music journal *Melos* described the piece as "spontaneous, explosive rhythm" with "bold, shrill, albeit very tastefully tempered colors."[52]

It was an American recording of Ellington's "Ring Dem Bells" and "Three Little Words," made in Hollywood in August 1930, that became Dietrich Schulz's first jazz record. In February 1932, upon successful completion of his Gymnasium matriculation, he received ten marks from his mother. A single disc cost RM 2.50; in all, he bought four. During that month in Magdeburg, ten marks would buy one hundred eggs![53]

Ellington, in fact, was one of two black American favorites among the aficionados, the other being Louis Armstrong, who had cemented his international fame with a great recording of "West End Blues" by his Hot Five band in June 1928. But Armstrong's German admirers were aware of more than just that selection. Kurt Michaelis preferred the trumpeter's rendition of the widely popular German hit "Armer Gigolo" ("Just a Gigolo"), and in 1928 young Günter Boas of Dessau was introduced to Armstrong's recording of "Basin Street Blues" by Paul Klee's Bauhaus student Paul Impkamp, a boarder in the Boas household.[54]

The redoubtable "Tiger Rag," performed by various native and foreign groups, was yet another tune that became a collector's item; Michaelis made a cult of collecting as many as he could, regardless of the artist. This points up one of the difficulties in the musical initiation of these fans: by dint of its structure that rag, like any ragtime tune, was awkward as a jazz piece, being a vehicle for humorous gimmicks rather than for improvisation, which was, after all, the essence of jazz.[55]

Because records were expensive, they were habitually shared among the fans and traded like postage stamps. Sometimes used records could be bought rather cheaply, perhaps fifty pfennigs apiece, but the gems among those were few.[56] As gramophones improved, they also became more accessible to these circles of friends, who would gather at the house of the fortunate owner. From bulky contraptions with mechanical drives and metal funnels in the early 1920s, gramophones developed into compact portables for outside use or handsome home consoles, electrically driven and amplified, and were marketed most auspiciously by the record firm Electrola in the late 1920s. New, such machines fetched more than a hundred marks in the stores, but could sometimes be bought used for less than half that price.[57]

The year 1929 represented the peak in new gramophone purchases; thereafter, because of the depression, consumption declined. Record purchases also slumped because they became too expensive for many buyers. For the young jazz fans, however, this crisis was mitigated by the richer choices in radio, both from the German networks and from certain foreign stations.[58]

The German broadcast system had begun in Berlin on 29 October 1923 with a live classical concert performance. By 1930 there were twenty-eight regionally dispersed stations in all of Germany, transmitting on standard ("middle-wave") frequency, so that one could listen anywhere in the country to at least one program. Dance music, which would of course include what jazz there was, was usually broadcast late at night; in the summer of 1924 this type of entertainment was favored by nearly half the listening audience, ranking just above opera.[59]

The reception medium in the early twenties was the crystal set with headphones; for youthful jazz lovers with scant pocket money, it remained the main vehicle to the outside world of music until late in the decade, because of the costliness of tube desk radios. Like gramophones, crystal sets were improved over the years and also became more economical. But by January 1933, 93 percent of all German receivers in use were electronic tube models, and one such apparatus was usually found in every middle-class home.[60]

Ironically, the first jazz-inspired program was broadcast on 24 May 1924 from Munich, hardly a mainstay of the new music. It was a live recording of a band playing at the Regina-Palasthotel. Jazz, in the narrower sense of the word, became a more frequent staple of radio after Paul Whiteman's Berlin success in 1926. By 1927 well-known German dance orchestras were broadcast live toward midnight on select days, with jazz holding a somewhat uncertain position amid a plethora of pop tunes, of which the great majority were German, not American.[61]

This state of affairs is well reflected in Berlin in Hans Blüthner's assiduously kept diary of nightly listenings from March 1929 to the beginning of 1932: bands like those of Etté, Weber, and Béla predominate, with the lesser-known but rather more jazz-oriented orchestras of Fred Bird (Felix Lehmann) and Ben Berlin making sporadic appearances. Young Hans evidently was impressed with the Weintraub Syncopators, who played on 29 August 1929, featuring Al Jolson's "Sunny Boy" and Kahn's "That's My Weakness Now" (along with more commercial dross), for he glued a picture of the group into his diary, embellishing it with his own drawings.

In June 1930 Blüthner listened to a fox-trot composed by Ellington and vocalized by the Comedian Harmonists, a German male sextet emulating the Revellers. And later in the month he could enjoy Sam Wooding's "Negermusik," as he termed it, with a whole diary page reserved for an unnamed black saxophonist's photograph. Increasingly thereafter Jack Hylton appeared, likewise with favorable annotations.

By 1930, too, these live performances tended to be replaced by record replays, so that "Jazz Hours" were a regular part of Blüthner's program. Now a mixture of artists was becoming more common, Louis Armstrong followed by Ellington and the tacky German band of Paul Godwin (March 1931), the white American trumpet player Red Nichols followed by German pianist Peter Kreuder, Whiteman, and again Duke Ellington (June 1931).[62]

When the much stronger tabletop receivers entered homes, young jazz fans had an opportunity to listen to foreign stations such as BBC London and Radio Toulouse, and, after autumn 1930 and mainly in the Rhineland, commercial Radio Luxemburg, which beamed an excitingly modern repertoire to the British Isles that was easily picked up in Germany.[63]

Significantly, as soon as their tastes had matured, these young friends of jazz appear to have shown a predilection for American black musicians, especially Louis Armstrong and Duke Ellington. On the other hand, German jazz artists ranked much lower on their scale. Over time, an acculturation process had taken them from simple popular German ditties they might have preferred in their early teens to the substantial compositions of an Irving Berlin or Jelly Roll Morton, and the generic blues form. Hence they came to know, or to feel, what was genuine jazz flavor and what only masqueraded as such. Yet if one had asked them then to define "jazz" for scientific purposes, they would certainly have been as much at a loss as musicologists are today: it is virtually impossible to give an exhaustive and totally satisfactory definition of this music.

What, indeed, is jazz? Gunther Schuller, the former president of the New England Conservatory of Music, has succeeded better than anybody in defining it. Schuller's credentials are formidable. Not only is he a classically trained hornist and noted composer and conductor, as well as a superb musical theorist, but he also once was associated with jazz musicians such as Miles Davis and John Lewis. For decades, Schuller has provided astute analyses of jazz music and in so doing has decided authoritatively that the most important criterion of jazz is whether it "swings" or not. Yet while he has said this in one book, he has conceded in another that some music, for instance that by Duke Ellington, could well be classified as jazz, even though it did not have "swing."[64]

If someone like Schuller can waver in his judgment, one must also consider the fact that the best jazz musicians themselves are subject to changes, not only from one style to another, but also between qualitative stages. Thus saxophonist Coleman Hawkins, probably the greatest the world had seen until the advent of Charlie "Bird" Parker, needed ten years to figure out the full capabilities of his instrument. Only by 1933 had he "developed a tone that had never before been heard on a saxophone."[65] Louis Armstrong, on the other hand, is said to have approached the nether areas of commercialism by 1928, after having passed his great innovative period, which, in the opinion of Schuller, he was never to reach again.[66]

Although any attempt to define jazz inevitably seems haphazard, it is generally considered valid to impute four main qualities to the music that is jazz. One is rhythm. Yet if jazz rhythm is conventionally called syncopic, this is not the whole story. "Downbeats" and "upbeats" mean that notes can be played with rhythmic variations from the main beat so subtle that they elude notation; if musicians are not born into an Afro-American culture, they may have to spend a long time acquiring this skill.

A second property of jazz is melody. Jazz melodies, artificially composed as well as naturally grown ones (like the work song in the cotton fields), in their linear or horizontal flow utilize scalar elements that are not exclusively triadic and diatonic, or Western. They incorporate flatted thirds, sevenths, and ninths in a manner that is strange to a traditionally attuned ear, until it has learned to accept this.

The third feature of jazz is harmony. In jazz harmony, jazz-melodic construction is duplicated in a vertical fashion, so that a chord supporting a particular note in the melody might contain the peculiar flatted notes (or raised ones, as the case may be). The jazz-specific art of improvisation means on-the-spot melodic and harmonic variations from the prefigured (composed) line by the artists, within the practices accepted in their day (or even beyond that, if they are pioneers like Armstrong or later Charlie Parker). Often this may involve the substitution of one musical key pattern for another, such as raising a four-bar run chromatically by a halftone, thus superimposing it on the original.

The fourth ingredient of jazz, and again one that is germane to the music's Afro-American roots, is tonal inflection. The serenity of sound so valued in classical music is frequently mutated to an ambiguous or "dirty" state deriving from the ever so slight and merely momentary flatness of a saxophonist's pitch, the sliding or smearing of a bass note on the string bass, or the impurity produced through the "wa-wa" of the trombone's mute.

All of this taken together is greater than the sum of its parts. In essence jazz thrives on the resolution of various tensions invoked deliberately during the playing of a tune, as for instance in the tension created by harmonizing a line in parallel perfect fourths, or in a brief polyrhythmic pattern that seeks a return to a more quieting unirhythm. The ultimate excitement of jazz, its very "swing," consists in the prolongation of this tension up to the last spot where resolution is still possible without permanently corrupting the entire structure of the piece. The ability to build up the dynamics of this tension, and to postpone the resolution, is the mark of the true jazz player.

Little of this was known to routine German dance-band musicians to whom a changing, Anglophilic fashion dictated that the new music of "jazz" be played. In the absence of such knowledge, and with no one around to instruct them but a handful of American expatriates, the average German dance-band instrumentalist played something resembling jazz, usually as he had come to hear it on some record. He took what he thought to be the most distinctive quality of jazz and attempted to reproduce it on his instrument. Bandleaders might do this collectively for the entire band.

This became most apparent in the area of rhythm. Analysts have forever commented on the difficulty for new jazz initiates of keeping the pulse, that is, maintaining the even flow of time that is the criterion of the accomplished jazz artist. This applied particularly to the German popular musician approaching jazz, who was used to march time with its emphasis on the first ("strong") beat of each bar, rather than the jazz tradition with its equivalent weighting of all beats.[67] The German musicians of the republic compensated for their lack of inner feeling for a secure pulse with excessive noise, mistaking the drum set for the preeminent jazz tool and loudly expressed *Rhythmus* for its quintessence.

In the German context the confusion of jazz with noise, and the identification of noise with drums, led to the strange and continuously misleading phenomenon that the drum set itself was called "a jazz." The function of "the jazz," then, primarily in the early twenties, was to generate as much noise as possible, regardless of an inherent rhythmic pulse. Many would-be musicians took up "the jazz," because to them this seemed the easiest element in this attractive entertainment novelty and because its show attributes, such as a cowbell or Tibetan woodblock, would make the drummer the most desirable member of a band.[68]

The buffoonery of the early German drummer, with his funny hats and phony cardboard nose, was then transferred to other band musicians, who would make these antics a constituent of their playing. Witness the faked laughter of the alto saxophone (as well as the leaden drumming) in Eric Borchard's 1924 recording of "Aggravatin' Papa"![69] Indeed, jazz-band musicians by definition were expected to provide a good time, tell jokes and, as musical clowns, introduce the most questionable instruments to play on, such as singing saws, harmonium violins, and the lotus flute.[70] In this sense, it may be said that the music was no different from yet another form of commercialized jazz in the United States, the so-called "nut jazz," where distorting humor was paramount.[71]

The more serious among Germany's young jazz musicians did not like these aspects. Georg Haentzschel is on record for expressing his disenchantment even with the famous Weintraub Syncopators, whose constant gimmickry he thought so unmusical that he left the group after a few months. In his opinion, their gyrations perennially took place at the expense of overall musical quality.[72] It was only in the second half of the twenties that the comical and noisy aura of jazz abated somewhat. Undoubtedly, the influence of performers from America, where refinements had already set in, was now increasingly prevalent, and this met with more refined consumer tastes in German society itself.[73]

Another factor detrimental to the development of jazz in Germany was the admixture of genuine jazz elements with residues of the continental salon dance style. Salon dance-band musicians were classically trained and often frustrated concert-hall soloists who knew how to sight-read music and who commanded a repertoire of medium-to-light classical pieces, such as the *William Tell Overture* or Bach-Gounod's "Ave Maria."[74] Hence what one got for dancing in the republic usually was a potpourri: salon tunes of semiclassical vintage, frequently operetta and waltzes, and imported modern dances, sometimes in an original American version like the fox-trot "Out of Nowhere," but more often in the guise of casual German ditties like "Where Is Your Hair, August?"[75] They were all played by the same orchestra with varying instrumentation. Most violin players, for instance, possessed a working knowledge of the saxophone or trumpet, and cellists also might engage the tuba.[76] Stringed instruments were characteristic of the traditional coffeehouse and salon orchestra, and when the new dance numbers "à la jazz" were called, violins still proliferated, lending a saccharine timbre to the overall sound.[77]

The great German dance-band leaders of the twenties and early thirties were all products of this older tradition and, significantly, most of them had mastered the violin, as did Etté, Weber, and Béla. Apologists for Etté even lauded the maestro's signature style, supported with strong, sweet violins, as having expunged all "alien acidity" to become noble and uniquely German.[78] Ironically, the prescient and commercially clever Etté had been the first to promote the most genuine American jazz possible, evidenced by his journeys to the New World and his hiring of American musicians. All German bandleaders emulated Etté by recruiting the best jazz players they could find, for reasons of prestige, even if they had to compromise their personal tastes, as did Weber, who actually hated jazz and understood even less about it than Etté or Béla. However, in this case the dictates of the fad provided extraordinary opportunities to younger musicians like Georg Haentzschel. Employed by Weber in 1928, he was careful to do his real jamming, with the hard core of American jazzmen in the band, as soon as the leader had left for the night! Naturally, he also was featured on Weber's perfunctory jazz record dates for Electrola.[79]

The nascent German jazz musicians toiled hard to acquire the right American touch, which was so often overwhelmed by their lustrous European technique. Improvisation did not come easily even to those with a good ear; for a long time they remained copyists who imitated Bix Beiderbecke or Red Nichols—chiefly white musicians since, unlike many fans, musicians remained strangely oblivious to the creative black man at the center of this music. Often they would transcribe original solos from imported records and then read them note for note during a performance. At other times they would adjust their style to what they thought was the mode and then play freely, and no doubt most awfully.[80] Listening today to the German pianists, probably Spoliansky and Haentzschel, in Lud Gluskin's and Dajos Béla's bands of 1927–28 is revealing. In Gluskin's "Crazy Rhythm," as much as in Béla's "Deep Henderson," their brief solos are halting, unsure in the execution of the harmonic changes, and lacking in the firm percussive approach of native American players.[81]

For commercial reasons, many German musicians pretended not only to be able to play jazz but actually to be Americans, adopting English names. Entire bands joined in this scam, shrewdly banking on the inability of most German entertainment critics to detect their deceit. In early 1925, for instance, a German musician who had probably never set eyes on the Statue of Liberty called himself "Herr Mike Sottnek aus Neuyork" and advertised his outfit as the "amerikanische Jazz-Tanzkapelle." Yet whatever there was in the music that was sincere and had truly evolved in tandem with the American jazz scene was gratefully acknowledged by enlightened German musicians and musicologists.[82]

Chief among the latter was Alfred Baresel. He had studied music in Leipzig and in 1920, at the age of twenty-seven, became a piano teacher in the conservatory. Soon thereafter he started writing music critiques for Leipzig's important dailies, and his musicological articles were printed by progressive music journals such as *Melos*.[83] Baresel was the first German music teacher and critic to take jazz absolutely seriously, publishing in 1925 a jazz exercise book, designed to aid musicians in the art of improvisation, and even in the composition of modern dance pieces. In 1928 he followed this up with jazz études intended for the piano, in which he attempted to stress the genre's distinctive approach to rhythm and harmony. This was succeeded, a year later, by an updated version of his 1925 *Jazzbuch*, now enthusiastically describing jazz as "the most original of the music arts in our day." Baresel called special attention to the unique rhythm of the Negroes and warned against an overemployment of the violin in any true jazz formation.[84] In respectable journal articles, he proved himself an inveterate defender of the new idiom, patiently explaining the significance of orchestras such as Jack Hylton's.[85] Among the proponents of modernist music in the republic, Baresel's equally eloquent colleagues Eberhard Preussner, Hans Heinz

Stuckenschmidt, and others agreed with him that jazz was a dynamic new art form that had to be treated with respect rather than dismissed out of hand.[86]

What impressed most of these critics about jazz was its potential for rejuvenating classical music gone stale in the works of postromantic epigones such as Engelbert Humperdinck or Wilhelm Kienzl. They were joined by such modernist composers as Paul Hindemith, Kurt Weill, and Ernst Krenek, who consciously incorporated elements of jazz into their own creations. Indeed, Krenek's hugely successful opera *Jonny Strikes Up* (1927) constituted a near-perfect symbiosis of the two musical styles.[87]

For the musical modernists at the republic's apex, jazz was a godsend. At least this was the opinion of one of the principal music educators in the country, Humperdinck's former student Dr. Bernhard Sekles. As director of Frankfurt's prestigious Hoch'sche Konservatorium he instituted an academic jazz class in January 1928, especially because German musicians were thought to lack rhythm.[88] The class instructor was Dr. Matyas Seiber, a twenty-three-year-old pupil of Zoltán Kodály, who before long was to publish a modern exercise book for drummers. Seiber taught theory and ensemble playing, schooling his pupils in the conventional jazz instruments. One of these students in 1932 was jazz fan Dietrich Schulz from Magdeburg.[89]

The idealistic Seiber was convinced that jazz had important uses in youth education at all levels, since its rhythmic properties were especially attractive to children.[90] But he was not the only one to think so. Among the many pedagogical experimenters of the Weimar Republic was Ernst John of Leipzig. In 1927 he engaged the local Heini Wenskat dance band to perform for nine hundred youngsters who, spontaneously and predictably, reacted to the beat. Five years later Leipzig's Karl Marx primary school integrated jazz into its curriculum.[91] Enlightened, left-leaning branches of the republic's youth-movement culture were also pervaded by jazz, whose regenerative virtues were cited in the struggle against an outmoded bourgeois value system.[92]

Apart from its most immediate usefulness for recreation, many creative spirits of the Weimar Republic saw in jazz the essence of the era's modernism, an influence toward greater quality and emancipation—in short, democracy for Germans. They imputed to jazz a therapeutic attribute of social dimensions that fitted the New Objectivity of a Hindemith or of the Bauhaus artists. It is no coincidence that after 1925 the Dessau Bauhaus supported its own student jazz band.[93] The technical precision of jazz in its ideal state indeed was comparable to the functionality of Bauhaus painters like Paul Klee and their postexpressionist friends, some of whom, such as George Grosz, adored this music.[94]

Jazz was "the music of this decade," observed the brilliant young historian Eckart Kehr at the end of the republic, before he set out for the United States, where he was to die in the spring of 1933 of a heart ailment, a bitter foe of the ascending National Socialists.[95] With its ring of modernism, jazz was as much a beneficiary of the postwar German passion for American accomplishments as it was its catalyst. To some it was the very incarnation of American vitalism. One of many testimonials to this was its interdependence with the carefree, optimistic chorus-line culture of the cabarets and revues of Berlin.[96] Even fundamentally pessimistic German authors in a Spenglerian vein such as Hermann Hesse became caught up in this attitude. In his celebrated novel *Steppenwolf* the auto-biographical hero Harry Haller, a self-confessed European, at first rejects the idea of the "gramophone and Jazz and modern dance-music . . . the latest rage of America let loose upon the sanctum where I took refuge with Novalis and Jean Paul," but then he succumbs to it.[97]

However, even in the liberal atmosphere of Weimar democracy, the public and private attitude toward blacks, including Afro-Americans, was an ambivalent one, and this reflected on the few black jazz musicians in Germany. The pervading racism of the day did not countenance blacks, no matter what their social station or where they originally hailed from.

Nationalistic student fraternities, for example, did not accept student members who were colored or were married to colored females. When Margret Boveri, later one of the preeminent, and critical, journalists of the 1930s, had an affair with a visiting black American scholar, she was shunned by her colleagues and friends. Eccentric figures from the stage or the arts found it easier to sustain liaisons with colored lovers, as did the Jewish author Joseph Roth, himself an alcoholic outcast from society.[98]

The German star cult around black personalities such as Josephine Baker really was an inverted form of racial prejudice: it was considered safe by good German burghers to flirt with this symbol of Eros as a manifestation of potential immorality, but the mere taste of temptation was satisfying enough. Notwithstanding the sensuality of all of Berlin's lighter culture, La Baker was popular *because* she was an outsider who afforded audiences the titillating illusion of sin while never endangering the moral standard. For her, behind the facade of popularity, lurked the grim reality of rejection as a racial alien.[99] The same disingenuous sufferance underlay the regard ordinary Germans had for Sam Wooding and his black musicians, whenever they made their frequent rounds. "We'd have a crowd of people following us all down the street," remembers Wooding's trumpet man Doc Cheatham, for these American blacks conveyed to Germans, irrespective of their expertise in jazz, a most exotic impression.[100]

In France the acceptance of black artists like Baker and Sidney Bechet was always a total one, not least because the French had a tradition of regarding their own colored colonials as rightful citizens. Hence the development of jazz music there became lastingly influenced by the true originators of that idiom, very much to its benefit.[101] In Germany, as to a limited extent in England, however, the disdain for and fear of blacks relegated them to the periphery of the jazz scene. Among the foreigners employed by German dance or jazz bands, there were extremely few blacks, as for instance in the Borchard band of 1928.[102]

Blacks of German nationality, commonly descendants from the former African colonies, were used in dance formations in the manner of a circus attraction—preferably as noisemakers on the drums. They were obviously expected to play the role of the black "boys" in the American South; native simpletons subservient to their white superiors.[103] This is aptly illustrated in an advertisement of 1926: a pair of Negroes was wanted by a Rhenish hotel, one as a funny waiter and the other as a funny drummer; the two future employees were warned not to expect "fantastic wages."[104]

In 1932, when nationalist sentiment stiffened, the autocratic Papen cabinet forbade the hiring of colored musicians altogether.[105] At the time, Papen's government was supported by all the conservative musicians and music critics who had been denouncing jazz as a product of what was called "nigger" culture. It was "nigger noise," said one critic, thinking it ludicrous rather than humorous. The only purpose of "nigger music" was to introduce obscenities into society, said another.[106] Such vicious polemics reached an initial climax when respectable personalities of the musical establishment such as Hans Pfitzner and Siegmund von Hausegger, in chastising Sekles for the institution of his Frankfurt jazz class, excoriated "nigger blood" and the "rhythm of belly-dancing Negroes."[107]

Sarcastically, music critic Paul Schwers conjured up images of lewdly dancing black boys and girls in the service of procreation.[108] This was meant as a broadside against what was seen as the fulcrum of the Negro's primitivism: his exaggerated sexuality. Such a vision implied that within the black race instinctive, lower forces always got the better of morality and reason as the white man understood them. Moreover, since sensuality had an affinity with dance and unquestionably permeated the jazz of black origin, as did the characteristically ribald lyrics, that music was deemed to be morally and aesthetically inferior to high German culture.

In the German context, so humiliating a view of jazz was a direct consequence of the inability of the losers of World War I to come to terms with a compromising colonial past, especially where native peoples were concerned. Here lay the seeds of a kind of racism that eventually led, from Negrophobia by way of anti-Semitism, to the Nazi liquidation camps.

Long before the Great War the German conquerors had treated their native subjects with patronizing contempt, while at the same time claiming that their attitude toward the colonials was immeasurably more humane than that of the British or the French.[109] Apart from the alleged inability to control their sexual drive, African blacks were singled out by a whole bevy of German Social Darwinists, as well as by colonial administrators, for their disorderliness, want of emotional depth, lack of imagination, laziness, brutality, and compulsion to lying and theft.

Intelligence of the European kind was something they lacked entirely, said anthropologist Eugen Fischer, and his colleague Fritz Lenz augmented this by averring that "accomplishments of genius, in the European sense, have never been shown by a Negro." In a hierarchy of races, German colonial blacks were placed well below the white man and in the proximity of primates, with mulattoes occupying a somewhat more favorable position. Correspondingly, Nordic Germans were positioned at the pinnacle of the human racial pyramid.[110]

Until 1918, antiblack prejudices had become ingrained among German rulers through the African experience. Ordinary Germans only saw colored people again in January 1919, by which time several thousand Senegalese, Sudanese, Malagasies, and North African Arabs were serving with the occupying French Army of the Rhine. The darkest-skinned of those, the Senegalese, were withdrawn to Syria by June 1920; after the spring of 1925, twenty-five hundred nonwhites remained on German territory alongside regular French troops.

With a vengeance German popular opinion, incited by growing propaganda of the radical right, now blamed the black occupation forces for all imaginable social ills, particularly sexual transgressions against innocent girls and women. A Freudian interpretation would hold that behind this was the German male's fear for his own potency, bad enough in colonial times, when the blacks had been near slaves, but hugely enlarged in a situation where blacks commanded a position of power on home terrain. The distortions became so commonplace and were so deep-seated that even Fritz Giese, an influential, enthusiastic champion of American revue culture and admirer of black jazz rhythms, joined in the general condemnation of the French provocation of the Germans' "natural, human racial sentiment."[111]

German opinion of American blacks, bolstered by pseudoscientific research, was scarcely more flattering. Eugenicists such as Fischer and Lenz eagerly embraced the findings of American colleagues, allegedly proving the inferiority of American blacks, and enriched such findings with their own wisdom. Lenz in particular repeated the stereotype about the blacks' "infamous lack of sexual control," while at the same time acknowledging their talent for jazz music. The juxtaposition of sexual voracity and propensity for jazz once again reduced this music to a mere function of base impulses.[112]

Simultaneously, a link was forged between racially inferior blacks and Jews. The latter were recognized in jazz not just as musicians and composers, but also as commercial managers and middlemen of the music. In Germany after the Great War, Negrophobia merged easily with preexisting anti-Semitism and actually gave it renewed impetus, because Jews were often portrayed as racially akin to blacks and possessed of similarly objectionable characteristics. Motivated by the same sexual jealousy, German men in 1919 distributed leaflets warning their women of "Jews, Negroes, Russians, Mongols." Jews also had to share the blame heaped on the French for waging a "Negro-Jewish war" on Germans.[113]

That Jews were especially gifted jazz artists is a truism, grounded as much in their socioethnic as in their diversified religious tradition; it is frequently emphasized by Jewish analysts themselves. Incontestably, Jews in the Weimar Republic stood out as protagonists of new art forms such as jazz, cabaret, and film, and they were in the vanguard of modernism both as creators and impresarios.[114] Thus the majority of jazz dance-band leaders were Jews, often from Eastern Europe, as for instance Béla, Weber, Efim Schachmeister, Paul Godwin, and Ben Berlin. This also applied in large part to the leading jazz combo of the era, the Weintraub Syncopators, and to the Comedian Harmonists, the jazz-inspired vocal group. Mischa Spoliansky and Friedrich Hollaender, whose talents moved between jazz, revue, and cabaret, were Jewish, and so was Paul Hirson, a former waiter and jazz devotee who in the late republican years acted as a casual but very efficient job broker for scores of Berlin's ensemble players.[115]

Some of the younger Jewish musicians, who appeared to have a feel for the essence of jazz and who mastered the challenge of playing hot choruses with relative ease, included the trumpeters Adolf ("Adi") Rosner (intermittently a Syncopator) and Rolf Goldstein (with Borchard in 1931–32). Also Jewish were the pianist Martin Roman, himself a former Syncopator and accompanist for Sidney Bechet in 1929, and the saxophonist Freddie Schweitzer, whose superb credentials persuaded Jack Hylton to lure him across the Channel to Great Britain.[116] A significant proportion of the jazz record collectors in the Berlin fan club were Jewish, and one of the favorite Düsseldorf dance bars, the Tabaris, was jokingly referred to as "Tanz-Bar Israels," even by the Jews themselves.[117]

Thus the massive attack on Bernhard Sekles and Matyas Seiber for having polluted the Frankfurt conservatory with a jazz curriculum was partially motivated by anti-Semitism, because both musicians were Jewish. To a large extent, however, the affair was grounded in the philistinism of the classical-music establishment. While Sekles was looked upon as a blinded idealist wasting his energies on a dubious pastime, his collaborator Seiber, a classical cellist with prior exposure to jazz in the United States, was regarded as an unconscionable opportunist interested only in his career. Spearheading the anti-Frankfurt campaign were leading composers and conductors—Pfitzner, Hausegger, and the Cologne professor Hermann Abendroth.[118]

Throughout the twenties Pfitzner led the war against jazz on behalf of all his high-culture colleagues by repeatedly publishing invective. This elderly man, who professionally was clearly losing out to the modernists, fought jazz as the "musical expression of Americanism." To him the music was a form of obscenity.[119]

Richard Strauss and the conductor Karl Muck, though more civilized in their comportment, essentially shared these sentiments.[120] Strauss's friend Siegfried Wagner, Richard Wagner's son, who not only was a composer in his own right but also, through the Bayreuth Festival, controlled much of Germany's musical life, typically vilified jazz as the manifestation of "nigger rhythms" and deplored its influence on the modern composers.[121]

This last point was something traditional music critics felt especially keen about. To them it was blasphemy to have the main character of Krenek's opera *Jonny Strikes Up,* an American Negro playing a jazz fiddle, emerge victorious at the end of a tortured plot, throughout which Western classical music was derided and white heroines succumbed to the black musician's charms. George Antheil, the young American composer and Berlin habitué, was reprimanded for incorporating "Negro jazz, mechanical pianos, etc." into his chamber music.[122]

Conservative critics had as much trouble with the harmonic liberties that jazz was assuming as with the new sounds of the classical modernists. The "blue-sound" microtonal pitch inflections of a jazz saxophone were as annoying to them as the quarter tones produced by Alois Hába's specially built piano.[123] The venerated music historian Alfred Einstein's denunciation of jazz as the "invention of a Nigger in Chicago" and "the most disgusting treason against all Occidental civilized music," summarized in its pungency the various objections that abounded, and was potentially damaging because of its authoritative ring.[124]

In the much wider landscape of the republic's conservative opposition to most forms of modernism and democracy, jazz became a potent symbol of cultural decay. It is true that such sentiments converged with various feelings of abhorrence expressed by bigoted traditionalists in the United States, but there can be no doubt that military defeat and the resulting wound to national honor rendered an espousal of jazz an even greater sacrilege in Germany.[125] There, conservative theologians of Günther Dehn's stature ascribed to it the same decadent qualities as did patriotic veterans' associations such as Jungstahlhelm, the Young Steel Helmet. Their scathing condemnations were eagerly seconded by reactionary critics of Alfred Hugenberg's press empire, chief among them Friedrich Hussong.[126]

Educators and youth movement spokesmen no less than theologians tended to single out the danger of sexual corruption endemic in that music and the nightclub atmosphere it was associated with, a danger that conservative physicians were linking to the whole phenomenon of a self-destructing life.[127] Jazz was equally scorned by the reactionary student fraternities at the universities.[128]

Many of these critics were already secret or open followers of the National Socialist movement, which stood in total opposition to any manifestations of modernity. Fascist-leaning veterans of World War I and of the anti-Semitic Freikorps such as the aristocrat Ernst von Salomon and the medical student Kurt Blome joined other members of the radical right in denouncing Jews and blacks. Their "Nigger music" was perceived as the ruse entrapping Nordic German womanhood in sordid sexuality.[129] *Völkisch* authors Gerhard Schumann and Edwin Erich Dwinger wrote stage plays and novels depicting young white girls yielding to the lures of the erotic saxophone, and Gothic blond heroes seduced by the lascivious jazz songs of cheap prostitutes.[130] A eugenically inspired racist, the eccentric youth leader Muck Lamberty collected boys and girls in what he termed a Higher Breed Campaign. Like Charles Manson four decades later in California, he had sexual relations with the females, getting several of them pregnant, all for the sake of racial rejuvenation and Adolf Hitler, and against Jews, blacks, and jazz.[131]

Nor were these Nazi pundits absent from musicians' circles. At a time when several neoclassical composers—the epigones of Beethoven, Brahms, and Wagner—were on the defensive, and not even traditionalists of Pfitzner's ilk could hold their own against serialism, atonality, and the New Objectivity of the republic's moderns, many a third-rate musician was tempted to blame it all on the pervasive jazz culture. Joseph Snaga, for instance, who composed innocuous operettas under titles such as *The Portrait of the Concubine,* prided himself on using only "Aryan" artists whenever a work of his was premiered, and did so in protest against "Jewish music and Nigger songs."[132] Music critic Dr. Alfred Heuss publicly castigated atonality and the "orgies of Negro jazz" as early as 1920, a year later becoming editor of the *völkisch* music journal *Zeitschrift für Musik* in Leipzig, which hailed the Führer and thrived on fulminations against jazz and the modernism from which it sprang.[133] Hugo Rasch, another music critic and disciple of Hitler, launched one of the heaviest assaults ever on jazz and Bernhard Sekles's supposed anti-German conspiracy.[134]

Gradually, this hatred of jazz and its subculture spread throughout the Nazi party structure that Hitler and his associates were at pains to erect, after he had been released from Landsberg prison in late 1924. It permeated the Hitler Youth, which was intent on driving a wedge of discord into the bourgeois German youth movement.[135] The hardy fighters of the Brown Shirts espoused it to the same degree as did National Socialist teachers and women's leaguers.[136] And for emphasis the National Socialist Physicians' Union assiduously pointed out the consequences of an increasing birth rate among blacks in South Africa.[137]

Adolf Hitler himself is not known to have made any specific pronouncements on jazz in the Weimar Republic. What is certain is that as a follower of Richard Wagner he did not like modernism in the arts, including music; in the Nazi party's program of February 1920 he threatened future governmental measures against decadent tendencies in art and literature. On the other hand, he offered no concrete plans for the rejuvenation of a Germanic culture as such. Surely jazz, as an allegedly degenerate product of Negroes and Jews, was anathema to him, but not important enough to be worthy of discussion. What he did refer to repeatedly in his early public speeches was the "black shame" on the Rhine. This was of course fashionable among all right-wing politicians at the time. As might be expected, his references to the Senegalese are abrim with insinuations about the sexual and eugenic danger posed for innocent German women. Moreover, according to Hitler it was the Jews who had offered these women to the Negroes, after doing everything in their power to corrupt them sexually in the dance halls. To judge from all of this, Hitler's opinion about jazz must have been linked to his strong views on a racial hierarchy, with jazz at the very bottom.[138]

The Führer had two advisers at his side who were to become instrumental in shaping a new cultural policy: Joseph Goebbels and Alfred Rosenberg. Goebbels had received his doctorate in German literature from Heidelberg. Named Hitler's Gauleiter in Berlin as of November 1926, he was a keen observer of the arts, a journalist with a penchant for scintillating prose, and an amateur pianist of moderate talent.

As his diary of the last republican years well illustrates, Goebbels took time out to play the piano, mostly popular classical pieces, and he savored the capital's busy concert life. In light entertainment he favored operetta (as did Hitler) and occasionally a large revue show in the Scala.[139] As he writes about Berlin's pulsating night life, it becomes obvious that he is more revolted by this "Babylon of Sin" than attracted to it, although, womanizer that he was, he could not escape its sensual lure altogether.[140]

During Goebbels's exposure to some of the more emblematic manifestations of the jazz culture in its wider sense, the prejudices of a small-town, petit-bourgeois racist, a hater of Jews and blacks, assert themselves: a black revue, probably by Baker, disgusts him, and so do the songs of the Revellers on Berlin Radio. "Negrodom, the art of the subhuman"—such is Goebbels's condemnation. His judgment regarding the film *The Singing Fool,* in which the Jewish actor Al Jolson portrays a black singer, is as decidedly cutting as that of the Kadeko, where he sees only the Jew at work. *The Blue Angel,* featuring Hollaender's music score and, briefly, the Weintraub Syncopators, also invokes his wrath; for him this is "offal," spewed out by the fetid city.[141]

It was clear to Doctor Goebbels, as it was to Hitler, that after a change in government he would assume responsibility for Germany's cultural renewal at the ministerial level. In conversations with the Führer in January and then again in August 1932, when it seemed likely that the Nazis would be called to power, Goebbels was promised jurisdiction over film, radio, art, and culture generally, together with a new revolutionary office of propaganda. But before this came to pass, the doctor had to outmaneuver his rival for that post, the Baltic German Alfred Rosenberg, who was the editor-in-chief of the Nazis' national daily newspaper, the *Völkischer Beobachter.* [142]

Munich-based Rosenberg had taken a much closer look at jazz than Goebbels or Hitler ever bothered to do. To the pseudo-scholar that he was, this cretinized American art form symbolized everything that was insidiously evil in a Jewish-Negro plot to undermine Germanic culture. [143] To counter this plot, and at the same time recruit conservative, educated, upper-class members of German society for the Nazi party, Rosenberg in early 1929 founded the Kampfbund für deutsche Kultur (Combat League for German Culture), which he dedicated to the defense of German values by stressing the connections between "race, art, and scholarship." Its mission was to fight against the further "disintegration of our cultural foundations." This concerned the visual arts as much as theater, film, radio, and of course music. Significantly, Dr. Alfred Heuss of the Leipzig racist *Zeitschrift für Musik* and Richard Wagner's daughter-in-law Winifred were among the Kampfbund's earliest members. [144]

As the Kampfbund was spreading throughout the Reich and particularly in the capital, Goebbels could not but feel that he had been left out in the cold. After attending one of the Kampfbund's Berlin meetings in 1932, he was full of malice about its mixed bag of offerings: "bad singers and a competent magician . . . this, then, is 'German culture'!" [145] All the same, the Gauleiter did have a liaison in the organization, an early Nazi fighter by the name of Hans Hinkel, who was on the staff of Goebbels's Berlin newspaper *Der Angriff.* Hinkel, as it turned out, was the administrative mastermind responsible for the impressive success of the Kampfbund until 1933; his relationship with Rosenberg cooled to the same degree that he was winning Goebbels's confidence. [146]

Under Hinkel's direction as general secretary, the Kampfbund embarked on a vicious campaign against all things Jewish, demanding instead increased creative activity by truly Nordic artists who would shun decrepit modernism. Henceforth stately matrons and honorable gentlemen were invited to any of the Kampfbund's regional gatherings to present Schubert lieder or chamber performances of Beethoven quartets. In contradistinction and true to Nazi form, the black man and his music were treated as a racial aberration, and his sexual aspect was deplored. This, to the Nazis, was Weimar culture: "Niggers, belly dancers, bordello crooners, all as spiritual leaders." *Völkisch* imperative instead called for the effacement of this evil: jazz had to be expunged. [147]

In this the Kampfbund was indirectly furthered when the National Socialists took over the Thuringian state government in January 1930. In April an ordinance against "Negro culture" was promulgated, prohibiting "jazz band and drum music, Negro dances, Negro songs, Negro plays." Jazz thus joined the modern paintings of Paul Klee and Wassily Kandinsky in being banished from public notice. This ban remained in effect until the Nazi government was voted out of office one year later.[148]

At the beginning of the 1930s, in Germany, jazz found itself in an ambiguous position. Not originally a German art form, it fell under the same shadow of suspicion as did other American imports into postwar German society, imports that were generally regarded as outgrowths of modernism such as rationalized methods of factory production or democracy itself. The democratic manner in which jazz musicians were wont to improvise among themselves—all being essentially equal as members of the group—reinforced this negative impression. On the one hand, the presence of Americans in the jazz and dance music scene antagonized German nationalists; on the other, however, even good-willed republicans were painfully reminded of their own imperfections in making and comprehending this music. The support structure of fans was thin and tenuous, while defense efforts emanating from enlightened corners of the establishment, as the case of Professor Sekles shows, were as naively conceived as they were clumsily executed. The seriousness with which the Frankfurt conservatory pushed through its jazz class was characteristic of a stern German mentality rather than of American lightheartedness. And jazz's potential for being identified with ill-suffered minorities or pariahs of German society, the demimonde, the depraved, blacks, and Jews, rendered it forever suspect in the eyes of social and racial bigots, even if they were privately tempted to relish the peculiar aesthetics of this music. To a large extent, jazz shared this fate with other facets of postwar modernist art: postexpressionist painting, the Bauhaus, and atonal music.

The economic depression starting at the end of the twenties exacerbated these difficulties as well as creating new ones. For dance and jazz music, the actual depression was foreshadowed several years before the fall of 1929 at various levels. In their notorious state of professional nonorganization, musicians easily fell prey to economic vagaries even after the stabilization of the currency in early 1924. Since the light-entertainment business was an extremely volatile one, ensemble musicians always were the first to feel the pinch, as the consuming public, agents, and restaurateurs would invariably pay them last, if ever.

Consummate dance-band musicians who also were competent jazz performers were no exceptions to this law. Although fiscal relief was slowly coming from the new Rentenmark and more and more Germans used it once again to finance a good time, restaurant and club owners were still burdened by exacting local and regional entertainment taxes, which cut down on their end profits. A one o'clock police curfew in most major cities, including Berlin, which deterred patrons from enjoying themselves well into the night, further hindered profits. Hence musicians were paid much less than they should have been, and their dismal self-organization meant that no system of professional examinations would weed out incompetent yet brazenly competitive intruders. As the army of entertainment artists grew, prospective employers enjoyed a position of relative strength in hiring only the cheapest bidders, in the absence of an official wage scale. Compared to prewar conditions, the musicians' real wage was much smaller on average, and there was unemployment even in 1925–27, a prosperous period for most other breadwinners in the land. Exceptionally bad seasonal stretches, as during the inclement summers of 1925 and 1926, did their share in destroying the work always sought after in health spas and seaside resorts.[149]

As the tax and curfew burdens were gradually lifted from mid-1926 on, more Germans came to patronize live entertainment, to the financial benefit of entrepreneurs and musicians alike. The climax in this development was reached during the carnival season of 1929, when a "bacchantian dance frenzy, a lust in the whirling rhythms of music" was noted.[150] However, luxury taxes and curfew restrictions were never entirely removed. This was thought to be an important reason for the severity of the depression, paralyzing most musicians under the restrictive Brüning, Papen, and Schleicher cabinets after March 1930.[151]

Yet another predepression circumstance that inconvenienced musicians earlier than most other occupational groups in Germany was the introduction of sound film during the first half of 1929, that is, before October's Black Friday in New York. The talkies cast into the streets scores of instrumentalists who had been playing in the pit bands of movie theaters—up to eighteen musicians in the luxurious cosmopolitan ones, and anywhere from a piano player to a quartet in the smaller cinemas. Budding jazz musicians like Georg Haentzschel and Ernst Höllerhagen had worked in theaters in their student days, and many even of the jazz-inclined, not talented enough to land a spot with a famous dance band or in a Berlin recording studio, continued to play there well into 1929.[152]

The earliest of the German "sound films," like their American counterparts, were silent movies overlaid with speech and music. The first of these, premiered in Berlin in January 1929, featured the voice of the famous tenor Richard Tauber. Most of the eleven sound pictures produced in Germany during 1929 were of this kind, but the first true German talkie, *Melody of the Heart* with music by Paul Abraham, was shown in December to overflowing critical acclaim and the consternation of most ensemble musicians.[153]

In the spring of 1929, as some cinema owners began to replace their pit bands first with gramophones and then with movie sound equipment, the first musicians were fired without notice. From then on things deteriorated very fast. Thus the large Berlin Ufa theaters, which had employed two hundred orchestra players in 1928, two years later only had fifty left, for the few remaining silent movies. In the fall of 1930 there was mention of eight thousand unemployed musicians in all of Germany, on account of the movie revolution. By the beginning of 1933, these cinema casualties had almost doubled.[154]

Moreover, from the end of 1929 on, because of decreasing wages and mounting loss of jobs, Germans tended to stay at home rather than enjoy themselves in dance halls or beer parlors. Consequently, more instrumentalists were dismissed, adding to the number of already idle theater entertainers. Musicians' wages plummeted. In those days it was not unusual for a player to accept an evening's work with an assorted band, just to avoid the dole, and then to learn that, after deductions, he had made no more than his expenses.[155] By February 1930 "bring-your-own-sandwich" balls had become the rage in Berlin, depriving hotel and club proprietors of possible earnings from clients' food and drink. Large dance establishments, like the Palais de Danse in Berlin, had to close their doors; cafés, clubs, and hotel lobbies resorted to the radio or record player for background music. Public dancing was further discouraged by government decrees. Many musicians now reverted to different occupations, inasmuch as they were able to, as did the young Berlin drummer Max Rumpf, who in bourgeois life was an optician.[156] Record consumption also slumped, as all kinds of recordings were becoming unaffordable, and the Berlin studio scene was showing signs of the downturn.[157] Throughout all this, only the very best musicians and those with established connections could support themselves. Among them were Georg Haentzschel and his friend Franz Grothe, pianist Fritz Schulze from Magdeburg, and the Berlin trumpeter Rolf Goldstein.[158]

These adversities bore down heavily on the many foreign instrumentalists in the German dance and jazz scene. With the growing political presence of the National Socialists, especially after the general elections of September 1930, not only did a hypernationalistic spirit of intolerance discriminate more heavily against the Jews in the country, but non-German nationals were also blamed for taking jobs away from Germans.

Foreign musicians had entered Germany virtually unchecked, after currency stabilization in 1924, because it had been lucrative for them. Most of these were Hungarians, often Jews, who quite literally played on the Germans' penchant for Gypsy music. Some Spaniards and South Americans had taken advantage of the growing tango craze, and Americans and British had capitalized on the public's hunger for jazz, or what passed for such. There were no restrictions on the numbers of those foreigners, for the Treaty of Versailles had mandated an open-door policy on the part of German governments. Besides, even though there were ample complaints from German musicians, the well-informed knew that if the republic clamped down on the foreign guests, then Germany's neighbors would retaliate against the thousands of German ensemble players of good reputation who traditionally worked there. With specific reference to jazz, the well-informed knew also that German instrumentalists could learn from the Anglo-Saxons, and that a German band's overall attraction and financial success would be enhanced by the presence of just a few American colleagues.[159]

But the mood even of the reasonable became more ugly after the fall of 1929, when more German musicians faced dismissals. Militants demanded that Germany pass laws against the foreign competitors or that previously issued permits be rescinded. Some pointed to heightened chauvinism in neighboring states that was putting German musicians out of work, as happened to Haentzschel with Lud Gluskin's band in Paris in 1930: while the Americans were celebrated, the Berliner was expelled. And as some observers were mistakenly asserting that the quality of German jazz had improved immeasurably, none other than the universally admired big band of Jack Hylton was maligned in the pages of *Artist,* a German musicians' trade journal.[160]

On the jazz circuit, key British and American players began leaving the country by 1931, as they became subject to xenophobic harassment by colleagues and authorities alike. Among them, Haentzschel's friend Teddy Kline returned to New York, and Howard McFarlane went back to England. Until 1933, only a few of the foreigners held out: the guitarists Mike Danzi and Harold Kirchstein, the reed players Billy Bartholomew and Danny Polo. From Denmark, Belgium, and Holland, jazz musicians like Kai Ewans, Fud Candrix, and Jack de Vries still managed to enter the scene, but only temporarily. A significant exception was the Romanian James Kok, who by 1932 led one of the most sizzling big bands in Berlin, staffed largely with German players.[161]

Toward the end of the republic, it seemed that the art of jazz in Germany was on the decline in more ways than one. In the somber atmosphere of the depression, while cynics or the carefree might call for a dance on the volcano, the general public returned to a more romantic musical repertoire, as was also reflected in the costume and musical film productions of the era. In the early thirties the sentimental kitsch of commercial song and the old salon and coffeehouse style of music predominated once more, with the waltz replacing the fox-trot. Outmoded instruments such as the harmonium, which could produce a deceptive orchestral sound controlled by only one player, reappeared for reasons of economy as well as taste. Traditional bandleaders of Bernard Etté's standing publicly forswore jazz and instead hailed the good, old German dance forms.[162]

It is certain that jazz in Germany at that time could not but reflect a general crisis of the music in the United States that, as Schuller informs us, began after artistic exhaustion in 1928 and thereafter was intensified by the economic decline.[163] There was consensus even among the most benevolent of German critics that jazz had spent its vitality by forsaking the art of improvisation, that it had become stale and bereft of all resiliency. It had failed to inspire the classics, as was evident in the concurrent difficulties some modernists were now experiencing.[164] If the composer Karol Rathaus had spoken as early as 1927 of the "dusk of jazz," music educator Matyas Seiber noted cryptically three years later that for the future the genre held few surprises.[165]

As the outspoken enemies of jazz gleefully recorded the death of the music, it did indeed appear that this art form had become as much a victim of antimodernist reaction as had the avant-garde Bauhaus or other manifestations of the experimental attitude in serious music, the graphic arts, or literature.[166] Frankfurt critic Theodor Wiesengrund-Adorno, himself an avant-gardist, a pupil of Sekles and Alban Berg who happened to dislike jazz, thought that this music had failed in the end because of its immodest claim to recognition as an original art. Patronizingly, Adorno consigned jazz to the arts and crafts.[167] But in this case, that brilliant pundit's analysis was corrupted by his private prejudice.

Without question, during the gradual smothering of the republic, jazz too was suffering a tortuous setback. Indeed, had it not been one of the most prodigious offsprings of the Weimar spirit and the hope of many who deemed themselves enlightened? Yet what Adorno and all the cognoscenti did not know was that jazz, this unpredictable and ambivalent culture, was going to spring back to a healthy life, ironically under a dictatorship and not without problems and compromises, but nevertheless in sufficient fortitude to assure its longevity in Germany beyond the catastrophe of 1945. For in the last half of the 1920s, whatever its imperfections, jazz had anchored itself too securely to be blown over by the storms of political change.

On the Index: The Third Reich's Prewar Campaign

Ideological Foundations and Polemics

"Now you can go packing with all your jazz!"[1] The musician who said this to a jazz-motivated colleague was a longtime follower of Adolf Hitler, and he said it on 30 January 1933, the very day Hitler took power in Berlin as chancellor of the German Reich. Forthwith Prof. Fritz Stein, director of the Berlin conservatory and a devotee of folk music, banned jazz from his hallowed domain.[2]

It was at a time when conservative essayist Friedrich Hussong could write that Berlin's central avenue, the Kurfürstendamm, had become synonymous with the Weimar Republic. It symbolized the whimsies of the era, wrote Hussong, the perversions and impotence of its theater, "the death of music in the jazz band, Nigger song and Nigger art, criminals glorified, the cult of the proletariat, rootless pacifism, bloodless intellectuality, proabortion histrionics, armchair communism, black-red-golden representational pomp, futurism, cubism, dadaism," in short, "the rot of a decaying society."[3] These conditions were thought to be swept away, now that Hitler had taken control.

Professor Stein deemed himself to be supported by an official rejection of jazz in the Third Reich, and in this he was correct. Figuratively speaking, jazz was placed on the Index: it was denigrated as much in music journals as in daily newspapers and illustrated broadsheets, government directives and the radio ranted against it, and public opinion maligned it as "Nigger jazz."[4]

Such polemics were linked, at one level, to the National Socialist disdain for most things of American origin, unless they were of a technical variety such as automobiles or films. On a related plane, these polemics were rooted in the Nazi racist ideology that discriminated heavily against non-"Aryans"—in particular, blacks and Jews.

While in power, the Nazis always misunderstood and misrepresented the

American psyche and its culture, and remained blind and deaf to any form of enlightenment on this subject. They steadfastly believed that the United States constituted a corrupt people devoid of sophistication, with a childlike mentality that countenanced fun and games but was incapable of profundity or erudition. Hitler and Goebbels above all despised the Americans for the relatively large degree of tolerance they extended to the racial minorities that were being expunged from the German *Volksgemeinschaft,* the blood-based *völkisch* community—namely, blacks and Jews.[5] America's national culture was said to reflect the destructive influence of those minorities. As Goebbels once put it, "Everyone knows, America's contribution to the music of the world consists merely of jazzed-up Nigger music, not worthy of a single mention."[6]

On the surface, the Nazi contempt for the black, whether of American or African origin, found its expression under the best of circumstances in a patronizing attitude toward Negro social life or culture as manifested within the boundaries of the Reich. In good missionary tradition, African blacks were dubbed "the chocolate people," credited with modest talents and therefore ready for the gift of German culture, if not religion, and always seen as on the brink of perdition from a failure to control instinctive drives.[7] Even though Hitler remained equivocal on the future of the German colonies in Africa, in principle he claimed sovereignty over the former native subjects in Togo or in Cameroon, and this was fuel for the fire of eager German imperialists, who viewed blacks as exploitable.[8]

After 1933, colored offspring of former colonials, living legally in the Reich in tiny numbers as German citizens, were subjected to daily offense, and their integration into society was forcibly prevented. Usually their activities were relegated to the circus; they were supervised like immature minors. In 1936 a circus entrepreneur sought to take advantage of a group of independent German-colonial blacks who had been performing vaudeville acts throughout the land. On the characteristic pretext that because of "sexual excesses" they had posed a considerable disciplinary problem, he asked for government permission to fence the blacks in and thereby guarantee their "morally impeccable" conduct.[9] What he really wanted was to exploit them in his own business.

Blacks of foreign citizenship also met with insults. The most notorious example of this was the demeaning manner in which Hitler treated black American medalists during the 1936 Olympics in Berlin, when he refused to shake champion Jesse Owens's hand, for instance, and turned his back on the celebration of other black winners. Goebbels joined Hitler in his open scorn.[10] From such discriminatory practice the Muses were not exempt. The famous black American classical singer Marian Anderson was banned from giving concerts in Germany while on a wide European tour in 1935–36, because of "the color of her skin as a Negress."[11] Black artists from the jazz world such as Duke Ellington, Louis Armstrong, and Coleman Hawkins fell under the same indictment, and thus were never heard in person in Germany until after 1945.

As in the 1920s, this distaste for blacks was expressed according to the pseudoscience then in vogue, but in a more radical fashion. Joachim Mrugowsky, later to be hanged by the Allies as one of Heinrich Himmler's leading criminal physicians, wrote in 1939 that the ideas of the Enlightenment were abrogated, in that today it was possible to discern the "natural differences" between blacks and whites. He was supported in his view by prominent racial hygienists such as Munich professor Theodor Mollison, Auschwitz doctor Josef Mengele's first mentor, and Prof. Ernst Rodenwaldt, who taught race science at Heidelberg.[12]

More than ever, race hygienists now believed in the primacy of hereditary factors. No environmental pressure in the world could turn a Negro into a "Frisian farmer," and such a Negro "could wash himself as long as he liked, he would never become white."[13] Since as a result of sexual relations between blacks and whites the black hereditary mass would always dominate, interracial union was forbidden by the Nuremberg Blood Laws of September 1935.[14] One of the first consequences of this legislation was the forcible sterilization in 1937 of the Rhineland Bastards, colored children whose fathers had been dark-skinned French colonials serving with the occupying Army of the Rhine after World War I.[15]

Against this background, Nazi polemics denounced the presence of blacks in jazz. Four arguments were employed, but since the Germans possessed little fundamental knowledge of jazz, they had trouble with all but one of them.

First, musicologists could not agree as to whether the African continent or the United States should be deplored as the historic home of jazz. This failure detracted from their credibility as experts on a genre that needed concise definition in order to be lastingly obliterated.

Second, the rhythmic device of the syncope was identified and attacked as the core ingredient of the very rhythm that typified jazz, and one that was unsuitable for marching. Unlike Germans, "Negro tribes do not march!"[16] But this approach foundered when musicologists remembered that even J. S. Bach had utilized the syncope. They then agreed that it was not the syncope as such, but the context in which it was used, that was to be condemned—an unconvincing compromise.

Third, the saxophone, that highly specialized jazz tool, presented itself as a natural culprit, in particular since German dance musicians had been learning it slowly and imperfectly only since the mid-1920s. This, however, quickly brought the German musical instruments industry into the fray, when their saxophone sales began to slacken, so again the tack was changed. It was declared that the saxophone was the nineteenth-century invention of a German, Adolf Sax, who had migrated to Belgium, with the result that his instrument became first known through the classical compositions of neighboring Frenchmen such as Claude Debussy. Nonetheless, Richard Strauss also was fond of scoring for it, so the unfortunate instrument itself was not at fault, but the manner in which blacks exploited it in jazz, debasing its originally noble tone and abusing it to accentuate the already arousing rhythms. This argument, too, was weakened by the universal knowledge that Sax had really been Belgian (his first name was Adolphe) and that, while jazz-specific sounds such as bent blue notes were thought to peal with particular effect from a saxophone as mastered by a black, the essence of that horn could hardly be ascribed to a nativist black culture, whether American or African-based.

The fourth argument once more targeted the insidious sexual powers of jazz. If produced by promiscuous primitives in a time of racial indictment on eugenic grounds, the alluring sensuality of jazz had to be viewed as corrupting national morality. Because no counterargument could be advanced against this point, music critics were most comfortable with it.[17]

Besides, this charge of wanton sexuality blended all too well with the Nazis' concomitant diatribes against Jews. As opposed to the anti-Negro/Jewish arguments of the Weimar Republic, those of the Hitler dictatorship were more differentiated and also more pernicious, largely because of the elevated pseudoscientific level at which they were aired. Whereas it was averred by racist anthropologists that Jews contained a significantly large proportion of negroid blood (a judgment that stemmed mainly from the amateur but influential Jena scholar Hans F. K. Günther), the Jews were thought to range above the blacks by dint of their mental powers, coupled with a strong sense of determination—the obverse of the happy-go-lucky animal state of the blacks.[18] A high degree of rationality had endowed the Jews with the gift of theoretical abstraction, which, in contradistinction to the brainless blacks, rendered them capable of peculiarly "Jewish" cultural accomplishments: "Jewish physics," for instance, as noted by Heidelberg Nobel laureate Philipp Lenard or, in music, the rational perversion of atonality, said to be exemplified by Arnold Schoenberg.[19]

Since the Jews were perceived as comprehending both art forms, the Nazis' ready juxtaposition of atonal modernist music with jazz was no coincidence. The connection was made obvious to the German public in the spring of 1938, when posters advertising a Düsseldorf exposition of "degenerate music," patterned on the notorious exhibition of "degenerate art" a year before, featured a monkeylike Negro, decorated with the Star of David, tooting a saxophone. The exposition guidebook, with an identical image on the cover, discussed at length the dreaded modernist composers and, in that connection, mentioned jazz.[20]

Nazi musicologists acknowledged the skill of Jewish-American composers like George Gershwin and Irving Berlin as contributions to the jazz world. But they thought their musical creations cleverly contrived copies of the original articles associated with blacks.[21] According to these Nazis, the crucial role Jews played in jazz was that of publicizers, middlemen for commercial consumption, advertisers for a mass market. Jewish jazz musicians typically were arrangers, conductors, or business agents, said the Nazis.

Even Benny Goodman was discovered, by 1938, to have cloned an intellectualized version, called "swing," from the black archetype. Goodman had simply manipulated the preexisting medium toward a specifically Jewish complexity and then marketed it internationally! Since the Jews had forced the blacks into humiliating partnership, the label "Nigger-Jew jazz" was as justified as ever. Ingenuousness had been married to cunning, "Niggerism to Jewish frivolity."[22]

As one Hitler Youth leader summed it up in 1936: "The Nigger has a very pronounced feeling for rhythm, and his 'art' is perhaps indigenous but nevertheless offensive to our sentiments. Surely, such stuff belongs among the Hottentots and not in a German dance hall. The Jew, on the other hand, has cooked these aberrations up on purpose."[23]

The proposition was more simplistically stated by an ocean liner's band musician who wrote home from Brazil: "Negroes and Jews have thrown trash at the German people for almost fifteen years, and it's my wish to help clean it out."[24] And if the blacks were thought to use the sexual ingredient of jazz naively and without racial design, the Jews were perceived as making it part of their systematic plot to poison the blood of German girls and women by seducing them through acts of "musical race defilement."[25]

Who, then, were the men that spewed out such invective? Chief among them was the former Kampfbund für deutsche Kultur functionary Dr. Fritz Stege, who regularly contributed a malicious column against all "un-German" music to the musicians' trade journal *Artist*.[26] Born in 1896, Stege had lost his father in World War I. Impoverished, he had studied classical piano and taken up music journalism. Although he only joined the Nazi party in 1930, he had claimed an "unerring political leaning" toward the extreme right since 1920.[27]

Somewhat less ubiquitous was Dr. Herbert Gerigk, nine years younger than Stege, with an aspiration in the late 1920s to become a music professor. Because of a scarcity of academic positions, he too had drifted into journalism; by 1933 he had joined the party and the storm troopers and allied himself with Alfred Rosenberg, who gave him a job as music critic of the party's daily, the *Völkischer Beobachter*. Gerigk coauthored a book on Jews in music and joined the SS in April 1939.[28]

It is clear that these men and others like them were driven early into the Nazi camp by a combination of socioeconomic uprootedness and radical-right proclivities—a very common phenomenon among young intellectuals toward the end of the republic. They then simply stuck to their chosen creed and made a career of it until the end in 1945.

Other cases, however, were more complex. One was that of Alfred Baresel, the well-established Leipzig musicologist who in the twenties had been a herald of jazz.[29] Perhaps because he sensed that, as an exposed friend of this idiom, his days as a piano teacher at the Leipzig conservatory might be numbered, early in 1933 he lauded the regime's new cultural policy. Having once upheld the black man's ingenuity as the essence of jazz, in 1936 he argued against "negroid drum rhythms." And in 1937 he joined the party—none too soon, for a year later Max Merz, a genuine antijazz crusader, accused Baresel of collusion with Jews.[30]

Baresel became a turncoat perhaps out of existential necessity. Whether he really wished jazz to go under may reasonably be doubted. Other musicologists were convinced, however, that with Hitler's arrival the end of jazz was near. One of them was Theodor Adorno. Having hated jazz with a passion even at the end of the republic, early in the regime he was enthused over the prospect of the Nazi authorities forbidding the music altogether—a strange position for a Jew who was to emigrate to England in the spring of 1934.[31] But Adorno was in for a disappointment; despite all the polemics, jazz never would be officially banned.

First Public Controls

At the beginning of the Third Reich, Hitler had entrusted to Joseph Goebbels the censorship of the nation's entire cultural life, excepting education and the Prussian theaters and operas. In his office as Reich propaganda minister Goebbels erected, by September 1933, the Reichskulturkammer (RKK), or Reich Culture Chamber, with sections for radio, theater, film, creative writing, the press, and music. This organization owed its origins directly to Rosenberg's Kampfbund, which Goebbels had begun to infiltrate in 1932 with the aid of his stooge Hans Hinkel, once Rosenberg's creature but long indispensable to Goebbels as manager of his Berlin broadsheet *Angriff*.[32] While Goebbels made himself president of the new body, Hinkel became its executive secretary in the spring of 1935. By appointing the thirty-four-year-old Hinkel—a man who had never taken his university examinations and had neither a working background nor a demonstrated interest in the arts—to this most important post, Goebbels reemphasized his intention of using culture merely as a propaganda instrument in the manipulation of public opinion.[33]

Under Goebbels's presidency, the Reichsmusikkammer (RMK), or Reich Music Chamber, as one of the RKK's six sections, was initially headed by the world-famous composer Richard Strauss. He had the assistance of more politically minded musicians such as Prof. Peter Raabe, the third-rate conductor of the Aachen symphony and predecessor there of Herbert von Karajan, but in October 1935 Strauss was himself replaced by the sixty-two-year-old Raabe because he was not a bona fide Nazi.[34] Already in February 1934, during the first convention of the RMK, Raabe had held forth about the rejuvenation of German music in the spirit of National Socialism. He talked about reviving *Hausmusik,* music performed by family members in the home, and the need for repressing the foxtrot and other examples of "bad taste." Just as programmatically, Raabe berated the influence of Jews, especially in the distribution of inferior music. In a well-designed publicity gesture, he announced his sympathy with the many thousands of musicians still out of work as a result of the economic dislocations.[35]

From the fall of 1933 to 1938 the RMK administrators set about the task of centralizing music and musicians in the Third Reich. Given the previous state of disarray, this was no easy matter. In a country of 66 million, by the summer of 1933 there were approximately 94,000 employable instrumentalists and singers of all persuasions and qualifications. Some were still organized in disparate groupings, but most were totally free-floating.[36] Certainly more than half of those were in the light-entertainment industry.

The degree of professionalization of musicians in Germany until that time was such that practically anyone with a modicum of musical skill and working on the rarest of occasions, sometimes for next to nothing, could be called a musician. There had been no certifying examinations and no predefined routes of specialization as mandatory criteria for professional musician status. Thus the rankest of amateurs, perhaps the weekend zither player in a Bavarian hamlet or the milk delivery man turned jazz drummer in Berlin, could mingle, in the sea of musicians, with the conservatory student of the cello or flute who aspired to a full-time career as member of a symphony orchestra or eventually as soloist. During the depression the negative effects of this condition were felt when amateur players, especially in the light-entertainment business where performance standards were laxer, snatched jobs away from more qualified musicians with formal training, because they had connections or used a variety of ruses.

Hence one of the first proclaimed aims of the newly appointed bureaucrats was to weed out the untrained players or hobbyists from the professional musicians. This accorded well with the corporative notions of National Socialism, which attempted similar differentiations in medicine (to separate lay practitioners from academically trained physicians) and law (to enhance the lawyers' standing vis-à-vis the paralegals).[37]

At first, to cement its monopoly, the RMK treated all musicians as automatically belonging to its realm. Musicians received requisite membership cards with the obligation to pay monthly fees.[38] But the selection began immediately and took years. Until 1938, thousands of questionnaires were distributed by Hinkel to musicians of every caliber so as to collect personal and educational data on them.[39] In cases where credentials looked dubious, provisional members were subjected to professional, albeit rather arbitrary, examinations administered by locally appointed committees. If members failed these theory and performance tests repeatedly or did not take them in the first place, their names were to be struck from the RMK rolls, or they could be relegated to the inferior category of occasional players.[40]

Significantly, the examinations could also be turned against undesirable musicians, as for instance players of jazz, if necessary under false pretenses. This almost occurred to jazz drummer Hans Klagemann, who despite insufficient formal training had for years been working with some of Germany's most prominent combos, and who was granted RMK status only in March 1936, after several attempts to pass the qualifying test. Most likely here, in an outgrowth of xenophobia, the Nazis wanted to discriminate against a former collaborator of British jazzman Billy Bartholomew.[41] Yet not infrequently these controls were evaded or ignored, sometimes after the bribing of RMK officials.[42]

It stands to reason that in this protracted process of screening Goebbels would have wanted to impose his own personal standard of quality and taste in music, or perhaps, insofar as he was aware of it, even that of the Führer. After his promotion to political power, Goebbels had much less time for the piano, using it mainly to seduce women from the screen and stage. His musical tastes essentially remained the same: light classics, some operettas, revue scores. He disliked popular hit tunes, yet sometimes appreciated their efficacy in controlling the public mood. Likewise, he indulged disciplined dance music offered by star bands such as Jack Hylton's, more mediocre German orchestras like Emanuel Rambour's, or even jazz-inspired performances like those of the Peter Kreuder combo. Such music was for public occasions like the annual press ball or receptions, or to impress his women, including his beautiful wife, Magda.[43] Yet the minister, who had located the "essence" of all music in its "melody" (implicitly, one of the most common anti-jazz arguments available), personally remained as firmly opposed to this art form as ever—as firmly, in fact, as he disapproved of modern atonal compositions.[44] Repeated rumors that he secretly collected hundreds of jazz records were based on misinformation.[45]

So while Goebbels, through his RKK, implicitly set musical guidelines that were undoubtedly influenced by his personal tastes, the actual degree of this interaction is very hard to ascertain. For often, as became particularly apparent during the war years, the minister had to make allowances in the interest of high policy, perhaps to the detriment of his private preferences. The possible role played by Hitler's personal musical tastes is even more imponderable. The Führer was both more narrow in his tolerance—witness his singular stress on march music, selected operettas, and any quantity of Wagner!—and yet—a seeming paradox—more removed from the business of steering the public's cultural propensies, a chore he chose to leave to trusted underlings.[46]

The first group of musicians to suffer in the novel regulatory aura of the RMK were the foreigners. Among them, jazz players were especially prone to scrutiny, for their music was as little German as they were themselves. In light of the economic complications militating against the entire German music scene, this was hardly surprising. Like the Weimar Republic itself, foreigners were treated like scapegoats in national adversity, but now their situation was more serious, for the government had placed itself squarely behind their enemies.

After January 1933, Germany continued to agonize over a scarcity of jobs for ensemble musicians, especially for persons over thirty-five. Available positions were often strenuous and ill-rewarded, and never guaranteed. The numerous taxes imposed by all strata of government on the entertainment industry, especially restaurants, were not reduced for several years. At the beginning of the regime, the slack holiday seasons of 1933 and 1934 yielded little for musicians in mountain resorts and at the seaside, for Hitler's consuming public still was strapped for cash for nonessential activities.[47]

By November 1934 the total number of employable musicians—those who had been anonymously registered with census bureaus—had been whittled down from almost 94,000 in 1933 to approximately 86,000; thousands had dropped out of the work force. But the figure for the unemployed still was at 12,000 (as opposed to 24,000 a year before). Moreover, the vast majority of active musicians were not even earning RM 1,200 a year, an income considerably less than that of coal miners.[48]

Accordingly, the RMK identified job creation for its certified members as one of its first priorities.[49] By 1935 some progress had been made by eliminating the undesirables, encouraging the creation of new jobs, and tiding over the indigent with a minimum of funds. And while it was estimated at the end of the year that the number of the unemployed had again been cut in half, still about one-fifth of all German musicians remained idle, and the absolute figure for the lowest earners had hardly changed.[50] Only in 1936, with a harnessed economy and the Olympics generating a flurry of activities, did the situation improve noticeably. By that time mandatory contractual agreements between musicians and their employers helped standardize wages and working conditions, and simultaneously, the checks on foreigners and other unwanted individuals were producing results.[51] The year 1937 appears to have been the first in a long time when the want ads seeking musicians in the papers outnumbered those for jobs.[52]

By 1 November 1933, as part of its first ordinance, the RMK specified that foreign musicians be subject to the same stipulations as those governing the professional life of native Germans. This compelled permanent residents of the Reich to be indexed in the central registry and to carry one of the brown RMK identity cards entitling one to work. Ideally, they also had to fill out Hinkel's questionnaire and indicate thereon their religion and "Aryan" status.[53] Another series of ordinances from October 1935 on forbade the use of foreign names by German artists.[54] In September 1937 foreign musicians had to be specially registered with the RMK by their German employers, and three months later the distribution of "all alien music" sheets was prohibited, unless specifically approved by the propaganda ministry.[55]

However, in 1933 National Socialist dance musicians had themselves begun to harass their foreign colleagues, irrespective of any official sanctions against them. In the immediate shock of Hitler's takeover, several more foreigners left the Reich, emulating the example of the earlier victims of the depression.[56] Thereafter, the standard Nazi justification was that the non-Germans enjoyed an ill-deserved edge over the native players and were exploiting this to their economic advantage, to the point where foreigners were getting a 60 percent fare reduction on the railways![57]

Xenophobia reached ridiculous heights in cases where ensemble leaders of foreign nationality were accused of skimming wages off their German employees, and of causing their dismissal from the engagement and the financial collapse of their contractual sponsor to boot, as allegedly occurred in 1934 in Tilsit.[58] Why was it that, as someone calculated, in 1936 all 61 active guest musicians in Düsseldorf were earning RM 6,768 a year on a prorated basis, whereas 388 local colleagues went begging?[59] The American guitarist Mike Danzi recalls the reluctance on the part of his German jazz pals, who wanted to play with him as usual, but now feared official repercussions. British oldtimer Billy Bartholomew, too, experienced much ill will; in 1937 he chose to sign on only Germans for the jobs that still came his way, and in late 1938 sailed back to England.[60]

If permanent alien residents like Danzi and Bartholomew were complaining, foreign visiting band musicians could fare equally badly, for a variety of reasons. In the case of Swedish swing master Arne Hülphers, it was degenerate sounds and exclusive fees that were criticized. The Swiss René Schmassmann along with his Lanigiro [Original] Hot Players was suspected of playing sultry jazz in the "Jewish" vein.[61] The most successful big band sound of the late 1930s, that of the Bern saxophonist Teddy Stauffer, was calumniated in one of the Nazi trade journals as "Jew jazz" and the "sabotage of German culture" in the fall of 1936. This came after Stauffer's Berlin triumph during the Olympic Games and was, of course, inspired by sheer envy. Only after Stauffer had added a trite, nonjazz composition by Hans Brückner, the editor of that journal, to his repertoire, did he suddenly receive much praise. In Berlin and Hamburg he continued to dare the Nazis with musical insults of all kinds and generally obstreperous behavior, relying solely on his fantastic popularity. Hamburg actually banned him. Then, in Leipzig in 1938, he jazzed up the Nazi "Horst Wessel

Lied." Thereupon, his presence in the Reich became precarious; the summer of 1939 saw him back in Switzerland.[62]

The Jewish references were germane, for they targeted any and all visiting musicians who, it was said, either had not revealed their Jewish identity or secretly were doing the work of the Jews. Although it was practically impossible, ardent Nazis would have liked to check the pedigree of every guest musician for its "Aryan" content, or rather the lack thereof.[63] After the Blood Laws of September 1935 had defined Gypsies, next to Jews and Negroes, as racially undesirable, they too were included in the witch-hunt. For not only did they produce objectionable tones (some of them akin to jazz, as evidenced in the music of Django Reinhardt), but they were of an elusive racial type: Gypsies could be (foreign) Hungarians or Jews or both, or they could be Romanian or Slavic, or they might deny their racial origins altogether and pose as decent Germans.[64]

Raiding Jews and Jazz

The removal of Jewish musicians, including the acolytes of jazz, proceeded haphazardly and with much difficulty, but as ineluctably as the proscription of the foreigners. Because no German musician had been centrally filed by name, all Jews were compelled to register with the RMK, created in the fall of 1933, by January 1934. But not all Jewish musicians appear to have complied. For Jews were difficult to define in terms of either ethnic background or religion, and their identification was not as easy as it had seemed at first.[65] Several times before 1939, Goebbels thought that the overarching organization, the RKK, was rid of all its Jewish artists, only to be sorely disappointed. According to his diary, he met with unforeseen obstacles particularly in the RMK.[66]

Possibly, one cause of this trouble was that Goebbels's most determined henchman, Hans Hinkel, did not join the RKK until the spring of 1935 and had too many other offices to look after.[67] Since nobody knew the "Jewish Problem" in German culture better than he did, no one else quite had the dynamism to deal with it. To be sure, anti-Semitism was an article of faith for Hinkel, who had become one of Himmler's SS troopers in March 1931 and had acquired expertise in the early anti-Jewish campaigns of the Kampfbund für deutsche Kultur.[68] Immediately after the political changeover, Minister President Göring had appointed Hinkel state commissar in the Prussian ministry of education, in which capacity he oversaw much of the cultural role of Jews in the nation. Then in July 1935 Goebbels entrusted Hinkel with the purging of Jews from all German cultural life, which gave him additional momentum.[69]

Another likely reason was the cumbersome process prescribed by the purge. It entailed complicated bureaucratic sequences and legal considerations, all of which were time-consuming; but the regime wanted to legislate its anti-Semitism rather than hound down the Jews in a frenzy. Hence questionnaires were handed to Jewish and non-Jewish musicians alike, prompting them to declare both religion and so-called Aryan status. But it was possible to conceal the truth until the bureaucracy caught up with one.[70] Musicians felt no obligation to disclose their backgrounds voluntarily; in most cases, RMK officials were at pains to request musicians suspected of being Jewish to provide family documents. Frequently Jews were ordered to take the qualifying examination as well, and predictably, their failure rate appears to have been high.[71]

The basis for final dismissal from the RMK was paragraph 10 of a regulation of 1 November 1933, according to which the RMK president—first Strauss, then Raabe—denied the "right to further professional practice," but it too could be appealed, even in a court of law, until definitively upheld.[72] In the case of the three Jewish members of the jazz vocal group Comedian Harmonists, it was only in February 1935 that they were irrevocably excluded from the German music scene.[73]

Even given all this, it was possible to avoid the finely spun spider's web. Time and again non-"Aryan" musicians were caught by RMK controllers in the act of performing music, in which case criminal proceedings might be initiated for contravention of the original RKK law of September 1933. Berlin singer Margot Friedländer, whose father was Jewish, performed illegally in the capital without a brown certification card, apparently with the complicity of a club owner who cynically underpaid her. At that time she was not found out.[74]

Yet a third reason for the slowness of the Jewish raids was that they were badly coordinated with the overall Nazi anti-Semitic policy, which itself was not consistent. The three climaxes in the Nazi persecution of Jews were the 1933 spring boycott; the months after the Nuremberg Blood Laws of September 1935; and all of 1938, gearing up for November, which with Goebbels's connivance brought forth Kristallnacht, the November pogrom usually called the night of the broken glass.[75] In the spring of 1933 Jewish musicians were not affected because the RMK was not yet in existence and its party forerunners lacked authority. On the other hand, the 1935 laws clearly had an impact on Jewish musicians in general, and the indictment of jazz in particular. By that time, too, Jew hunter Hinkel had been empowered. But the influx of foreigners to attend the 1936 Olympics caused difficulties, as for instance in the case of partially Jewish musicians such as Friedländer, because anti-Semitic activities were toned down or stopped. This certainly applied to Berlin with its enormous show business.[76] But by November 1938 the "purification" of the RMK had been all but completed; most Jewish musicians had left the Reich or, if still in Germany, were eking out a living in some other, unrelated occupation.

Very few Jewish musicians—probably less than a hundred, and in their midst even fewer dance and jazz musicians—were afforded a chance to perform their music legally in the Third Reich, after their identity had been noted. One who could do so was the trumpet player Sigmund Petruschka, who, with a partially Jewish band named Sid Kay's Fellows, had performed since the late republican years in the Berlin Haus Vaterland and then in Dresden until 6 April 1933.[77] After that he worked mainly as a composer and arranger, largely for the big band of James Kok, who recorded Petruschka's fox-trot "Flying Hamburger" with Deutsche Grammophon in early 1934. Petruschka also arranged Theo Mackeben's tango "Speak Not of Faithfulness," which was played at the Berlin Press Ball in the spring of 1935, ironically under the auspices of Joseph Goebbels. A few months later, Petruschka recollects, he was notified by the president of the RMK that definitive membership "in this august organization was refused and that I hereby immediately lose the right to engage in the musical profession."[78] Since the Nazi record keepers had thus caught up with him, Petruschka could consider himself lucky to continue a career of sorts within the dubiously protective framework of the Kulturbund deutscher Juden, the Jewish cultural organization established with Hinkel's help and under Gestapo endorsement in 1933. The Kulturbund provided a variety of entertainment—from classical theater to Yiddish folk tunes—for the increasingly ghettoized Jewish communities, mainly in the larger centers such as Berlin, Frankfurt, and Hamburg, using only Jewish artists.

Petruschka, whose Fellows were moderately influenced by swing but stressed elements of Jewish folk music as well, produced a dance record with Hebrew lyrics sung by Ferris Gondosch, formerly known as Ben Berlin's big band drummer Friedrich Goldstein, which was sold only to Jews through Jewish outlets on the exclusively Jewish record label Lukraphon. Illicitly, Petruschka kept on arranging for other "Aryan" clients, almost until January 1938 when he was finally allowed to leave for Palestine.[79]

If most Jewish dance and jazz musicians left Germany voluntarily in the first two years of Nazi rule, they did so for two reasons. One was that they were too well known to conceal their identity, having already been identified by vociferous Nazi propaganda against "Nigger-Jew jazz" in the republic. The other reason was harassment and physical abuse by Nazis after January 1933.

To the first category, those Jews singled out long before January 1933, belonged the celebrated champions of German café society such as Dajos Béla, who in March 1933 went to Amsterdam, thence to Paris, eventually to settle in Buenos Aires. He was immediately joined in emigration by Marek Weber and the even more dance-music oriented bandleaders Efim Schachmeister, Ben Berlin, and Paul Godwin.[80] Rudi Anhang, the guitarist who had once accompanied the obscene dancer Anita Berber, held out because he was shielded in the band of prominent dance-band leader Bernard Etté, but early in 1936, after the Nuremberg Blood Laws, he accepted an invitation by Béla to join his Argentine radio orchestra.[81]

The celebrated Weintraub Syncopators had performed in Frankfurt in January 1933 and were back in the capital's Wintergarten in February. But in March they started a European tour that took them first to Prague, all of Switzerland, and Copenhagen. Evidently during their subsequent stay in Rotterdam in September 1933, they decided not to return to Germany. Instead, they embarked on a world odyssey that saw them in the Soviet Union, Japan, and finally Australia, where Stefan Weintraub himself retired. Whereas his onetime pianist Franz Wachsmann ended his career in Hollywood as a celebrated film composer, Weintraub's former trumpeter, Berlin-born Adi Rosner, ended up in Russia, after long detours to Belgium and Poland soon after January 1933. Later he was banished to Siberia by the Stalinist regime.[82]

Rosner belonged to that second category of Jews, those experiencing various degrees of molestation by the Nazis. Others in that group were the brothers Charly and Gert Reininghaus, who had led a band called Charly Gertyn's Blue

Boys, and then left for Holland; much later, they perished in a Nazi concentration camp. Likewise Rudi Grünauer, who had played with Erich Börschel's band in Königsberg, the trombonist Hans Lachmann, and the promising Berlin trumpeter Rolf Goldstein all went to Holland.[83] After having been questioned by the Gestapo, the Berlin amateur agent Paul Hirson, who had helped so many jazz musicians out when the going was rough, fled to Dajos Béla in Buenos Aires in 1937.[84] "The Jews were vanishing," recalled pianist Georg Haentzschel at his Cologne apartment in 1988; "it was certainly noticeable in the violin sections."[85]

There were several kinds of humiliation Jewish jazzmen had to endure at Nazi hands before being allowed to leave. Adi Rosner, for instance, had been beaten by storm troopers at a bar near Berlin's Alexanderplatz before departing for Belgium in 1933.[86] Goldstein had been beset by musician representatives of the Nazi trade union, NSBO, while playing in the Palm Garden of Haus Vaterland, from which he saw the Reichstag burn on 27 February 1933.[87] Pianist Martin Roman was leading another band in the huge Vaterland complex at that time when SS men stopped him at the entrance to the hall. Once past them, he was informed by his violinist, Peppie Marcel, that as a representative of the Nazi party it was his own band now. Totally taken aback, Roman was physically threatened by Marcel, so he decided to sue the usurper. The pianist would probably have won in court, had not his mother persuaded him to flee to Amsterdam instead. There Roman hid out until, much later, he was almost killed in Auschwitz.[88]

In those early Nazi years James Kok became a cause célèbre. The half-Jewish Romanian had arrived in Germany in 1929 and by 1932 had built up the best Berlin big band, one that usually performed in the swank club Moka Efti. In November 1934 Magdeburg's piano wonder Fritz Schulze had joined him, and Kok employed other excellent young jazz players such as reed men Erhard Bauschke and Kurt Wege, formerly of Petruschka's Sid Kay's Fellows.[89] Then, in late January 1935, Jack Hylton once more arrived to regale Berlin jazz fans on his first visit since the Nazis had taken power. Because of xenophobic prejudice and jealousy, he received bad reviews in the official press. In a show of sympathy the admiring Kok and his co-musicians sent him a wreath with the audacious inscription: "In defiance of all bearded critics, please come again, Maestro Hylton!" It is not known who the "bearded critic" was, but the incident caused a storm of protest from Nazi sycophants.[90]

At Kok's next performance in the Moka Efti, piano man Fritz Schulze recalls, Brown Shirts appeared shouting "Down with the Jews!" It was only then that fastidious Nazi researchers had ascertained Kok's half-Jewish ancestry. His engagement at the Berlin club had been contractually secured beforehand till the end of April. But he was never to fulfill his next contract, for a summer stint on the Baltic island of Rügen. The RMK expelled him and in May, after narrowly escaping persecution by the SS, he found refuge in England. In the Third Reich he left behind a legacy supported by the fond memories of his musician friends as well as some stunning recordings, many of them scored by Petruschka. Kok survived the war and eventually settled in Switzerland.[91]

The man who had brought James Kok's non-"Aryan" background to light was Hans Brückner, the Nazi who put pressure on Teddy Stauffer. In 1935 he was a corpulent thirty-eight-year-old tenor, a veteran of the Great War and of provincial operettas. He owned and edited *Das Deutsche Podium,* a bimonthly broadsheet in a lighter vein for National Socialist musicians. The Munich-based Brückner had joined the NSDAP in 1928; an admirer of Jew-baiting Nuremberg Gauleiter Julius Streicher, he proved an avowed foe of jazz, blacks, and Jews.[92] As far as he was concerned, the regime's anti-Semitic policies did not go far and fast enough; in particular, he resented the fact that the RMK's purge of the Jewish dance and jazz musicians was fraught with delays and procedural inefficiency. Thus he dedicated his publishing career to driving from the business as many "music Jews," as he termed them, as he could possibly expose. This was not always easy, not only because Jews, like many in the entertainment field, used pseudonyms, but also because they frequently could not be distinguished from their "Aryan" colleagues by either physical appearance or comportment.

Hence Brückner willfully ignored the Führer's decision, after the Röhm purge of June 1934, that the Nazi revolution was to be halted, that the regime's future nationalization policies had to occur within proper bureaucratic tracks, and that in consequence no party members should take the law into their own hands, least of all against Jews. Instead, Brückner aided anti-Semitism at the grassroots level when his reporters physically pulled Jewish musicians off a stage or defiled them in his newspaper, on charges of displacing "Aryan" Germans.[93] He targeted them in an unrelenting crusade that ruined them professionally before any law could apply.

One of his intended victims was the violinist Paul Weinapel, who in April 1935 was working in Berlin's fancy Sherbini-Bar, along with other non-"Aryans." While Weinapel was slandered in *Podium,* his Jewish pianist was replaced by Fritz Schulze, just released from Kok's big band and undeniably "Aryan." Weinapel's group then moved to the neighboring Ciro-Bar, and Brückner could announce that the Sherbini finally had offered employment to "full Aryans."[94] But now he had to place the Ciro on his index, and by the beginning of 1936 "the Polish Jew Weinapel (Woynapel)" had quietly been reemployed by the Sherbini![95]

If Brückner faced obstacles in catching his quarry, the repercussions of his smear campaign were wide. Harold Kirchstein, the German-American guitarist who had helped found the successful jazz septet Goldene Sieben, or Golden Seven, was a habitué of all the recording and sound film studios and consistently received rave reviews in the Nazi press. He was brought down, probably by Brückner's minions, because of his Jewish-sounding name. Pressed in vain to prove his "Aryan" heritage before the Nazi authorities, Kirchstein, whose mother's genealogy was Polish, with the help of Georg Haentzschel one day in 1937 left Germany hurriedly overnight for this American homeland and eventually settled in Hollywood.[96]

Meanwhile Brückner had a problem. No sooner had he earmarked a Jewish combo for expulsion than he found, to his chagrin, that many a German musician was still playing Jewish dance numbers. And it bothered other Nazi censors such as Fritz Stege that tunes by Irving Berlin and George Gershwin were still in several German band repertoires. Thus the neophyte Berlin bandleaders Hans Rehmstedt and Kurt Widmann, already experts in the swing idiom, were sternly warned by Brückner in the fall of 1937.[97] Counterarguments that audiences often asked for such music were refuted on the grounds that it was the duty of "Aryan" musicians to educate their listeners by consistently presenting non-Jewish programs.[98]

To Brückner's further dismay, his purges were hampered by what he perceived to be networks of international Jewish publishers who imported undesirable sheet music to the Reich via hidden channels from abroad. Viktor Alberti, for instance, who had owned the miraculous Alberti music store on Berlin's Rankestrasse, a treasure source for every jazz buff, after his post-January 1933 emigration to Budapest had left the management of his shop to a relative, Nikolaus Weiss. According to Brückner, Weiss was receiving Jewish imports both from Alberti in Hungary and from his Italian-based cousin Ladislaus Schugal.[99] Some formerly Jewish music-publishing outlets in Berlin, Leipzig, and Hamburg, after "Aryanization," were said to be smuggling in Jewish contraband from new headquarters in Vienna, until the Anschluss in March 1938 put a stop to this. Before that date, Austria was supposed to have had merely three non-Jewish music publishers! In particular, Irving Berlin's tunes were suspected of being marketed in Germany by the Viennese Bristol Publishers of Felix Ehrenfreund. But New York Broadway producers such as Shapiro and Bernstein and similar Jewish firms in London were also charged with infesting the German market.[100] Therefore, when "alien" music was officially proscribed in late December 1937, this order was loudly hailed by the Jew hunters, whose xenophobia was fueled by anti-Semitism.[101]

By the spring of 1937 Brückner was receiving grateful letters from Nazi bandleaders who had been able to identify the insidious Jews in dance music, with the help of a lexicon he and Streicher's confidant Christa Maria Rock had compiled and marketed in 1935. It was called the "Musical ABC of Jews" and contained the names, birthdays, and origins of thousands of non-"Aryan" musicians and composers internationally. James Kok was in it, and so were Dajos Béla, Paul Weinapel, and the "Weintraub Syncopaters" (*sic*).[102]

At this time, German musicians were already referring to the second edition published in 1936. The first one had been full of errors—92 of them among 4,782 entries, Brückner conceded later, but probably there were many more.[103] Ralph Benatzky, for instance, a German composer of operetta and popular song, who had protested to the authorities already against the "libel" of a Jewish identity in September 1933, was falsely documented in 1935 as being a Jew. The second edition of 1936 had corrected this mistake, since Frau Rock, a Düsseldorf dentist's wife, and Brückner himself were at great pains to publish regular corrigenda in the *Podium*. The 1936 edition had mentioned Irving Berlin but forgotten his original surname Balines; this was set right in a *Podium* list of February 1937. Also printed there was the name of one Benny Goodman, "jazz musician, director of a jazz band in London." Goodman's alter ego on clarinet, Artie Shaw, was missing in all lists (his real name was Arthur Arshawsky), evidently, as rumor had it, because the Nazis, Rock and Brückner included, believed him to be the son of former Irish music critic G. B. Shaw![104] Brückner, who at great cost to himself had published his third edition in 1938, became the laughing stock even of the party. Nonetheless, by 1941 the NSDAP had issued its own certified Jew guide, although this time around, jazz musicians were ostensibly neglected.[105]

Such a milieu proved extremely trying for the few non-"Aryan" dance and jazz musicians who were allowed to stay in Germany and work. Almost without exception, these were half or three-quarter "Aryans," whom both Goebbels's RKK and the originators of the September 1935 Blood Laws tentatively tolerated. When applying for RMK status, as was mandatory, the one-quarter Jews invariably were successful, even though, as in the case of trumpeter Hans Berry, there might be difficulties, whereas the half Jews could fare either way.[106] The fine half-Jewish tenor saxophonist Eugen Henkel seems to have been temporarily stopped by a RMK performance ban, but other than that he had no trouble, even after patrons of a club he played in had complained about his "Jewish nose."[107] Constantinople-born drummer Fritz Brocksieper, who witnessed that event, himself was a quarter Jewish, and so far as is known was not molested.[108] Budding jazz singer Evelyn Künneke enjoyed some protection, for although her mother was half-Jewish, her father, the great operetta composer, stood in Goebbels's and Hitler's personal favor.[109]

Because the Nazis so conveniently paired Jews with jazz, a campaign against the one tended to involve an indictment of the other. Broader ordinances against dance and jazz musicians received added momentum to the extent that anti-Semitic policy itself strengthened over time, up to and beyond the prewar climax of November 1938. Conversely, official and semiprivate anti-Jewish offensives could be inspired by mounting revelations about the nature of, and actual incriminations against, jazz. This radicalization, whereby interdependent variables determined one another, however unevenly, typified the very dynamics of the Hitler dictatorship.

The race legislation of September 1935 had not a little to do with that reciprocity. But so did the changeover in the RMK presidency from Richard Strauss to Peter Raabe, seemingly a coincidental affair. While Strauss had been no friend of jazz, he did not hate it with a vengeance, and his own daughter-in-law as well as his favorite librettist, Stefan Zweig, were Jewish. Unlike the world-famous Strauss, the provincial symphony conductor Raabe was a fervent National Socialist who applauded Hitler's every racial measure and expressly called for German music to be rid of alien elements. It became one of his declared aims to "remove completely foreign jazz and dance music and to replace it with the works of German composers."[110]

From January 1933 on, all dance and jazz musicians were subjected to pressure at various stages in their professional career, and by a multiplicity of agencies. Such pressures increased as time progressed, the reed player Franz Thon has recalled. For trumpeter Charly Tabor, "the fear, the fear was there, always."[111]

Because of the polycratic nature of the Nazi regime, yet also on account of the cosmopolitan quality of jazz, prohibition orders against it emanated first, and primarily, from the provinces at local administrative levels. Weeks and months before the institutionalization of the propaganda ministry and the RMK respectively, live jazz performances were indicted by NSDAP officials in Frankfurt, Regensburg (home of the ultra-Nazi Bosse music-publishing house), Passau, and Bamberg, the latter adjacent to the Bayreuth shrine. In Frankfurt, Professor Sekles's jazz class at the Hoch'sche conservatory had been canceled by the end of February 1933.[112] Then there was a lull in the prohibitions because the RKK needed time to consolidate its activities, and several extraneous developments, such as the Olympic Games of 1936, counseled caution. But if the RKK was reluctant, the Blood Laws had nonetheless been passed, so more radical elements at regional levels prevailed once again, and the Gauleiter of Pomerania forbade the playing of jazz in a wordy edict of November 1938. This edict preceded the Kristallnacht by four days, and while there was no generic connection between the two events, it evinced the mood of heightened intolerance at this particular point in the regime's development.[113] In that same year the police chief of Freiburg, Nazi-controlled entrepreneurial (restaurant) lobbies in Stuttgart, and party authorities throughout Württemberg, Franconia, and Thuringia passed similar laws for their jurisdictions. These were followed, in March and May, 1939, by decrees issued by the Gauleiter of Saxony and the municipality of Cologne.[114] The ban was duplicated in the ranks of party cadres such as the German Labor Front and the Nazi Student League; German youth hostels had abjured jazz as early as August 1933.[115]

At the pinnacle of the administrative hierarchy Minister Goebbels, meanwhile, had exhibited a certain reluctance to issue centrally binding prohibitions through his RMK, despite popular pressure from the provinces that he could easily monitor.[116] So as not to alienate certain sectors in the population unnecessarily, he favored persuasion and conversion over outright restriction; this, in fact, was the actual philosophy guiding his ministry and but another quality of the haphazard totalitarianism of Hitler's regime.[117] The otherwise impatient Raabe reflected this caution when he repeatedly admonished that "public self-education" was preferable to "administrative embargoes and regulations."[118]

Hence the relative paucity of the RMK's ordinances, and their reserve. From the interdiction against the use of foreign names in 1935, which eventually included a ban on the English-language term "drummer," to technical restrictions on tours abroad in 1937 (which affected not just jazz musicians), few pronouncements against live jazz appeared.[119] Then, two months before Kristallnacht, Goebbels himself forbade the music of Irving Berlin, the performance of Friedrich Hollaender's score for the film *Jungle Princess,* and—the epitome of Jewish-nigger jazz—Sholom Secunda's popular "Bei Mir Bist Du Shein."[120] That song by the composer of Yiddish musicals for the New York stage had lyrics that said in effect, "To me, you are beautiful." This provoked Raabe to announce an index of "undesirable and harmful music" in the spring of 1939, followed in July by a decree against the playing of swing-oriented dance scores and, a month later, by the president's specification that "the performance of works by Jewish composers" was undesirable.[121]

The enforcement of the various controls matched the diversified pattern of their origin: radical executioners in the provincial backwaters of party and police on the one hand, and more circumspect yet also more authorized warders in the RMK on the other. The efforts of the two groups were never coordinated. Hence early in the regime and locally, owing to the controversial publicity, SA men would knock the saxophones out of the mouths of dance-band players, or at the very least, SS personnel could prohibit use of the instruments, whereas the RMK had never called for this.[122] In 1938 the jazz flutist Eddie Unger was arbitrarily hauled from the stand of a Timmendorf beach bar by a local police contingent, and the Gestapo on its own authority closed the Frankfurt Hippodrome Café after hearing strains of the swing tune, "A-Tisket, A-Tasket."[123]

Even though the enforcers of the RMK were physically less dangerous, they possessed an aura of omnipresence and omnipotence, especially in the capital, where jazz was rampant. Here seven or eight agents usually swarmed out until midnight to the Ciro, the Barberina, the Sherbini, or the Quartier Latin, and less famous places, ostensibly to check for the RMK brown card, for moonlighters, Jews, and foreigners, and to see whether dues had been paid. Their real purpose, of course, was to intimidate musicians in all bars and dance establishments into not playing jazz by confiscating their sheet music, arresting them on minor charges, and generally being a nuisance.

Especially menacing was Erich Woschke, a sometime piano player with a modest mastery of the organ and accordion, and also Otto Föhl, a party member since May of 1933.[124] Through their machinations, jazzman Walter Leschetitzky was excluded from the RMK, because he had said that, in one way or another, every German musician was dependent on either Jews or blacks. When, one year after the Olympic Games, Berlin big-band leader Heinz Wehner was harassed to an unbearable extent for his scalding swing performances, he chose temporarily to escape to New York.[125]

Broadcasting and Recordings

Radio, that fast-growing medium from the middle years of the Weimar Republic, became an integral part of Joseph Goebbels's propaganda machinery, for Goebbels early on had realized its value in manipulating public opinion. After a purge of its old personnel, the minister appointed his own cronies, mostly fanatical young men whom he could mold and trust completely. By personal cross-appointments, radio was anchored both to the propaganda ministry and the RKK, where, analogous to the RMK, a Reichsrundfunkkammer (RRK), or Reich Radio Chamber, was established. After July 1933 the chief of all broadcasting stations in the Reich under Goebbels was Eugen Hadamovsky, like Hinkel a university dropout and a ruthless agent of the new dictatorship. In March 1937 the insensitive Hadamovsky was replaced by the head of Radio Cologne, Dr. Heinrich Glasmeier, who was less dynamic and less offensive to other Third Reich bureaucrats, and, if more boring, also more conciliatory. Under both men the policy toward jazz was essentially censorial, if vacillating.[126]

Broadcasting under Goebbels made giant strides. From 1932 to 1943 the number of listeners in the Reich grew from four to over sixteen million; even in

1937 almost one-third of those were tuning in to Superhet receivers—the strongest radio sets available. In 1937 Germany's total number of listeners, then over eight million, surpassed that of Great Britain.[127]

Like the RMK, the RRK and the Reichs-Rundfunk-Gesellschaft, the new umbrella organization of German stations responsible to it, were faced with an ideological problem of personnel and content control, but their task was not quite as difficult, because they had to deal with much fewer people, most of whom were on their payroll. After a preliminary purge of known Jews in the spring of 1933, the broadcasting bureaucracy made concerted efforts to create a central Jewish registry in the manner of Rock and Brückner in 1934–35, so as to catch the lesser known Jews; foreigners were also discriminated against.[128] To ensure coordination between the performing arts and radio, a liaison committee was established in the summer of 1936 at the behest of President Raabe, which was appropriately directed by Dr. Fritz Stege, who regularly published diatribes against non-"Aryan" music in *Artist*.[129]

As soon as Goebbels had an overview of the reorganized domain of broadcasting, he decided to follow a policy of quality light-entertainment music at the expense of more serious content for two reasons. One was that he had divined that the great majority of listeners, continuously reinforced by members of the less educated and culturally less demanding social strata, were in need of simple, trivial diversions after putting in a hard day's work for the national economy.[130] From the point of view of those interested in jazz, this potentially could provide a protective cover for that music as camouflaged by the dance genre, depending on how the latter was defined.

Second, and more crucial to jazz, Goebbels was aware that powerful foreign stations, as for instance Radio Luxemburg, were beaming more sophisticated light music, including New Orleans–type jazz and the new type of jazz called "swing," into the homes of those Germans who were seeking such programs out. Moreover, the greater danger was that these programs might be framed by news in English, and anti-Nazi propaganda to boot! To counter this threat, the minister was forced against his will to accept a minimum of German-sponsored jazz productions, perhaps at safe hours late at night, on his own stations.[131]

Goebbels was walking a tightrope here: he eschewed a concentration of heavy-content offerings, Beethoven and lectures on philosophy, on one side of the consumer spectrum, while on the other side rejecting the military marches that Germans had been subjected to on the airwaves immediately after the Nazis came to power.[132] In the golden middle he was for measured light entertainment, but since this still could include the much-hated jazz, he had to sail around those rocks with circumspection. As the coming years were to show, he managed this only with moderate success.

Because Goebbels, in contrast with the live music scene, controlled the medium of radio sufficiently, he was able to apply the carrot-and-stick principle: taking something away from the public that he deemed unsuitable, he replaced it with something else as a pacifier. Concerning jazz, his policy till the beginning of the war more or less alternated between these two extremes. Before the minister's reorganization of radio in the Reich, the Berlin station Funkstunde had totally abolished jazz from its broadcasts in March 1933, and Stuttgart's station was considering a similar measure. So Goebbels, lest he alienate a certain segment of the population needlessly, initially decided on compromise.[133] Berlin's long-wave Deutschlandsender could be received all over Germany. Here Goebbels launched the Golden Seven as a sort of model orchestra, staffed by jazz musicians of impressive qualifications but tamed by written arrangements and a Nazi boss. This boss was twenty-nine-year-old Willi Stech, a classically trained, superbly competent dance pianist with Nazi party credentials. He wrote many of the arrangements, in some of which he was assisted by guitarist Harold Kirchstein (whom he later tried to help, unsuccessfully, to obtain an "Aryan" pedigree). They were both joined by Adalbert and Waldemar ("Waldi") Luczkowski on violin and drums respectively, Franz Thon on reeds, Kurt Hohenberger on trumpet, and Erhard Krause on trombone. This studio band began to function in December 1934.[134]

It was obvious that the adjective "golden" in the combo's name indicated the golden middle intended by the propaganda minister. But did these musicians play jazz, or did they not? Even today opinion is divided. Georg Haentzschel, who ought to know, says: "Jazz it was not. These were in part some very clever arrangements for a small combo, American-inspired especially by Kirchstein." Yet a 1987 West German swing magazine is much more enthusiastic. About one of the group's renditions, it waxes: "A well-honed swing arrangement! Experiments with Anglo-American colors, accentuated with genuine swing rhythm from Waldi Luczkowski. A dry, pungent trumpet solo from Kurt Hohenberger, and clarinet phrases in a jazzy final chorus."[135]

Fifty-five years ago the disparity between judgments was the same. Whereas the Nazi music press lauded the group as one that loosened up the "bombastic jazz sound," hence acknowledging its didactic function, its studio sound engineer thought that it always managed to smuggle in an American quality, to see how far its members could go "without being arrested the next day." However moderately Goebbels and his men may have ruled this music, it was still swinging enough that the discerning British jazz tabloid *Melody Maker* classified the band as "the very best German musicians at their best."[136] Preserved samples of the music seem to corroborate that verdict.[137]

Probably it was this relative jazz quality of the Golden Seven that caused the concern of at least one important German radio functionary and led to its removal from the Deutschlandsender in the summer of 1935. Thereupon the band signed a commercial recording contract with Electrola, and Haentzschel replaced pianist Stech, who as a regular broadcast executive was allowed no outside employment.[138]

To follow up the purge of the Golden Seven, the ambitious Hadamovsky, with Goebbels's certain acquiescence, scheduled a wholesale proscription of jazz music on all German wave bands on the twelfth of October. This was announced in Munich at a general assembly of all radio station directors, a few weeks after the racial laws, which explains Hadamovsky's direct reference to "cultural-Bolshevist Jewry." To drive home the message to practicing musicians operating beyond the broadcast stations, a select group of composers had also been invited.[139]

On that occasion a special commission was appointed as a screening device for music to be played on German radio that was *not* jazz. It was staffed by relentless enemies of jazz such as Stege, the Hitler Youth (HJ) music chief Wolfgang Stumme, and Secretary Heinz Ihlert of the RMK, but also—here Goebbels's flexibility was once more evident—by the more indulgent Nazi pianist Stech.[140]

To leave no doubts in anybody's mind and to get the committee off the ground, Otto Fricke, the director of Radio Frankfurt, in December demonstrated to his colleagues not only the dubious history of jazz, but also criteria for recognizing it, using an American Negro recording of "Dinah" and other illustrative live-band music. This lecture was broadcast nationwide, so that jazz fan Dietrich Schulz, then studying economics at the University of Königsberg, was able to make a note of Fricke's utter horror at the "terrible disharmonies."[141]

With Fricke's admonitions ringing in their ears, Stege and his fellow censors proceeded to ban pieces such as Raymond Scott's "Christmas Night in Harlem" (marketed in Germany by the Berlin subsidiary of New York–based Francis, Day and Hunter), and "Alle meine kleinen Wünsche," a perky composition by the German swing pianist Franz Mück.[142] To make absolutely sure that none of the radio dance bands ventured too deeply into forbidden territory, a number of party spies were assigned to them.[143]

Theoretically speaking, control of the recording industry was an even more efficient method of subduing jazz music than was radio, because records were listed with their producers, and they in turn were registered with departments of commerce and of trade. But it was precisely the ongoing trade with foreign countries that tied the Nazis' hands, for long-standing agreements that internationally based recording companies such as RCA Victor had forged before 1933 could not be broken overnight, even by Hitler's dictatorship. The regime depended on international commerce for precious foreign currency, and if German records of Beethoven symphonies conducted by Wilhelm Furtwängler were to be marketed abroad, then British Decca or American Vocalion jazz records featuring the black Louis Armstrong and the Jewish Jean Goldkette had to be allowed into Germany.[144]

This did not exclude the possibility of semiofficial harassment of the kind that Hans Brückner was so fond of; indeed, the Jewish influence prevalent in the internationally connected German recording industry was repeatedly excoriated by him and other party wardens.[145] In 1936 Fritz Stege scolded the Telefunken company for christening the Heinz Wehner big band "Swing Orchestra," and jazz buff Dietrich Schulz around that time observed SA troopers trampling on jazz records enjoyed by young people on a Baltic beach near Königsberg.[146]

Individually, German-Jewish jazz artists disappeared from German records to the extent that they stopped working and were blacklisted by radio. This fate befell the longtime German resident James Kok after he had gone to London in May 1935. Still, on the fifteenth of that month *Artist* had lauded his latest

Deutsche Grammophon recording (of the German RCA-Victor branch), the single "Jungle Jazz—Harlem," as "a paragon of 'hot' arrangements." Then, one year later, in a review of current German dance music records, all his nationally admired singles were simply ignored.[147]

Foreign jazz records could generally be bought in the better music outlets, such as Berlin's Alberti store, unless there were shortages. In purchasing these records, it was always prudent to do so quietly and without fanfare, for plainclothes policemen could be around to take notes. In the uncertain terrain of Nazi legality, such transactions might later be interpreted as misdemeanors, especially in combination with hard, indictable offenses. Of course, to avoid both shortages and harassment, it was best to go abroad and buy such items there, or to have them sent by foreign mail-order firms, which was possible up to the modest amount of ten marks per month.[148]

For the treasured foreign jazz recordings, whether imported directly or marketed by German-licenced firms, the ax fell in December 1937. On the ninth Goebbels entrusted to his diary his satisfaction that "the remains of the recording industry will now be Aryanised."[149] On the fourteenth, five months after George Gershwin's well-publicized death from cancer, Goebbels's ministry issued a directive that "all records created through the efforts of non-Aryan authors or artists shall be prohibited from sale in Germany, effective 1 April 1938."[150]

Certain events lay behind these developments. After a two-year silence on the "Jewish Question"—conditioned to a large degree by the Olympic Games—Hitler had resumed his public attack on the Jews during the party rally of September 1937. In particular, he ranted against Jews in Bolshevism and condemned their alleged role on the republican side of the Spanish Civil War. According to British historian Ian Kershaw, this set the tone "for the new wave of anti-Jewish action and propaganda which began in the last months of 1937 and continued throughout the following year," eventually to culminate in Kristallnacht.[151]

In October 1937, the American King of Swing Benny Goodman, whose Jewish background had been known in Nazi Germany at least since February of that year although not widely circulated, is reported to have played a benefit concert for General Franco's adversaries in New York. Even though this concert cannot be verified today, it is certain that Goodman would have had the opportunity to stage it, for his band was back in New York at that time, having just completed a tour of California and Texas. Goodman was then receiving national and international ovations as the most brilliant jazz musician ever.[152] Goodman, "one of the best clarinetists in the world," as Electrola's 1937 "Swing Music" folder acclaimed him, whose swing records had been advertised in Germany on a fairly wide scale for the past year and a half, was immediately singled out by Goebbels's minions as the chief perpetrator of "Jewish jazz," and his music was banned. This affected the sale of his recordings, whether imported or German-pressed on franchise, as well as his compositions as performed by other artists or published as sheet music.[153] Also banned were the records of all other known Jewish jazz musicians and, not much later, those of classical composers as well.[154]

These prohibitions were augmented, through 1939, by the various ordinances against other Jewish music and musicians, such as Irving Berlin tunes.[155] Königsberg student Dietrich Schulz remembers shopping at a Berlin Electrola record store in 1938. Goodman and Gershwin records were already gone, but there still was some Mendelssohn left on the shelf. Compleat music lover Dietrich bought it all.[156]

After the spring of 1938, therefore, German jazz record collectors entered a period of potential crisis. However, since the Nazi authorities typically handled the foreign-jazz record proscription very unevenly, it was often possible to slip through the holes of an imperfect net. One could still order records from abroad and hope that ignorant customs officials might be fooled, as Schulz did successfully in provincial Magdeburg. Others smuggled in records across the border at considerable risk to themselves, as did Teddy Kleindin, a member of Heinz Wehner's formation on his way back from Sweden.[157] Alberti's, long on the Nazi index, continued to sell Anglo-American jazz records clandestinely, having glued phony German labels onto the originals.[158]

The affluent young jazz lover Hans Otto Jung from Lorch-on-Rhine, himself a proficient swing pianist, brought back forbidden records after visits to Italy, and beyond that he prodded the internationally connected German record companies. To Electrola he wrote in June 1938: "It is a great pity that lately you have had to strike from your lists so many items because they are allegedly of non-Aryan origin. Friends of swing (myself not excluded) deplore this, especially since such masters as Benny Goodman and Fletcher Henderson have been taken away from them." While he received no reply to this complaint, German Brunswick informed him in writing that singles from their collection, including Duke Ellington's composition "In A Sentimental Mood" played by Jimmy Dorsey, were now unavailable. A year later Kristall Records, a large Berlin retailer, consoled Hans Otto with copies of an outdated catalog that still contained—by then a mere memento—an entry for Benny Goodmann (*sic*)![159]

Significantly, Jung was pining not just over the loss of the Jewish Goodman, but also over that of black big-band leader Henderson. The proscription of 17 December 1937 implicitly had targeted black artists by virtue of their non-"Aryan" status, notwithstanding the Nazis' considerable difficulties in trying to identify all foreign blacks. At the end of November the SS had denounced Goodman, Irving Berlin, and George Gershwin, as well as "half a dozen Negroes."[160] In the end it was sheer ignorance that induced the propaganda ministry to forbid certain black players and allow many others to pass, and to show slackness even in the treatment of singular individuals. Whereas Jung had given up trying to find any Henderson records by June 1938, that bandleader's recordings still were included in a Brunswick catalog of March 1939.

Ellington's "Sentimental Mood" may have been deleted, but several of the master pianist's works, for instance "Caravan" as performed by the black vocal group The Mills Brothers, continued to be carried by Brunswick, according to the March 1939 catalog. In point of fact, the Mills Brothers' version was expressly forbidden only in July of that year.[161] Such Nazi inconsistency might benefit some black artists for a while, but conversely it could also victimize non-"Aryans" who were mistaken for Jews or blacks. This happened to the accomplished American alto saxophonist Frankie Trumbauer, who was "of German descent" according to the 1936 Brunswick catalog. Because Goebbels's experts mistook him for a Jew, his name had vanished from the German labels' rosters by 1939 at the latest.[162]

Attempts at "German Jazz"

Goebbels's controls of jazz through live performances, broadcasting, and the recording industry had been negative measures, which well befitted Hitler's dictatorial regime. But not least because of both the Führer's and Goebbels's own desire to be perceived as popular leaders, these measures possessed a tentative rather than a definitive character. Hitler and Goebbels despised jazz and did not *want* to compromise on the issue, but they were forced into necessary compromises both by their unwillingness to foster the image of a tyrant, and by the inadequacy of the bureaucracy at their disposal. Goebbels's post-1932 diaries are filled with expressions of a real or imagined love for the people, as well as indignation over the incompetence of his administrators in all echelons.

To bolster the impression of benevolence, which was in keeping with the leaders' vision of themselves as Caesarist revolutionaries constructing something new, they decided to supplement the negative policy against old-style jazz with a positive one toward the creation of a new-German idiom, a sort of "German Jazz." Yet this attempt was doomed to failure from the start, for it amounted to the proverbial squaring of the circle. Goebbels may have realized that jazz in Germany was an elitist music that appealed to a small, upwardly mobile lower-middle class as well as some upper-class segments of the population of less than middle age—in short, those sectors from which future leaders ideally were recruited. One of the problems of jazz, however, was that it was often imbedded in vulgar dance music of a kind embraced by a large cross-section of the populace, which militated against elitism. Even in nondictatorial times this involvement with dance music had often come close to undermining jazz as an art form.

Not only were the original German efforts to fabricate Nazi-specific jazz outmoded, in that the Nazi composers and arrangers had recourse to old-fashioned German music styles and formats, but the now very pronounced populist intentions neutralized all those special ingredients of jazz that had effected its sophistication. The Nazis rendered the new music melodically and harmonically simplistic and employed crudely conventional instrumentation and intonation, thus hoping to broaden its appeal as dance music for larger crowds. Although even National Socialists curiously continued to call jazz by its original American name, as is evident from the professional journals, thereby implicitly broadening the concept to include a wide variety of dance and entertainment genres far removed from New Orleans or Chicago jazz, they decided to dissociate their new creations from the old, detested nomenclature. In their first effort to generate a novel Germanic art form they termed their prospective product Neue Deutsche Tanzmusik, or "New German Dance Music."[163]

The installment of the Golden Seven combo in radio late in 1934 had been the prototype attempt at establishing role models for German dance and jazz musicians. However, since those musicians had failed in their mission by still sounding too American, Hadamovsky had introduced his jazz proscription on the broadcast network in October 1935, coupled with the censorship bureau. But these ordinances were interpreted by listeners and musicians alike as unnecessarily drastic, so that Goebbels's ministry came under pressure. His deputies therefore hit upon the idea of inaugurating another, fresher model for German jazz, one to serve for all time to come.[164] A radio-sponsored contest would be initiated, inviting German bands to qualify for local and regional competitions and for a final one in Berlin, with adjudication by both an interested listening audience and a round of expert judges. The first prize was a three-month contract with the national radio network worth eighteen thousand marks; two runner-up bands would get similar, albeit shorter, engagements.[165]

The enterprise received the warmest blessings from Germany's top two dance-band leaders, Barnabas von Géczy and Oskar Joost.[166] They themselves could not participate in the contest for three reasons. First, only novices without prior radio commitments could apply. Second, and more important, Gézcy and Joost already were too well known for a venture of this kind and could not stoop to it. Third, and somewhat ironically, their music already had proved unsuitable as ersatz jazz, having failed to catch the ear of the younger, purist crowd.[167]

Not that they would have been unacceptable to the authorities, quite the contrary! The thirty-eight-year-old Géczy was a classically schooled Hungarian who favored strings over reeds and brass and conducted his often schmaltzy society orchestra with a discipline most pleasing to the Nazis. This former Budapest concert master had fiddled himself into the most illustrious circles of official Germany; a favorite of Goebbels and Hitler, he commanded the steepest fees in the most exclusive ballrooms of the nation. Not exactly a Nazi, he was an opportunist who made well known his policy not to perform any Jewish compositions.[168]

Oskar Joost, one year Géczy's junior, was somewhat different in that originally, in the republic, he had been a promising jazz bandleader, but then had adapted his style to what he sensed were the regime's new guidelines. He knew jazz well and had jazzmen in his employ, among whom the trumpeter Kurt Hohenberger and the pianist-arranger Franz Mück were the most creative. But this violinist and sax player, originally a right-wing nationalist veteran of World War I, made no secret of the fact that he hated Jews; he had joined the Nazi party in April 1933. From 1930 on his band played in one of Germany's premier hotels, the Berlin Eden, and in October 1935 it started a new stage show at the giant Femina ballroom. Such credentials plus a small, honorary party post made Joost well acquainted with Berlin broadcasting executives as well as culture bureaucrat Hans Hinkel.[169]

From the outset and during its execution, the new German music contest was flawed in several important respects. First, it was confounded by cross-purposes: although the event's real mandate was to find a contemporary German music style, in practice it called for hitherto unknown dance bands to present themselves. Moreover, the judges at the national level included men inherently prejudiced against anything resembling the essence of jazz, so that to connoisseurs the outcome had to be a foregone conclusion. Eugen Hadamovsky himself was the chairman of the assessment committee. The classical composer Prof. Paul Graener of the RMK, like his newly appointed chief Peter Raabe, was a declared enemy of jazz. Dr. Willy Richartz of the Berlin broadcast central was the very man who had caused the downfall of the Golden Seven, and Dr. Fritz Stege, who joined somewhat belatedly, was long notorious for his antijazz campaign.[170] To curry favor with the judges, many bands during the three-tiered contest would endeavor to perform Richartz's own compositions, the works of a man who cherished "melody," as he himself once professed to Stege, and who had penned such pedestrian pieces as the fox-trot "Melodie der Liebe" and the *Marschfoxtrott* "In der Krone ist grosser Manöverball."[171]

The contest lasted until early March 1936. Everywhere in the Reich it was sloppily organized. In Königsberg strings were missing from the grand piano; in Hamburg one band was allowed to perform in its customary setting and thus unjustly collected all the votes from its fans; the adjudicating public often began to dance rather than evaluate the music earnestly—all might be considered trifles.[172] But while eventually some five hundred bands from all over Germany participated, at least one regional station, Cologne, recognizing the farce for what it was, never bothered to send finalists to the capital.[173]

The ultimate scandal during the final confused round, appropriately at the Berlin zoo on 13 March 1936, was indicative of the censorial intent of the administrators and exposed Hadamovsky as a heavy-handed zealot. Radio Hamburg's winning band, Fritz Weber's—a comparatively steamy formation even by critical German standards and already playing in some of Germany's better clubs[174]—appeared to all true jazz fans, both those in the audience and those listening in on the national broadcast system, as the favorite, and was touted for days as the sure winner. But since such an outcome would have been embarrassing to Goebbels's staff as reinforcing the old values to be scrapped, the final vote was manipulated so that a totally unknown orchestra, that of Willy Burkart (sponsored by Radio Frankfurt), ended up with the first prize, though never to be heard from again. An equally innocuous band came in second, and Weber was consoled as the third.[175]

When it all was over, nobody was satisfied: neither the regime leaders, who had failed to find a viable substitute for modern jazz; nor the organizers, who had lost face in the production of a scam; nor the many mediocre musicians who had merely been duped, spending their own money and time to acquire a transient and mostly local publicity. To be sure, Weber and his fans had the last laugh: he had not needed this boost in the first place, and thereafter was kept busy playing to full houses all over Germany.[176] "Once an institution has rooted itself as strongly as jazz has," mused Stege, "it is virtually impossible to get anywhere with mere prohibitions, unless one can replace the jazz band with something better." For once, this Nazi music critic spoke the truth.[177]

Nonetheless, even after this fiasco the Nazis' attempts to create "German jazz" did not subside. From the summer of 1936 until early 1937 Oskar Joost was working out a deal with Hadamovsky and Richartz for the establishment of a paragon dance band under his direction, as well as a new department in the RMK that he would head. The flexible bandleader, who had ingratiated himself with the regime in the spring of 1936 by doing voluntary reserve training in the newly formed Wehrmacht, already had a contract with the long-wave Deutschland-sender where his band played in such a manner that other dance musicians would be impelled to learn from it. Almost certainly, the reactionary Richartz had been behind this.[178]

In the fall of 1936 Joost was ready to present a detailed proposal to Hinkel, whose cooperation he needed, if his plan with the RMK was to go ahead. Backed by Hadamovsky and Richartz, Joost planned to head a "model orchestra respon-sible for the entire German broadcast network."[179] As such, Joost would deter-mine, as closely as possible, how German dance music—not to mention jazz—was to be performed by his own and other German bands. His own big band was to have no more than four saxophones (here the classic antijazz attitude surfaced again), but would sustain eleven strings, including six violins. Special composi-tions and arrangements were to be written, in paradigmatic fashion, "so that even the last band in the land, however small, can orient itself on the basis of the programs of the proposed orchestra as well as its performance style." Each of his model musicians was to be salaried by the Reich to the tune of about 700 marks a month, with a special bonus to be negotiated for its leader—at a total cost of RM 200,000. The musical arrangements would cost extra.[180]

By mid-November Joost's plans had crystallized further. Since, as Ger-many's future jazz policeman, the bandleader needed "ordinances of an au-thoritative nature," Hinkel was to commit himself regarding the institution of that special RMK dance music section. Joost was particularly determined to remove the influence of the Jews, "those well poisoners"—men like Friedrich Hollaender, Mischa Spoliansky, and Viktor Alberti, whose middleman control was still palpable through the backdoor sheet-music business. His new RMK office would have to be invested with National Socialist leadership authority, argued Joost, under the immediate supervision of President Raabe. In his multi-ple capacity as censor for dance music on radio, recordings, and the stage, throughout the music-publishing business, and eventually in film, Joost hoped to apply a pass-or-fail grade such as "musically valuable" or "rhythmically not suitable" to every piece submitted to him for examination. Only such radical cleansing action, maintained Joost, would have any chance of saving German light-entertainment music from progressive deterioration.[181]

The negotiations between Joost and the capricious Hinkel dragged on well into 1937, but at this particular time radio boss Hadamovsky's star was already falling. On 17 March Joost told Hinkel that "Dr. Richartz asked me once again to move on with the matter, for otherwise the project would founder this year." But two days later Goebbels appointed Cologne's radio chief Heinrich Glasmeier to replace the clumsy Hadamovsky, whereupon Joost's grotesque chimera dissolved into thin air. The bandleader carried on in the society ballrooms of the nation without special authority for or against anything, until he died of pneumonia after serving on the Russian front during World War II.[182]

Even this escapade did not yet end the national reconstruction. There was one additional, even more comical attempt at replacing jazz with artificial sub-stitutes. It was made by Wilhelm Hartseil, a trusty forty-six-year-old Brown Shirt stalwart with a checkered past who, in Goebbels's reshuffling of broadcast posts in March of 1937, became Leipzig station's new director.[183] Hartseil's brain-storm was to obliterate jazz through social dancing, by publically performing various "new" German dance pieces with suitable orchestras, with the participa-tion of professional dance instructors. On a smaller scale than the 1935–36 contest, these events would be aired on radio, albeit merely for Saxony, by Reichssender Leipzig.

The series began in January 1938 and dragged well into the fall of that year, moving to many local dance halls in Saxony and even adjacent regions. Letters to the station from listeners were encouraged, and the response was mostly positive, for only those who approved of the banal music in the first place ever bothered to write; what use was it to criticize? Self-servingly, the station director then had the most flattering excerpts mimeographed. Unsurprisingly, these letters testified that Jewish and Nigger jazz was awful (but had, thanks to the Nazis, now vanished at least from Leipzig's station); that there *were* German musical alternatives, what with compositions for the newly created "railway dance"; and that such heartening exercises should be repeated much more often.[184] On the other hand, Hartseil probably knew only too well that this venture had been more than naive and had certainly not touched the hearts and souls of the people who really mattered in this: the dedicated New Orleans jazz and swing musicians and their uneradicable fans in Germany.

Apart from ludicrous, isolated, last-ditch offensives engendered by the storm troopers and the HJ in the last months before the war, this was the finale in the Nazi struggle for jazz substitution.[185] Jazz had been placed on the index, it is true, but neither could it be suppressed, nor could the regime leaders come up with an even vaguely viable equivalent.

Jazz Defiant
The Reassertion of a Culture

Jazz Alive

Jazz in the Third Reich turned out to be a resilient art. Because of the imperfection of controls, improved conditions after the economic depression, and the centrality of Berlin, which ostentatiously hosted the 1936 Olympics, this music continued not only to exist, but to flourish in Germany after January 1933, right up to the beginning of the war. Enemies no less than lovers of jazz music have attested to this fact with graphic clarity, thus dissolving the lingering postwar myth that after the Games jazz fell back into a period of repression.[1]

"It is true: jazz is still with us, in spite of prohibitions and decrees," lamented Fritz Stege in March of 1937. The Brown Shirts noted one year later that Germany was suffused with swing "in the noblest night clubs of the capital and the provinces." Toward the end of that year austere Nazi university students identified similar culprits: "Jazz blossoms in the most representative hotels, which serve as advertisements of the German Reich for foreigners, as well as in bars that open their doors only after sundown." Musicians and fans agreed, but with reverse sentiments. "In Berlin there is much of this nerve-racking, vulgar sound around," was the ironic message of a visiting Leipzig aficionado to his friends back home, after a torrid night at the Femina in December 1935. And in regards to the Olympics Otto Stenzel, the sovereign bandleader of the Scala orchestra, reminisced some years before his recent death: "There was a lot going on then, and it was wonderful, and we could play as hot as we liked; it was the swing of the Americans."[2]

Yet was it really "the swing of the Americans"? In the United States, jazz music had experienced something of a metamorphosis since the late 1920s. As Gunther Schuller reminds us, a creative crisis in the music of leading stylists such as Louis Armstrong had coincided and merged with the economic malaise

57

of the Great Depression, creating a double predicament for jazz. When the music recuperated in the early thirties, it did so on the basis of the old melodic, harmonic, and rhythmic conceptions, but it reasserted its strength in a different, more progressive form.

Important elements of this change were a novel use of the traditional rhythm section, where antiquated instruments like the tuba and banjo finally gave way to new ones, in this case string bass and guitar. Pianists and drummers no less than bassists and guitarists were assuming more constructive roles both in the rhythm section and as solo performers. Rhythmically, a transition occurred from a two-beat-per-bar to a four-beat articulation, executed on string bass (the "walking bass") and bass drum. The riffs—repetitive two- and sometimes four-bar phrasings—were introduced. And melodically there appeared a greater elegance in solo choruses, making more imaginative use of boldly innovative harmonic constructions such as extended chords and altered notes. Since the postdepression economic climate increasingly allowed for such luxury, jazz combos tended to include more members, so that the typical swing formation of the late thirties was a big band, up to sixteen instrumentalists conducted by the leader. This called for arranged scores charted individually for the sections—brass or reeds or even strings—thus somewhat limiting opportunities for solos. But as solo vehicles saxophones, especially the tenor, became predominant. Other instruments, previously seldom heard as lead carriers, came to the fore: the guitar as a solo voice, the vibraphone, the clarinet. All these instruments now executed solos with greater precision and a new, albeit relaxed, brilliance; improvisational lines became much more fluid, leaving the often jagged, rough-hewn patterns of New Orleans jazz well behind. Jazz's very sound texture was made smoother and richer by the new mode of playing called swing.

Today it is a truism that no one did more to herald those epochal changes, authoritatively defining the essence of jazz until the subsequent developments ushered in by bebop in the mid-1940s, than the white Chicago clarinetist Benny Goodman. Still, it is well to emphasize that Goodman's sudden fame after that singular Palomar (Los Angeles) stand in August 1935 was somewhat accidental, for the black pianist Fletcher Henderson, though much cruder in his overall sound, had laid the foundations for swing music several years earlier, without being himself able to reap the benefits. Henderson's pioneering role in swing is starkly obvious, for instance, from his 1934 recording of "Wrappin' It Up." As far as the music world, the world of entertainment, and certainly the world of social dancing was concerned, Benny Goodman, soon to be celebrated as the "King of Swing," had singlehandedly invented this music; few people cared to know that he had actually used—and continued to use—Henderson's arrangements.[3]

There are, then, two main reasons why swing in Germany could not have had the same significance in the context of the country's indigenous culture and was, in fact, a significantly different thing from swing in America. One is, self-evidently, that the Germans (like other Europeans) did not create the swing idiom or help toward its evolution in any way; as they had done previously with jazz, they at best copied the new style from American originals. Yet another reason is that a necessary ethnomusicological condition for the development of swing, as witnessed in the United States, was missing in Germany. In America, as Schuller has observed, after severe economic trials "a special identity between a people and its music" had been galvanized; swing became almost a national or folk music to which masses of Americans could relate—and demonstratively dance to![4] By contrast, in Germany only small, quasi-elitist segments of the populace knew swing; it represented anything but a mass phenomenon, even though its clangor and coloration influenced much of the prevalent social-dance milieu even on the most trivial of planes.

Germans and non-Germans alike have commented on these differences in subjective but nevertheless revealing fashion. Self-critically, German dance musicians identified the drums as the main culprit in causing faulty rhythm, especially fouled-up syncopation; because pointing to the Americans was risky, they cited British big-band drummers as models for improvement.[5] With reference to melodists, one journal noted disparagingly in 1933 that the total number of true improvisers in Germany could comfortably be seated "in one of our larger taxis."[6] Helmut Zacharias, that violin wunderkind active in German jazz toward the end of World War II, opined about jazz and German musicians that "it certainly was not in their blood."[7] Most serious fans concur. Today they attest that even the best of German jazz players did not interest them then because the alternative, American recordings, was always accessible. Even the Golden Seven, officially indicted for "hot" playing, "were somewhat lax, not as exact as the Americans" (Hamburg fan Panagopoulos); indeed, they were "too German" (Baden-Baden impresario Berendt). Made-in-Germany jazz reminded Berlin's Hans Blüthner of marches; it was "chemically sanitized," Frankfurt's saxophonist Emil Mangelsdorff recently observed.[8]

Knowledgeable outsiders were even harsher. American guitarist Mike Danzi was generally disdainful of German drummers.[9] Martha Dodd, the daughter of the U.S. ambassador in Berlin, stated that "only a few night clubs attempt to play jazz and they are very bad."[10] The most convincing verdict stems from a well-placed New York record collector who corresponded somewhat irregularly with a Leipzig fan. After having received Telefunken recordings featuring Kurt Hohenberger's combo, he liberally dispensed criticism. "The records are very interesting and show that the idea is there," he wrote his pen pal in August 1938. "However, there is very little inspiration present to make them give out right from the hearts. The men play well from the music and technically they produce danceable stuff, but I must admit the right hep stuff is still here in the city of N.Y., also Chicago and Kansas City." He had spun the discs for some friends, "musicians like Eddie Condon and Mezz Mezzrow and it didn't click. Too restrained and void of sincerity. . . . After all Jazz is a typical American product and is part of us here."[11] But more damning is the omission of German jazz musicians, even the finest, from Charles Delaunay's famous second edition of *Hot Discography* of 1938, while at the same time Delaunay saw fit to include among the hundreds of Americans his own Frenchmen such as Alix Combelle and Stephane Grappelly, Britons like Ted Heath and Spike Hughes, and even the Dutch group Het Ramblers.[12]

This said, it is important to note that in those years Germany was not alone in being a second- or third-rate jazz power. Oberlin College historian Frederick Starr has provided persuasive examples of how even more horribly contemporary Russians performed, and even the British, ranking among the best in Europe, had their wobbly moments.[13] None of these musicians, whether English, German, Russian, Swedish, or Swiss, did what Coleman Hawkins has singled out as the stock-in-trade of every truly inventive jazz musician: "I find myself playing a lot of things, changing them around and playing them completely different than what I would perhaps have played them a year before. . . . I've never stopped, you know."[14] The Germans stopped early, and then again and again.

Yet it stands to reason that such a blanket judgment will never suffice completely; for the prewar Third Reich a ranking of groups of musicians by quality must be attempted. At the very top ranged a handful of jazz players who were able to improvise in the vein of their adored American paragons, even if they could never contribute anything to be truly called their own. Improvisation on the original melody or "head" still was not something German jazz musicians took for granted in those days. When Erwin Lehn, today the doyen of German big-band leaders, attended a provincial conservatory in the mid-1930s, he and his compatriots were reading written-out jazz choruses, to the scorn of their Brown-Shirted teachers. "Only later did it occur to us that we could improvise this stuff ourselves," says Lehn, and obviously, their talent proved them right.[15] Yet merely as superb copyists the peak professionals often came remarkably close to American originals. The best of them mastered improvisation in the American style. By the consensus of surviving musicians, clarinetist Ernst Höllerhagen, who during most of the thirties was the undisputed star of Stauffer's Original Teddies and was therefore sometimes removed from his native Germany, improvised in a fashion very close to Benny Goodman's. Today one cannot mistake his smooth, seductive sound for anybody else's, as in Stauffer's performance of "I Left You for the Leader of the Swingband," or Kurt Hohenberger's rendition of "What Will I Tell My Heart," of December 1937.[16]

The reigning pianist of the Nazi era was Magdeburg's own Fritz Schulze, who until the spring of 1935 was with James Kok and then in various Berlin small bar settings—the Ciro, the Sherbini, the Patria—until in 1937, at the luxurious Quartier Latin, he joined up with Kurt Hohenberger's combo, which then overlapped with the Golden Seven (for which Schulze also performed).[17] Various sample recordings today convince us that Schulze's near-genius made him sound like a carbon copy of Teddy Wilson (whose recordings were suggested to him by Kok), but sometimes also of Billy Kyle. Listen to his freely swinging solos in the loosened-up versions of Kurt Hohenberger's "Jammin' " and of "Limehouse Blues" (1938)![18] Schulze was known to copy arrangements or transcribe solos from American recordings; he then internalized these and played in the mold of the demigods.[19] In December 1937 the key American jazz magazine *Down Beat* hailed him as "by far the greatest Swing musician" in the Reich, "one of the finest on the entire continent"; given the opportunity, in America "he could become one of the foremost Jazz pianists."[20] *Down Beat* was right. Schulze himself tells the story of how Jack Hylton frequently came to his club to hear him; Hylton would lodge solidly behind a whiskey glass, and as he was leaving would say: "Boys, it was great!"[21] Schulze, who resembled Frank Sinatra in looks and carefree life-style, found his professional match only in Art Tatum, whose mind-boggling harmonic modulations he could not emulate.[22] But who in the United States could do that?

Number three on the list would have to have been the guitarist Hans Korseck, not as gregarious as Schulze the playboy and not as brooding as the pudgy, alcohol-addicted Höllerhagen, but, with his wire-rimmed glasses and straight-combed hair, seriously introspective. His Berlin widow Hilde Korseck has provided a loving personal memoir of the man. Korseck, born in 1911, was from a sternly religious Prussian family. He had started out as a university student majoring in medicine; the plectrum Gibson guitar became his second passion. In the early thirties he played with an obscure Berlin band called the White Ravens, but soon found himself in Stenzel's Scala band and in Peter Kreuder's excessively commercial jazz group. After Harold Kirchstein's flight in 1937 he replaced him in the Golden Seven band and through it also frequently performed with the offspring Hohenberger combo. Intermittently, with his friend the pseudojazz accordionist Albert Vossen, he went to New York, where his idols Benny Goodman and Tommy Dorsey personally allowed the enthralled young man to audit their rehearsals. "Those impressions overwhelmed him, determined him, and set standards."[23]

Hans Korseck, who during the research for this book was unanimously mentioned by his surviving peers as the foremost German jazz guitarist of the 1930s, may very well have been the Reich's first guitar player who improvised in linear fashion à la Charlie Christian or Django Reinhardt, rather than strumming chords in the manner of the banjo players still popular until the early thirties, and the long immortal Freddie Green of the Basie band. Unfortunately, the evidence for this hypothesis is scarce: in the few surviving recordings of the Kreuder and Hohenberger bands, his instrument is somewhat subdued, while strumming is in fact quite audible.[24] But all his former colleagues as well as his widow have asserted that he could improvise in the most modern way, and the raw swing influence on him is evident from his personal record catalog.

This document is a rare testimony to all the German musicians' agility in evading Nazi content controls, no less than to Korseck's individually refined taste. There is no reason to doubt Hilde Korseck's assertion that his playing was heavily influenced by copious study of recorded music that he often got from Alberti's surreptitiously. On the roster we find the names mostly of American musicians: the Boswell Sisters, Joe Venuti, Eddie Lang, Ellington, Armstrong, Lunceford, and Artie Shaw. A good one-third of the entries are by the King of Swing and Tommy Dorsey. Most tunes are typical swing songs, among them several "Jewish" numbers by Gershwin and Irving Berlin. Fred Astaire sings Gershwin's "Shall We Dance" and that composer's perennial favorite "I've Got Rhythm"; the British Jew Bert Ambrose performs Berlin's "Isn't It a Lovely Day" and Sophie Tucker, also Jewish, even belts out "My Yiddishe Mama."[25]

As far as one can tell, Höllerhagen, Schulze, and Korseck were what may be called pure jazzmen, musicians who never compromised their standards in the light-entertainment field, so that even when they played for social dancing, perhaps at the popular Baltic Sea resort of Timmendorf, they basically engaged in their beloved swing. Into the same category of purists, although not of the same musical order, fell several other musicians, all of the Berlin scene, who freely moved in and out of the existing big bands, availed themselves of what studio work there was, and joined colleagues in small combinations for club dates.

Munich drummer Fritz Brocksieper was one of them. He had come to the capital only in the summer of 1938 and then sat in for Waldi Luczkowski, also a good jazzer, as drummer for the Golden Seven, but was soon at home in establishments like the Ciro bar.[26] Brocksieper's craving for swing drove him uncritically to adopt one of the faults of his exemplar, Goodman's drummer Gene Krupa, who was known for his inordinate noise, which, even so, was somewhat in the German tradition of drumming.[27] Brocksieper's elders in the business, by the summer of 1939, included Hans Klagemann, who used the opposite percussion dynamics, usually as a mainstay of the Kreuder group, and characteristically was known as "Cat's Paws," if not as everyone's favorite jazz percussionist.[28] Also prominent was Willi Kettel, who was working in the Hohenberger combo by the time the war started.

Among other reed men of note, who improvised well but not in the class of Höllerhagen, was the half-Jewish Eugen Henkel, an alumnus of Seiber's Frankfurt jazz seminar and a Hawkins acolyte who impressed Hylton sufficiently to get a job offer from him. There was also Höllerhagen's prodigious pupil Detlef Lais, as well as Franz Thon, Kurt Wege, and Herbert Müller, whom they called "Mouse Tooth" for a glaring dental gap.[29]

Stellar pianists in the Schulze style were Haentzschel, Wernicke, and Mück. Under the influence of his old friend Franz Grothe and his mentor Theo Mackeben, the veteran Georg Haentzschel turned more and more to film scoring in those years, although with equal virtuosity he would accompany the Golden Seven or soloists like vibraphonist Kurt Engel, the Red Norvo of the Third Reich, more prosaically in charge of timpani at the state opera.[30] At his peak, Helmuth Wernicke played excellent piano for Heinz Wehner, and Franz Mück, when not reading Oskar Joost's more sedate scores in a society dance band, moved around freely as a much-sought-after swinger. For string bass accompaniment one would call on Otto Tittmann, Paul Henkel, or Rudi Wegener.

One of the best trombonists was known to be Walter Dobschinski, who throughout this time played with Stauffer but was sufficiently often in Berlin to handle side gigs. Dobschinski, on a steamer with Stauffer's Teddies, had been befriended and influenced in New York by Pee Wee Hunt, by his own admission of German descent.[31] Then there were Erhard Krause, also of the Golden Seven set, and Willi Berking, who excelled on several other instruments and performed a great deal with Albert Vossen, Korseck's accordionist friend. Not quite Korseck's equals on guitar but with much drive and potential were the stateless Armenian Meg Tevelian; the refugee Russian Serge Matul, who was wont to smash brandy glasses against the ceiling; and Hans Belle, a native of the Reich. Belle starred in a surprisingly modern combination of piano, guitar, and accordion that cherished American Swing tunes such as Ella Fitzgerald's "A-Tisket,

A-Tasket." This Bar Trio seems to have been the favorite of many of Berlin's beautiful people, including cosmopolitan film idol Willy Fritsch, whose screen marriage was with the British Lillian Harvey.[32]

It is a somewhat complicated business to assess the trumpet players of this period, if only because of the predominance of the oft-mentioned Kurt Hohenberger. This Swabian was twenty-seven in 1935, the time when the Golden Seven signed a potentially lucrative contract with Electrola, and thus with regard to publicity and commercial success he unquestionably dominated the trumpet scene of Germany's jazz capital. His style was modeled on Red Nichols, but because he played in a quieter, cleaner vein and was not known to improvise in the strictest sense, preferring arrangements instead, critics have tended to dismiss him as a genuinely swinging musician. There can be no doubt that both in the Seven as well as in the later Hohenberger combo musicians such as Thon, Haentzschel, and Schulze, rather than Hohenberger, constituted the hard-core swingers. In the United States, Nichols himself, of course, had sustained a fairly commercial mode before the coming of classic swing. At the Quartier Latin in July 1937, Hohenberger's music was "pretty hot," wrote the *Podium*'s critic Heinz Roger acidly (which furnishes another reason why, put in historical perspective, the Nazis always suspected the Seven). But three surviving expert witnesses aver persuasively that Kurt's trumpet was at best "tasteful" (Gunter Lust), "very soft" (Werner Daniels), or "diffident" (Franz Heinrich).[33] On the neat, tautly arranged "What Will I Tell My Heart" of December 1937 Hohenberger blows eight bars of a pleasant, but very likely preconceived solo.[34]

Admittedly, there were at least two lesser known trumpet players, in and out of Berlin, who played a more biting horn as facile improvisers. One was the aforementioned Hans Berry; the other was Charly Tabor. The discriminating German amateur impresario Hans Blüthner in 1947 noted about Berry in the Swedish journal *Orkester Journalen* that he had been the Reich's "ranking trumpeter." If nothing else, Berry was much more urbane than the Stuttgart homebody Hohenberger. He had experience with Billy Bartholomew, the Swiss Lanigiro Hot Players and, of course, Teddy Stauffer. Not only that, but in 1935 in Geneva, he was working with Hawkins, and later, in the Belgian resort of Ostend, with the black band of Willie Lewis. In 1934, the *Artist* called Berry's burning style "unheard-of" for a trumpeter thus far, and a little later its editorial office still thought him, if snidely, "a very hot boy." That was before Berry's Israelite grandfather had been pulled out of the closet, for because of the already described circumstances there is no official mention of him further on.[35]

Born in Vienna in 1914, Charly Tabor played with the Italian band of John Abriani all over Germany and Holland and then arrived in Berlin after his Munich jazz buddy Brocksieper had beckoned him to come. When the Harry James disciple got there, he was supposed to start an engagement in the Carlton bar, with an "extremely respectable, refined band, and for them I was too hot. I was supposed to play much more melody." Interestingly enough, the leader of that group was Albert Vossen, which reflects as much on that accordionist's conventional mode as it does, in comparison, on young Charly's unbounded jazz temperament.[36]

The Carlton bar certainly was one of those exalted places where jazz or pseudojazz was being performed in the capital. Between 1933 and 1940 this happened in several such venues all concentrated within perhaps five thousand square meters along Berlin's pleasure mile, the Kurfürstendamm to the west of the Kaiser Wilhelm Memorial Church.

Other cavernous haunts were the Sherbini, Königin, Roxy, Uhu, Kakadu, Rosita, Patria, Ciro, and a dozen lesser ones. Liveried doormen chased away any but the most chic and distinguished-looking customers, thus also keeping a check on the hated RMK spies, who were invariably shabbily dressed. (If the spies forced their way in to scrutinize the music, the players had already been warned by a secret bell and now displayed phony song captions on their sheet music, such as "Schwarzer Panther" for "Tiger Rag.") "Vaguely akin to the 52nd street Swing saloons, these bars are minute night clubs, luxuriously outfitted and never containing more than two rooms of microscopic dimensions, which cater to unquestionably the best public in the city," sneered *Down Beat* magazine. International and German film stars were regularly sighted there, such as Robert Taylor and Brigitte Horney (the daughter of German-American émigré psychiatrist Karen Horney), who had a much-vaunted liaison with the racy Stauffer. Aristocrats high and low as well as the monied gentry met in that El Dorado, along with the demimonde, industrialists, and military aces like Luftwaffe colonel Ernst Udet. "Drinks begin at a buck a gulp," *Down Beat* continued its dubious laudation, "and one can partake of excellent food at prices which are also unpleasantly high."[37]

The Quartier Latin, that habitual cave of pianist Fritz Schulze, was said to be "by far the most exclusive . . . Berlin's swankiest, smoothest and snootiest night spot, which is not only Germany's finest *boite de nuit,* but indeed one of the most select establishments on the continent." Schulze too recalls the "exclusive clientele, international, and, in particular, ambassadorial." An ordinary beer was so expensive here that even moderately well-off patrons could hardly afford it. Prince Bernhard of Lippe-Biesterfeld, consort to Dutch crown princess Juliana and today one of the richest men in the world, was once observed nursing the cheapest cognac the bar had to offer, after getting his spirits high with cheap booze from a tavern across the street.[38]

The Quartier Latin was owned and operated, until 1937 at least, by Herr Dajou, of certifiably exotic (Romanian but not Jewish!) extraction. Sherbini's took its name after the Egyptian proprietor and jazz drummer Sherbini, who was married to the stepdaughter of Count Conny Frankenberg. And Herr Ahmed Mustafa, yet another Egyptian, owned the renowned Ciro.[39]

On the other side of upper-crust recreation, but often still featuring quality jazz, especially with an international flavor, were the grandiose Haus Vaterland complex, the Wintergarten, Scala, Delphi-Palast, and Femina. Haus Vaterland sported many style and period rooms in which anything from a Bavarian *Schrammel* band to a small swing group was wont to play, usually for dancing and bolstered by regional cuisines. For instance, John Abriani's ten-piece band worked in the Vaterland-Palmensaal in the fall of 1937.[40] Wintergarten and Scala were home to popular variety shows that could include the famous Swiss clown Grock or Italian opera tenor Benjamino Gigli, but had some jazzlike offerings interspersed. Otto Stenzel's house band at the Scala was known for its jazz proclivities; Stenzel employed many genuine jazz musicians such as Korseck and Karl Hohenberger, Kurt's less prolific trumpet-playing brother. As in the Weimar Republic, emphasis here was on showmanship, the dazzling display of skills, rather than on musical content per se, and of course one could not dance. The Delphi and Femina came closer to the sumptuous hotel dancing establishments such as the Eden-Dachgarten or Adlon ballroom in that big bands played there for the merriment of social dancers, but here, in contrast to the fine hotels, the crowds were larger, younger, and solid middle class. One could visit in pairs or—and this was the clue—as a single, hoping to find a friend for dancing and perhaps for courtship. The Femina was actually unique for several reasons. For the man or woman who espied a potential dance partner across the hall, there were 225 table telephones with instructions in German and English, as well as a letter shuttle system by which to exchange amorous notes. Daily there were four orchestras (among them inevitably a major swing band), which enraptured fifteen hundred dancers on three platforms. During summer nights, a huge sky dome opened up to reveal the firmament—an incredible spectacle for the festive crowds. Once Dietrich Schulz watched the zeppelin *Hindenburg* gliding overhead, "majestically, noiselessly."[41]

It was at the downtown Moka Efti (there was another such club in the suburbs), in similar but rather less opulent environs, that the "Aryanized" James Kok band continued its illustrious career, although with some noticeable deficits. Kok's group had of course been the leading German big band until the spring of 1935. Apart from a couple of Dutchmen, the Romanian had employed only German musicians, outstanding ones like Schulze on piano, the reedman Kurt Wege (soon to join the Golden Seven as well), and the reed player, pianist, and scat singer Erhard ("Funny") Bauschke, who, despite occasional antics on the bandstand, handled his horn professionally.[42]

It was Bauschke who decided to carry on with the Kok band as its frontman, so that the planned engagement on the island of Rügen during the summer of 1935 could be honored.[43] Bauschke somewhat reconstituted the band, luckily keeping Wege and acquiring the fledgling multi-instrumentalist Erwin Lehn as well as the ambitious young trumpeter Günter Herzog, who later played with Stauffer. The bandleader then signed a contract for January 1936 with the downtown Moka Efti, where he would remain until 1942. In fact, he became an institution in Berlin, where dance-crazed youths would sing, to the melody of a famous swing tune: "Erhard Bauschke spielt im Moka Efti einen Swing, Goody, Goody. . . ."[44]

The existence of this ditty is further proof of the porosity of Nazi anti-jazz measures. And whereas in late 1936 the Nazis lauded Bauschke for avoiding all "foreign exaggerations," and Hans Brückner a year later even thought that apart from a few English items he preferred "good, old German productions," Bauschke stealthily moved to adopt mostly American swing tunes for his repertoire. For example, he was the first in Germany to perform and popularize the classic Benny Goodman vehicle "Organ Grinder's Swing."

That tune is what Dietrich Schulz heard when he checked out the band one evening in 1937. Dietrich, ham that he was, noted that Bauschke played an arrangement by the British Jew Bert Ambrose that was still available in the Reich on the German Brunswick label. The "Goody, Goody" of the fans' ditty was Goodman's own arrangement on Electrola, and in addition the band played Irving Berlin's "Alexander's Ragtime Band" according to the Casa Loma orchestra's arrangement on Brunswick. That evening, Bauschke also intoned the "Tiger Rag," "Basin Street Blues," and "Whispering," but also included a few tangos and two fox-trots to provide some German numbers and serve as a pro forma concession to the powers that be. "Now no one has any more reason to complain about the lack of good bands in Germany," Schulz wrote to satisfy himself. "Through the transcription of recorded arrangements the orchestra has been able to find a style, a precision, and a sense of swing, as it would never have been possible by any other shortcut."[45]

Bauschke could always profit from the former reputation of James Kok, but by 1937 at the latest he was rivaled as Germany's paramount jazz big-band leader by the up-and-coming Heinz Wehner. The beginning of national prominence for this twenty-nine-year-old alumnus of the Hanover conservatory dates from the spring of 1934, when his big band played engagements in Hamburg and at the Timmendorf resort, performing, like Kok's band, in the pervasive Casa Loma style. In the summer Wernicke, Berking, and Müller joined his organization, and on 1 September Wehner premiered at Berlin's Europa-Haus, another large dance establishment. Using this as his base, Wehner and his boys then moved back and forth to Hamburg, Leipzig, and Düsseldorf, the Reich's other three important jazz centers. With his Telefunken Swing-Orchester he also cut many records.

In the winter of 1936–37 Wehner was on tour in Sweden, and thereafter, with the exception of his sojourn to New York in the summer of 1937, he became a fixture both at the Delphi and the Femina. By the summer of 1939 Müller had left, but two other superior players had joined the band, Teddy Kleindin on reeds and the Dutchman Henk Bruyns on trumpet. A well-known foreign big-band leader said about Wehner at the time that he was eminently comparable to the British show bandsman Henry Hall.[46]

As a matter of fact, Wehner's musical style has frequently been compared to the disciplined English manner of big-band performance. *Down Beat* magazine accorded Wehner's band the epithet of "best large band in the Nazi Realm." As such, it was a suitable yardstick with which to measure the output of other German orchestras. However, it is a measure of the overall quality of jazz in Germany in this period that in itself, Wehner's band was very uneven. The Swedes in January 1937 scoffed at the official Telefunken name tag "Swing Orchestra," good-humoredly downgrading it to "a well-prepared dance orchestra." They characterized the rhythm section as "heavy and mechanical," and even star trombonist Willi Berking impressed them as "somewhat antiquated." Maestro Wehner, whose school instruments were violin and trumpet, was chided as much for his faulty vocalizing as for his nervous stage manner. With regard to his comportment, the *Down Beat* critic Douglas McDougall had similar qualms, and Wehner's arrangements he thought "for the most part pretty pompous." The Swedes, once more, found his repertoire old-fashioned. If one listens to

Wehner's most popular tune of the day, the Wernicke fox-trot "Fräulein Gerda," one cannot help agreeing that the execution of the music is disciplined yet dense to the point of sterility, with a wooden, marchlike beat sustained by a leaden, uninspired rhythm section. German jazz at its best? The knowing Schulz thought in 1937 that Wehner was rather inferior to Bauschke.[47]

Undoubtedly, at certain times some of the lesser-known bands of the Berlin jazz scene—those of Hans Rehmstedt, Georg Nettelmann, Fritz Weber, Kurt Widmann, Walter Schacht, and especially Max Rumpf—surpassed Wehner in pure swing, although on average their productions were much more spotty, with the truly spicy highlights being few and far between.[48] Small wonder, then, if German and foreign experts alike preferred the Reich's small and elastic jazz combinations over the big bands, even though, strictly speaking, these small groups were not the hallmark of true swing. Moreover, when it came to big bands, the foreign visitors—Teddy Stauffer, Arne Hülphers, Henry Hall, and Jack Hylton—were considered princes.

To be truthful, after January 1933 Hylton's star was falling in Germany, as livelier, more titillating foreign bands entered the realm, in particular Stauffer's. After his spectacular tour of early 1935, which led to Kok's demise, Hylton returned twice more to Berlin, in February 1937 and exactly one year later, thus prolonging the powerful Hylton cult. But the Briton's stilted style, which now favored the more common pop tunes rather than classic American jazz compositions by Henderson, Ellington, or Gershwin, allowed little latitude for the controlled abandon of swing and hence could not sustain him as an institution with the growing number of connoisseurs of that music. Hylton became outdated. As far as the regime leaders were concerned, his presence in the Reich after the Kok affair was not exactly welcome, even though Hylton had organized a benefit concert for jobless RMK musicians in 1935, but after all, he was also envied for the large fees that he demanded for himself in hard, foreign currency. Furthermore, although in 1935 he had knowingly left the visiting Coleman Hawkins behind in Holland, the presence of Jewish musicians in his band—such as the German expatriate Freddy Schweitzer—did nothing to benefit the maestro. During one of his Berlin visits Hylton was instructed by Goebbels's office that if Hitler and his entourage should attend a performance, any Jews were to be placed at the back of the band. Allegedly, Hylton disregarded this order; the Führer is not known to have visited a jazz recital. In any event, it is clear that because of the international concert exchange agreements and the lack of tangible anti-foreigner legislation Hylton could not be effectively kept out of Germany.[49]

To a certain extent one can say that Hylton's place was occupied in 1939 by Henry Hall, the London BBC bandleader, who visited Berlin for four weeks in January and February. Today some critics hold that Hall was even more rigid in his mode than Hylton.[50] Besides that, he seems to have been much more accommodating to the dictatorship than Hylton ever was, for he pointedly left his Jewish band members at home,[51] and, after having performed in the Scala and on German radio, he wrote a flattering article about Germany in the British journal *Rhythm*. Noting the hundreds of uniforms in the street, he still assured his countrymen that the Germans "certainly don't want war"—and this after Prime

Minister Chamberlain's recent martial cry that appeasement was over! Hall was full of praise for a state that appeared to be giving its workers ample opportunity for recreation (deduced from his observation of near-free concerts on Sunday mornings). Moreover, Hall had the "thrill of seeing a torch-light parade of Hitler's Storm Troopers, and it was a tremendous sight, made all the more impressive by the fervour of the fanatical civilians for whose benefit it was staged." Remarking on the creative presence in Berlin of the "grand clarinettist" Ernst Höllerhagen, Hall, who after all had hired Benny Carter as his arranger in London, also rendered the hardly surprising verdict that in Germany "the bands, taken by and large, are rhythmically much inferior to our own." Although he judged orchestral and instrumental skills as being "extremely high," he said that altogether "Jazz in Germany is notably deficient in swing."[52]

If nothing else, dyed-in-the-wool Nazis would not have been put off by such a collection of thoughts. They were in any case positively pleased with Hall's shrewd Jewish band policy, rejoicing that he had never employed Jews in the first place, and also with his constrained, inoffensive musical style. By his own admission, Hall, like Hylton, was rewarded handsomely in pounds sterling.[53]

Among those foreign big-band leaders, then, Teddy Stauffer and Arne Hülphers were considered to be the serious swingers. Both men, in fact, pushed their swing to the limit, Stauffer in a consciously reckless fashion, Hülphers inadvertently so. Stauffer had played around Germany off and on since 1930, until his July 1936 Olympic Delphi grandstanding put him on the jazz map as number one. He himself was deficient on the saxophone and clarinet and could hardly show off on his original instrument, the violin. But he had extraordinary charisma as a leader, inspiring his very best musicians to excel. Clarinetist Höllerhagen, of course, was the star, but Walter Dobschinski on trombone and the Swiss pianist Buddy Bertinat (later Jack Trommer), often flanked by Kurt Hohenberger, Kleindin, and Thon, shone in section-playing as well as stinging swing solos, the latter at times vacillating in quality. This is evidenced by recordings of "Limehouse Blues" (1937), "The Big Apple," and "St. Louis Blues" (both 1938). Much of Stauffer's success was due to Dobschinski's many arrangements; so if handsome Teddy scored highly with the young women of his large German swing congregation, the more swarthy Walter could compensate by knowing that he had the true believers on his side. The Original Teddies, while in Germany, were even more ubiquitous than Wehner's men: after the Olympics they often went to Hamburg, but also Leipzig and Düsseldorf, apart from occasional stints in their homeland.[54]

In retrospect, Swedish swing ace Arne Hülphers impresses the musicologist as much as, if not more than, the son of Bern. Hülphers's was by far the best Swedish jazz band, in the impressive Scandinavian tradition of Hakan von Eichwald, Kai Ewans, and Aage Juhl-Thomsen (the last two being Danish). Unlike his Scandinavian peers, however, who often played commercially and were purposely devoid of swing, Hülphers compromised on nothing. Unlike Wehner and very much like Stauffer, his titles were, exclusively, original American swing tunes, to which he, as much as the Swiss, had immediate access. From

1936 to 1939, Hülphers came frequently to Berlin, sometimes accompanied by Greta Wassberg, the singer.[55]

Wassberg constituted a phenomenon Germans could never cope with and actually neither understood nor cherished: the human voice in jazz, especially that of women. For whereas there were a few male singers working with German groups—preeminently Peter Rebhuhn and Horst Winter—their style was noticeably immature, and there were no women vocalists to speak of. The genius of soloist Ella Fitzgerald, for instance, then just coming to the fore, was something a few purists tuned into, but no German musician in Berlin or any of the other jazz venues ever tried to copy her the way they would copy Goodman or Harry James.

Despite this skeletal textbook description of the German jazz scene from 1933 to the beginning of the war as being a uniform development concentrated in Berlin, the reality was much more heteromorphic. Apart from weekly and monthly agendas, which appeared smooth on the surface, there were anomalies and irregularities, and to no small extent they involved the inadequate policing efforts of the regime's leaders at all levels of the bureaucracy. These irregularities aided the progress of jazz in Fascist Germany. Three examples should suffice to illustrate this situation.

First, although jazz and jazz-inspired dance music were mainly centered in Berlin, they found a limited haven in certain provincial hubs such as Münster, where they were supported in local hotels and restaurants by a fairly active club scene.[56] Leipzig, Hamburg, and Düsseldorf have already been mentioned as jazz centers, and even the comparatively backward Bavarian capital of Munich was not immune, particularly since some of the intermediary bands such as Georg Nettelmann's would visit there.[57]

Second, jazz sometimes appeared in surprising political environs. In the summer of 1939 one young aficionado, sponsored by the Nazi party's "Strength through Joy" program, visited the Baltic seaside resort of Warnemünde. Once there, he found that the small-town beach hotel he was staying in was resounding with the most arousing solos. In the hall downstairs, a small trio led by a young violinist was jamming it up; clearly, the musicians had listened to the Hot Club de France's Stephane Grappelly. The hall was decked out with swastika flags, and brown-uniformed men and their wives were obviously enjoying the scintillating rhythms of "Tiger Rag," "Dinah," and "Sweet Georgia Brown." The highest-decorated Nazi there then warmly thanked the young bandleader, who turned out to be none other than eighteen-year-old Helmut Zacharias. Four years later Zacharias was Europe's premier jazz violinist, ranking only behind Grappelly and the Dane Svend Asmussen. Having played in this steamy style all week long for grateful summer guests, Zacharias, the talk of the small town, had been hired on his day off by the local party chapter![58]

A third sign that jazz was alive was that, totally contrary to Nazi protocol, there was even the odd black left to play jazz in Germany in those years. Around 1936, in Berlin's posh Sherbini bar, the American trombonist Herb Flemming, formerly with Sam Wooding, was the main attraction besides his accompanist

Fritz Schulze. It is said that Flemming performed there by dint of an Egyptian passport, but even though he may have had Arab parents and therefore was strictly speaking not black, he definitely was an American citizen and considered to be "colored" back in the United States. U.S. ambassador Dodd had personally intervened to secure a work permit for Flemming; his rationale is unknown, but it could have been contingent on the permissive aura of the Olympics. Flemming eventually left Germany in June 1937.[59] Inexplicably, in a place in Hamburg called Block House a black pianist was churning out boogie-woogie, blues, and related sounds. And a black drummer named Jimmy from German South-West Africa was entertaining patrons with an otherwise all-white band in the capital's Kajüte bar, upstairs in the Berolina-Haus, as late as the summer of 1939.[60]

The Jazz Congregation and Its High Priests

In Germany as elsewhere, jazz could not be performed in a vacuum: it had to be heard and enjoyed. And as in the United States and England, jazz music in Germany during the thirties required, for its existence to be assured, two sources of support: a large listening and dancing public that geared itself to the music's more commercial qualities, and a small, elitist core of purists who considered jazz as an art form, studied the music seriously to the point of attempting to play it, and always adulated its creators. In Germany these cultists were of acute importance because the most active of them not only lived jazz as a life-style but actually approached the status of impresarios. As such they exerted an inestimable influence on the course of this music under Hitler, one that proved to be crucial to its survival.

A pivotal figure in this filigree network, with a covert center in Berlin, was Dietrich Schulz, the former Magdeburg high-school student who even in late Weimar days had tried to master the trombone under Seiber and Sekles in Frankfurt. Schulz was a peripatetic young man. While still in Frankfurt in 1932, his main occupation became the study of economics at the university, for he had realized that his talent as a jazz trombonist was limited. Early in 1933, of course, Seiber's class had been canceled. During the summer and fall of 1933 Dietrich attended University College of the South-West of England in Exeter, where he perfected his English. In the summer of 1934 he moved to Königsberg in East Prussia to continue his economics courses at the university there. He received a state diploma, the equivalent of a master's degree, in December 1935 and a doctorate in May 1939.[61]

But this résumé merely constitutes the bourgeois shell of Dietrich Schulz's persona. His inner passion always was jazz, "the elixir of my life," as he confessed much later. Significantly, he composed his dissertation on the subject of the international recording industry, with heavy emphasis on jazz and dance music, and it is a work that still is eminently readable today.[62] Research on this topic conveniently took him to Berlin often enough to find a foothold in the esoteric world of jazz music and the more lucrative one of the German record industry.

Since republican times, the bespectacled, multilingual Schulz had been an ardent reader of foreign jazz journals, the French *Jazz Tango Dancing* and, especially, the British *Melody Maker*. Through the former he learned much about the catalytic role of that budding French doyen of jazz music, Hugues Panassié, and through the latter equally much about the Irish musician-cum-critic Patrick ("Spike") Hughes. Panassié had been largely influenced by the American reed player Milton ("Mezz") Mezzrow, who had perchance met the young Frenchman while recording in Paris in 1929. Subsequently Panassié was to owe Mezzrow a huge debt: after his first book, *Le Jazz Hot*, had been published in 1934, it influenced not only Schulz but even American musicologists of the caliber of Gunther Schuller. By 1934 Panassié had also become one of the cofounders of the vastly influential Paris-based Hot Club de France, which launched the meteoric careers of Django Reinhardt and Stephane Grappelly.[63]

In 1934 Schulz's enthusiasm with regard to Panassié's work culminated in his decision to translate the book into German, a task that he was not to accomplish. But after corresponding with the French impresario—they were then both callow youths of twenty-two—Dietrich became the first certified German member of the Hot Club in November 1935, and in the late summer of 1936 he was able to visit Panassié at the parental castle just east of Bordeaux. Proudly he wrote to his father: "I am spending my days sleeping and eating, loafing and listening to records, in order to gain new strength for my stay in Paris." At this Château de Gironde Schulz met Panassié's friends Pierre Nourry and Charles Delaunay, who had both cofounded the Hot Club. Later, in Paris, Dietrich met his idol Django Reinhardt, and he revisited Django on the occasion of the World Fair held in Paris in 1937, where he also happened to listen to an unknown nineteen-year-old American trumpet player with the name of John Birks Gillespie. By 1938 Schulz's contacts with Panassié and Charles Delaunay—son of the famous postcubist painters Robert and Sonia (Terk) and an artist in his own right—had solidified to the extent that during the war Charles acknowledged Dietrich's cooperation in compiling the second edition of what was becoming the bible of jazz purists all over the world, Delaunay's classic *Hot Discography*.[64]

Indeed, his youthfulness notwithstanding, Dietrich Schulz was on the way to becoming Germany's most knowledgeable and most distinguished jazz critic. In 1933, during his sojourn to England, he had visited the former bassist and arranger Spike Hughes, who by that time was turning more and more to jazz journalism and was the moving spirit behind Schulz's treasured *Melody Maker*.[65] Schulz was already emulating Hughes, Delaunay, and Panassié as the paragons and impresarios that they were. After listening to James Kok's band in the Berlin Moka Efti club in early November 1934, he chatted with the maestro about personnel problems in the band. Kok told him that one of his two pianists was leaving him. Schulz then proposed that Kok try out his Magdeburg school chum Fritz Schulze, for he was uncommonly good. Fritz was immediately summoned from the province, examined by Kok for a session or two, and hired on the spot.[66]

Moreover, inspired by Panassié's and Hughes's polished record reviews in the journals, Dietrich wrote to Deutsche Grammophon in Berlin, applauding the firm's jazz sideline, a product of the German Brunswick label. Boldly he said that he found the remarks of the commentator, the weighty classical musicologist Hans Heinz Stuckenschmidt, rather wanting because they were "interchangeable." Deutsche Grammophon replied forthwith, offering him Stuckenschmidt's prestigious job and sending along a box of sample recordings. This marked the beginning of Schulz's long and prodigious career as a jazz record production adviser in Germany; the Berlin firm was glad to have acquired an expert. In September 1935, for example, Dietrich suggested that Brunswick issue certain records by American jazz musicians that were so far available only in their country of origin, yet he also plugged the big band of Heinz Wehner (soon to sign with rivaling Telefunken), which was thought to be, by the Grammophon executive, "the complete equal" of Kok's band.[67]

By early 1936 Schulz's authority with German Brunswick had grown, commensurate with his own enthusiasm as a jazz critic. Hence he was able to organize three public lectures at the Delphi-Palast, that shrine of German jazz aficionados, in which he sought to explain to large crowds "what swing was all about." On 20 January he used Brunswick recordings by Spike Hughes, Ellington, and Bert Ambrose to illustrate his discourse, which he repeated again in variation during March and April. Judging by the preserved protocol of the first session, these speeches were overly scholarly, if not to say bookish affairs. The March lecture, for instance, distinguished between swing, instrumental, commercial, and vocal categories rather academically; Ambrose and the Dorsey Brothers were rated as "commercials," while Benny Goodman had not yet appeared on the scene.[68] Schulz topped these achievements by coauthoring the official Brunswick jazz record catalog later in 1936, featuring artists like Ellington, Ambrose, Henderson, Grappelly, and Hawkins. About Goodman he now noted that only lately did he have "his own orchestra," with a photograph showing the King of Swing smilingly tooting a clarinet.[69]

Nazi censors had by this time caught on to the Paris Hot Club—and to Dietrich Schulz. Yet the exuberant impresario was himself to blame for that. In a less than modest letter to the American popular-music magazine *Metronome,* he had written in near-perfect English that swing was "progressing rapidly in Germany and I am working on a big campaign for Swing Music just now. . . . Clubs will be formed all over the country, record recitals will be held, more and better records will be issued." The three very successful Delphi lectures would be repeated in other places such as Hamburg and Cologne. "I am proud to have made Germany Swing-conscious," Dietrich bragged. "A few months ago the word Swing was almost unknown, but now all the great recording companies are using it: Electrola . . . and, of course, Brunswick, the releases of which I control."[70]

Dietrich Schulz the Swing Dictator of Hitler's Germany? This was too much for Fritz Stege, the party's bona fide music critic. After having blasted the Hot Club de France and its quintet in mid-September, Stege embarked on a personal attack on Schulz one month later. Germany now possesses a "swing reformer," he wrote derisively, with direct reference to *Metronome.* Germany should awaken and become aware of the gift of Negro swing, courtesy of Herr Dietrich Schulz. All German musicians will be grateful to Schulz, mocked Stege, and if this Nazi official was not any more threatening at that particular point in time, it was surely due to the phony spirit of international fraternity conjured up by a publicity-hungry Third Reich, the host of that year's Olympic Games.[71]

In early 1937 the self-assertive Schulz sent yet another letter to the American music journal *Tempo,* in which he stated that he had "founded three Rhythm Clubs in Germany, in Berlin, Konigsberg and Magdeburg."[72] This, too, was an exaggeration, for whereas Schulz played an undisputed role in all three fan groups, he had not actually founded any, and there is doubt whether Magdeburg ever had anything like an organized unit. A former member of the Königsberg jazz club has indicated that this East Prussian group was always very loose; young people interested in jazz were visiting each other's homes casually and irregularly, so that one day Dietrich Schulz was being introduced by a friend. The circle consisted mostly of university students who exchanged jazz records, relishing and discussing them infrequently in the company of like-minded confrères.[73]

Located deep in the backwoods, Königsberg could not support a live jazz scene; the local clientele in cafés and bars went for the usual commercial schlock, even though Erich Börschel, who led the radio station dance band, was an ambitious jazz-inspired musician.[74] At any rate, no sooner had Schulz joined the Königsberg group early in 1935 than he took charge of it as "president," authoring, on the model of the Paris Hot Club's circulars, regular broadsheets filled with record information and suggestions such as how to create a disc inventory.[75] Schulz may have been overly Teutonic in his systematic approach to jazz—he has sometimes been called the "chartered accountant" of German jazz—but he was, after all, dealing with equally systematic Germans who took such an attitude in stride and were actually grateful for Schulz's well-meaning, didactic methodology.

There is no question that Schulz was an earnest proselytiser who sought appreciative converts to his music wherever he could find them. His contact with the Berlin jazz denizens occurred as a consequence of his energetic publicity in the Delphi-Palast in January 1936, for one of his listeners there was Hans Blüthner, the equally dedicated, if not nearly as learned, connoisseur of dance bands of the late republic.[76] Blüthner then inducted Schulz into the Melodie-Klub, of which Fritz Schulze, Dietrich's old chum, also was a sometime member. Schulz naturally attracted these aficionados, and they respected him for his encyclopedic wisdom and his personal ties with the grandees of Paris and London. In late 1935 Schulz, too, had received a letter from Kurt Michaelis, who had seen one of Dietrich's frequent communications in an English journal; Schulz then met with the idiosyncratic Leipzig "Tiger Rag" collector in Berlin, where on 18 January 1936, just before the first Delphi lecture, they spent a night of revelry at the Sherbini, entranced by the swing of Fritz Schulze and of U.S. trombonist Flemming.[77]

Right around then Michaelis was a mandarin of the Leipzig Hot Club, and Dietrich Schulz was able to pass on to him his serialized, typewritten broadsheets, explicating jazz and especially Brunswick's new offerings. Preserved samples of this series demonstrate that, perhaps knowingly, Schulz advertised several American Jews when their music had been forbidden for some months. In the fall of 1938 he sang the praises of clarinetists Meyer Weinberg and Artie Shaw, bassists Art Shapiro and Artie Bernstein, drummer Godfrey Hirsch, and trumpeters Manny Klein and Charlie Spivak. Only Benny Goodman's name—too notorious to print—now was conspicuously absent. After Berlin and Leipzig, yet a third sphere touched by Schulz in this way was that of Hans Otto Jung in Lorch on the Rhine. Soon to be the spiritual leader of a Frankfurt-based jazz circle, pianist Jung also became one of Schulz's thankful jazz news clients through the mediation of Blüthner.[78]

Hans Blüthner, once the "hit parade man" of his schoolroom, continued into the Third Reich his regular visits to Berlin combos and big bands, the year-to-year diaries of which were just as meticulously kept as Schulz's record inventories.[79] Twenty years old in 1933, Hans's formerly superficial, if not to say innocuous tastes were sharpening with age, definitely in the direction of eclecticism. He was acquiring the discriminating penchants of a jazz collector. Blüthner's log of the bands he investigated from 1931 to 1938 is astonishing both for its methodicalness and for the way in which it reflects a cultural maturation process. Thus on 2 February 1933—Hitler had been in power for a mere three days—Blüthner patronized the Kirchhöfer orchestra in the Schiller-Saal, a non-band as far as jazz was concerned. These entries continue with the names of Arkadi Flato, Dol Dauber, Gerhard Hoffmann, and Harry Borgend—all indisputably vacuous. Then on 12 August Hans listened to the swinging Georg Nettelmann formation with Helmuth Wernicke on piano and vocals, already a vast improvement.

The listings of quality groups then increase (until September 1935) with the mention of Bartholomew, James Kok, Jack Hylton, and Kurt Widmann. Blüthner did not fail to attend Kok's historic last concert at the city Moka Efti, on 30 April 1935, with Wege, Bauschke, Schulze, and the guitarist Meg Tevelian. On 10 May 1935 Blüthner caught the neophyte Wehner in the Europa-Haus and thereafter sampled him again repeatedly. Erhard ("Funny") Bauschke became a permanent favorite with Hans as of January 1936 when he began his new contract at the downtown Moka Efti.

Also appearing in the diary is the Flemming combo that Dietrich Schulz listened to earlier with Thon, Schulze, and Sherbini himself on drums at the Egyptian's exclusive Uhlandstrasse hideaway on April 23. (By this time the two premier jazz fans were already well acquainted.) The Dane Aage Juhl Thomsen played the Femina three days later. And then, of course, there were the Original Teddies! Although the Berlin summer of this Olympic year was chock full with genuine swing options, Stauffer dominated all billings. Blüthner enjoyed him at the Delphi no less than three times in July, again in September, and four times in October. At the front of the diary Hans enumerated all the members of that sterling band by name and instrument, a distinction no other orchestra received. The rest of the diary until September 1938 contains only brand names save a very few, altogether potent testimony that Hans Blüthner's jazz education was complete.[80]

Blüthner became the kingpin in the Berlin Melodie-Klub, the most authentic and thoroughly organized gathering of jazz fans in the capital. (In this large city there were other, smaller groupings of very little import.)[81] Its origins are traceable to a 1934 publicity effort on the part of Adalbert Schalin, the "Aryan" manager of Alberti, the increasingly compromised, Jewish-owned music store in the Rankestrasse. The musician-arranger Schalin, editor of *Musik-Echo,* the firm's own music tabloid, had been animated, possibly as early as 1932, by the multitalented Jewish amateur musician Robert ("Bob) Kornfilt, originally from Turkey, who at the time of the political changeover was a close friend of Blüthner's.[82]

Young Hans continued to frequent Alberti's as he became a bank trainee in the fall of 1934. He purchased more and more fabulous records there with the money he now earned and thus was enticed by Schalin to join the club later on. A select group of club members—no more than twenty or so—was meeting at Café Hilbrich on the Kurfürstendamm to ingest the choicest recordings, invariably of American vintage. The membership was cosmopolitan and included several of Berlin's erudite Jews, among them Kornfilt himself, Heinz Auerbach, and Franz ("Franny") Wolf. Dietrich Schulz visited off and on after January 1936, exchanging records with the likes of Wolf. About twelve months later Schulz introduced to the Melodie-Klub a seventeen-year-old half Jew by the name of Gerd Peter Pick, whom he had come across as an expert salesman at Televox, a small but important record-producing and retailing Berlin company.[83]

By that time the club had already split into a hard-core purist and a more permissive commercial section. The purists, among them Auerbach and Wolf, proceeded to withdraw to private quarters after the convenient café lease had expired. Blüthner and a handful of his followers, including Pick, who did not wish to become dogmatic in this art, sought a similar abode for themselves.

Their faction, which now called itself "Magische Note," was reinforced in the summer of 1938 by a new but distant member from the Rhine, Hans Otto Jung. This not quite eighteen-year-old pianist, whom Hindemith had blessed as a child, was about to study economics at Frankfurt University to prepare himself for the eventual takeover of the ancestral winery. Swing enthusiast that he was, he had sent a letter to Electrola in Berlin asking for a certain Benny Goodman record. Blüthner, who like Schulz was advising Electrola every now and then, had been commissioned to handle this request. On 22 May 1938 he had written to Jung: "We have a swing club here called 'Magic Note.' If you are interested, I would like to tell you about it. Are there any swing fans on the Rhine? I should certainly hope so." Jung had duly received the illegal Goodman record and in March 1939 was to find himself in the possession of a Magische Note membership card, though as number 15, it was a sign of the club's shrinking fortunes.

Jung and Blüthner had met in Berlin in October 1938 to attend thrilling Wehner and Stauffer concerts. Roughly ten days after that, the Jews of Germany were crushed during Kristallnacht. Already by this time it was clear that the fate of Berlin's preeminent jazz club was sealed. The dissenting faction was in the process of dissolution. Auerbach saw fit to move to Buenos Aires and Wolf caught the last boat to New York, where he teamed up with Alfred Lion, another émigré Berlin Jew, who had just founded the Blue Note jazz record company. Lion and "Francis Wolfe" later made Blue Note into the pioneer for the emerging bebop style. In the last months before the war, only Blüthner himself and the half-Jewish Pick were holding out in the capital, visiting each other clandestinely in their apartments. By the war's beginning it had become a risky business to be involved in anything like a jazz club.[84]

When Blüthner sent his postcard to Jung in May 1938, Hans Otto had just been drafted into the Reichsarbeitsdienst (RAD), Reich Labor Service. However, he was released on 26 October and was able to join Blüthner briefly in Berlin. The atmosphere was tense, remembers Jung, despite the Munich Accord that had just staved off war. After having been conscripted for military duty, Jung was traveling through Cologne on the tenth of November en route to his Wehrmacht posting. There he saw the destruction perpetrated upon the Jews of the city by the storm troopers. What brutality, thought Jung; what sort of people would do a thing like that? Was this at all within the law?

Jung was by far the most sensitive and, despite his youth, potentially the most sophisticated of these jazz disciples. A near-prodigy with perfect pitch, he had started playing the piano in 1925 at the age of five and then was tutored over the years by Paul Hindemith's confidante and fellow performer, the pianist Emma Lübbecke-Job, who was also a family friend of the cultured Jungs. Hence Hans Otto came to jazz above all as a relatively mature musician, who faithfully and joyously practiced Beethoven sonatas and Chopin études, and who by 1933–34 intensely disliked the pop-tune fad of the day and whatever else he heard over German radio. Records and foreign stations put the youngster in touch with the international world of swing. His intimates were his younger brother Rudolf and a lone like-minded school pal. Hans Otto and Rudolf performed in the school orchestra, and every once in a while the older sibling chanced a blues or boogie-woogie on the school piano. This awed his classmates, who, not surprisingly, failed to understand completely this tall, thin boy who was an enemy of the crude jokes and rough sports so much favored by Nazi diehards.[85]

By the summer of 1936 the teenager was correspondingly proficiently with German, French, and English record firms and was collecting international re-cord catalogs and brochures. Hans Otto was urbane enough to order hard-to-get swing platters directly from London or Paris. "Your esteemed favour to hand this morning," replied the Fleet Street music retailer City Sale & Exchange to Jung on 27 April 1937, "we shall be pleased to forward any order with which you may favour us, on receipt of your remittance by cheque or International Money Order."[86]

In this way Jung came into the possession not only of printed record infor-mation by German Brunswick, Electrola, or Alberti, but also by English Brunswick, RCA Victor, and Vocalion. His copies of the London "Gramophone record" contained "a monthly review of recorded and broadcast music edited by Leonard Hibbs."[87] The painstakingly detailed descriptions in these brochures, no less than the foreign records themselves, motivated Jung to participate in a readers' poll announced by *Melody Maker,* to which he subscribed as a matter of course. In the fall of 1937, with unconcealed excitement, he wrote to London that black pianist Herman Chittison had "such a marvellous touch and 'bounce' as nobody else. His 'walking bass' in the left hand and his phrases in the right hand are really terrific. . . . Herman Chitison [*sic*] gave me my first impression of swing music." With uncanny expertise he chose Roy Eldridge, Tommy Dorsey, Johnny Hodges, Hawkins, Goodman, and Reinhardt as his other favorites. On bass he liked Bob Haggard, while on drums the dynamo Krupa impressed him. Lionel Hampton was his choice on vibraphone, and Armstrong and Ella Fitzgerald were his top vocalists.[88]

Hans Otto's collecting activities were interrupted by the labor and army services, both of which he loathed. Stationed in a Wehrmacht training unit in Westphalian Gütersloh, the frail young man could stand it only for ten days. He was luckily transferred to a more bearable posting near Stuttgart, close to his grandparents. And here he got together with an amateur drummer and a classical violinist, for whom Jung put jazz parts in writing. They called themselves the Jungle Rhythmicians and played for the after-hours elation of their comrades. Then Jung contracted pleurisy and spent four months in a sanatorium. It was during this period that the war broke out.[89]

In the meantime, the Jungs had moved down the Rhine from Lorch to Rüdesheim, a stone's throw from Frankfurt. In this metropolis on the river Main jazz did not exactly flourish, although the Weintraubs and later some of the better German big bands are known to have visited there.[90] And, of course, this was the home of Sekles's experimental Hoch'sche Konservatorium! In 1932–33, one of Seiber's jazz pupils had been a saxophone student, the gifted Rudi Thomsen, who had befriended fellow student Dietrich Schulz. Thomsen initiated a Frankfurt cousin, Carlo Bohländer, into jazz, and soon Carlo was a rookie trumpet player. Schulz met him as a lanky boy of fifteen while in Frankfurt in 1934.[91] Like his much older cousin, Carlo wished to become a professional musician, and in 1935 he won a fellowship to the Konservatorium for four years. He learned harmony, trumpet, and piano but became disappointed with the rigid course of studies and never took his final examination. In August 1936, overpowered by swing and longing to visit the land of its birth, Carlo got himself hired as a deckhand on the oceanliner *Deutschland,* just bound for New York from Hamburg. Carlo was in New York only for five days, spending most of his time on 42nd Street; when he wanted to repeat the venture, he was prevented by the outbreak of war.[92]

Emil Mangelsdorff also lived in Frankfurt. Barely eight years old when Hitler came to power, he got attuned to jazz on the radio, and it stuck. Besides, Ellington's 1932 recording of "Dinah" proved to be a seminal influence. Emil taught himself to play the accordion, hardly a jazz instrument, and with other street-smart teenagers from his working-class neighborhood he formed an amateur band. During the summer of 1939 they played dance music in the poorer suburbs; they had neither the financially supported resourcefulness of a Jung nor the formal training of a Bohländer, but they satisfied their lust for American tunes. Then Emil was inducted into compulsory farm service, and before he knew it the war was on.[93]

Meanwhile, dental technician Kurt Michaelis of Leipzig had turned twenty in 1933. Already he was in the center of four or five young men of like mind, who held informal jazz meetings on what they called "Blue Mondays" in their modest rooms every fortnight or so. As in Berlin or Königsberg, they would gather around a gramophone and sample American, British, and German recordings, in that order. An older, wealthier acquaintance with a car occasionally would take them to the capital, a few hours' drive, and here they would spoil themselves with much-vaunted show-business marvels: an afternoon tea dance in the Femina or Moka Efti, an expensive club date well into the small hours, or a music film. These activities would repeat themselves in Leipzig on a much smaller scale. That prosperous city of commerce and of trade fairs was endowed with two or three venues for social dancing and hence enjoyed irregular visits by prominent jazz and show groups, such as those of Abriani, Stauffer, or Wehner. In the late summer of 1936, at the leading Café Drei Könige, Michaelis and his friends even savored the sounds of a lesser-known Viennese band, Karl Ballaban's Dance Symphonists, who nonetheless performed pseudojazz based on "Jewish" compositions by Gershwin and Berlin sufficiently well to incur the wrath of self-anointed censor Hans Brückner.[94]

Through the systematic perusal of *Melody Maker* Michaelis, who had been christened "Hot-Geyer" (hot vulture) by his best friend, Joachim-Ernst ("Fiddlin' Joe") Frommann, found out about a London chap by the name of Carlo Krahmer, a semiprofessional drummer also specializing in the collection of "Tiger Rag" discs. This man Kurt had to meet! In July 1934 Hot-Geyer embarked for London for the second time in his life and stayed with remote relatives in the outskirts. The Cockney-accented Carlo lived on the other side of town, and Hot-Geyer had to commute by train to consort with him daily. Carlo, of distant German ancestry, was nearly blind; he was well respected by the London jazz and dance crowd and through him Michaelis met Max Abrams, the Jewish drummer of the Hylton band, a very friendly sort. But once, in a London jazz club, having taken in the British Armstrong adept Nat Gonella after hours, a group of young English Jews accosted Michaelis; he had to be a spy for Hitler, or else why would he be allowed to travel outside Germany! Carlo returned the visit during July 1936 in Leipzig, taking along his friend, the alto saxophonist Gerry Cane. A couple of years later, back in London, before he founded his record company Esquire, Carlo Krahmer became the drummer for Claude Bamptons' Blind Band, the pianist for which was a certain George Shearing.[95]

Like his Königsberg compatriot Dietrich Schulz, Kurt Michaelis got into the habit of sending notes and letters to Anglo-American trade magazines in order to attract international attention. In September 1937, judging by his own experience, the patriotic Hot-Geyer sought to dispel the stubborn rumor that Hitler had banned jazz in Germany. Kurt published a technically correct statement in *Tempo* for fans in California that "it is not true that we have no Jazz in Germany for there are many Jazzbanders. We have Brunswick records of all the famous hot stars, Armstrong, Red Nichols, the jazzy Mr. Ellington, and the Red Hot Benny Goodman's boys. American newspapers are not telling you the thruthfulness about our Jazz world over here."[96]

A year and a half later the young British pianist and jazz journalist Leonard Feather conveyed news to *Melody Maker* readers from his "correspondent in Leipzig" to the effect that German laws had now become stricter. Feather had tried to obtain a very rare Goodman record through Hot-Geyer, who apologized for his failure to deliver, "for obvious reasons." But Feather also cited Michaelis as saying that "platter 'Home-cookin' in private homes" was still possible. Hot-Geyer expressed his intention to "come over to jammy London in late-summer, and wish to get in acquaintance to you, Mr. Feather."[97]

Even though Hot-Geyer never met Feather, who was to do so much for American jazz in subsequent years, in 1937–39 he sustained a very fruitful correspondence with two U.S. collectors whom he probably would have visited had the war not intervened. After another letter to *Tempo* asking for record exchanges, a New York dentist by the name of Henry H. Sklow, most certainly Jewish, approached him in the fall of 1937. This Tufts and Harvard graduate, Hot-Geyer's senior by nine years, was delighted at the prospect of friendship. "I certainly was very pleased to hear from you so soon and I feel that we are going to have some swell times writing to each other so far across the sea. I am sure our exchange of ideas pertaining to that thing called 'swing' and other bits of person-al notes will prove most interesting to both of us." Sklow had a fairly good practice on Holland Avenue and was married, with a baby daughter; however, he wrote that "marriage . . . does not interfere with my hobby, SWING." His sym-pathies were with Ellington, Goodman, Bob Crosby; he also favored Norvo, Chick Webb, and Basie. In fact, he liked only American musicians, and it must have come as something of a shock to Michaelis that the dentist displayed no interest in German or even British contemporary bands and that it was actually difficult to satisfy him with caches of Third Reich Brunswick reissues of U.S. musicians—the ones Dietrich Schulz had selected for the firm—for the originals were sometimes still sold in New York.[98]

Thus Michaelis probably profited more from this exchange than Sklow ever did. For one thing, he received choice collectors' items from New York such as Teddy Wilson's "Blues in C Sharp Minor," which Henry sent as a Christmas gift because he knew "how you must save the pennies these days in your state and I here perhaps can find it a little easier to make you happy."[99] Michaelis was also provided with a superb opportunity to brush up on his English, the quintessential vernacular of jazz, for unfamiliar phrases like "inferior" or "in cash" he could underline and replace with German dictionary translations. Alas, this did not always work with slang, for he never understood the meaning of "nuts," which he took literally to refer to the popular indehiscent fruit.[100] Hot-Geyer must have been green with envy to read about Sklow's personal jazz contacts in the Big Apple, for example with Mezzrow and Condon, or his private chats with Good-man. Then, on 16 January 1938, Goodman's historic Swing Concert in Carnegie Hall was staged. Henry wrote Kurt all about it, so that the jazz vulture was able to impress his own Blue Monday friends with an exclusive, firsthand report: "Every number is a Killer and Benny obliged with several 'Evergreen' encores. There was at least 4000 people in the hall and you can imagine the 'cats' going to town both on and off the stage."[101]

Michaelis's other American pen pal was a young man from California, again one who had seen fit to reply to the vulture's *Tempo* letter. He was more particu-lar than Sklow and hence less easily satisfied, finding that the German

Brunswick catalogs Hot-Geyer had sent him were "a little disappointing."[102] But he also had much less money and was socially somewhat uprooted. A graduate of the University of California, he was recently divorced and had "tried a number of things ranging from social welfare work to taking pictures for a newspaper for a livelihood, all without too much success." In the spring of 1937 he was twenty-eight years old, roomed in Los Angeles, and was attempting to be a sports and detective story writer, delivering mostly to nickel-and-dimes magazines.[103]

In between this and his record collecting—he preferred Armstrong, Fletcher Henderson, and clarinetist Frank Teschemacher but was slowly getting sold on Goodman—he sought to gain experience in police work by helping to solve the much-publicized case of the Dyer triple child murder in Inglewood. His big break came later, in 1937, when black pianist Luis Russell took him along on a California concert tour with his band, co-led by "Sachmo" Armstrong.[104]

Early in 1938 the young drifter was able to write about this singular experience and start a publishing career in jazz. It was a fortuitous moment for a man who, in the mid-forties, would found Dial Records, a mainstay for the emerging bebop style. Later still he would become famous as the biographer and somewhat controversial promoter of one of his recording artists, Charlie "Bird" Parker. The name of this man, who thus made jazz history, was Ross Russell.[105]

There thrived two other significant jazz congregations that were not in any meaningful way related to Dietrich Schulz or to the Melodie-Klub, although incidental contacts did exist. These were the fraternities revolving around Werner Daniels in Düsseldorf and Dieter Zimmerle in Münster, somewhat to the north. Other fan clubs are said to have existed, at least intermittently, in Breslau, Hamm, Rostock, Eisenach, Dessau, Darmstadt, and even Munich, but the very fact that the evidence is sparse would seem to indicate that often these were just small groups with little formal organization. However, in more general terms the existence of these clubs underlines the universality and popularity of dance and jazz music throughout the entire German Reich, not just its capital, even if this complex is tangentially connected with the "Swing youth" phenomenon, to be introduced later in this chapter.[106]

Werner Daniels was born in Düsseldorf in 1919 and left school at fifteen to apprentice with a business firm. Again, like so many of his peers, he came to like genuine jazz via dance music through radio and German recordings, first the more banal, national variety, then the more intriguing foreign stuff. Düsseldorf, that arrogant and ritzy financial hub of the Ruhr, was nevertheless comparable to the more humble Leipzig in that Stauffer, Wehner, Hohenberger, Schacht, and Hülphers would come irregularly to perform there, in places like Tabaris, Café Cornelius, Kaskade, and Café Mainz. By luck the odd, swingy local combo might work in more intimate places such as the Carlton-Bar and Bei Toni.[107]

While still in Gymnasium, Werner had encountered a few jazz enthusiasts who would listen to radio and records with him, and in 1936 the International Swing Rhythm Club was founded, of which Werner became the nucleus. In spite of there being no statutes, of which the order-loving Germans are so found, membership dues were collected for the purpose of subscribing to *De Jazz-*

wereld, the paramount Dutch jazz journal. (Düsseldorf's Lower-Rhenish dialect is akin to Dutch.) In retrospect, this aggregation of teenage buffs bears similarity to an American school gang, meeting after supper for a game of Cops and Robbers; this was still very much a juvenile world of fantasy and make-believe.

The members all adopted English names, used greetings such as "Swing High," and tried to identify as closely as possible with blacks in Harlem and the rural American South, rather than the Hitler Youth most of them belonged to. And there were signs of German fastidiousness. Carefully printed membership passports featured English-language rubrics for "name," "dwellingplace" (*sic*) and "nationality"; there was space for a "certifate" (*sic*) to guarantee that the affixed photograph "represents the possessor of this statement and is subscribed with his own hand. The possessor is member of this club. The admission attest"—in this artifact's case "James Bristol" and "Oliver Kingston." A "contribution card" at the back of the passport registered membership dues, per year, and included a stamp marked "Germany." Ironically, as in the case of the founding of the Nazi party in the year that Daniels was born, the membership numbers were artificially inflated to make the club appear larger; Hitler's original number until November 1923 had been 555 (in actuality 55); Werner Daniels's was a round 100.[108]

Club members met twice monthly to audition records, study foreign jazz journals, playact in scenarios adopted from England and New York, and write anonymous letters to the editor containing criticisms of the daily papers' critiques of visiting bands such as Hylton's. Last but not least, from fall 1937 onward they associated themselves with an amateur jazz band. These Fürstenwall Gymnasium boys played from sheet music, commercially still available at retail outlets such as Suppan's on Karlstrasse, and there was no improvisation to speak of. Several players doubled on instruments as best they knew how, for example Gustav ("Utta") Königstein on trumpet, violin, and drums, or Artur ("Lang") Aengenvoort on alto sax and piano. Rehearsals were scheduled in their school or in the beer parlor Neusser Hof, and often, with the help of a good deal of beer, they degenerated into "swing parties." Semiprofessionals dates, which could generate a bit more than just pocket money, came through at sports clubs or annual school events.

Werner ("James") Daniels himself played rhythm guitar. He composed several pieces, some with German text, but also the textless "Jammin' James" and the pubescent "Red Week Blues," which alluded sexually to demure girls revered from afar. In late 1939 he linked up with gifted hobby pianist Theo Hoeren, whose privately recorded rendition of "Honeysuckle Rose" and some hapsichord pieces (1940) in the style of Teddy Wilson and Fats Waller today almost belie the amateur. The Rhythm Club broke up, as had the Frankfurt and Rüdesheim groups, when in the spring of 1939 several members were drafted into the RAD; before the breakup they had authored typewritten circulars discussing, ingenuously enough, the quality of visiting bands and other musical trivia.[109]

Compared to the Düsseldorf Rhythm Club, Dieter Zimmerle's Münster club in 1936 was a more dilatory affair, where the spirit of the movement took the place of puerile obsession with registries and formal etiquette, or, for that matter, innocent girls. In this sense, then, the twenty-year-old Zimmerle's mates were much more mature than the Düsseldorfers: three years in adolescence did make a difference. And although the Münster devotees did not play instruments, they spun their records seriously, mostly sides from Berlin, at the Café am Domplatz, right near the Gothic cathedral. They enjoyed the camaraderie of visiting musicians, rare as they were, such as the prize-winning Fritz Weber. They would meet them at one of two important venues in this university town, the Roxel and the Kaiserhof. In Berlin, where he had grown up and where his sister lived, Zimmerle frequented the Femina or Europa-Haus to hear Hülphers and rub shoulders with Heinz Wehner. After hours he would join them at the Insel on Innsbruck Square, a relaxed, bohemian place serving bratwurst and beer to jazz fans and musicians alike. On one of these Berlin junkets Zimmerle once also met Schulz, probably through the Melodie-Klub; Dieter and Dietrich recognized one another at the train station, each with *Melody Maker* in hand.[110]

After a description of these disparate flocks and their shepherds, it might be helpful to analyze those units according to the presence, or absence, of certain sociocultural commonalities. With regard to the social sector of jazz fans, Eric Hobsbawm has held that, at least according to British typology, there was a very strong middle-class infrastructure, with the upper as well as the working classes noticeably underrepresented. He also pointed to a median age range from the late teens to about thirty, and to signs of a cohort revolt, if not against parental authority, then against the reigning (middle-class) material and cultural value system.[111] Some, but not all, of these observations can be validated in the case of Third Reich jazz aficionados.

By and large, these fans hailed from the solid middle class, with few representatives from the elite and the proletariat. Middle-class jazz fans typically were using this new cult to improve their station over and above their elders, and thus were upwardly mobile. In our scenario, the most striking example of this is Dietrich Schulz. His father was a public school teacher, an archetypal lower-middle-class occupation in Germany, and the son was determined to propel himself into the elite by acquiring a doctorate. Moreover, in the admired English manner, he applied in 1938 to have his last name changed from Schulz to Schulz-Köhn (the affix being his mother's maiden name), undoubtedly because he found "Schulz," a name like "Smith" in England, too common.[112]

If this is a clear example of upward mobility, where jazz may have played a crucial role, cases where mobility was negligible or uncertain (again in the lower middle class) were also typical. In these cases, possibly, jazz was used to dispel a sense of uncertainty. Hans Blüthner had lost his lower-middle-class father, dropped out of Gymnasium to become a bank trainee, and then joined a small family business, with his own future in the balance. Leipzig's Fiddlin' Joe Frommann had begun as a music sales clerk in the late 1920s, but during the heyday of the Leipzig Hot Club he was selling coffee (apart from pianistic odd jobs in local bars). In this connection one could also mention Carlo Bohländer of Frankfurt. His parents had an antique furniture store, and although he aspired to an academic diploma at the conservatory, he did not end up receiving it.[113]

Then there were several jazz buffs who knew they were in the process of descending socially and deliberately used the jazz culture as a sign of (albeit questionable) respectability. One such individual was Werner Daniels. Although his father belonged to the elite as a university-trained architect, Werner left the prestigious Gymnasium at fifteen to start a middling bank clerk's career. Another was Dieter Zimmerle, who managed to obtain the Gymnasium diploma with difficulty and failed at the university (his father was a high-placed army colonel). Others in this group were Kurt Michaelis, the son of an academic Gymnasium teacher, who ended up in the comparatively lowly spot of a dental technician, and Dessau's Günter Boas, the child of a regional gas works executive, who eventually would try but then quit medical school.[114]

The proletarian exception to this white-collar and pencil-pushing throng was Frankfurt's Emil Mangelsdorff, the child of a bookbinder. Significantly, Emil remained isolated from his middle-class jazz peers until the war years, when he got to meet Bohländer, Jung, and others, who would then constitute the "Harlem" group. Jung himself was a picture-book scion—unlike Mangelsdorff, who was at the opposite end of the social spectrum—and thus represented the elite exception. There were a few more Berliners who qualified for this category: Olaf Hudtwalcker, heir to a shipping fortune, and Günter von Drenkmann, of lower nobility and already a lawyer, the son of a superior justice official.[115] To Mangelsdorff's sense of social belonging jazz must have been incidental, as it certainly was to Jung and the few others of his class.

In a special class, and socially not easily classifiable, were the Jews and half Jews in these groups; by Third Reich standards, they were true pariahs, irrespective of their economic circumstances, their families' positions, and their own educational backgrounds. In their objectively precarious situations, they were hoping to support themselves through membership in these jazz clubs, as did Pick, Wolf, and Kornfilt in Berlin and one or two of the Leipzig fans, the comrades of Hot-Geyer and Fiddlin' Joe. Their position was ultimately hopeless, however, for realistically they could not expect to gain what was uppermost on their minds: not so much conventional social improvement as simply the sustenance owing to regular, even traditional, members of German society.

By far the majority of these club members thus conformed to middle- and upper-middle-class values and deportment; socially ambitious, they took on the affectations of the parvenu. The fact that English jargon, however faulty, was de rigueur assured a modicum of formal education and kept out the coarser laboring classes.[116] For those with the ambition to perform and a need for adequate meeting places, modest family fortunes were important, as the Düsseldorf fans found out when purchasing instruments and transporting members to job dates in their fathers' cars.[117] In the ritualized settings of the more established clubs, notably of Berlin and Leipzig, there was a certain formality observed at meetings (which was aped by the juvenile group at Düsseldorf), with tea and biscuits being served in Leipzig, and the stilted "Herr" and "Sie" employed in Berlin experts' discourse. Alcohol was eschewed, even though at least one of the Berlin habitués, Carlo Boger, was a drunkard and the Leipzig buffs cooled their heated moods with beer or wine after dance or concert events.[118]

Dress was punctilious, and certainly in Berlin and Leipzig jackets and ties were obligatory. In Schulz-Köhn's stern regimen at Königsberg, a "business suit" was required for an evening lecture by the "president" on swing music, which was usually followed by a film and a formal dance.[119] It is significant that the peculiar German sense of orderliness prompted both Schulz-Köhn and Michaelis to make a special note of the fact that Gypsy guitarist Django Reinhardt, during the 1937 World Fair in Paris, was attired like a vagabond, although Schulz-Köhn generously conceded that his divine music "allowed you to forget all this."[120]

This meticulousness approached fetishism in some of the younger crowds, such as those in Münster and Düsseldorf who kept their hair longer and flaunted well-tailored overcoats and white scarves.[121] Yet to construe this behavior, according to Eric Hobsbawm's model for Britain, as a token of rebellion either generational, political, or social, would be faulty, for without exception these young men all enjoyed good relationships with their parents and wished to accommodate themselves to society. Jazz served as their instrument of standing, or vehicle of movement, whatever the case may have been—and to them this was legitimate.[122] Politically, the situation was somewhat more complex and must be dealt with more fully in the next section, but it is appropriate to state at this point that attitudes ranged from mild disapproval to indifference and sometimes even a measure of support—in short, anything but revolt against the Hitlerian dictators.

Nevertheless, Hobsbawm's astute observation regarding age obtains for the German fans as well; they were seldom more than thirty, as jazz always tends to appeal to the more excitable blood flowing in youthful veins. His judgment is also germane with regard to the sexist attitude toward young women, which was demonstrated by virtually all of our young men. Says Hobsbawm: "By tradition the Jazz-musician (and by imitation, the Jazz fan) goes for women just like the traditional Italian operatic tenor." And as he has explained, jazz fans were almost exclusively male. Although they had a benevolent contempt for girls where their purist collector ambitions were concerned, they were not prepared to deny their natural biological urges and hence were willing to keep girls as paramours, even at the risk of having to compromise their jazz dogma by being forced to dance to swing.[123] However, to put this more in perspective it is necessary to point out that maintaining a social divide between males and females by emphasizing gender distinctions was not just a pronounced National Socialist goal, but had been the time-honored practice of any but the least conventional German men in the republican and imperial past.

Nevertheless, the easily suggested correlation between male jazz purism and misogyny is broken if Berlin is used as criterion, for here, among the purist jazz fans, there were a few bona fide female members in the Melodie-Klub.[124] On the other hand, Blüthner maintains for the capital what Michaelis has asserted unequivocally for Leipzig, namely that "the position was simply, women and jazz don't mix."[125] But Hot-Geyer and Frommann had regular girlfriends, nicknamed "Wasp" and "Bonzo" and "Bee-Hive"; they good-naturedly went dancing with them, naturally to the sounds of swing, and on their stag Blue Mondays they also swapped cavalier stories.[126] Blüthner escorted girls to the famous Berlin afternoon tea dates; whether he danced is unknown.[127] On the more promiscuous side may have been, not the Düsseldorfers (they were too young and too properly reared), but the Münster group led by Zimmerle. He and his friends even enjoyed dressing up for girls, and when in Berlin they absolutely delighted in the table telephones and letter shuttles of the Femina, seeking erotic adventures to the tunes of Stauffer's Swiss Teddies.[128]

It is an anthropological fact that female interference with male pursuits is often feared, even in less traditionalist societies, whether these activities be fishing, computer hacking, stamp collecting, or, for that matter, the serious discussion of jazz. The purists among jazz buffs in the Third Reich seem to have held pride of place in Berlin, perhaps owing to the existence of sophisticated Jews there and the overweaning presence of Alberti's, that resourceful record shop catering to the discerning jazz lover. In the sanctum of the Melodie-Klub, there was the air of a secret society, as indeed it was, with its quasi-illegal, well-nigh conspirational activities. Here the purists, led by Auerbach and Wolf (who later prolonged his eclecticism with his New York programming for Blue Note), tended to suffer only "black" jazz, a narrowness eventually shared by France's Panassié, and nothing "modern."

When Blüthner joined in late 1934, he brought as his initiation record "Swingin' Uptown" by Jimmy Lunceford's band. The music had been recorded in January, safely before the suspect, populist swing movement. The advent of the swing style around that time, with its modern ring, superb danceability, and commercial appeal, was to cause the dogmatists much pain of conscience, for was this identifiable as "jazz"? Blüthner heard of a person who had sold his entire Jack Teagarden collection after learning that the master trombonist was white! Gerd Peter Pick, who joined the Melodie-Klub at the start of 1937, introduced something more contemporary than Blüthner had and was immediately censored by, if not barred from, the by now fragile organization. After the division, the liberated "commercials" led by Blüthner and Pick accepted "black jazz" (Henderson, Ellington, Fats Waller) as well as the "white" variety; on their lists of favorites for 1938 we find entries for the British big-band leaders Ambrose and Lew Stone, but also for the white Casa Loma band and, it is true, Kok and Wehner.[129]

The Leipzig rites were less stringent, but here too a theoretical difference was made between a purist's predilection and, albeit forgivable, softer preferences. The more gregarious Leipzigers, who sometimes stayed up until seven in the morning in the town that Goethe had called his "Little Paris," allowed for each others' idiosyncracies, for example Hot-Geyer's interest in "Tiger Rag," a tune that in jazz terms was somewhat questionable. Kurt even collected a satirical American version of it by the "Schnickelfritzers" sent to him by Ross Russell (Ross to Kurt: "It's so bad you will die laughing!"). Some of the Leipzig buffs liked Liszt "Liebestraum" jazz versions; they also listened to the occasional Hawaiian guitar (which Armstrong fooled around with in 1936–37). The schmaltzy Guy Lombardo and his Royal Canadians were taken in, usually at the end of a hard-working night, because Hans-Hugo Helbig ("Dreamy-Hot") just happened to love him so.[130]

Collecting records was thus a necessary requirement for all these jazz fans. "Every Jazz fan is a collector of records, within his financial means," writes Hobsbawm.[131] It is obvious by now that domestically produced recordings could not have been these buffs' first options: discs by the valiantly swinging Kok, Wehner, Bauschke, Hohenberger (Golden Seven), or even Bartholomew and the Teddies.[132] Record companies like Telefunken, Electrola, and Odeon, not inveighed against by Hadamovsky's radio ordinance of October 1935, produced them in bulk not just for home consumption by the less discriminating, but in particular for export to Germany's neighboring countries, such as Poland and the Baltic republics.[133]

Instead, the German fans' preferences ran to black, white American, and British artists, in exactly that order. The most precious originals they obtained, by various subterfuges if need be, directly from the source, ideally New York. But neither did they spurn the best that Germany's recording industry itself could make available. And here, owing to the ignorance of the regime leaders, it is amazing how much forbidden fruit was still entering the country legally on foreign masters, to be processed further by German firms. Long before the watershed of 1 April 1938, which marked the indictment of non-"Aryan" record artists, banished musicians of Jewish origin such as Lud Gluskin, Marek Weber, and the former Weintraub Syncopator Adi Rosner were still (or again) marketed by businesses such as Electrola—to the chagrin of Hans Brückner, who kept an eye out for the most blatant indiscretions.[134] The Nazis even kowtowed to British Jews such as Ray Noble, Joe Loss, Harry Roy, and Bert Ambrose, because they thought their big-band swing a bearable alternative to the more insidious American staple, and at the same time had no idea about these men's ethnic background.[135] In fact all those British Jews, including also Roy Fox and Lew Stone, probably the most passionate swinger of them all, were marketed on German labels and regularly advertised in Third Reich trade journals through the spring of 1938. And implicitly advertised were the Jewish musicians who played with them, such as Max Goldberg, the trumpeter; Monia Liter, the pianist; and Joe Crossman, the saxophonist.[136]

But even after 1 April 1938 the proliferation of English-Jewish jazz artists in Germany continued, for the Nazi enforcers in their stupidity found no sure-fire method of identifying "Aryans." German Brunswick carried right on, obliging all its fans in the Reich with "So Rare," played by Lew Stone in February 1938; "Cherokee," performed by Noble in January; and "Deep Henderson," offered by Ambrose in May 1939. The Electrola and Alberti house labels sold similar selections.[137] Many of these were purchased legitimately in German stores by the likes of Hot-Geyer and Blüthner. After the withdrawal of Goodman titles, the American Jew Artie Shaw appeared on German records at least until April 1939, just as openly as many black American artists such as Teddy Wilson, Ellington, and Hawkins.

Or pianist Luis Russell. In December 1937 his white namesake Ross Russell had started his jazz author's career by bribing the pianist into getting him a seat on Satchmo Armstrong's tour bus. He had given Luis a 1936 reissue of the latter's own ten-year-old single "Sweet Mumtaz," now part of the Germans' new

"Classic Swing" series, which he had obtained from Kurt Michaelis.[138] Then there was the emerging vocalist Ella Fitzgerald, whose "A-Tisket, A-Tasket," recorded with mentor Chick Webb in May 1938, had become the rage in German swing circles by the end of that year. As with most of the black artists, the Nazi government did not have a clue that this girl got her start in the Harlem ghetto— which was to the ultimate benefit of the Reich's jazz aficionados.[139]

In October 1938 Dreamy-Hot of the Leipzig club hosted a large fete to celebrate his departure for Istanbul, where he worked on intermittent assignments as an interior designer. The international forays of these German jazz fans were surprisingly far-reaching, and in this magnitude and for that class of people, very untypical of corresponding male cohorts in the currency-deficient Third Reich. Naturally, the American origin of jazz and its continuing Anglo-American lifeline were the basis for such cosmopolitanism. By definition, a German jazz disciple had to look to New York, London, or Paris, as the examples of Schulz-Köhn, Bohländer, and Hot-Geyer himself have already shown. Michaelis was in London again in the summer of 1937, having visited the Paris World Fair and there having met Delaunay and Panassié, something that really impressed Ross Russell. In between he was in Torino, Italy, where he fawned on his idol Armstrong.[140]

Hans Blüthner, too, was a notorious globetrotter; whenever he could he went to England, Scandinavia, even Mediterranean countries; and of course he was in Paris in 1937. He exchanged letters with the British impresario Ralph Venables, was mentioned in a Brussels music tabloid "as a founder of the Jazz Club," and sought out further correspondents in Sweden.[141] Jung traversed to England and Italy, and the Düsseldorfers and Münsterners gravitated strongly to nearby Holland, which then, as now, had a formidable jazz reputation. Zimmerle tells the bittersweet tale of how in 1935 he and his friends took the train to Amsterdam to hear Coleman Hawkins, but were taken off in Hilversum on the ridiculous charge of having attacked a truck driver. Finally freed, they missed Hawkins in the Dutch metropolis, though they were able to listen to some sizzling local bands instead. Their money having run out, they walked to the train station in the wee hours of the morning and there were cursed by sailors, who recognized the German accent in their self-conscious English. "The sailors jumped up and bellowed 'Heil Hitler,' and we ran away as fast as we could. Laughing it off, we said: Why us, who are so against the Nazis?"[142]

The interrelationship between cosmopolitanism and tolerance explains the ties of friendship (once again not typical) that jazz created between "Aryans" (like Leipzig's Michaelis and Frommann) and their Jewish club compatriots. One of these Jews was Hermann Ucko, who immigrated to Palestine just before Kristallnacht in the fall of 1938. Another half-Jewish friend was Heiner ("Fats") Kluge, who was still safe in Leipzig in July 1938, at least for the time being. This jocular Leipzig fan club even organized jogging races in surrounding forests, "Aryans against Jews," as if to mock the Nazis' racial policies.[143]

Apparently there were no Jews in the Düsseldorf, Münster, and greater Frankfurt groups. By contrast, in Berlin's jazz fraternity, the Jews set the tone until the schism in 1936–37. Not surprisingly, the capital's large young Jewish population had a special affinity for jazz. Even before Blüthner joined the club, he would frequent the Wannsee beaches to meet confrères, all with portable gramophones, and six out of ten of them were Jewish. When in London in 1936, Hans visited his old school chum, Werner Perdeck, a Jewish émigré. The fate of his friend Pick profoundly moved Blüthner; Pick's Jewish father was being sheltered by a Russian-Jewish lady in Berlin-Grunewald, who was herself protected by an honest policeman of the old sort. Then Gerd Peter's Jewish aunt and her "Aryan" husband committed suicide, and young Pick himself had encounters with the Gestapo on trumped-up charges of homosexuality. Gerd Peter and Hans became inseparable, bonded by their passion for jazz.[144]

This appreciation of the foreign element deriving from the jazz culture was buttressed by a love of American films characteristic of all these club members. Well into World War II Goebbels allowed many American films to be shown in the Reich because he admired them and wanted the Germans to copy this cinematographic technique as closely as possible.[145] Revue and adventure films starring Clark Gable, Dick Powell, Greta Garbo, and Marlene Dietrich abounded and were shown in the great movie palaces of the city centers. Very popular were flicks with singers Nelson Eddy and Jeanette MacDonald. On the German label Electrola MacDonald and Eddy sang "Indian Love Call" and "Farewell to Dreams," tunes not spurned by German jazz musicians.[146]

The pristine sensation for jazz fans, however, and an unanticipated phenomenon in the Goebbels ministry, was the extraordinarily clever musical film *Broadway Melody,* in which the irresistible Eleanor Powell tapdanced to swing. "You Are My Lucky Star" became a world hit and a favorite of dance addicts as well as jazz fans. Metropolitan teenage girls especially developed a fondness for Eleanor and her colleague Frances Langford. Seventeen-year-old Margot Hielscher, who entered the German jazz milieu during wartime and was buying swing records at Alberti's even in 1936, saw the German premiere of the film in the Berlin Marmorhaus theater; she was beside herself with excitement. She would play hookie at school for days on end just to see this movie over and over again. Leonore Boas, who as a Düsseldorf Gymnasium student was a fan of Kurt Hohenberger at the time, remembers that for her entire school class Eleanor was "God." The success of that film was rivaled but not surpassed by others of that genre, Cole Porter's *Born to Dance* and Irving Berlin's *On the Avenue,* as well as *Swing High, Swing Low,* and the 1938 sequel to *Broadway Melody.*[147] During stays in the capital jazz connoisseur Frommann repeatedly saw the first version of that film in the Marmorhaus in April 1936 and rated it "unbelievably good." Blüthner's pals enjoyed the sequel there exactly two years later. They also sampled *Jungle Princess* with Dorothy Lamour, a movie the Leipzig fans could admire in their local Capitol cinema. The Leipzigers were no less discriminating than the Berliners. For after watching the Franco propaganda film *Heroes in Spain* a few months later, Michaelis and the fellows judged it "tiring."[148]

Another foreign source of inspiration was radio. After the fall of 1935 Goebbels had made certain that no jazz or jazz-related music would be broadcast on the German airwaves (not that there had been much before then). But at the same time, he had as yet found no way to keep citizens of the Reich from tuning into foreign stations. By far the most favorite station for jazz lovers was Poste Parisien, a private outfit in the French capital with the respectable transmitter power of sixty kilowatts (the same power as the Munich station). Details about the Paris station were spread around in Berlin jazz circles—for example, Willie Lewis's band, anchored since 1934 in the Paris Chez Florence club, was a Saturday evening regular and included Benny Carter, Herman Chittison, and Bill Coleman.[149]

Also popular was Radio Luxemburg, after Radio Moscow now the strongest station in Europe. Still beaming much popular music, including that of English swing bands, in the direction of the British Isles, if was also easily received throughout Germany.[150] Other foreign stations, regionally accessible and always superior to the German ones, were Sottens and Beromünster in Switzerland, Swedish, Danish, and Dutch channels, some American short-wave signals, and, of course, BBC London, with features by Ambrose, Hall, Roy Fox, and Stanley Payne.[151]

Much of this music served as a model for those fans with the ambition to play. Hans Otto Jung honed his swing style religiously after careful samplings of those broadcasts. Fiddlin' Joe Frommann of Leipzig is said to have mastered the piano almost equally well, well enough at least to make an income on the side. The Düsseldorf amateurs, too, needed these paragons. In fact, almost every one of the fan clubs had one or two members who were hobby musicians, although few were, like Jung, invested with potential for greatness. In Berlin, Bob Kornfilt proved himself so proficient as an amateur arranger that Bauschke performed one of his charts.[152]

What mattered most to all these fans, then, apart from record collecting and catching the spectacular foreign radio programs, was the close personal contact with the musicians themselves, be they German or foreign. It was a criterion of jazz in those years that it could grow only through the reciprocity established between performers and their audience; the one was lost without the other. This was particularly applicable to Nazi Germany, where jazz was constantly threatened. Dieter Zimmerle and his pals befriended many of the younger band musicians and, whenever in Berlin, joined them at night at the Insel, where informal discussions took place about all aspects of the music. In Leipzig, the Blue Monday fraternity always sat close to the bandstand, enjoying with their musician buddies what Hobsbawm has called the "conspiracy of appreciation." Musicians loved to oblige when asked for their autographs, as did Stauffer when he and his Teddies all signed a card for Hot-Geyer follower Herbert Becke.[153]

Of greatest significance was the control the genuine cognoscenti assumed in the presence even of the best performers. Zimmerle instructed visiting bands in the Münster Kaiserhof to play "Dinah" or the old standby "Tiger Rag" and was duly obeyed.[154] Blüthner, who hobnobbed with Fritz Schulze and Hans Korseck, actually scheduled a ceremonial farewell visit for the corporate members of the Magische Note on the occasion of Stauffer's departure. By that time his prestige among musicians had risen to the level where Teddy or other prominent bandleaders would watch closely for his every reaction when a certain number was played. Arne Hülphers rewarded such know-how with insiders' presents: American records from Sweden at a time when Berlin stores would not sell them anymore, no matter what the offer.[155]

Jazz Within Politics

In the summer of 1947 Hanns Mohaupt in Berlin received an urgent letter from his brother, the émigré composer Richard Mohaupt, from New York. Richard asked Hanns for the whereabouts of a certain Siegfried Muchow, once a pianist at the Scala revue. "For years this swine has denounced me to the Gestapo," wrote Richard Mohaupt, "his insinuations got me an impeachment by a Nazi special court." Mohaupt wanted the man prosecuted.[156]

The case of Richard Mohaupt and the Scala, with all its reverberations, illuminates the delicate subject of the relationship between dance and jazz musicians and everyday politics in the Third Reich. The accused Siegfried Muchow, born in 1906 and presumably a close relative of Reinhard Muchow, founder of the Nazi trade union NSBO, had become a pianist at the Scala in April 1931. A fanatical Nazi and representative of the NSBO among National Socialist Scala employees in 1932, he instantly clashed with Scala musical director Otto Stenzel. Since 1930, when Stenzel joined the famous variety show, he had been on excellent terms with the show's founder and owner, Jules Marx. For the continued success of their revue Marx and Stenzel relied heavily on international artists and musicians of high caliber, and this during the depression, when xenophobia in the German entertainment industry was rampant. Siegfried Muchow resented it. After his arm had been injured in a street brawl with Communists in 1932, Marx and Stenzel used this as an excuse to get rid of him.

But no sooner had Hitler occupied the chancellery than Muchow was reinstated. In May 1933, after Marx's departure for Paris under storm trooper pressure, the non-Jewish artistic director Eduard Duisberg took the Jew's place. Because of his political clout (but without Duisberg's doing, for he was an anti-Nazi), Muchow schemed successfully to become Stenzel's deputy as conductor of the Scala orchestra in July 1933. Since Muchow did not cease his intrigues against the cosmopolitan management of the revue, Stenzel wanted to keep him at as low a profile as possible and insisted on paying him merely a token honorarium for his auxiliary deputy conductorship.[157]

Partly to counterbalance Muchow but also to help Richard Mohaupt out, Stenzel hired Mohaupt in 1934 as an understudy and arranger. This was hardly an adequate position for the twenty-nine-year-old, but already he was heavily compromised politically and needed shelter. In the late republic this gifted pianist and composer had been a musical avant-gardist and, as a collaborator of Hanns Eisler, Kurt Weill, and Bertolt Brecht, had been in the midst of Communist party politics. Together with his Russian-Jewish wife, the violinist Rosa Gottlieb, he had completed a successful concert tour of Asia and the Soviet Union in 1931.[158] After January 1933, Mohaupt undertook what work he could find as a film composer; the sympathetic Stenzel then supported him with the express backing of the urbane Duisberg, with whom Stenzel saw eye to eye.

Muchow's later accusation, that Stenzel favored Mohaupt by awarding him lucrative arrangements (many of them "Jewish" pieces), thereby preempting incremental income for Muchow himself, presumably was well founded. Thus for the sake of revenge on Mohaupt and on Stenzel, Muchow decided to keep a careful log of the anti-Nazi utterances that proliferated among the free spirits of the Scala. He also kept a log of anything that would lend itself to substantiate the charge of a "Jewish policy" regarding the Scala's personnel management and artistic repertoire. By October 1936 he had collected enough evidence about Mohaupt's own anti-Nazi remarks to sustain proceedings against the composer by one of the dreaded Nazi special courts, resulting in stern warnings for the defendant. Subsequently, Mohaupt rallied to his aid musicians from the Stenzel band, which had the effect of isolating the handful of confirmed Nazis in the Scala organization. Hence Muchow had to plot further. In the spring of 1937 he leaked an earlier anti-Streicher remark by Stenzel as well as details about Mohaupt's racially suspect marriage to Nuremberg Gauleiter Streicher's pornographic rag *Der Stürmer*. He also complained heavily about Jewish compositions such as Gershwin's *Rhapsody in Blue* being regularly performed. Thereupon *Der Stürmer* published a stinging invective against Scala, Mohaupt, and Stenzel at the beginning of May 1937.[159]

And now the affair acquired momentum. Since Muchow had apprised the RMK of his findings, it commissioned its chief vigilante Erich Woschke with an official investigation. Throughout the month of May Woschke scheduled hearings for the actors in this drama, in particular Muchow and Stenzel, while he himself was able to substantiate every Muchow charge. It was easy for Woschke to secure Mohaupt's immediate expulsion from the RMK, thus depriving him of his main livelihood.[160]

Meanwhile, Goebbels himself had become interested in the case. Since republican times, he had been a faithful patron of the Scala, whose electrifying program he often attended after a stressful day, sometimes accompanied by his wife Magda and even the Führer. Whenever Stenzel was forewarned by the propaganda ministry that Goebbels would attend, the orchestra leader was able to make prearranged adjustments to his "Jewish"-skewed program. While Goebbels and his entourage were entering the auditorium just before the show started, ordinary Germans had to rise, extend the Nazi salute, and wait until the high company was comfortably seated in the plush front row.[161]

Goebbels was therefore nonplussed to read in *Der Stürmer* not only the various accusations against Stenzel and his colleagues but also the information that "the 'hot' music (Jewish jazz racket) is stopped and replaced by more decent music," as soon as regime dignitaries were sighted. Indeed, Goebbels's first reaction was one of disbelief; never a friend of the obscene Streicher, he was sure that the Gauleiter's attack was groundless. It was only on the second of June, when the RMK probe had been under way for some weeks and his own men had discreetly reconnoitred the compounds, that he conceded Streicher a point or two. Three days later Goebbels was convinced that "cultural Bolshevism" had pervaded the Scala: "Now I shall intervene." At the beginning of October this minister, who was otherwise not a prudish man, had detected sexual innuendo on the Scala stage. Four weeks later he had resolved to "Aryanize" the place completely. Hitler himself endorsed this plan, which was to be carried out at the beginning of 1938. At the same time the Führer wanted to see a law drafted, altogether prohibiting Jews from attending "German theater and cultural events"; it came into force in November 1938. Already by January Goebbels's lieutenant was able to report that the Scala's program had become "really tame, just as we wanted it."[162]

Not surprisingly, the first victim of this by now supremely authorized purification was Richard Mohaupt. After his ejection from the RMK in late May 1937, the arranger used a pseudonym under which to deliver further work to Stenzel. Most certainly through the mediation of Stenzel and Duisberg, who were on good terms with Scala enthusiast Hinkel, that culture warden provided Mohaupt with special permission to carry on his musical scoring for the revue. Mohaupt was, after all, not just anybody; in November it was made public that his new opera *Die Wirtin von Pinsk* would be premiered early the following year in Dresden under the direction of none other than Karl Böhm, one of the darlings of the Nazi cultural establishment. That premiere occurred on 10 February 1938 as scheduled, but after an acrid critique in Goebbels's Berlin weekly *Der Angriff* only one other performance was staged. It was clear that the minister, in cahoots with President Raabe, had overruled his lackey Hinkel; by June Mohaupt's personal licence was withdrawn. Intrepidly, Mohaupt continued his Scala tasks, but he now was considering exile. After further harassment from the RMK and even the Gestapo, which Hinkel could divert no more, the Mohaupts left for the United States in winter of 1938.[163]

Evidently the Scala was singled out for aspersion by Nazi diehards because it was one of those rare institutions in the Reich totally dependent on international collaboration, something that went against the grain of the official ideology. Only a few of the top Varieté acts Duisberg was booking were native German, and if even fewer may have been foreign Jewish, virtually all these artists relied for their musical accompaniment on at least one or two pieces originating with a Jewish composer. This tainted them in Nazi eyes. The racial stigma adhered, similarly, to Jewish musicians in visiting orchestras, for instance those that Hylton brought over in 1935 and 1937. Stenzel knew the artists' needs well from the days before Hitler came to power; it was under the entrepreneurial Jules Marx that he had developed his own taste for George Gershwin, Jerome Kern, and Irving Berlin, and had formed friendships with many Jews. And because Stenzel and Duisberg were quite aware of the fact that the Nazis required the Scala not just for the private diversion of the propaganda minister, but for the international prestige of the entire country, especially during the Olympic year, they dared to push for as much "Jewish" content as possible. Much like the controversial orchestra conductor Wilhelm Furtwängler, they felt they could take a few more liberties in fraternizing with or protecting Jewish artists than could any of their lesser colleagues from the German world of show business.[164] Many of Stenzel's musicians thought likewise, and so Woschke was justified when in May 1937 he charged that, with negligible exceptions, the entire Scala orchestra was "averse to the set goals of National Socialism."[165]

The American guitarist Mike Danzi, a regular with Stenzel's band, has said that in any given combination of some twenty players there usually was a resident hard core of nine musicians capable of playing jazz music, even if they could not always do it in the nightly diversified programs of the Scala.[166] To be sure, Franz Thon, Kurt Wege, Paul Henkel, Erhard Krause, Kurt and Karl Hohenberger, and Hans Korseck were counted among those, at one time or another.[167] Ernst ("Bimbo") Weiland, the menacingly versatile "trick drummer" who added to the circus suspense of tight-rope acrobatics (he was working when teenager "Prince Louis" fell to his death in October 1934), was well-nigh capable of playing swing and showed it at a record date with Billy Bartholomew's combo in August 1938, even if much of this was more for dancing than for listening.[168] Although Stenzel—classically trained like his colleagues on Broadway at that time—was rarely called upon to produce New Orleans–type jazz or swing, he at least had the option of doing so in the company of so many talented instrumentalists and was a jazzman at heart, especially since he understood and loved that music.[169] Even Mohaupt had arranged the "Tiger Rag" for him, and Mohaupt's successor as head arranger, Horst Kudritzki, was an expert at swing, although he was better known by his "commercial" reputation.[170]

It is therefore not surprising to find that Stenzel had a predilection for the company of red-blooded jazz players, be they Germans or visiting foreigners. Not unnoticed by his deputy Siegfried Muchow, in February 1937 Stenzel attended a private party thrown for Jack Hylton and some of his boys, including the émigré Jew Freddie Schweitzer, at the apartment of society dance-band leader Eugen ("José") Wolff. Also at the party were Bimbo Weiland, swing bandleader Georg Nettelmann, and, significantly, the confidant of all Berlin dance musicians, the Jewish job broker Paul Hirson. When interrogated about this incident by RMK officials, Stenzel was impelled to concede that he knew he was supposed to avoid contact with undesirable Jews, and that in future he would heed this regulation.[171] To Stenzel at the time this was a painful reminder that his position in Germany was precarious.

Stenzel's partial involvement in the jazz culture and his exposure as a friend of the Jews were bound to render him permanently suspect with Goebbels and his ministry. But in related areas of show business he was forcing things against certain limits in a way that potentially compounded his already difficult situation. His "Crazy Show," as he called it, one of his and Duisberg's inventions, featured vaudeville nonsense American-style, which Goebbels would find kitschy, or, at worst, degenerate. In one of these 1938 presentations Stenzel himself, projecting the image of a homosexual, dressed up in white tights, black patent leather boots, and an idiotic wig; to the music of Jewish Fritz Kreisler, he tossed a huge ball to the similarly attired film comic Theo Lingen. The choreographer of this was not a German but a Polish-American by the name of Anthony Nellie, which was grist to the mill of Nazi xenophobes. For Goebbels, who thought males in ballet effeminate, this was a stark provocation.[172]

The American aura of the Scala was nurtured by the presence of other U.S. citizens such as Mike Danzi and Terry Castellani, the captain of the irresistible, long-legged revue girls. This pro-Americanism was aided and abetted by artistic director Duisberg, who engaged the young, quarter-Jewish tap dancer Evelyn

Künneke under her nom de guerre Evelyn King because of her overpowering "American style." Moreover, Duisberg complemented his American orientation with a peculiar pro-British spleen; to him the London musical was the epitomy of quality light entertainment.[173] In connection with the Mohaupt affair Duisberg was ordered to the propaganda ministry in autumn 1937 and given a dressing-down. Seemingly impervious to such treatment, a year later he engaged the film composer Hans Sommer, who was married to a Jew. Two weeks into the Scala show the Gestapo arrived, reprimanded the director, and threw out Sommer. Sommer immediately left for Hollywood.[174]

Duisberg and Stenzel were both courting disaster in yet another way by favoring the cabaret set. Especially since the middle of the Weimar Republic and concomitantly with the rise of right-wing politics, German cabaret had acquired a sharp political acumen. In the supportive fabric of democracy this entailed only a modicum of personal risk for the performing comedian. But by temperament, these sardonic jesters were reluctant to change after Hitler's takeover, so that at the height of World War II a regime voice ascertained that "unfortunately, they had not been filled with the new spirit."[175] The ultimate that could happen to these ongoing critics of the powers-that-be was eerily illustrated in the North American television series "Hitler's SS: Portrait in Evil" of the mid-1980s, in which the monocled cabaret character Putzi gets tortured and finally murdered by the SS as a "decadent."

Until the depression, the most cutting political satire of the republic had been staged at the Kabarett der Komiker, founded by the Viennese Jew Kurt Robitschek in 1924. After 1930 Robitschek had had to tone down his skits, depoliticizing them for fear of political radicalism, which would ultimately affect box-office sales. The Kadeko was leftist and predominantly Jewish; it had declared itself against the emerging National Socialists. From the beginning it was jazz-oriented; Mischa Spoliansky, Friedrich Hollaender, and the Comedian Harmonists were early collaborators.[176]

Two stand-in comedians at the Kadeko, who continued right into the Third Reich with their scathing commentary after the Jews had gone, were the chansonniers Claire Waldoff and Loni Heuser. Both were close friends of Stenzel and always welcome Scala guests.[177] Waldoff, a squat, small woman who had been Marlene Dietrich's lover before 1932, held a huge popular appeal for Berliners: although she stemmed from the Ruhr, she could impersonate suburban street urchins in perfect Berlin dialect. She was the little man's friend. At the Kabarett der Komiker she sometimes teamed up with Heuser, an elegant brunette who was married to Theo Mackeben, one of the giants of German operetta and film music. Mackeben was suspect in his own right because before 1933, like Mohaupt, he had been close to Brecht, Weill, and the proletarian singer Ernst Busch.[178]

Waldoff's specialty at the Scala, for which Berliners virtually loved her to death, was a song in which she mocked Hermann Göring's penchant for uniforms, his rotundness, and his office as minister president of Prussia. It was the parody of another limerick that she had made famous during the republic and thus doubly funny. The publicity-conscious Göring himself accepted the song good-naturedly when it was first performed in 1933, yet this did not prevent the storm troopers and Hitler Youths from menacing Waldoff. In 1936, when Claire appeared once again at a Scala premiere, Goebbels was so beside himself that he threatened Duisberg during the intermission.[179]

Heuser does not seem to have offended anyone under the giant Scala roof. But at that revue's somewhat less imposing rival institution, the Wintergarten, she sang some couplets in late 1936 that got her into trouble. Apart from jostling Göring once again (because he seemed jovial as well as ridiculous, he was a favorite target of these comedians), she used veiled language to assail Labor Front leader Dr. Robert Ley's drinking problem and the general Reich dictum that one should refrain from any criticism. She was promptly censored by Goebbels's tabloid *Angriff* and by the RKK itself.[180]

Werner Finck was the most acerbic of the wits. He was able to capture the essence of a situation and excoriate it with puns that in the German cabaret culture remain unsurpassed to this day. Purely an intellectual, he combined the talents of Bill Cosby and Peter Sellers. Once he shouted to Gestapo spies he had detected in the audience the impromtu remark: "Are you following me, or shall I follow you?" Finck last performed at the Scala in 1932 but was often in the Kadeko and had his very own cabaret, the Katakombe, which was situated, appropriately enough, right in the Scala building on the Lutherstrasse. However, every time Finck scored with a one-liner, he did so under considerable danger to his own safety, and he was in Esterwegen concentration camp from May to July 1935. His Katakombe having been closed, he once again worked in the Kadeko in 1937–38, but in February 1939 the enraged Goebbels had him expelled from the RKK altogether.[181] At that time the propaganda minister also issued tight, new guidelines restricting political satire. This came at the conclusion of a lengthy process of policing the Kabarett der Komiker, a process that was deliberately synchronized with the cleansing of the Scala operation.[182]

It is clear that over the years Otto Stenzel's relationship with critics of the Hitler dictatorship had made him a highly politicized figure. But how deepseated were his anti-Hitlerian sentiments and how typical was he of the other musicians in the light-entertainment field—and jazz in particular?

With reference to its Southern black origins, Eric Hobsbawm has described the propensities of jazz as a vehicle of protest and rebellion in the socioeconomic, generational, racial, and political realms.[183] Intrinsically an art form redolent of liberty, the evangelism of jazz has been used over time by politically and culturally oppressed minorities in several modern states, not only in Bolshevik Russia in the 1940s and 1950s, but as late as the mid-1980s in Communist Czechoslovakia where the "Jazz Section" adopted an open policy of artistic freedom and got punished for it by the single-party dictatorship of Lubomir Strougal.[184] Cuba's Fidel Castro, one of the currently surviving dictators, has always found jazz subversive.[185]

The situation of jazz in the prewar Third Reich was more complex, however, for here the music, its musicians, and its admirers were not automatically elevated to the consecrated plateau of political resistance. It constitutes something of an anomaly that, while Nazi jazz haters disliked this medium because of the prominence of blacks and Jews participating in it, German jazz lovers, musicians and aficionados both, did not necessarily espouse jazz because they might have championed the cause of blacks and Jews. Or, putting it differently, they did not necessarily like jazz simply because a dictatorial regime happened to have placed Jews and blacks on some index. Nazi racist propaganda notwithstanding, the figure of the Negro was too abstract to bear any relevance even for politically aware young Germans, and while the Jew was much less abstract, he was perceived merely as a peripheral figure in the music. At all events, the ideal-type of a person who predicated his or her active involvement in the jazz culture on a pronounced antagonism to the Nazi regime—never existed in the flesh. And if jazz-inspired Germans did not, as a rule, rebel for racial or political reasons, they could be even less driven by generational or socioeconomic maladjustments.

Mixed categories, however, did exist, and in such cases elements of political or social nonconformism invariably came into play. An individual's reluctance to conform to the predominant political and cultural patterns of the day frequently was the result of distinctive socialization at home (and sometimes also in the classroom) and then could lead to acculturation in jazz as a restrained form of personal protest.

A number of jazz fans were appalled by Hitler Youth service, having previously been conditioned by religious or otherwise firmly indoctrinated elders. Werner Daniels and Hans Otto Jung both were born into strict Catholic homes with ties to the Vatican-geared Center party. Before 1933, Jung's father had been a Center party worthy in Lorch; during Hitler's rule, he would congregate with his educated Jewish friends and perform chamber music on the first of May— now a Nazi holiday—on which occasion they would critically review the regime. In Düsseldorf, the senior Daniels suffered career setbacks for his strong Center party connections. The father of Emil Mangelsdorff in Frankfurt was a dedicated socialist who imbued his teenager with working-class tenets while sensitizing him with details about Nazi concentration camps. Dessau's Günter Boas was influenced at home by liberal Bauhaus artists and in school by a left-wing socialist teacher. Dieter Zimmerle and Carlo Bohländer became nonconformists because paramilitary drill in state youth groups and intellectual arrogance in school frustrated them.[186] Joachim Ernst Berendt in Berlin, a loner of a boy too young and shy to be in the Melodie-Klub, had a not so distant Jewish ancestor; his father was a Lutheran minister who also directed a large foundation that included medical institutions contrary to Nazi eugenic aims. Storm troopers and SS regularly searched his house, and in December 1938, after a very explicit sermon, Pastor Ernst Berendt was marched off to Dachau, with his young son watching the arrest in horror.[187]

Apart from dodging Hitler Youth service, which was possible until inscription became truly compulsory in March 1939, jazz fans showed no signs of counterdisciplinary activities. The understandable exception was Hans Otto Jung, who in school produced cardboard cartoons of Hitler (as a praying monk) and other Nazi greats that fell into the hands of Brown Shirts, resulting in a police hearing.[188]

There was even less of this humanitarian, social, or political consciousness (let alone conscience) among musicians than among fans, probably because of the musicians' utilitarian way of life, their mundane concern with getting a gig, making a buck, finding a girl for the night. These activities precluded involvement in matters of the mind (after all, many had risen from rather primitive social and professional settings) and commanded them, instead, to sing the tune of the rulers when asked. The frequently vented conviction that at heart they were "apolitical" reflects this fundamental concern, and in principle it applies to the dance and jazz instrumentalists to the same degree as it would to classical and other musicians, as studies about Strauss and Furtwängler have lately shown.[189]

This would be in keeping with F. Scott Fitzgerald's classic aside that in the United States the Jazz Age "had no interest in politics at all."[190] The notable exception to this in Germany was Hans Korseck, that particularly gifted and sentient artist who, like Berendt, hailed from a staunchly Protestant home and hated the Nazis to the point of wanting to shoot Goebbels at point blank. (As guitarist for the Kreuder group, he periodically saw Goebbels at official functions.) Korseck had lost a Jewish girlfriend, who had emigrated to Brazil, and when he met his wife-to-be in the summer of 1939, she too had recently been left behind by a Hungarian-Jewish conductor; a declared enemy of Hitler, she had already been a victim of Gestapo interrogation.[191]

If jazz in these cases was a consequence of political noncompliance, however moderate, that causal relationship could be reversed to the extent that the promotion of jazz as an aesthetic commodity caused fans to regard totalitarian politics with grave suspicion. The redoubtable Hans Blüthner has repeatedly gone on record with the axiom that as a devotee of jazz, it was impossible to accept National Socialism and its Reich: "The championship of jazz was identical with democracy and freedom."[192] This socialization through jazz, if it can be acknowledged as such, was something that may have occurred to more than one member of the cultist Melodie-Klub, where the rituals were stringent enough to determine one's worldview. The alcoholic Carlo Boger, one of the resident geniuses of that club—he was a short-story writer, splendid graphic artist, and connoisseur of fine literature and theatrical plays—lived by the maxim that tyranny was anathema to artistic freedom.[193] Boger was later drafted and killed at the front.

Among the musicians, a kindred soul may have been Fritz Brocksieper, for whom jazz drumming was a passion beyond which only women and gambling held some merit. He, too, maintains that *because* he and his musical compatriots thought jazz the ultimate form of existential expression, anything that might impede its progress was harmful. Arguably, Nazi politics would fall under that rubric by default, not by design. Because jazz necessitated individuality, Nazi uniforms and swastikas symbolizing uniformity were the bane of Brocksieper's creative art.[194] Despite such reflection, however, one would be hard put to characterize this consummate swing artist as a political animal in the mold of Korseck or of Boger; if the latter two were more like wise men, Brocksieper lived far more instinctually.

As an intermediate verdict, then, it is important to revise what Horst H. Lange said more than twenty years ago in his pioneering work about German jazz during this prewar period, namely that especially within the bastion of the Berlin fan club, jazz was a source of "spiritual resistance" under Hitler.[195] A more pertinent and trenchant judgment comes from Dieter Zimmerle, who has re-marked that anyone who loved jazz for its own sake had nothing to fear from the regime, yet in combination with anything else that was objectionable, a Jazz penchant was potentially fatal.[196] This is why the non-"Aryan" jazz practi-tioners, Pick or Wolf or Eugen Henkel or even the temerarious Brocksieper, were always so much at risk.

For other jazz devotees, their commitment to jazz music as an ideology was partly or even totally abstracted from the political reality in which they lived. Paradoxically and frighteningly, this abstraction, the removal of jazz into a vacuum, could thereupon enable the protagonists themselves to enter the realm of Nazi politics in one way or another; in extreme situations they proceeded to lead the improbable double life of Nazi jazz lovers. Opportunism as a moti-vational force could never be ruled out.

Shades of this can be documented. Drummer Hans "Cat's Paws" Klagemann performed often with Hans Korseck and Peter Kreuder. With a self-professed "tendency toward the unpolitical," he is nonetheless far from denying that he was comfortably adjusted to Nazi mores. That was in his best interests, for it must be remembered that he was hassled by the RMK because of profes-sional qualifications.[197] Although Klagemann was not a member of the Nazi party, he dutifully moved out of the apartment of Jewish landlords after having been reprimanded by a regime official in 1936, and he naturally offered the Hitler salute, apparently more often than was necessary.[198] Klagemann's much younger colleague, the violin prodigy Helmut Zacharias, was not socialized against the Nazi regime either at home or in school; with Professor Gustav Havemann, one of the leading musical functionaries of the regime as his main teacher, he experi-enced all the thrills of Hitler Youth service as a teenager. At the Berlin conser-vatory he joined the Nazi Student League. He loved the camaraderie, the outings, the camp fires. He remembers that he "neither liked the Nazis nor disliked them. We knew nothing, even about the concentration camps, apart from the fact that they existed and that they held prisoners, as jails would." In 1938, when the wizard had to fiddle something for Adolf Hitler (Zacharias miraculously com-manded the conventional classical violin repertoire as a mere lad), he was ob-viously flattered and found the Führer quite human, certainly not crazy. Young Helmut never even gave it a thought that the jazz he was beginning to become expert at could compromise him morally.[199] Should he have done so?

In another scenario Hot-Geyer, who insists that his Leipzig club friends rejected NSDAP membership, lived out strong nationalistic feelings of his own when in 1935 he volunteered for the RAD. For six months he helped to build the autobahn near Leipzig, acquiring a handsome suntan and loving it all every week. Today he claims to have used this voluntary service as an excuse not to join the party when they asked him to later on, yet even then he should have known that the NSDAP never could force anybody to become a member.[200] When in London, he was appalled by Jews taunting him for his loyalty to Germany, and for the benefit of Californian *Tempo* magazine readers he de-fended what he understood to be the Berlin government's jazz policy.[201]

Another category of jazz followers went Nazi either from conviction, or

Weintraub Syncopators at a ballet rehearsal in Berlin, 1931. Leader Stefan Weintraub is holding the bass drum. (Ullstein Bilderdienst, Berlin)

James Kok Band in Berlin, 1934–35. Fritz Schulze is at the piano. Erhard ("Funny") Bauschke, Kok's successor as bandleader, is seen behind the maestro's right shoulder. (Ullstein Bilderdienst, Berlin)

Golden Seven Band at a Berlin studio session in 1935. From left: Adalbert Luczkowski (violin), Erhard Krause (trombone), Kurt Hohenberger (trumpet), Franz Thon (saxophone), Willi Stech (piano), Waldi Luczkowski (drums), Harold M. Kirchstein (guitar). (Ullstein Bilderdienst, Berlin)

Logo for Sherbini nightclub in Berlin, mid-1930s. (Private Archive of Kurt Michaelis, Dreieich)

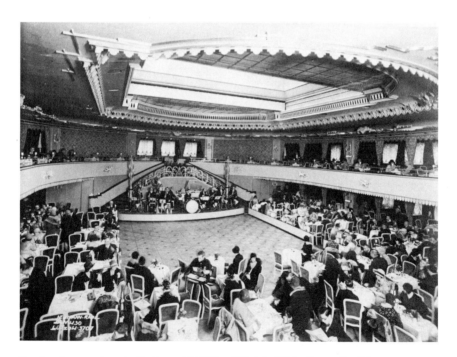

Femina dance palace in Berlin, mid-1930s. (Ullstein Bilderdienst, Berlin)

Jack Hylton Band during its February 1938 tour in Berlin. (Ullstein Bilderdienst, Berlin)

Teddy Stauffer during a visit to Berlin in 1956. (Ullstein Bilderdienst, Berlin)

Jutta and Inga Madlung with their younger brother, Hamburg, early 1942. They are dressed up in sacks. (Private Archive of Inga Madlung-Shelton, London)

After a night in the Sherbini nightclub, 19 January 1936, at 3:00 A.M. From left to right: Dietrich Schulz, Herb Flemming, Joachim-Ernst ("Fiddlin' Joe") Frommann, Fritz Schulze, Kurt ("Hot-Geyer") Michaelis. In front: an unidentified black employee of the nightclub, said to have been a cigarette vendor. (Private Archive of Kurt Michaelis, Dreieich)

Members of the Leipzig Hot Club at one of their Blue Monday meetings, March 1934. From left: Kurt ("Hot-Geyer") Michaelis, Joachim-Ernst ("Fiddlin' Joe") Frommann, Hans-Hugo ("Dreamy-Hot") Helbig. (Private Archive of Kurt Michaelis, Dreieich)

A typical Hamburg Swing scene, ca. 1939. Leading Swing Alfred Dreyer is standing fourth from left, Helga Rönn and Hans-Joachim ("Tommie") Scheel are fifth and sixth. On the far right is Ursula Nielsen. The group typically includes foreigners, such as the Italian Aldo Patzono (standing third from left), and an English friend (eighth from left). (Private Archive of Hans-Joachim Scheel, Mississauga)

On the Berlin Scala stage, 1939. Otto Stenzel is on the right, next to the clown. Notice the Asian artists. (Ullstein Bilderdienst, Berlin)

sheer opportunism, or an undeterminable mixture of both. By all accounts that we have, Willi Stech, the crafty pianist and cofounder of the Golden Seven, was a party member and faithful Nazi from early on, but Haentzschel vouches for his good cheer even when the anti-Hitler jokes of musicians like Kirchstein and Krause (betrothed to the leggy American Scala captain Terry) got a little out of hand.[202]

Another kettle of fish was Peter Kreuder, the overly commercial but sometimes adroit jazz pianist who concertized all over Germany. In his memoirs, Kreuder makes much of his anti-Nazi stance before and throughout the Hitler dictatorship, but fact is that for insurance he joined the NSDAP as early as August 1932, a month after an election had made it the largest party in the Reichstag. For hitherto unknown reasons, Kreuder left the party again in October 1934, and, as will be shown below, was to have his share of trouble with the regime in subsequent years, but hardly because of politics.[203]

And then there was gallant pianist Fritz Schulze who, it is difficult to believe, joined the SS at the beginning of 1933 when he was still in Magdeburg. When asked about it recently Schulze explained that he had been persuaded by school pals, who thought he might get some gigs. Admittedly, this was still happening in the throes of the depression, when even the best of the musicians toiled hard to make ends meet. As it turned out, no jobs were forthcoming, for the SS danced to different tunes. Schulze conveniently developed appendicitis and dropped out of the hated SS field service. In the fall of 1934 he moved to the capital to play with Kok. For years thereafter the SS pursued him, dragging him out of bed early on Sunday mornings when he had just turned in from the bars, and disturbing his paramours. But as ingenuously as Schulze had entered Himmler's elite corps, he was able to leave it again. One of the higher SS leaders was a regular fan of his notorious swing mode in the Quartier Latin. So one night Fritz approached him and begged to intervene. Finally, in January 1938, a SS general officially thanked him for "all past services rendered" and honorably discharged this part-time Black Shirt back into his own glitzy world.[204]

Schulze claims that, by and large, he had absolutely no idea what the SS was all about; he was in a communications unit using Morse code, and it was only wine, women, and song that sustained his interest. A caricature of the "unpolitical musician"? At least Schulze admits that the idea of SS-organized concentration camps was beginning to bother him, and he could not have escaped the anti-Semitic jargon that resounded throughout the Black Order. He also concedes his opportunism and the fact that because he loved his freedom, as the SS experience had taught him, he resisted subsequent attempts to pull him into the party.[205]

All this may still be fairly comprehensible; here was a man naive enough not to have ever been bothered by a shadow of a doubt about whether jazz and the Judeophobic SS were at all reconcilable. Indeed, young Fritz was anything but an intellectual given to metaphysical reflection; an unflappable vitalism propelled him. However, a much more complicated problem is presented by the broodingly analytical Dietrich Schulz-Köhn. As the chief surviving witness, however, he finds it impossible to aid the historian's quest to dispel the enigma.

The enigma is that Schulz-Köhn, this crusading defender of American jazz, joined the storm troopers in the fall of 1933 at the age of twenty-one, while studying at Frankfurt University.[206] Now it is known that during that particular year the Brown-Shirted SA had tremendous power in every German university, so that more than half of all the male students joined at that time.[207] Schulz-Köhn does admit to conformism; it was easier to give in to the pressure, for the sake of his future career.[208] On the other hand, there were those students who found ways to resist this pressure, and why was Schulz-Köhn not among them?

In all probability the answer is that Dietrich could not conceive that jazz and strong German nationalism were mutually exclusive ideals. Every indication to date points to the fact that like many of his peers, this is what he saw in Hitler's movement about all else: a strong nationalistic impulse with admittedly ugly side effects that one had to dissociate oneself from by simply blanking them out.[209] Nobody who knew Schulz-Köhn then and who knows him now would ever have accused him of being in any sense a "Nazi," much less an anti-Semite. But his unbending nationalism seems to have been passed down to him by his nationalist-conservative father, the public school teacher, who was in fact less a fan of Hitler than of Bismarck.[210] Somewhat like Michaelis, who took no action on his own political behalf, Schulz-Köhn must have believed that jazz and a strong National Socialist fatherland were indeed compatible, warts and all. Though an intellectual, Schulz-Köhn's mind was blocked off when implicitly challenged to consider the consequences of such a compromise for the Muse he heralded.

But this is only part of the picture. Schulz-Köhn temporarily suspended his SA membership some time early in 1936 to have more time for his studies.[211] After his lectures on jazz at the Delphi-Palast, innocent enough and with what might pass as verbal concessions to the regime,[212] he was attacked in the leading SS tabloid, albeit anonymously, as "the advertising chap of the Brunswicks."[213] Pursuant to this, three months later in October, Stege published his diatribe. And only one week after that, the storm troopers themselves picked up where Stege had left off and publicly threatened their former comrade with brutality. The SA would form "a small swing commando," one that would specialize in going after "dear Dietrich." They planned to submerge him in water, with unpredictable results. There was no telling what those thugs might do.[214]

Possibly as a precaution against these dangers, Schulz-Köhn decided to enter the Nazi party itself in February 1938; his entry became retroactive to May 1937.[215] But this imputed motive—the most noble one could ascribe to Dietrich—is based on pure conjecture, for the jazz doctor himself today cannot recall any details. Was it his father who pushed him? Was it crass careerism? The latter would not be so implausible because as an aspiring recording industry executive, Schulz-Köhn would have benefited from Nazi party membership—as he had, arguably, from the SA earlier on.

Or did Schulz-Köhn join the party to deflect attention from his involvement in jazz? This particular possibility, avers Schulz-Köhn in all sincerity, would not have made much sense, "for as a student I was fairly independent" (nor did he need a party tag to bolster his chances of passing his university exams for the doctorate, as his superior thesis shows).[216] So when all is said and done in this part of our inquiry, the enigma remains unbroken. In any event, Dietrich's 1938 party entry would have been in keeping with his earlier SA action, since his patriotic views had not changed. In fact, they would strengthen as the war commenced, and, paradoxically, so would his love for jazz.

The juxtaposition of jazz as dogma and National Socialist ideology was thrown in stark relief whenever professional Nazis consumed this music. They may have done so cynically, the way Hitler might have been reading *Das Kapital,* chuckling to himself from one page to the next. Even though jazz was often disguised, riding piggy-back on the more conventionally acceptable dance music, there is no getting away from the fact that bona fide Nazis who abhorred manifestations of Americanism, blacks, and Jews could be in love with the tainted Muse all the same. The SS general who rescued Fritz Schulze from SS service is a case in point. Other staffers of Himmler's Black Order were known to be habitués of the Quartier Latin. Polished SS officers in their tightly fitting black uniforms, often from the social crème de la crème, mingled easily with the beautiful people of the capital who frequented the extravagant swing bars.[217] The Königsberg jazz club hosted at least one SS man as well as a former Nazi university student leader.[218] After Goebbels's abortive affair with Czech actress Lida Baarova, his aide Karl Hanke, who was in love with Magda Goebbels, repeatedly took his boss's wife to the Ciro in 1939.[219]

Even the proverbial rowdies of the Nazi movement, the storm troopers, partook of the forbidden fruit. SA commander Count Wolf-Heinrich von Helldorf, the police president of Berlin and a neighbor and close friend of Goebbels, adored the Quartier Latin. The half-Jewish singer Margot Friedländer, who illegally performed American evergreens in such Berlin bars as the Orangerie and Patria, once was picked up for the night by a handsome, elegantly attired SA colonel, certainly in ignorance of her ethnic background. This was none other than the nobleman Diether von Wedel, Goebbels's own adjutant, who, in Friedländer's recollection, was "crazy about anything American" and constantly hung around the nocturnal jazz dives.[220] Ironically, in 1934 the SS and SA also attended one of the last concerts of the vocal group Comedian Harmonists, in Stuttgart, before they were disbanded for their partial Jewishness.[221]

The example of the Warnemünde Nazi party hacks who listened to Helmut Zacharias's trio in the summer of 1939 shows that even the common foot soldiers of Hitler's movement exposed themselves to the blacklisted music, again with the knowledge of doing something mischievous.[222] But forbidden fruit usually is doubly sweet, and here the Nazi regime was no exception. Fritz Brocksieper tells one last characteristic anecdote. Although in Munich he was still working in dance outfits with little chance of playing straight jazz, Gauleiter Adolf Wagner and Hitler's adjutant, SS-Obergruppenführer Julius Schaub, were partying in a public place to the tunes of Brocksieper's dance band. They were in the company of prostitutes from the Schillerstrasse and living it up with a good deal of liquor. Wagner then made a request, a song by the Jew Emmerich Kálmán. As it was being performed, Schaub shouted "Jew Music!" Wagner then turned around, insisting that *he* had demanded it. Thereupon the band went on with swing-type dance music, including any number of English and American tunes. The Nazis reveled in it until the drunken Wagner stumbled onto the bandstand in a stupor, nearly breaking a violin, at three o'clock in the morning.[223]

In conclusion we should consider the politically subversive behavior of the "swing youth" in Hamburg. This phenomenon requires more than an historical approach as far as jazz in the Third Reich is concerned, for in one sense it belongs to the wider problem area of the contemporary youth culture and is best dealt with by psychohistorians, historians of pedagogy, or sociologists. In another sense it has to do with Hamburg's peculiar situation within Germany as a commercial port with traditional cosmopolitan leanings that was controlled by a powerful mercantile elite harboring largely Anglophile sentiments: this calls for the skills of demography. Third, that movement occurred in direct response to certain developments in the entire German social-dance scene and was not relegated to the Elbe river town; here the analyst of fashion might come in.

To begin with the last-mentioned item: from the final years of the republic Germany possessed a large proportion of social-dance instructors (*Tanzlehrer*) who were reactionary to the core, if not politically, then certainly with regard to their craft. It was customary for youths of the better families to attend dance classes for several months, often alongside Gymnasium, as a necessary part of an all-round education. Hence the *Tanzlehrer* envisioned for themselves a preceptorial mission of great moral, even patriotic scope, which many of them saw realized under nazism. In the restrictive era of late Weimar one of their representatives had held that "today's societal system requires more than ever the command of distinctive forms of deportment . . . as expression of a balanced inner composure." A good floor dancer was supposed to be aesthetically pleasing; in a cryptoracist manner the instructors posited an interrelationship between such bodily aesthetics and character development.[224]

After the creation of the RKK social-dance instructors were incorporated into the subdivision of the Reichstheaterkammer (RTK), or Reich Theater Chamber, and thus were under the propaganda minister's thumb by 1935.[225] From then until early 1938, social-dance functionaries of the Reich were straining for a German alternative to the foreign, allegedly "Nigger" and "Jewish"-inspired dances such as the fox-trot or Charleston, which were seen as manifesting lurid sexuality. These efforts were intimately tied to the attempts to replace jazz, the ideal vehicle for the modern dance genre. Both the Reich contest to create a "German Jazz" idiom in 1935–36 and the Radio Leipzig competition of early 1938 really had the twin aims of a new dance form on the one hand and a complementary music for this dance on the other. And because both events failed miserably, dance instructors in the Reich were placed in limbo; they resented the official pressure on them to go with the times, yet they also had to admit to their own incompetence in contributing new social-dance concepts.

The shabby compromise they struck consisted of an artificial revival of long-outdated German dance forms that stressed the desired communal animus at the expense of individuality and eroticism: the *Deutschländer,* performed as a group dance, or the stilted pair dance *Marsch.* Other resurrected period dances were the aseptic *Rheinländer* and *Polka;* the traditional but already sterile waltz was of course desirable. In keeping with the collective goals of the dictatorship, instructors sought to utilize as many elements of German folk music as possible; whereas the more modern fox-trots and tangos were still tolerated, emphasis now was on a more wooden, sanitized German fox-trot version called the *Marschfoxtrot,* and the originally seductive tango became schoolmarmish and unerotic.[226]

Matters came to a head when by 1938–39 the state-sponsored Hitler Youth, whose leaders had been waiting for new dance patterns for some years only to be disappointed, decided to throw its weight in the direction of the artificial German dance revival. It was forced to do so, for since the middle of 1937 or so a new "social dance" called "swing" was in the process of being appropriated by the carefree, fun-loving young Germans of large city centers. The swing dance was based on the American Lindy Hop of the late 1920s and emphasized loose movement of all limbs; it was executed in pairs, vaguely like a fox-trot. Partners sometimes danced slowly and tightly cheek-to-cheek, but usually they followed the hectic speed of the propulsive band, jiving to and away from each other and exuding sexuality. The music was the swing of the Swing Era, ideally Benny Goodman's. Most probably this dance style had found its way into the Reich via the films *Broadway Melody* and *Born to Dance.*[227]

Membership in the HJ organizations (for ages ten to seventeen), while strongly recommended, was not yet obligatory, and the leaders realized that they had to proffer some attraction in the area of social dancing in order to keep their present city flocks contented and to recruit new members. For this purpose they could have adopted the swing dance. But of course it was noxious—degenerate, American, and tied to the damnable jazz—and so they resorted to the freshly touted new-German community dances, to the accompaniment of mandolin, zither, harmonica, and recorder. Yet they should have reckoned that this would only exacerbate their difficulties by effecting the very opposite of what was intended: instead of embracing Hitler Youth pastimes, city girls and boys crowded the swing dance joints. Reaction bred counterreaction and further reaction. In 1938 a spiral began, the end of which was impossible to foresee.[228]

Nowhere was this more acute than in Hamburg, where a self-contained little colony seemed to evolve solely on the basis of the swing dance. But evidence of the swing-dance craze was in virtually all large and often even medium-sized towns. The purist jazz record collectors and connoisseurs of live bands understandably looked down on these *Stenze* (pimps) and their "piss carnations," as burghers sometimes called these lads and their girlfriends. Whereas the collectors cherished jazz, not excluding its more commercialized swing version, as art for its own sake, those loafers were abusing it for the idle pleasure of the swing dance.[229] This perceptual division, whether justified or not, is one of several reasons why the swing youth, as a political spectacle, deserves treatment in its own right. It is true that within the framework of straight jazz history the "Swings" were at opposite ends from the hardliner Melodie-Klub, but they had something in common with the Münster and even the Leipzig fans, who all liked dancing, and there were many collectors among even the "Swings."

To describe these largely teenage hoppers as "Swings" was not contemporary usage, but a post–World War II invention. They were officially known as "Swing-Heinis," a name they contracted from the authorities; among themselves they favored an Anglo-American nomenclature: "Swing-Boy," "Swing-Baby," and so forth. Their political quality derived originally from the fact that they ignored express prohibitions of the swing dance, with varying degrees of risk to themselves, then or during wartime.

Characteristically, in parallel and sometimes even synchronized actions against the outright playing of swing music, these prohibitions were promulgated locally or regionally, at all events without express backing from the Berlin government. The first such ordinance on record is one issued by the dance division of the RTK in Gau Essen and Düsseldorf; it commanded the Düsseldorf wine bar Bei Toni, one of the more likely places to feature jazz in the Reich, to stop this style of dancing. That was in November 1937. The police president of Freiburg followed through with an action for his entire jurisdiction half a year later, and after another six months Gau Weser-Ems officials blanketed all of Bremen.[230] The beginning of 1939 saw interdictions for the town of Osnabrück and the Ruhr Valley; by June the net had been cast over large parts of Germany.[231] Not to be outdone, party and state agencies—the Wehrmacht, RAD, SS, Deutsche Arbeitsfront (DAF), or German Labor Front, and Nazi student organizations—followed suit.[232] The HJ leadership waited relatively long with its own decree because it wished to coordinate any embargo with its positive, albeit ultimately futile, encouragement of new Germanic dances at the beginning of 1939.[233]

In Berlin, by 1938, there were signs posted all around Erhard Bauschke's dancing palace Moka Efti, warning that the swing dance was verboten. Waiters politely sequestered delinquents, but with few lasting results, for Kurt Widmann at the Imperator with its thousand club chairs was also attracting fanatics, and they were in evidence even at the noble Femina.[234] Corny Ostermann's swing orchestra boldly announced a new dance number, "Ich tanz mit Fräulein Molly Swing." Another new standard, performed widely at the time, was entitled "Come, Dance Swing Time With Me, My Darling." Billy Bartholomew had not shrunk from recording the doggerel for Odeon in August 1937.[235]

Once again Goebbels himself was to blame for the inadequacy of the dragnet. In the first place, he had allowed various agencies of party, municipality, and government, including some from his ministry, to act on their own accord, without any centralization. Second, when he did step in, he did so only half-heartedly, with no serious consequences until the beginning of the war. Prompted by repeated, publicly vented complaints about the situation from two cultural overseers, President Raabe of the RMK and Paul Graener, head of its composers, the minister had the presidents of both the RTK and RMK issue a lukewarm ordinance in spring of 1939, making the performance of any social dance contingent on a special "declaration of nonobjection." But how this act was to be implemented was never made explicit.[236]

In Hamburg, social-dance functionary and RTK warden Franz Büchler condemned the swing dance as "one of the most terrible outgrowths of the Negro dance period" yet to have surfaced. This happened in January 1938. Eighteen months later the port city issued its own indictment of this "Nigger-like cacophony from the USA."[237] Now the stage was set for one of the most curious protest movements of the Third Reich.

At the height of World War II, the Hitler Youth command reported that in Hamburg during the winter of 1937–38, boys and girls from the social elite, who knew each other from Gymnasium or exclusive sports clubs, had formed an "ice-rink clique." "They would frequent specific taverns, clad in conspicuous costumes and fancying English music and English dances."[238] Although the "ice-rink clique" in the downtown Planten and Blomen park was incidental rather than organized,[239] this was a fairly accurate assessment of what had in fact been transpiring in the last two years before the war. "English music and English dances" correctly referred to the vibrant Hamburg jazz scene, second only to Berlin's, and, of course, to the swing dance then in vogue.

While Hamburg had few indigenous dance and jazz orchestras, virtually all the German and international formations of note came to visit, sometimes repeatedly and for lengthy engagements. For instance, among the more prominent bands was that of Heinz Wehner, who premiered in Hamburg in May 1934 and then returned a year later. He played at the Faun, one of the less reputable places popular with dance crowds. The gilt-edged establishment in town was the Café Heinze, which hosted Bartholomew in September 1935, while Bauschke was at the Faun. Max Rumpf performed there in January 1937, and in the fall the Tarantella-Bar of the upscale Esplanade hotel had the swinging combo of clarinetist and singer Horst Winter. Swedish jazz ace Arne Hülphers was at the Faun in December, and he was rivaled at Heinze's by the Swiss Lanigiro Hot Players. Kurt Hohenberger's fine swingtet regaled the holiday guests at Timmendorf, the Baltic sea resort near Lübeck, a virtual Hamburg preserve, in the summers of 1938 and 1939. The Dane Kai Ewans came to the Faun in December 1938, when Rumpf was at another favorite spot, the Trocadero.[240] Two of the bands most sought-after by juveniles enthralled by swing dance were the Dutch group of John Kristel, who had started here with a classical salon repertoire but was becoming tarter by the month, and, not surprisingly, Teddy Stauffer, who, from March 1935 to the end of 1938, was employed either by the Trocadero or Heinze's café.[241]

The Hitler Youth survey had correctly identified the upper-echelon origin of the Hamburg swingsters. As a group of jazz music fans, the Hamburg Swings were different from the hot clubs of Berlin, Leipzig, or Königsberg, not least because their core members hailed largely from a monied patriciate quite unique to this city. Their coherence was not based on the formal unity of a jazz club, but derived fundamentally from a common fraternity and sorority in highly restrictive sports clubs and elite schools. They were also in their teens, and in that sense they resembled the fans of Münster and Düsseldorf. If the parents of these juveniles were not bankers, insurance or real estate brokers, import–export merchants or shipping magnates, they were well-placed professionals such as physicians and lawyers. Those parents were traditionally cosmopolitan and, in particular, Anglophile, and many a Hamburg Swing had been to England or America, sometimes accompanying their fathers on business trips. Hence there was a large degree of socialization going on in the sumptuous parental homes located in Hamburg's finest districts, Nienstedten and Harvestehude, Uhlenhorst and Flottbek. The parents sent their children to famous schools with names like Gelehrtenschule des Johanneums, or Marienau in the Lüneburg heath, directed until the Nuremberg Blood Laws by a polyglot humanist, the Hamburg Jew Max Bondy. He had encouraged jazz, the appreciation of atonal music, and Bauhaus art among his pupils since the Weimar Republic. These families emphasized cultured entertainment, sophisticated enlightenment, relaxed living supported by expensive tastes, and liberal politics—a time-honored value system diametrically opposed to what the Nazis stood for. After all, upper-crust Hamburgians were the descendants of those proud merchant burghers who, in the thirteenth century, had made their city one of the pillars of the politically and commercially dominant Hanseatic League.

The sports clubs, such as the yacht club Norddeutscher Regatta-Verein (NRV) or the water-sports Klub an der Alster, as well as a couple of tennis, ice-hockey, and skating establishments, served equally important social functions. Their role in the broadly liberal education of this affluent youth cannot be overestimated: here the boys and girls got to know each other through festivities and friendly competitions in which they learned rules of fair play, but they also learned to associate and communicate easily with their role models, the parents of their friends, the friends of their parents. At the frequent social functions, Anglo-American music was favored, so that in the sports clubs alone, the teenagers were early on exposed to one form of jazz or another.[242]

Before the war, this was a self-contained, homogeneous community into which members of lower social strata initially had no entry, but which, characteristically enough, included prominent foreigners and non-"Aryans." Associates of the large and often commercially weighty diplomatic corps were generally welcome. A few very rich Greeks and Iranians, who had settled in Hamburg through wholesale trade, raised their progeny in these environs and were themselves on the periphery of this genteel culture that centered on private clubs. Dutch-born Andreas Panagopoulos came to Hamburg as a toddler, the son of a Greek tobacco wholesaler; he never learned his mother tongue until adulthood. Demitrius ("Kaki") Georgiadis was the son of a Cypriot father, who owned the mammoth Leopold Engelhardt cigarette company, and a German mother; he himself was born in Bremen but carried a British passport. Kaki was eighteen when in 1937 he was called upon to be executor of his deceased father's estate and suddenly found himself in control of a fortune.

Because Kaki was a trifle older in years and had unlimited wealth at his disposal, he became a sort of liaison between the teenagers gradually being initiated into the Anglo-oriented yachting culture and the more seasoned men of the world already of some accomplishment, who were on the threshold of their thirties. One of these was the half-Jewish Fritz Simon, a successful perfume manufacturer; others were Bobby Dependorf, who owned Germany's largest dry-cleaning firm; the industrialist Ernst Carstens; and the would-be singer Axel Springer, whose liberal-minded father published a newspaper in exurban Altona. The shipowner Erik Blumenfeld was also half-Jewish. Significantly, all of them had become close friends of Teddy Stauffer, who resembled them in good looks and in his taste for all manner of refinements, not excluding erotic adventures. Springer even sang in his band. Hamburg regular Stauffer became the walking symbol of this close-knit group's international proclivities, expressed through its passion for jazz.[243]

From 1937 to the outbreak of the war, which was to change his life dramatically, Kaki was the uncrowned king of the swing youth in Hamburg. There must have been more than a hundred of those by early 1939, and if he did not know them all, they certainly knew him well: the dapperly dressed young gentleman with the soft facial features, the magnificent Horch convertible, the weakness for fine restaurants, beautiful show girls, and, of course, American swing. He was admired from afar by scores of younger men, scions some of them, with the best in manners and tastes, and probably not much poorer. But he was also feared by them, since he was recognized—as was the genial Axel Springer in the somewhat older set—as an irresistible attraction for everybody's girlfriend.[244]

These privileged youths indulged in jazz and the swing dance the way modern, ordinary adolescents might become beholden to the pop charts and a disco. But because the activity of the dance itself was just as important as the music, if not more so, their interest in jazz per se, historically and musically, always tended to be superficial, and it naturally favored contemporary Goodman-type swing (Stauffer's brand of jazz) rather than vintage Armstrong or middle-period Hawkins. Yet, all the same, records were purchased, treasured, and exchanged, particularly since one needed them for that specialty of the Hamburg swing scene, the private parties in spacious villas, usually under the supervision of the parents and sometimes when the trusting elders were away. The magnet at such celebrations were the Madlung sisters, two lovely young girls, daughters of a half-Jewish lawyer of great distinction. They were very musical, and together with their younger brother they were stunningly able to imitate the American Andrews Sisters, who had succeeded the Boswell Sisters with an even more closely knit harmonic style of vocalizing. Both Inga and Jutta were the toast of every swing party, not just for their singing, but also their great charm and, not least, their known tolerance in matters of casual sex, which proliferated at these gatherings.

These permissively educated boys and girls avoided permanent relationships, or "going steady." Actually, they were much more ready to engage in sexual experimentation than were their socially inferior cohorts, and they had a good ear for the aphrodisiacal quality of jazz, which also served them well for the rather more unfettered swing gyrations on a hotel's ballroom floor.

Apart from private quarters, the clubs, or rented halls, swing-dancing was best done at the large Café Heinze, in the Trocadero, or in the more cramped, Ciro-like nightclub Tarantella. A local pianist named Schröder, who called himself Teddy Sinclair, fired up the rhythms in the Vierjahreszeiten-Keller, hidden in the illustrious hotel of the same name, another great favorite. Stauffer, of course, was the star, and because of his connections with the more mature Swings, he was approachable for the younger Swings as well, certainly for the girls. When the indisputably sexy eighteen-year-old Inga saw him perform in 1938 at the Trocadero, she became infatuated with the considerably older rogue on the spot. Bent on conquest, she managed to catch his attention, and then coaxed her father into buying her a saxophone. For weeks thereafter Inga and Teddy met daily at his Vierjahreszeiten room, allegedly for saxophone lessons. The eternally alluring Inga's recollection of the maestro is still poignant: "Everytime I entered his hotel room, he was dressed in a red lounge robe, perfectly matching his blond hair." And: "A real man, and always tanned, with snow-white teeth, and classy." Today she says that the meetings were innocent; her father never found out.[245]

The obsession with aesthetically pleasing things and people was as much a hallmark of the Hamburg Swing youth as were its sensual preoccupations, and it went far beyond the formalities of the more serious jazz clubs elsewhere. This desire not only to be different from the madding crowd but to be constantly perceived as different manifested itself in their behavior at home, at school, in the sports clubs, and certainly in public. Appearance and comportment became a ritual that held these adolescents captive. Of utmost importance was dress code. Not short of pocket money, the boys bought custom-tailored suits, sometimes with glen-check patterns, expensive crepe-soled shoes, trenchcoats, and white silk scarves of the finest materials. To lend their garb a British flair, they sported felt or homburg hats and tightly rolled umbrellas, even under the brightest sun. They wore their hair rather long, and accoutrements such as a little Union Jack in the lapel and *The Times* under the arm rounded off the apparel. The gentlemanly countenance of the boys was to be matched by a pronouncedly feminine look among the equally fashion-conscious girls, who wore short skirts, silk stockings, and attractive blouses. Lipstick and lacquered fingernails were the norm. The girls' hair had to be long and shiny; homespun braids and German-style rolls were out of the question.

This dress had to be shown off in public, and so the Swings developed the habit of leisurely sauntering up and down Hamburg's most fashionable streets, typically the thoroughfare Jungfernstieg, in late afternoon during rush hour. To demonstrate solidarity among themselves, they whistled Swing refrains as greetings and spoke to each other in what English they knew. "Hallo, Old Swing Boy!" was a favorite salutation. The richer boys, Kaki in the lead, would drive their cars to and fro, ideally filled up with pretty "Swing Babies." For the evening, assorted groups would repair to one of the chosen hangouts, to enjoy the pleasures of the swing dance and to commune with other Swings, or else to the Waterloo cinema where films such as *Broadway Melody* were shown. Private parties and the clubs also offered amusement. Well-behaved Swings were always home before the parentally imposed, albeit liberal, curfew.[246] King Kaki lived by his own schedule.

Where, then, lies the political import of the Swings? In retrospect, almost all of them have denied a rebellious intention, certainly for this prewar phase. Yet from their reports, however subjective, it is clear that their ostentatiousness was meant as an explicit challenge to a dictatorial regime that punished individualism and rewarded drab collectivism. That consciousness of being superior to the rest of Hamburg's population had of course always been the fulcrum of the Hanseatic patriciate's snobbily relaxed, elitist life-style, without any overt intent to antagonize. Hitler's takeover of power had changed nothing in this regard, even if a few of the municipal plutocrats, like Carl Vinzent Krogmann or the coffee importer C. C. F. Meyer, had joined the rat pack early on.[247] But as the Führer's regime tightened, Hamburg's cosmopolitan haut monde became alarmed. Anglo-American commercial ties appeared threatened, and the mounting anti-Semitism offended the elite's open Jewish propensities. It was in this atmosphere of suspended dissidence that their children, the Swings-to-be, were socialized.

That cohort, born between 1920 and 1925, found itself by the end of 1936 in a situation where official pressure to join the Hitler Youth increased, for Reich

Youth Leader Baldur von Schirach, in an ordinance promulgated on 1 December had stated his resolve that all of German youth henceforth become part of the Nazi organization.[248] This may be taken as the actual birth date of the Swing youth phenomenon throughout the Reich, particularly in Hamburg where resentment in upper-echelon circles already was rife. But Hamburg also had a large proletarian populace whose youngsters resisted HJ pressure to a similar degree, if for different reasons. Thus the unanimous decision of the individual Hamburg Swings *not* to give in to Schirach's appeal in 1936–37 constituted their first, however conscious, act of defiance, and from then on, the dialectic process of reaction and counterreaction ran its prefigured course. "Sailing was more important than Hitler Youth service," as one former Swing has phrased it; the Swings' hedonistic philosophy with its emphasis on fashion, sexual licence, jazz, and the swing dance, was meant as provocation, subliminal or deliberate, against Schirach's equalizers. The latent political tension resulting from this opposition to Hitler Youth service was supercharged in March 1939 with Schirach's announcement that such service would be compulsory, a message which the Hamburg Swings again ignored. Since at the same time they were stepping up their suggestive mannerisms, their situation was precarious and became all the more so, after Hamburg's own swing dance prohibition had descended on them in July of that year.[249]

The cosmopolitan composition of Hamburg's Swings, inasmuch as it reflected the urbanity of their elders, caused a special problem in the Hanseatic metropolis. As in the professional music business, this nourished the xenophobia of the Nazis. Young Hans Engel, the son of an internationally connected travel executive, had returned from New York to Hamburg in 1935; he had several Jewish cousins and attended "Jewish" Marienau for a while. Since this blond teenager's American slang was better than his German and he was able to show off with a knowledge of jazz, he became the idol of his peers. When he poked fun at a Nazi teacher he was almost evicted from school.[250] Axel Springer, in 1938 a junior partner in his father's modest newspaper business, attempted to help their former politics editor, Dr. Hans E. Meyer, who had escaped from Sachsenhausen concentration camp. Meyer was caught and beaten to death, while Springer endured intense Gestapo questioning.[251] Andreas Panagopoulos and Kaki were always suspect because of their non-German status; when Andreas visited England, the Gestapo had him under surveillance.[252] Maurice Thomas was a Belgian citizen who, openly contemptuous of Nazi pomp and circumstances, befriended Hans-Joachim ("Tommie") Scheel. Tommie, at the Gelehrtenschule des Johanneums, demonstratively went to his classes in a white shirt and short pants whenever uniformed Hitler Youth paraded.[253]

It was worse in the case of the non-"Aryans," some of whom, like the quarter-Jewish Madlung sisters, could have opted for total integration into Hitler's *völkisch* community had they been willing to make some concessions. That the Jews had been legalistically defined as racial aliens by the Blood Laws of fall 1935 was bad enough. But to be partially Jewish *and* a Swing became downright dangerous by November 1938, during and after Kristallnacht. On such an occasion Dieter Zimmerle's dictum assumed its terrible meaning, namely that an affiliation with the jazz culture was damaging whenever other incriminating circumstances could be factored into a formula for persecution.

Kaki's future father-in-law Fritz Simon, only half-Jewish but a proclaimed older Swing, was hauled off to a concentration camp and returned with a shaven head before he could emigrate to London. Kaki's best friend, Hajo Hartwig, whose Jewish mother was already in Brazil, was harassed by the Gestapo for purported homosexual offences, a charge he could easily disprove with the help of a throng of "Swing Babies." Nonetheless, during 1939 the secret police incarcerated him repeatedly, sometimes keeping him in a large filing cabinet for hours. Hartwig fled to New York before the war broke out, but not without Kaki's help. He had initially been denounced by a squalid Nazi spy for blaring jazz records at a Swing party in his comfortable apartment, which was also attended by the Madlungs.[254] Another half Jew, Hans Hirschfeld, whose family owned a chain of clothing stores, was on training in Bremen on 10 November 1938, the time of Kristallnacht. Along with other Jews, including his visiting father, Hans was made to run the gauntlet through the length of the town and then thrown into a suburban penitentiary.[255] Like Hartwig, Hans might have emigrated had he known that eventually his father would perish in a death camp. Yet that was at a time when the political dimension of the jazz culture had become infinitely more complex, with a potential for live-saving as well as for nefarious functions that was unfathomed in 1938.

3

Jazz Goes to War
Compliance and Defiance,
September 1939 to August 1942

Demands of the Military

"Jazz is still alive!" agonized a music critic at the height of World War II. Indeed, Nazi faithfuls who might have thought that jazz music had vanished from the Reich could be proven wrong just a few weeks into the war.[1]

These Nazis were deploring a state of affairs which, unbeknownst to them, was in perfect accord with Propaganda Minister Goebbels's own directives. For the sake of social peace, but initially also because the war had been planned as a short interlude, Goebbels conjured up a myth of continuity, of normalcy, from peace to wartime. In order to mitigate the shock of hostilities that clearly were not popular with the vast majority of Germans, anything that reminded ordinary people of a caesura in their daily routines was to be suppressed in order to maintain the illusion of irenic conditions at home and at work. By blanking out the unaccustomed consciousness of stress and pain, the hardships of this new war could be more easily legitimized. Toward that goal, cultural events of all kinds, in content and in form not significantly different from their prewar proportions, would help the propaganda machinery that was busily at work on so many other facets of the nation's collective life. Scores of elegantly written articles in Goebbels's clever wartime creation, the tabloid *Das Reich,* reminded sophisticated readers that "life goes on as does one's work," and that unavoidable deficiencies represented nothing but a new style of existence. "Everything was supposed to remain the way it had been in peacetime," admitted *Das Reich* in January 1941. It was only one year later, after the Soviet Union and the United States had become belligerents, that Goebbels decided to change his tack. Assessing the much more somber public mood, he conceded that now it had become impossible "to play peace." "In two-and-a-half years we have turned into a people at war."[2]

At least until that juncture, all manner of cultural events were encouraged to promote relaxation and pacify the populace. As early as mid-September 1939 a RMK decree stated not only that concert life had to carry on as before, but also that lighter music had to have its place. Goebbels himself reiterated these principles publicly a few weeks later, and in the spring of 1940 the regime prided itself on the existence of no less than three hundred theater stages, eighty itinerant theater companies, and sixty-seven hundred cinemas. A year later the minister pointedly introduced special light-music performances in several of Berlin's beer gardens.[3]

As an integral part of this, Berlin nightclubs that featured jazz remained open as long as it was feasible, even though there were constraints. Among the more harmless of those, at least for the noble establishments such as Ciro, Quartier Latin, Carlton, or Patria, was the deteriorating quality and then quantity of liquor, especially by the time of the Soviet campaign, when caches of captured Polish vodka and French cognac had been spent and home-grown wine was running low.[4] More serious was the sudden necessity of total blackouts at night as an anti–air raid measure. This was enough to induce many patrons to stay at home altogether; and then the police curfew was lengthened by two hours. All cultural events in the land, therefore, started and finished much earlier in the evening, detracting, in Berlin, from the capital's former nightlife glamor.[5]

For a long time, of course, Germany and especially Berlin went relatively unscathed by air raids, a circumstance that aided the entire entertainment industry. It was only in August 1940 that severe British attacks occurred, with appreciable casualties at the end of the month. One of the first victims in the fall was the sought-after jazz bassist Paul Henkel. One day he told his friend Fritz Brocksieper that he had had a dream: a chandelier had come crashing down from the ceiling, narrowly missing him. During the following night a bomb hit his apartment, injuring him slightly. Henkel was rushed to the hospital in an ambulance, but the vehicle collided with another ambulance and Henkel was killed. The eerie tale of the two errant ambulances shocked the capital.[6]

During all of 1940 and 1941, only 448 Berliners died as a result of air raids (but casualties were much higher in more endangered areas such as the industrialized Rhineland). Because the German Luftwaffe successfully warded off British night raiders throughout 1941, Berlin, unlike less protected provincial centers such as Lübeck, Rostock, and even Cologne, enjoyed an ominous quiet during all of 1942. Despite a worsening housing shortage, the capital's population grew by one hundred thousand. Not least as a consequence of that, Berlin's cultural and light-entertainment scene flourished almost without interruption.[7]

The greatest danger to the capital's dance and jazz musicians consisted in military conscription, after some of them, notably drummers Brocksieper and Willi Kettel and saxophonist Eugen Henkel, had been laid off because of a temporary ban on social dancing.[8] If the jazz musicians were not interested in politics one way or the other, anything relating to war certainly was anathema to them, challenging their artistic, carefree ways and acutely threatening their livelihood. Some musicians were drafted right away, others in the course of the early 1940s. In this manner, entire big bands disappeared, such as those led by Max Rumpf or Erich Börschel.[9] A few players, like Swiss-based Ernst Höllerhagen, managed to stay outside the Reich when war broke out; others, such as Hans Berry, returned to Germany later during the war, only to be drafted then.[10] Heinz Wehner's showcase band had difficulty surviving the conscription of so many of its principals, until the maestro managed to save his organization, as well as his own career, by landing a Wehrmacht job at the German military radio station at Oslo in 1941.[11]

Several musicians, though drafted early on, were allowed to work in the capital until they were needed at the fronts: trumpeter Charly Tabor was deployed to Russia in late 1941, and violinist Helmut Zacharias was sent on a less threatening assignment to occupied Holland a year later.[12] Once inducted, musicians and jazz fans alike usually tried for commands with communications units, for those had powerful radios for listening to jazz, and the chances of actually having to use a shotgun were minimized.[13]

Many of Germany's best-known musicians continued to perform in the Reich in various combinations well beyond 1942. Chief among them was trumpeter Kurt Hohenberger, who teamed up with pianist Fritz Schulze and reedmen Detlef Lais and Herbert Müller, and then was joined by Kettel on drums and Walter Dobschinski—the latter a returnee from Switzerland. Hohenberger's combo, really an extension of the now defunct Golden Seven group, played in the well-known Berlin clubs until he was contracted by the Wehrmacht to perform for servicemen in Holland and Belgium, on the French Channel coast, and in Paris, along with Chilean singer Rosita Serrano.[14]

When in Berlin, musicians like Kettel and Lais joined the other Germans still able to enjoy a civilian existence, forming groups in ever changing combinations. Thus accordionist Albert Vossen, tenor saxophonist Henkel, and the pianists Franz Mück and Helmuth Wernicke were very much a jazz presence in the capital during the first two war years or so. More prominent now than even in peacetime was Horst Winter, who knew how to sing but was much more convincing as a tangy swing clarinetist à la Benny Goodman.

Hans Korseck remained the premier guitarist, but ultimately his fate turned out to be a tragic one. As a medical student his conscription was deferred until after his graduation as a doctor from Berlin University in December 1941. In January 1942 Korseck was sent to the Russian front, because physicians were in great demand. But at the same time, the RKK tried to have him returned to the home front, for his superb musical talents were indispensable for Goebbels's propaganda network. On 10 July, as he was serving with a medical unit near Orel, Korseck was informed of his impending return to Berlin the following day. His commander sent him out that night on a final mission and Hans was shot through the head, not yet thirty-one and with a pregnant young wife back home.[15]

But as the ranks of the German jazz musicians were slowly being thinned out, they were replaced in growing numbers by foreign, and often superior, jazz players. The new musicians hailed from countries like Holland, Belgium, and even Fascist-ruled Italy, which if anything had nurtured a more advanced jazz culture than the Reich's. As nationals of countries either allied with or occupied by Germany, they were not subject to the Wehrmacht draft. The great majority came on their own volition, having been lured to the Reich by promises of riches and of fame, though a few had been in Germany before the war broke out.

Whereas Anglophone denizens such as Flemming, Danzi, and Bartholomew understandably had left Berlin by the autumn of 1939, Milan-born Primo Angeli, who had enjoyed a classical conservatory education and already had good dance-band experience, had made it to Berlin in the first half of 1939 and there became an instant success with Eugen Henkel, Vossen, and Brocksieper. Indeed, this thirty-three-year-old pianist rivaled Fritz Schulze in the way he emulated Teddy Wilson, and he soon was a bedrock of jazz in exclusive bars such as Ciro and Königin, as well as in the recording studios.[16] Reed player Lubo D'Orio was a citizen of Axis-allied Bulgaria and had been with the likes of Max Rumpf and Fritz Weber since the mid-thirties. In 1940 he formed his own combo to liven it up in the Berlin Uhlandeck, soon to be notorious for its reckless swing.[17]

Two other superlative Italian players on the scene, working mainly in their own small groups and often with their countrymen, were Tullio Mobiglia and Alfio Grasso, who had come to Berlin toward the end of 1940. Tenor man Mobiglia, a Hawkins disciple, had a sextet in the manner of Hohenberger, which by the fall of 1941 was blowing up a storm in the Patria and Rosita bars and in the officially suspect Kabarett der Komiker. Mobiglia featured all the American swing standards such as "Honeysuckle Rose" and "Lady Be Good," sometimes superficially concealed under German captions.[18] Grasso was a multi-instrumentalist who excelled on tenor sax and guitar and became prominent in Berlin's West End bars by early 1942. Judging by critical reports of soldiers who sampled this sextet in the Patria, it was probably the best small jazz formation active in the Reich at that time. One telltale sign of this, so it has been said, was the absence of any sheet music whatsoever, signaling the sextet's complete ability to improvise on any item of the rich American repertoire.[19]

The most important big bands of the era, however, were led by Dutch and Belgian musicians. Eddie Tower, Jean Omer, Stan Brenders, and Fud Candrix were all from Belgium, and Ernst van't Hoff was from Holland. Pianist van't Hoff had a fifteen-piece band, mostly of fellow Dutch artists, but he also was known to employ Germans such as reeds specialist Herbert Müller. Until early 1942 he toured larger German cities such as Dresden, Düsseldorf, Frankfurt, and Stuttgart. However, after he performed concerts in the Swabian center, the Gestapo, wanting his band proscribed, accused him of having offered "wild or Jewish hot music." Goebbels's RMK knew better, however, and forestalled the indictment. Thereafter, van't Hoff was entrenched at Berlin's Delphi-Palast, to the exhilaration of hundreds of soldiers home on furlough.[20]

Many judged tenor man Fud Candrix from Belgium an even more exciting bandleader than van't Hoff. Candrix followed the Dutch orchestra leader at the Delphi in April 1942 and stayed until August, playing mostly for Wehrmacht personnel, who had to be in uniform to ensure entrance. Candrix's group of fourteen instrumentalists and a female singer had, like van't Hoff's group, total control of American jazz standards in up-to-date arrangements. Superficially, it was a carbon copy of the classic swing and already postswing formations from across the Atlantic.[21] Compared with the élan of van't Hoff and Candrix, the main three surviving German big bands of Kurt Widmann (who continued to hold forth in Berlin's Imperator), Georg Nettelmann, and Erhard Bauschke at the Moka Efti had to be considered strictly second-rate.[22]

In general, then, this was not a good time for the German jazz community to produce new native talent, or to let the old one grow—but there was one significant exception. This was Helmut Zacharias, the blond prodigy fiddler of the prewar years. In 1940 he was twenty years old and still a conservatory student of the classics. But word had gotten around about his fabulous seaside resort exploits of the years before, and so Helmut found himself sitting in with Horst Winter or Fritz Brocksieper in the Carlton or Ciro bars, until his doting mother forbade it. Later in the year, Zacharias was approached by Odeon records, and in November he made a small-group recording with Ernesto Romanoni, another expatriate Italian. He played hapsichord, because, as the string virtuoso recalls, "hapsichord and violin, that sounded fantastic, much better than with piano." That particular swing disc, with a tune composed by Theo Mackeben, vaguely in the tradition of the Quintet du Hot Club de France, was a novelty that became a huge success with the central Berlin and sundry Wehrmacht radio stations, and today it is regarded as one of the all-time classics of the European swing era.

Zacharias moved on to further recordings, with Georg Haentzschel and Hans Klagemann for instance, and in 1941 was a member of Lubo D'Orio's group. During this period, also, he was locally drafted, but still enjoyed leave to play. In 1942 he was posted to Hilversum, the Dutch radio center, and as a member of a Wehrmacht music corps he carried on with his art, mostly entertaining soldiers and some knowing Dutch fans.[23]

In terms of musical quality, Zacharias's uncontested originality notwithstanding, the German jazz players were now being eclipsed by the foreign musicians in their own land. At best, the natives remained passable imitators. Zacharias himself had borrowed his sound—as had the two or three guitarists in his band (Grasso being one of them)—from the Paris Hot Club's Stephane Grappelly and Django Reinhardt, respectively, and the novelty hapsichord timbre was obviously reminiscent of Artie Shaw's previously formed Gramercy Five.[24] The advantage of the Dutch and several Belgian big bands over comparable German formations consisted in American arrangements (Candrix evidently preferring Count Basie's), in a more felicitous instrumentation that shunned continental accordions and saccharine violins, and in a frankly, sometimes audaciously American repertory. The discipline of these Northwestern Europeans, especially in brass or reed section-playing, was exemplary, verily Anglo-Saxon in nature, bearing a strong resemblance to the technique of Jack Hylton and Henry Hall, the Britons of yesteryear. And if the solo work of the Dutch and Belgians, by technique, intonation, or melodic fluidity, was hardly superior to that of the Germans, the Lowlanders' sense of dynamics certainly was.[25]

The Dutch and Belgians, as well as the Italians, were demonstrating that the best of their German colleagues, be they in large or small formations, could hardly improve upon the standard, however high that had been, which they had achieved for themselves in peacetime, and now again were falling behind the rest of Europe. While Höllerhagen's clarinet performance got remarkably better as he was freely honing his skills in the haven of Switzerland, the once respectable competence of trumpeter Hohenberger, pianist Schulze, or drummer Brocksieper became arrested at its 1939 level. Psychologically if not physically more restrained than the reckless foreigners, who had no stake in a German fatherland and were not threatened by military conscription, the Reich natives succumbed to the seriousness of the martial environment and, heeding some RMK warnings, kept reins on their playing.

This constraint precluded opportunities for conceptual and technical advancement that ordinarily reward the wholly unfettered artist. Hence German improvisational lines of the early war years today sound timid, if not insipid, without the freshness acquired in a less confused society before the conflict. Innocuous German compositions such as "Men Are Worthy of Love" replace the previously favored American standards; accordions increasingly obfuscate a potentially pure jazz quality; heavy rhythm-guitar strumming overturns preexisting instrumental balances; arrangements appear flat as if memorized by rote. More seriously, careless synchronization by the rhythm sections conveys a feeling that the bane of German jazz, the dreaded "um-papa" sound, is creeping back in, as is audible in Kurt Hohenberger's 1941 piece "Improvisation." Sweet violins are overbearing, especially in big bands; impromptu solos give way to mindless, mechanical riffing; and the overall rhythm is thumpy and choppy. Worst of all, vocalists warble mindless lyrics to indelibly trite melodies.[26] What was happening here was that at a time when social dancing was intermittently prohibited, mere dance music, paradoxically, once more tended to assume the place of jazz.

It is instructive to juxtapose the indigenous German as well as the Reich-co-opted output with developments in jazz in the United States at that time. On 11 October 1939 Coleman Hawkins, recently returned from Europe, made music history with his recording of "Body and Soul," a tour de force of a solo improvised, in front of a mediocre septet, over sixty-four bars. Apart from pure musical invention, an unerring sense of pulse and time, and sheer beauty of tone, the element characterizing this creation even more than other contemporaneous American works was a sublime sense of transparency and relaxedness. This was the obverse of the frenzy that even the Belgians mistook for dynamics, and hence for swing.

Some of these spellbinding qualities are also obvious in the seductive "Moon Glow," recorded on 23 January 1941 by the maturing clarinetist Artie Shaw and his big band, with sparse piano and unobtrusive rhythm guitar and a quietly urging solo by the trombone. Some eight weeks later "Slow Down," recorded for Decca, surprised listeners with Nat King Cole's harmonically advanced piano styling and Oscar Moore's linear solo on *electric* guitar, which Reinhardt had never even used. Before that, the Nat Cole Trio had recorded "Sweet Lorraine," with Moore's guitar ending the song on a ninth chord with a flatted fifth, thereby anticipating bebop, with its more systematic emphasis on polyrhythm and chromaticism.

Finally there were Duke Ellington's epochal big-band recordings during the banner years 1941–42: the economy of the instrumental voicings, the translucent piano-comping of the Duke behind the solos, the unassuming yet strident rhythm guitar of Freddy Guy, the taut but never overbearing drum work of Sonny Greer! It is enlightening to compare Ellington's "C-Jam Blues" of 21 January 1942, which slowly builds to a sonorous climax after imaginative solos by Ray Nance, Rex Stewart, and Ben Webster, with the unstructured "Farewell Blues," recorded by Candrix in Berlin in April 1941, which shows off competent riff-playing and scorching clarinet and trumpet solos, but also oppressive drums. Candrix, in turn, wins after contrast with Kurt Widmann's messy "Hot Days" of November 1941, a blues in which twelve bars of solo are rattled off, one after the other, by trumpet, alto sax, piano, and so forth, backed by the chronically plonky rhythm guitar.[27]

Whatever the quality of their music in comparative terms, Candrix, Widmann, and van't Hoff were meant, by the propaganda ministry, to entertain the troops home on furlough, or those stationed in Berlin on a more permanent basis. Naturally, the capital's entire character had changed because of that strong military presence.[28] Enlisted men and officers in uniform enjoyed priority for admission to the mass concerts staged by the big bands in the Imperator, the Delphi, or the Femina, but those former dance establishments had now lost their original purpose: for men in uniform dancing was prohibited. The small bars, however, such as Carlton and Rosita, which featured combos such as Hohenberger's, Vossen's, or Winter's, still were exclusive enough not to countenance a uniformed presence at all. Wehrmacht aficionados who patronized them had to come in mufti.[29]

Goebbels not only allowed such exploits but, within limits, actively encouraged them, for, as much as he realized the need for mollifying the civilian population, he valued the spiritual well-being of the armed forces even more. There were two reasons for his attitude. On the one hand, he was a frustrated would-be fighter of World War I who had been prevented from entering battle by his deformed foot. Hence he identified very closely with true warriors, onto whom he projected his own personality. On the other hand, his policy toward the military was guided by the same cool considerations as that toward the public at large, which were valid even in peacetime: the more satisfied the soldiers were, the better they would fight for the Reich. This combination of private sentimentalism and sheer expediency dictated the minister's actions in making cultural events serve the martial requirements of the regime, and ironically, his conduct once again came to benefit jazz music.[30]

Goebbels realized his plan to humor the soldiers on a regular basis through a scheme called *Truppenbetreuung,* or troop entertainment, for soldiers at all levels of culture, whether they were formally educated or not, and irrespective of their degree of sophistication and taste. After a series of agreements between the propaganda ministry and Robert Ley's "Strength-through-Joy" organization, German artists, both male and female, were contracted to go on special troop entertainment missions, at first to home military bases, but increasingly to the occupied countries, such as France, Holland, and Norway.[31] Thus the Berlin Philharmonic Orchestra could be sent out, or a well-known municipal theater company, but also trapeze artists, comedians, and popular entertainers from screen and radio for purposes of a variety show. Remuneration, at up to RM 100 per day, was extremely generous; yet the real incentive for male artists lay in the possibility of avoiding conscription, for as long as their talents were needed.[32] For women, excitement and camaraderie with men beckoned, as did the possibility of seeing strange places, and sometimes the satisfaction of fulfilling a patriotic requirement. These junkets, soon under the personal direction of Hans Hinkel, remained welcome adventures as long as the German armies were victorious and safe. After the Nazi invasion of Russia in June 1941 this changed, however, for now the entertainers were often operating in the front lines, and they could always become targets for partisans. There were unforeseen accidents, too, as on the Mediterranean front, where one stage actor was seen to slip from a cliff and drown in the ocean.[33]

Goebbels knew well that the soldiers, enlisted men and officers alike, loved rhythmically accentuated dance music that covered the spectrum from badly performed amateur stuff right to the most proficient swing of a Wehner or a Hohenberger. As much as the minister disliked the pure-jazz extreme, it was difficult for him to draw a line between it and officially acceptable "German" dance music, and so the military fronts ended up indulging in whatever they wanted. Goebbels also knew that his commissioned artists were performing, technically speaking, in the jurisdiction not of his ministry but of the Oberkommando der Wehrmacht (OKW), or Armed Forces High Command, where his prerogatives were limited. Specifically, civilian RMK controls may have been of little consequence in the Reich, but by setting the mood they did serve as a psychological damper on jazz musicians that kept them from cutting loose, and in combination with other checks they were a nuisance, if not worse. These controls were totally absent from the casinos and officers' messes of the Wehrmacht, with the result that true jazz musicians could play unrestrained. Even the pompous Hinkel had to resign himself when he chaperoned Fritz Brocksieper's combo to a Channel coast concert. After announcing to the troops that Jewish and Anglo-American tunes were off limits, the men bombarded the general secretary with apples. Hinkel beat a hasty retreat, and the band churned itself into a frenzy over "Bei Mir Bist Du Shein."[34]

Understandably, in 1940–41 it became the declared aim of virtually every German dance and jazz musician to enter the troop entertainment ranks in order to save his own skin. Men of military age might attain a special civilian status (*uk-Stellung*) that allowed them to make contractual arrangements for a number of tours. Others, like Zacharias or Wehner, were in the employ of Truppenbetreuung even after their conscription. None of them knew, of course, when such a relative privilege might end and a gun would take the place of the saxophone or trumpet. For a very few, it seems to have lasted indefinitely, as it did for Kurt Widmann, who was popular with various encampments. To all intents and purposes, by 1943 Wehner's big band was safely locked in at Oslo. Fritz Schulze briefly joined him there, after stints with Otto Stenzel's orchestra in occupied Poland. But while Stenzel himself managed to repair to Fascist Spain in that year, Schulze was drafted after all, as was his old friend Hohenberger; both men saw combat until the end of the war.

Earlier, Brocksieper had been ordered to report to the garrison, near Berlin. When the final drill approached, the drummer swallowed a medication that induced vomiting just as he was standing at attention for the sergeant's inspection. What a scene, with the sergeant's uniform soiled! Brocksieper was dispatched to a Berlin hospital, where he malingered as an ulcer patient until his artistry was again called for elsewhere in the capital. Meanwhile, his original platoon had stepped onto a mine field on the Eastern front and all of his comrades were killed.[35]

It would be a legitimate if not entirely flattering generalization to say that German jazz musicians were cowards because the war robbed them of their freedom to engage in artistic expression. In the case of their fans, matters were more complicated. Jazz aficionados could not claim a need for artistic freedom in order to indulge their passion, even if they were loath to take up arms, especially for a Fascist regime. Yet some of them do not seem to have minded the potential for active combat, which may have been wholly in accordance with their pre-1939 patriotism.

Dietrich Schulz-Köhn volunteered for officer training even as a university student in 1937–38, during semester holidays; this way he could choose the service most congenial to his temperament. As a lieutenant second-class, he opted for the artillery because his nationalistic father had also been a cannoneer during World War I. Officer status meant prestige and social standing to this upwardly mobile young man; now he was again in charge. Did he find this detrimental to his jazz pursuits? Not in the least, avers Schulz-Köhn, for the more liberal forces tolerated and even aided his tastes, and opportunities for purchasing rare or forbidden jazz records abounded when he was stationed in occupied territory. In fact, "if you wore a uniform, this was like a protecting shield." For the first two years of the conflict, the young doctor of economics found himself deployed in Nazi-governed France, with plenty of chances to visit his venerated jazz clubs in Paris, which continued, some under cover, or by special German license.[36] Schulz-Köhn was no war monger; still it is true that once on call for his country, even a National Socialist one, the lieutenant did not shirk duty and eventually earned himself two medals. In his worldview, this was compatible with jazz.[37]

Some members of the Leipzig Hot Club, who were not as well educated or as aware as Schulz-Köhn, reflected even less on the possible compatibility of jazz with Fascist, aggressive warfare. Because of his fair knowledge of English, club chief Kurt ("Hot-Geyer") Michaelis was drafted early in January 1940 and sent to an air reconnaissance unit to intercept and decrypt British aviators' radio messages. Evidently he had never replied to a pensive statement from his New York pen pal Henry Sklow, who, in the last few days of August, when war was imminent, had sent a letter to Hot-Geyer to excuse his recent silence. Apologetically, the Jewish dentist wrote, "I don't want you to feel that there might be differences in political opinion which kept me away because I really feel that two souls like ourselves with such a common decent interest as swing know of no barriers. When it comes to art, and swing is an art, there are no lines." If anything, Hot-Geyer concurred, for whenever he was not deciphering English code, he was listening to the British swing bands with his earphones, utilizing the powerful Wehrmacht receivers on the sly. In June 1940 Michaelis was in Aarhus, Denmark, and then at various Norwegian bases. There, too, he visited the small-town shops and profited from the ready availability of jazz records, including valuable vintage discs from America and England. Hot-Geyer shipped them home by the sackful.[38]

Michaelis's best friend "Fiddlin' Joe" Frommann, now thirty-four years old, even assumed the life of a sybarite. Stationed, like Schulz-Köhn, in occupied France, but evidently endowed neither with the integrity that characterized the serious Dietrich nor with his puritan morality, the convivial Frommann unabashedly regarded France as a playground, and one that fulfilled his long-standing passion for jazz music. Indeed, if ever jazz was consumed as an apolitical, hedonistic commodity by anyone, it was then. And a jazz life-style had its side benefits. In the fall of 1940 Frommann reported from Rennes in the crass vernacular of the soldier: "Recently, this has been all we care about: what do you eat, who do you lay, where do you go on Sundays?" Having gotten used to the mode of Paris Hot Club saxophonist Alix Combelle, he had bought his records and those of Benny Carter, too. Half a year later, in Paris, he could nightly listen to Combelle in the flesh, sample the visiting Hohenberger combo, and rub shoulders with Fritz Schulze and Delaunay and Schulz-Köhn. To the background sounds of "Linger Awhile" his pen rhapsodized: "To do whatever one feels like, to live into the day without a care, just living, loving, hotting it up, would you believe it: I never had it so good even in civilian life." His hot-buddy Kurt believed it.[39]

Not everyone in the Leipzig circle had such an easy time. Their half-Jewish friend Heiner "Fats" Kluge had been inducted as an orderly somewhere, and nothing was heard from him. Another friend, whom they had named "Hot-Ibsen," also was silent now; he was stationed in Russia.[40] Unquestionably, in terms of a high life with wine, women, and jazz, the Eastern front compared to France and its fleshpots as Purgatory would to Paradise.

Several or Werner Daniels's Düsseldorf jazz compatriots also ended up in the inhospitable East. Private Daniels himself was in Dessau and then in Jüterbog near Berlin, where in the fall of 1940 he began a jazz newsletter to be sent, in several carbon copies, to his comrades all over the war arena. The entire 250-page document, preserved from autumn 1941 onward, is proof that while the Düsseldorf circle did not revolt against the inevitable fate of being drafted, it employed a cautiously critical approach to the Hitler regime. Part of this approach involved jazz, of whose precarious position it was acutely aware. Many of the news items were couched in ironic, even self-deprecating language; the bulletin itself was given the unassuming title of "Musikalische Feldpost" (Musical Field Post) so as to fool possibly malevolent censors.[41] Even granted the circumstance that military monitors were far less severe than party or police controls, Daniels and his friends were taking some risks in associating themselves in writing (they used their own signatures) so openly with a music that was, after all, more than ever identified with the British enemy and his American allies, among them blacks and Jews.

In addition to his core group of former Düsseldorf jazz club members such as Gustav ("Oliver Kingston") Königstein and Theo ("Wilson") Hoeren, Daniels managed to acquire new disciples, some of them active musicians, such as Hans Kolda, a reed player once working with Corny Ostermann. Perhaps the most significant manifestation of this clique's deep-seated skepticism concerning the war and its Fascist perpetrators, apart from the sometimes scathing jargon, was the lack of interest by any of these men in advancement to officer's rank: "We did not want them and they did not want us," states Daniels; the Hitlerites had realized "that we were not firmly rooted in the soil of National Socialism." Men like Daniels were considered a liability; they could not be trusted as officers. "In any case, we were known for our love of the blacklisted jazz."[42]

Editor Daniels signed each of the bimonthly circulars with a strongly etched "Heil Hitler!" and reproduced reviews by his pals. From Holland, Private Theo Hoeren sent his impression of the record "Black Boy Shuffle," by the Jewish Artie Shaw, "which cannot be purchased for love or money"; but Hoeren was hoping for a tobacco exchange with the shop owner. Corporal Hanns J. Maassen wrote from Bremen that he had enjoyed the persiflage in the "Feldpost" defining all swing music lovers as criminals. "I now feel like a traitor." And compiler-editor Daniels himself mocked the black creators of their cherished jazz pieces as "disgusting fellows in shirt sleeves and suspenders"—among them Chu Berry, the composer of everybody's favorite, "Christopher Columbus." There were timely columns on who played what jazz where, especially back in Berlin and the occupied Western countries, and readers traded tips regarding the best locations for rare and modern American discs. Not all the news was funny, useful, or sarcastic camouflage, for the close-knit ranks of these fans were being depleted. Thus in mid-February 1942 Daniels had to report the death in the field of Friedel ("Teddy") Korte and Heinz ("Chicken") Küster. Virtually every one of these friends could be the target of an enemy bullet the very next day.[43]

Daniels and his clan were on the borderline between compliance and resistance in a strong-arm regime that spurned their medium of cultural identity: American jazz. Yet by participating in the war effort, as the good Germans they considered themselves to be, they never did cross that borderline. To a large part because of prior sociocultural conditioning, other jazz enthusiasts, when put to the test, either resisted conscription or, in the manner of Fritz Brocksieper, devised means for escape.

Trumpeter Carlo Bohländer, transfixed by images of live New York jazz and the individual freedom this signaled, was inducted into the Wehrmacht in early October 1940. Chronically underweight, Bohländer thought of one ruse after another just to get an honorable discharge. Never having left for the front because of a combination of real and imagined ailments, he was finally dismissed in November 1942 and returned to his native Frankfurt. Hans Otto Jung's will to survival and his firm inner opposition to the Hitler state were also aided, paradoxically, by his failing health. Because of his ever-recurring lung disorder, he was home in Rüdesheim already in early 1940. Günter Boas of Dessau opted for medical studies in Berlin in order to avoid the barracks; there he was with a Jewish girlfriend who was later killed in a death camp. Berlin's Hans Blüthner, long a foe of the regime and under suspicion by the authorities because of his friendship with non-"Aryans" like Franz Wolf and Gerd Peter Pick, conveniently skidded on ice in March 1940 and broke his arm; from then on he was grounded at home.[44]

Yet another category of jazz followers could not escape the draft, whatever their excuse, and they lived dangerously. Soldier Joachim Ernst Berendt, whose father was in Dachau, kept a low profile merely to get by, first in Holland and then on the Russian front. Pick, called up for military service at first as were many half Jews, and stationed in occupied France, was at risk for his racial background *and* the Muse he cherished. On New Year's Eve in 1940 he was sent back to the capital as someone not worthy of the German colors; there he faced an uncertain future that could include forced labor. Arguably, ill-tempered Dieter Zimmerle fared worst of all. In late September 1939, twelve days into his term with the forces, he was court-marshaled for having been involved in the beating of a drill sergeant, whereupon he was dispatched to France and Russia, always in and out of punitive battalions. It was only in rare, stolen moments that this singular dissident in a Nazi tunic was able to listen to jazz records, which kept him going to fight another day.[45]

Jazz as Propaganda

As Joseph Goebbels had already discovered before the war, he was facing a grave problem in utilizing radio for totalitarian propaganda: that countries unfriendly to the Reich would rival his efforts in the use of cultural idioms such as music to captivate German listeners. For the minister, this difficulty was immensely compounded after 1 September 1939. Goebbels became acutely aware that the British were in a unique position to manipulate German audiences through their programming, for three reasons.[46] First, they alone among Germany's enemies still went undefeated at a time when broadcasting stations in France, Luxemburg, and the Lowlands already could be controlled by the Nazis. Second, the British knew how to transmit news, both in English and in German, that was eagerly sought by certain members of the Reich's populace, including Wehrmacht personnel. And third, London's information programs were often packaged with attractive music in order to catch the Germans' ears, music that was difficult if not impossible to tune into on ordinary Reich stations. Such music, of course, was of the Anglo-American dance and jazz genre.

In fact, London emitted a variety of signals perilous to the Nazi regime. By January 1940, the "British Expeditionary Forces Programme" was broadcasting jazz on standard wave; although aimed at British soldiers stationed in France under Lord John Gort, it could also be picked up by the stronger German receivers. On the eleventh, for instance, Henry Hall had a "Guest Night" spot, but there were also news and a sequence called "The Shadow of the Swastika." Sounds by Bert Ambrose rounded out that Thursday's offerings.[47]

As the Battle of Britain escalated, London founded various propaganda stations broadcasting from the United Kingdom with the aim of demoralizing German civilians and soldiers alike. The most notorious of these were Gustav

Siegfried Eins (May 1941) and Soldatensender Calais (fall 1943), the latter of which came to beam a lot of jazz. But the BBC itself transmitted an alluring mixture of jazz music and news in English; moreover, there was a special German-language program ("Bush House") featuring news items mixed with swing performed live by current British groups, such as the impressive Royal Air Force Band, under the baton of Dietrich Schulz-Köhn's paragon, Spike Hughes.[48]

Even though Goebbels had prohibited Germans from listening in on any foreign stations by an ordinance on 1 September 1939 and had begun to enforce this with draconic punishment, he was plagued by constant infractions from among the Reich's subjects. On one hand, the British and some other enemy stations easily penetrated the Nazi broadcast network because of locally wavering German signals and intermittent shutdowns owing to anti–air raid precautions. In this situation even the cheap *Volksempfänger,* the "people's receiver," proved ineffective, although it had been designed to keep German listeners tied to just a few, standard-wave Reich stations.[49]

On the other hand, English programs were simply too attractive for inquisitive German listeners to shun. Original Anglo-American dance and jazz music held a fascination for droves of Wehrmacht soldiers on the various fronts who were always close to a radio, be it their private small Philips receivers or the more powerful army equipment. Goebbels found it alarming that such jazz broadcasts were invariably followed by news. And at home, the already existing jazz fans found the music and the news equally intriguing; worse still, Germans initially interested merely in BBC news might become addicted to the hitherto neglected jazz. And what jazz there was out of London! During the first years of the war, for example, Hans, a Hamburg Swing boy inducted into the Wehrmacht, was able to listen to recorded Gershwin standards, but also other tunes such as "All the Things You Are," played by Henry Hall, and "I'm Nobody's Baby," performed by Harry Roy.[50] In 1943 the BBC estimated that between one and three million Germans were tuning in to its special programs for the Reich, at one time or another.[51]

Additional foreign sources of American jazz were Dutch, Belgian, French, Danish, and Norwegian radio stations, even after Germany had been victorious on those fronts. But Goebbels was less concerned about them because no anti-German newscasts were connected with their programs; Berlin had granted relative cultural freedom to the subdued broadcast stations on condition that they censor their contents. Still, this self-censorship was less than perfect. Hence certain of Hilversum's programs, even if they were never as good as those from London, became very popular with civilian and Wehrmacht jazz aficionados. Copenhagen and some French stations followed well in line.[52]

In Germany itself, Goebbels gained twelve million new native-language broadcast listeners between 1933 and 1943, owing, in part, to the regime's imperialist ventures, for instance the Austrian Anschluss. Already in 1941 the Reich possessed the largest number of listeners in absolute terms; in all of Europe, the rate of listeners per capita was superseded only in Sweden and Denmark.[53]

With this enormous mass-media potential on hand, Goebbels had to maneuver carefully to find the right balance between pure indoctrination and entertainment at all levels of intellectual comprehension, for the sake of public morale. Moreover, once again he had to choose carefully between the demands of the military and the civilian population, for their tastes in radio did not always coincide, and he was coerced into adjusting his programming to the competition posed by enemy—particularly British—radio stations. Altogether, it was an excruciating task to be maintained for the duration of the war with the aim of helping the "Final Victory," and in the course of this jazz music again made further gains, inadvertently and sometimes imperceptibly.

To all intents and purposes, German and foreign jazz had been banned from German air waves since Hadamovsky's spiteful decree in the fall of 1935. Because of the deteriorating international situation, musical programming fell behind other broadcast content, especially news, after 1937. This tendency was naturally aided after the outbreak of war in September 1939, with quantities of music now on the blacklists. By May 1940 Goebbels had realized that in keeping with the live cultural scene, changes in the direction of greater choice, with a premium on entertainment, also had to be initiated in radio. His veteran broadcast staff toiled as best it could to accommodate the minister's demands.[54]

Then, in October of that year, the Wehrmacht leadership passed on to Goebbels a timely reminder that the popularity of the British stations among many soldiers, with their crafty mix of swinging music and news, was posing an increasingly hazardous predicament for the Nazi war effort. It took the propaganda minister until the spring of the following year to contemplate more radical changes for his broadcast schedules, including the insertion of more "rhythmic dance music," even though he privately as well as publicly still abhorred "distorted rhythms" and "atonal melodies."[55] One week before the Nazi invasion of Russia, Goebbels, in a famous lead article published in *Das Reich,* reaffirmed that the taste of Wehrmacht personnel had priority over that of the civilian population, while asserting that "at war, we need a people that has managed to preserve its good humor."[56]

At this point Goebbels was intelligent enough to know that with the old radio cadres, largely trained under the crude Hadamovsky and the stuffy Glasmeier and hostile to more modern programming concepts, he would not be able to overhaul the broadcasting engine. At the risk of courting the illicit, he needed proven experts who were in touch with popular trends, who were efficient in their work habits, and, most important, were unobstructed by the blinkers of Nazi ideology. More likely than not, the new men would not even be members of the Nazi party or any of its formations, and they would not be in the sworn corona of "Old Fighters" who had helped the Nazi movement to power.

Hence between October 1941 and February 1942 a fundamental reorganization of the standard German broadcast system, the Reichs-Rundfunk-Gesellschaft, took place, supervised closely by Goebbels and administered, on a week-to-week basis, by his experienced aide, RKK secretary Hans Hinkel. Radio recreation, a Nazi opiate for the people, was accorded a new official preeminence. Ten innovative groups were formed, each to be directed by undisputed specialists in their fields: the conductor Rudolf Schulz-Dornburg as head of classics, the popular sportscaster Heinz Goedecke for troop entertainment. Late-republican jazz pianist Franz Grothe, who along with Peter Kreuder and Theo Mackeben had meanwhile become one of the leading composers of light music, especially for films, and was personally acquainted with Goebbels through the movie industry, was placed in charge of more sophisticated popular music such as operetta. Significantly, Grothe had his old friend Georg Haentzschel, who was steeped more heavily in the jazz milieu, appointed as head of Gruppe A, "light dance and entertainment music." What exactly the circumstances of this appointment were and whether Goebbels was fully cognizant of its long-term implications still has not come to light. But it is virtually certain that Goebbels knew of Haentzschel's qualifications and that therefore he approved of Grothe's choice precisely because he was painfully aware that for the moment, more "rhythmic music" was called for.[57]

Notwithstanding the fact that common folk, often in rural areas and small towns, had already complained about too much jazz programming on the German air waves, Goebbels's measures opened the door to more of the blacklisted music. To be sure, so as not to invoke unnecessary wrath from the broad majority of listeners, Haentzschel and his colleagues avoided labeling it "jazz."[58] One of the immediate consequences of the policy change was that early in 1942, the moderately swinging big band of Willi Stech, cofounder of the Golden Seven, was becoming more prominent. It was lodged at the long-wave station Deutschlandsender and, under party member Stech, provided protection and employment to a number of Berlin's finer jazz musicians, such as drummer Brocksieper.[59] In March Goebbels himself, commending the soldiers he so admired, managed a rather more conciliatory public statement regarding broadcast jazz, in which he conceded that rhythm is a "basic element of music," while still maintaining that "badly squealing instruments" were contemptible.[60] Now it was obviously up to Haentzschel to figure out how to create a new reprieve for the music he had helped to develop in his youth.

Goebbels knew that Wehrmacht personnel would be especially grateful for the results of the changes he had initiated. Since the beginning of the war, he had been constantly reminded of the special needs of the armed forces in radio entertainment. In his programming policy toward them, he soon found himself between the devil and the deep blue sea. Whereas on the one hand he donated thousands of radio sets to soldiers on the fronts to make their lives more bearable as well as to render them more susceptible to his own propaganda, on the other hand he could not prevent the fact that it was the soldiers more than anyone who continued to breach his dictum that no one listen to foreign stations other than those on conquered soil.[61]

To help resolve the quandary, Goebbels made several broadcast decisions with chiefly the soldiers in mind—decisions that would not, however, offend the civilian population either. Early in the war he created a regular Sunday program called "Wunschkonzert," something like a high-class hit parade, which featured popular songs and easy classics by well-known artists chosen according to soldiers' opinion charts. The music was interspersed with personal messages from family members, from the Reich to the front; names were mentioned; donations of clothing or foodstuffs were announced. The smoothly competent moderator was Heinz Goedecke, who, significantly, assumed official responsibility for the troops' radio entertainment in 1941–42.[62]

Typically German-style dance music had some place in these programs; jazz had virtually none. That became more the specialty of the new-style Soldatensender, or armed forces radio network, established by the Wehrmacht with the assistance if not always to the satisfaction of the propaganda ministry. Those stations soon existed wherever the Germans had taken control: Oslo and Bergen in Norway, Poland, the Balkans, and in conquered Russian territory. Knowing that 50 percent of all conscripted men had approved of modern dance music just before the war, some of the stations went a step further and, to the delight of jazz purists, broadcast the best quality of native-made jazz they could find.[63]

And so in the fall of 1941 Sender Weichsel was known, among aficionados, to spin swing records all day long, even those of British dance-band leader Harry Roy. Heinz Wehner's big band soon reigned supreme in Oslo. The station in Minsk, too, was a favorite with lovers of the swing genre. Sender Belgrad especially was known for its dance music and could, like some of the others, be monitored from certain corners of the Reich, to the excitement of homebound jazz fans.[64]

Still, Goebbels was not yet satisfied with the degree of psychological control over the army that he had achieved by mid-1941. It was at this time that he was painfully reminded that his most cherished martial heroes, the pilots, still were in particular danger, because their urbanity, their knowledge of English, and their legendary penchant for swing music inevitably laid them open to British propaganda during air combat over the Channel and in North Africa. Goebbels had been enchanted with airplanes and their pilots for a long time, since the republican "Time of Struggle," and during the initial air bouts against England he had come to marvel at the feats of air aces Adolf Galland, Hans-Joachim Marseille, and, especially, Werner Mölders.[65]

Dedicated Glenn Miller fan Mölders, at twenty-seven the most celebrated pilot among Göring's men, could never get enough of old-style jazz and swing. He and his comrades would frequent the Savarin, a special hangout near the Eden hotel, close to the exclusive bars in Berlin's West End, where they could enjoy their drinks to the sound of the choicest jazz records.[66] And when they flew out on their dangerous missions, they regularly listened to their favorite music on the British stations. Mischievous wits claimed that they would soar toward the BBC in order to bomb it into the ground, but not without making contact with its airwaves beforehand. The fact was that having missed their targets, they could take in the British news as well as the music on their retreats home.

At any rate, the often-told story has it that one day in the winter of 1940–41 Colonel Mölders was relaxing from his strenuous career in Zürs in the Austrian Alps. In the comfortable ski lodge on Lake Eibsee he happened upon Franz Grothe, who was vacationing there with his wife, the Norwegian singer and film star Kirsten Heiberg. Urged on by Mölders and his comrades, the famous Grothe sat down at the piano and offered his interpretation of modern swing. Enthralled,

Mölders confided to him that if only the German stations were broadcasting decent music in the American style, then Luftwaffe pilots could stop tuning in to the BBC. In principle, this was no problem, replied Grothe, since there were many musicians in the Reich capable of such music. Mölders and Grothe then conspired to lure Goebbels into establishing a special German big band for that purpose.[67]

By all the accounts, it was Mölders who approached the minister, on a routine occasion, probably in the early spring of 1941. And although the main onslaught by the German flyers against Britain was over in March of that year, and thereafter the Luftwaffe's energies were to shift more to the newly opened Eastern front, Göring's pilots could still pick up British radio signals during flights over the Balkan and North African war theater and, of course, also still in Western and Northern Europe. Hence Goebbels personally warned his radio staffers that increasingly, Luftwaffe personnel were listening to "racy music" from England; something drastic had to be done.[68]

The result was meticulous planning for yet another German-type jazz orchestra—after the much earlier demise of the Golden Seven, the Reich contest fiasco of 1936, and Oskar Joost's abortive proposal—which began in September 1941. That this planning coincided with the revision of the German civilian radio program was no accident, for Goebbels purposely wanted to take advantage of his two experts there, Grothe and his friend Georg Haentzschel. Indeed, it was these two proven musicians, indomitable followers of jazz, who were jointly put in charge of setting up a state band, the Deutsche Tanz- und Unterhaltungsorchester (DTU), or German Dance and Entertainment Orchestra, under a label Goebbels himself had chosen and once more with the organizational assistance of the resourceful Hinkel. The new orchestra was to be formed from among the best dance and jazz musicians in the country, men who in extreme cases might have to be requisitioned from the Wehrmacht. The band's status was to be highly official, comparable only to the Berlin Philharmonic in the classical sector, all of whose principals had been declared indispensable. Remuneration and living expenses were to be generated by the Reich finance ministry, and at more than a million marks per year, were more than generous; altogether, the DTU was supposed to be of such high musical quality that it would not only divert the Luftwaffe's (and other military units') attention from the British influence but satisfy civilian jazz friends as well.[69]

The recruitment of the best German musicians for the DTU occurred chiefly in the early months of 1942 and was complete by about 1 April, when the band staged its first rehearsal at the Berlin Delphi-Palast. "I would have run for my life, to be declared exempt from military service," said Hans Klagemann later; he was lucky enough to be signed on as one of the band's two percussionists, and indeed, given the characteristic aversion of jazz artists to the military, the DTU came to be regarded as a safe haven for jazz musicians and their art.[70] Grothe, Haentzschel, and their most intimate friends from the golden days of German jazz made the preliminary selection. Then RKK secretary general Hinkel managed the actual requisitioning, which was arduous at best, for some men, like guitarist Hans Korseck, were already in the army (and he had the bad fortune to die just before he was slated to join), while others, for example Willi Berking and Albert Vossen, were employed by Berlin organizations such as authorized theater or Varieté bands, which themselves claimed inviolability.[71] Others again, like twenty-two-year-old violinist Helmut Zacharias, then still stationed in Berlin, would have come, or at least his protective mother would have wanted him to, but the Wehrmacht gave him no leave.[72] As Hinkel's struggle for the best players became more frustrating, Goebbels himself intervened, and by the summer the Reich's swing elite was on a new bandstand, by the grace of the propaganda minister and subject to future good behavior.[73]

The list of these highly privileged musicians was impressive by German standards. On drums were Klagemann and Waldi Luczkowski, the latter of Golden Seven fame. Franz Mück played the piano, and on bass was Rudi Wegener. Some of the other known names—several from Stenzel's former Scala band, and from theater, radio stations, and film studios—were reedmen Herbert Müller and Detlef Lais; trombonists Erhard Krause, Walter Dobschinski and, of course, Berking; Kurt Hohenberger's Scala brother Karl on trumpet; and the temperamental Russian Serge Matul on guitar. Arrangers were the legendary Horst Kudritzki, also from the Scala, and Friedrich Meyer, a twenty-seven-year-old pianist originally from Bremen, an old friend of Gerd Peter Pick's from Berlin record shop and studio days and eminently eligible for the position because a head injury precluded his fighting at the front. Whereas Grothe was the musical director who, because of his many other responsibilities, acted more like a figurehead, Haentzschel did the day-to-day conducting, especially during studio rehearsals.[74]

After the war, Haentzschel and Klagemann both assured me that politically, no pressure was ever applied to those bandsmen, and that the two conductors themselves had seen to it that the DTU remained a virtually nonpolitical preserve just for art's sake.[75] This is not the entire truth, however, for two musicians were certified party members and one of these had been planted there as Goebbels's political stooge. Whereas Wegener was a harmless nominal Nazi who had joined, like countless others, in the spring of 1933, the violist Hermann Däubner had a proven right-wing record. An anti-Semitic Sudeten-German Austrian and a hater of the Czechs, he had been an illegal Nazi party adherent in clericofascist Austria and, after coming to the Reich, joined the storm troopers and then the German mother party in 1938. He was, remembers Klagemann, by far the worst musician of the lot.[76]

The DTU instrumentalists received comparatively large salaries—eleven hundred marks on average—which was in keeping with top compensation paid to leading entertainment stars in the Reich, but in this case also reflected the representative character of the venture. Georg Haentzschel alone was making seventeen hundred marks a month, plus two hundred for each publicly conducted performance, beyond the two thousand he grossed as Gruppenleiter A in radio.[77] In those times, a skilled German worker was earning over two hundred marks monthly.[78]

The symbolic character of the band was to manifest itself, by the original plan, in festive performances for regime ministries and authorities, not excluding

Hitler himself, and, of course, for the Wehrmacht. The band would also—after the Final Victory—represent Germany abroad and produce film scores and radio recordings. (In this sense it was to fulfill a function similar to Stalin's ill-fated State Jazz Orchestra of the 1930s, which was also a model band.[79]) But these latter ventures were peripheral, for the primary purpose of the DTU was, after all, to satisfy the Wehrmacht, in particular the pilots, with a kind of rhythmical music they could accept, and then, in a wider sense, to fulfill the long-standing dream of creating a paragon of specifically German jazz sound for the public and all dance bands at large.

This aim meant assuming the heritage of Oskar Joost. Significantly, that society bandleader had attempted, half a year before his death in May 1941, to revive his plan of a Nazi jazz band, with less than enthusiastic support from Hinkel.[80] Still, this explains why Joost's erstwhile band manager, the émigré Russian Sergius Safronow, became the business director of the DTU in May 1942. Since Safronow was also a confirmed, card-carrying Nazi, he was able to supplement the political control duties of the violist Däubner.[81]

As it turned out, the DTU gave extremely few public performances, for it was much too busy recording music on a newfangled "Magnetophon" tape recorder from Holland, to be broadcast by all the Soldatensender and civilian stations at select hours. The band did not even cut commercial records.[82] Naturally, the pilots were important; on one occasion, Goebbels himself, whose personal interest in this orchestra never abated, took twelve highly decorated Luftwaffe fighters along with him to one of its regular rehearsals.[83] As the big band settled into its weekly routine at the Berlin studio, it found ways of compromising with the regime. On the one hand, it remained on the edge of the comfortable, sweetish kitsch the Nazis liked to pass on as "German Jazz." On the other hand, Grothe and Haentzschel, realizing the tremendous pure-jazz potential that existed for the band by virtue of the qualified players involved, moved into the true modern idiom whenever there was a chance, if only for a few bars at a time. The resulting mixture was indeed a curious one, and the content dilution or distortion of basically good sound frequently was so penetrating that the post-1945 musical critique has been quite controversial: anything from "un-German swing" to "very, very tame."[84]

Predictably, the stalwart German jazz fans did not like the DTU.[85] The sound of strings abounded, and improvisation by solo players was all but absent. Yet the custom-tailored arrangements of the oftentimes mediocre German melodies by jazz experts Kudritzki, Adolf Steimel, and Haentzschel himself were swinging to a fault, even though not a single American title was allowed and the wartime standard of Widmann and Wehner, let alone the Belgian bands, was never reached.[86] For the time being the authorities were satisfied—what with rave reviews from Fritz Stege!—even though the Luftwaffe aces are on record for requesting a studio rendition of *Rhapsody in Blue* by Gershwin and departing disappointed when this was ignored.[87] As far as Grothe and Haentzschel were concerned, however, they had saved many of Germany's best jazz musicians from going to waste at the fronts; moreover, they had provided for them a secure income with the opportunity to hone their skills in an almost acceptable fashion.[88] Nevertheless, the moral implications of being a state jazz orchestra, really at Goebbels's bidding, could be bothersome to the more scrupulous.

One musician with whom Haentzschel had worked off and on in the studios and whom he had asked to come along was Fritz Brocksieper, the Munich swing drummer. Brocksieper told him that he was engaged in another musical mission for the Reich and that besides, the proposed orchestra would probably not swing stirringly enough for him.[89] Since early 1940 he had in fact been playing in an outfit named Charlie and His Orchestra, a special combination of sterling jazz players called together by Goebbels's ministry in the service of Nazi propaganda abroad. Charlie's Orchestra came to constitute the most bizarre phenomenon both in the history of Nazi popular culture and the Reich's strenuous propaganda effort. It was an attempt to reverse the damage done by the BBC to the Germans with their broadcasts by paying the enemy back in kind: American-type jazz was to be thrown back to the British Isles from Germany in order to confuse the king's loyal subjects. The orchestra was part of the grotesque "Lord Haw-Haw" scheme.

Would-be Oxford actor and onetime compatriot of the British Fascist leader Oswald Mosley, William Joyce had begun to broadcast pro-German commentaries, with an impeccable British upper-class accent, by mid-September 1939. His base was the German short-wave station on Berlin's Kaiserdamm, not far from the West End club scene. The entire program had been initiated by Wolf Mittler, a tall blond German from Poland who had a weakness for sports cars and women and who had learned his Oxford English while on an extended prewar stay in British elite schools. He was initially assisted by another British Nazi collaborator, onetime captain Norman Baillie-Stewart, who already had spent five years in the Tower of London for treason and, disgusted, had made off to the Continent in 1937. By August 1939 Baillie-Stewart had settled in Berlin; both he and Mittler ministered English broadcasts before the war began. But by the end of September it was clear that Joyce, originally a backup man for Baillie-Stewart, was more effective than the other two, and by January 1940 at the latest he was anchored at the British Desk and already well known in London as "Lord Haw-Haw."[90]

Goebbels got to love the Irish Joyce, particularly since, increasingly, this former British Fascist propaganda chief was wont to write his very own commentaries and did so with a sardonic verve that the minister admired so much in George Bernard Shaw. American correspondent William L. Shirer, who in the fall of 1940 boozed an air-raid night away with the alcoholic Joyce, found him "amusing and even intelligent," if an unreconstructed anti-Semite and reprehensible in a personal sort of way. Goebbels knew what he was doing in keeping this man on the job; in January 1940 already more than six out of ten Britons were listening to foreign broadcasts, with three out of ten turning to the English-language programs of German provenance.[91]

In January 1940 the directors of the short-wave station had the ingenious idea of adumbrating Joyce's anti-British vitriol, which was centered on the alleged corruption of Winston Churchill and his "Jewish" camarilla, with saucy sketches staged by professional actors capable of English jargon and catchy, unadulterated jazz of the kind the British were so used to. The music was meant as a bait. Goebbels and his team had no qualms over the fact that this latest idea would be thoroughly out of character for a well-aligned network that had actually been lauded abroad, from Cape Town to Vancouver, for its rejection of the universal "jazz fad."[92]

For reasons not yet clear the thirty-eight-year-old Lutz Templin, a relatively minor saxophonist originally from Düsseldorf, who had been playing with his own small group in and around Berlin for years and who was not even a party member, was commissioned to build up a versatile jazz band that could handle the most demanding tasks. Templin chose as his drummer the much-vaunted Brocksieper, who early in 1940 happened to be playing at the Carlton Club with Horst Winter, Detlef Lais, Charly Tabor, and Willi Berking. Eventually the core band that was connected with Joyce's broadcast "Germany Calling" later in the year comprised sixteen musicians, but others could be requisitioned as the various programs demanded it, so that it was possible for as many as forty men to perform in the short-wave studio at one time. Charlie's Orchestra was a "mixed bag," remembers Brocksieper; musicians as diverse as Helmut Zacharias, Albert Vossen, Franz Mück, and even the half-Jewish singer Margot Friedländer helped out over an extended period.[93]

Obviously, the premier players were getting very scarce and now had to be shared by the official agencies in accordance with their daily needs. By the end of 1940 the first foreigners had been signed on: Primo Angeli, who became the regular pianist; the Italian trumpeter Giuseppe Impallomeni; and the Dutchmen Barend ("Bob") van Venetie and Tip Tischelaar, who played saxophone and trombone, respectively. As Germans like Tabor were drafted and others such as Berking, Mück, and Vossen were shunted off to the DTU, more foreigners had to be hired, always Belgians, Dutch, and Italians: Mario Balbo on reeds and Cesare Cavaion on bass, for example, or Alfredo Marzaroli and Rimis van den Broek on trumpets. Yet as long as the DTU was stationed in the capital, personnel crossover was fairly common, especially to assist in putting some 270 titles on shellac recordings, in carefully limited editions, for eventual paratroop distribution behind British enemy lines and in German POW camps filled with English soldiers.[94]

Charlie's Orchestra was loosely integrated into Joyce's regular programs as a lavish extravaganza, with musical instruments of the finest quality being supplied by the propaganda ministry and, as in the case of the DTU later, grand salaries accruing to the artists. Brocksieper somewhat implausibly claims to have earned as much as five hundred marks a day, most of which he used to finance ever scarcer luxury provisions for himself and his small family (at rates that demanded something like thirty-five marks for a pound of butter on the black market by 1941, with genuine coffee costing twice as much). There were up to five expert and similarly high-paid arrangers for the band, among them Friedrich Meyer, who penned special charts based on stock arrangements of current American swing tunes and older evergreens procured at the highest level through neutral channels in Portugal or Sweden.[95]

These arrangements were thought, by Templin and his men, to be the most dazzling musical scores in the Reich at that time, and they were, of course, totally clandestine. The attraction for the British, especially the servicemen whose morale was to be undermined, was meant to be original modern jazz, played so well that Anglophones would have to think the programs came out of England, or perhaps neutral Scandinavia.

As a pièce de résistance, and not without a large measure of arrogance, Goebbels's staff designed songs that at first hearing sounded like jazz standards or evergreens in a jazz vein; they were vocalized in English by Karl ("Charlie") Schwedler, a shadowy official from the propaganda ministry. To maintain the enigma, the orchestra took Schwedler's name rather than using Templin's. No one knew Schwedler's true identity; Private Werner Daniels, having picked up the program one Saturday evening in March 1942, still thought the singer was Horst Winter.[96]

For his performances, Schwedler was handed the original text of an American standard, its first stanza to be sung straight to the swinging accompaniment of the band, whatever its size. At least in the second stanza political satire would replace the original; it was aimed invariably at Churchill, British "money bags," the Soviet ally (after June 1941), the U.S. friend, and, of course, the Jews; in short, the whole stock-in-trade of Goebbels's anti-British stereotypes. Conversely, Nazi Germany's military might was extolled. As far as his musical ability and pronunciation were concerned, Schwedler strutted his stuff in an almost professional fashion, but anyone listening more closely would be embarrassed to discover his German origin. In addition to all this, the orchestra tried to present well-arranged jazz that featured not only suitable accompaniment but acceptable solos as well, in unmitigated swing style, by any of the accomplished players.

A typical text rendition would be the following, based on "Onward, Christian Soldiers," and vocalized to that very melody:

"Onward conscript army,
You have nought to fear,
Isaac Hore Belisha,
Will lead you from the rear.

Clad by Mounty Burton,
Fed on Lyons Pies,
Fight for Yiddish conquest,
While the Briton dies.

Onward conscript army,
Marching on to war.
Fight and die for Jewry,
As we did before."

Speculation has it that Haw-Haw might have written all this. In another typical parody on the standard "I've Got a Pocketful of Dreams"—Long-Lease was already in place—the last few lines instruct the listener, "[I'm] Gonna save the world for Wall Street, / Gonna fight for Russia, too, / I'm fightin' for democracy, / I'm fightin' for the Jew."[97]

These songs were made to alternate with Haw-Haw's harangues and political skits, done by the actors in front of microphones, of the kind Brocksieper described to London journalist Michael Pointon in his broken English two years before his death: "Churchill are sitting in the bathroom, the water, and then comes a minister. He said, 'Ah, Mr. Churchill, we got bombed out, so many ships again . . . ' And so Churchill said, 'Give me a whiskey and cigar'—in the bathroom, you know, he lay in the water, like this kind of cabaret they make."[98] Each of those theatrical programs, together with the music, could last up to twenty minutes, and about four per day were made, first weekly and then six days a week; presumably Joyce later edited these recordings to fit them into his speeches.

Templin, Brocksieper, and their friends do not appear to have been the only jazz musicians in the Reich who were cynically used in the service of the propaganda ministry, nor were England and the POW camps, via radio or records, their only targets. In Berlin it was hoped that the short-wave signals would be picked up in the United States, and some of these broadcasts were beamed toward neutral Portugal, perhaps with the aim of catching some of the many unsuspecting foreigners passing through there at the time. Moreover, jazz that was specifically arranged in the Latin style à la Xavier Cugat was directed to South America, most certainly in conjunction with Spanish-language commentaries.[99]

And in April 1942 a rare event happened in Berlin: Fud Candrix's big band staged a public performance at the Delphi, introduced by none other than Lord Haw-Haw himself, replete with personal greetings from English prisoners of war to their families, who were mentioned by name as was the custom on "Germany Calling." Candrix was encouraged to play the steamiest jazz possible, and he obliged with the "St. Louis Blues," an Artie Shaw arrangement of "Begin the Beguine," then very much in vogue, and Chick Webb's chart of "My Heart Belongs to Daddy." According to one listener from among Werner Daniels's Wehrmacht circle who monitored this later on the German military station in Calais, the live audience's applause was "frenetic."[100]

In evaluating this odd music and its originators, one can make judgments using three criteria: artistic-aesthetics, efficacy, and morality. From an aesthetic vantage point, Brocksieper always maintained that with regard to technique and content, this jazz was at the peak of the art in the Reich. "We made the best music at this time," he told Pointon, and taking into consideration the resources in 1940–43 and the official constraints still in effect for other bands, notably the DTU, there is no question that he was right. Brazen solos by the likes of Tabor, Angeli, Impallomeni, and Brocksieper bear this out, as is apparent from reissues of some of those rare singles.[101] With the possible exception of Mobiglia and Grasso, who had the added booster of live public support, there was no better quality swing being played in the Third Reich in this period.

On the other hand, the postwar caveats of experts like Emil Mangelsdorff, the experienced musician, and Werner Daniels, the seasoned fan, must be heeded. Whereas Mangelsdorff has compared the music of Charlie's Orchestra with the contemporary American style and rightly found it wanting, Daniels has emphasized that in absolute terms it was really only pianist Primo Angeli who was outstanding, an opinion one would tend to agree with after listening to some random samples.[102] By April 1942, at any rate, Hans Hinkel for one was being plagued by doubts as to whether "copies of specifically British or American music" were entirely appropriate for Anglophones, since Germans were not truly at home in these idioms.[103]

In assessing the effectiveness of Charlie's jazz with the target group, one has to take into account the fact that the music could never stand alone, but always had to be heard in juxtaposition not only to political skits, but also to propaganda flashes in the "songs." Chiefly because of those two extraneous factors, but also because the actual singing by Schwedler was not up to universal jazz standards, the overall musical quality of Templin's combos as jazz formations consistently sustained serious damage. Inasmuch as Goebbels thought that his Haw-Haw programs were a terrific success because Hitler himself understood this to be so, Brocksieper, too, believed until his death in 1990 that the quality of his jazz was superb not only on a national, but also on an international level, in the degree to which it feigned Anglo-American origins.[104]

On both counts, this was a delusion. The British listened more to Joyce's broadcasts because the names of freshly captured Allied soldiers would regularly be spelled out, while at the same time they found Haw-Haw's bathos amusing, if not a nuisance. The humor of the skits alternating with Templin's pieces was heavy-handed in the Teutonic manner, certainly not with the typical British tongue-in-cheek or understated style. And the same goes for those witty songs of Charlie Schwedler.[105] Thus it comes as no surprise that English prisoners of war, who were given copies of the records, broke them to pieces after fair examination on German-provided gramophones.[106]

The ethical consideration in this case is the most difficult. It is clear that the messages against England and her Allies were hateful not only because of their belligerence, which is to be expected in war, but also because of their racism and in particular their anti-Semitism, which was the loathsome specialty of the National Socialists. Was it right for jazz musicians of Brocksieper's stature to prostitute their music, the creation of blacks and Jews, in the service of the dictatorial regime?

Whenever confronted with this issue, Brocksieper has argued that doing what he did constituted the lesser of two evils, the greater having been the danger of the military draft for all those musicians. In addition, he claims that as a quarter Jew he was more acutely at risk than the co-opted foreign colleagues.[107] While these twin arguments have some validity and certainly hold up to the rationalization used by Haentzschel and Grothe for the DTU, which posed much less of an ethical problem, it has to be recalled that Brocksieper himself eventually could not avoid conscription and most of his German comusicians were ultimately replaced by foreigners, until only four or five of them were left. As for Brocksieper's further explanation that he did not comprehend the nefarious texts of the songs or the skits (he never really had the opportunity to listen to Joyce), it is even less creditable. For the Dutch and Belgians almost certainly understood English and must have translated the material for him and the others, such as the Italians, who possibly did not know the language.[108] Even less tenable is the drummer's final contention that in terms of money alone, the regime had made him an offer that he could not refuse.

If one were concerned with the fate of jazz in the Third Reich, without considering the persons who played it, it might be legitimate to say that any means necessary for the preservation or even the development of this music in times of duress would have to be countenanced. But this thesis is based on strictly aesthetic grounds without any heed to ethics. It touches on the present debate about the history of the modern professions in Germany. Today there is consensus that professionalization, for instance of physicians and lawyers, should be accompanied by moral responsibility.[109] If this standard is applied to musicians in the Third Reich, then it becomes clear that performing their art in the service of tyranny was indeed immoral. The example of Charlie and His Orchestra demonstrates that jazz in Germany was given a chance to develop as an art, and yet its conversion into a tool of Fascist propaganda and ultimately aggressive war made it suspect as a vocation.[110] In principle, this occurred in the same manner, albeit not to the same degree, that medicine became criminalized in the concentration camps. The jazz musicians were hardly exempt from blame as collaborators, no matter how small their degree of compliance.

The War Inside the Great Germanic Reich

Joseph Goebbels may have supplied certain segments of the population as well as the military with jazz, a tonic they needed in times of stress in order to function as required. But these exceptions did not change his opposition to this music: essentially, he wanted it destroyed. As a clever strategist, however, he stated this aim only very rarely. One such occasion was in August 1942, six months after Germany had declared war on the United States, the source of that cultural flotsam. In characteristically contemptuous fashion, Goebbels reiterated his long-held view that America possessed no indigenous culture. "Everything is borrowed and perverted through Americanization." And he charged that Americans were capable of "converting a mature language into slang, and of turning a waltz into jazz."[111] In practice this meant that while protected musicians with *Truppenbetreuung,* the DTU, or Charlie's Orchestra did not have too much to fear, unless they stepped far out of line or had to be drafted after all, various agencies, including Goebbels's own RMK, tried to move up their campaigns against the jazz culture as much as circumstances would allow.

This made for a continuation of that double-edged policy already observed by the regime in the prewar era: reluctant tolerance on the one side and recriminations on the other. Such an approach did not constitute a split national consciousness, as Hans Dieter Schäfer suggested several years ago. Rather, both attitudes were strangely, albeit involuntarily, complementary, as were so many seemingly antithetical phenomena in that curiously riven dictatorship, in which preordained policies coexisted and momentarily clashed with ad-hoc improvisations.[112]

Nowhere was the admixture of goal-directed planning and subsequent involuntary abrogation more apparent than in the area of social dancing. The vacillating regime ordinances passed from September 1939 on reflected once more the insecurity of the authorities concerning the balance between bread and circuses and total entertainment abstinence that would best serve the war effort, but they also reflected the fortunes of the war itself.

The regime began with a complete ban on public dancing effective 4 September 1939, which contributed to the dismissal of several jazz musicians from the clubs until the courts had ruled in their favor. However, by the end of the month this had been modified to the effect that dancing was forbidden only before 7:00 P.M., probably because the government had quickly learned to adjust to necessary blackouts, which turned out to be rather infrequent, and because in line with Goebbels's policy on entertainment, there was no need to upset the population unduly. This explains why most of the Berlin jazz clubs and dancing establishments were able to resume their operations almost as in peacetime and continue in this way for many months. But when the Phony War was over by 10 May 1940, Goebbels, out of his deference toward the soldiers now busy defeating the Northwestern continent, reinstated the general indictment against public dancing. However, since the soldiers back home on furlough were the first to suffer from this, the policy was again modified in July 1940 to allow for dancing on Wednesdays and on Saturdays. This caused confusion among some civilians who could not appreciate the soldiers' needs. Until now, dance and jazz musicians had been in fairly regular demand.[113]

When the extended Battle of Britain commenced in earnest in August 1940, Goebbels saw no alternative but to reintroduce the blanket dance ban because of the increased need for nightly blackouts as an anti–air raid measure. But the public mood, and especially that of the soldiers, was so much against it then that Goebbels was impelled to make yet another alteration in December: public dancing was to be permitted three days a week. The correctness of his decision was borne out by the observations of one of his *Reich* reporters, who noted in March 1941 that "never has there been more passionate and more inspired dancing anywhere in the Reich than during this past winter."[114]

By now Goebbels had acquired some expertise in manipulating the social dance as a tool of public control. Dancing was again forbidden in conjunction with the German offensives in the Balkans. But this was once more reversed a few weeks later, on 10 June, to fool both the enemy and the German people about the impending invasion of Russia, because, as Goebbels slyly suggested in his diary, where there was levity, no offensive could be suspected. Nonetheless, as soon as the Wehrmacht had crossed the Soviet borders, dancing was blacklisted again.[115]

And this time, because "Operation Barbarossa" turned out to be no blitzkrieg, the ban remained in effect and was even reinforced in January 1942 when semiprivate dance activities, for example by sports clubs, were prohibited as well. In broadcast planning Georg Haentzschel was compelled to remove from the studio turntables records with texts that encouraged dancing, at a time, ironically, when he was just taking charge of the so-called German Dance and Entertainment Orchestra.[116]

Dance and jazz musicians were kept busy during many of these months, but in 1941–42 things were getting palpably tighter for them. Significantly, this was also a period when more of them were beginning to be signed up for active duty, as happened to Charly Tabor, and later to Kurt Hohenberger and Fritz Schulze. Moreover, for independently employed jazz players more decrees were put in place than ever existed in peacetime, and they tended to be more tenaciously enforced. Goebbels used the authority of Raabe's RMK to clean up English-language texts completely, so that eventually it became impossible to sing in English, the vernacular of the enemy, even in refrains. Unless extremely well camouflaged (as by Mobiglio and Grasso in the Patria), the melodies of original American jazz standards could no longer be played either, which explains why more and more of the inane German numbers were being performed and why they, and not the incomparable American evergreens, were consistently being recorded. By April 1940 every new composition along with its text had to be submitted to the RMK for examination, and could be entirely censored.[117]

In August 1941, moreover, the RMK issued what once again came fairly close to an actual prohibition of jazz music, which could be circumvented only through the musicians' knowledge that RMK spies like Erich Woschke still had not advanced their jazz know-how and were inept at detecting the genre: "hot and swing music in the original or copied . . . degenerate music by Jews and Negroes." Nonetheless, Woschke and his jazz policemen not only were making their rounds of the Berlin clubs and bars as usual, but they appeared more oppressive and relentless, so that the ever dwindling number of jazz musicians also took them more seriously.[118] There were corresponding RMK enforcers in large cities such as Hamburg and Frankfurt.[119]

For practical purposes, two qualifications that had been absent before the war now determined live jazz music. Although theoretically the foreign co-opted bands, such as those led by Grasso or van't Hoff, could play more recklessly because their members did not have to fear conscription (only expulsion or jail at worst), in reality they had to be more careful; precisely because of their known proclivities, they were singled out for controls and could be suppressed. Hence a Belgian scat singer was silenced by the RMK for spouting English jargon, and Grasso and his comusicians were jailed for thirty-five days for having overdone it with the "Tiger Rag."[120] No wonder that one day in May 1942 an old German swing fan in uniform was flabbergasted to find the spectacular orchestra of Fud Candrix holding forth in Berlin's Delphi, as demure as a church choir. It had just been reprimanded by the RMK.[121]

The other new danger was that the often toothless measures by the RMK now tended to be interfered with, or superseded, by the secret police, which was starting to take a special interest in foreigners like D'Orio and van't Hoff. Heinrich Himmler's Gestapo did not bother much with any decrees that might have been promulgated by Goebbels, Raabe, or anyone else, for it was guided by the SS's ideology, which inveighed very broadly against anything or anybody connected to Jews or jazz. Journalists Fritz Stege and Herbert Gerigk had done their indoctrination in Himmler's broadsheet, *Das Schwarze Korps,* long enough and fairly persuasively. The activities of swing-inspired youths in Frankfurt and

Hamburg soon prompted the secret police to commission specialists such as Heinz Baldauf and Hans Reinhardt (whom we will meet again later), and in 1941 a Gestapo seminar in Berlin deliberated on more effective tactics in combatting jazz. Musicians who flaunted their swing or misbehaved in other ways, perhaps in a drunken stupor, could be certain to face the Gestapo, over and beyond whatever the RMK had in store for them.[122]

After 1 September 1939, regime controls extended to musical records as well. During much of that month companies like Brunswick and Electrola still advertised prewar productions such as those by the American orchestras of Tommy Dorsey and Artie Shaw, and the English bands of Bert Ambrose and Ray Noble.[123] Although there was as yet no blanket prohibition against enemy English records, international companies had to stop importing them from London forthwith (though not yet from the United States).[124] English records were indicted selectively according to the confused, incomprehensible criteria of the RMK; for example, they banned all recordings by British trumpeter Nat Gonella, who was neither black nor Jewish. Included on that early September list were also some German and U.S. productions by Americans, such as the Jewish Charlie Chaplin's cocreation "Swing for Sale" on Odeon and Cole Porter's "You Never Know" (RCA Victor).[125] Spurred on by an officious polemic against "every English dance record and every English jazz music" in the official *Völkischer Beobachter* early in 1940 and by an article lambasting the general dearth of musical talent among the English, the RMK issued a second listing of forbidden records on 15 April 1940, which, among others, mentioned the standard "Frankie and Johnny" on Telefunken.[126] It was around this time that the Golden Seven combo, which had successfully marketed records with Electrola since 1935, was finally dissolved, because its Anglo-American renditions had been just too insidiously popular.[127]

With vicious polemics against jazz continuing, as in an article by a small-town music director entitled "The Jazz Bacillus," the authorities proceeded to rout record collectors. For Berlin, Goebbels initiated searches of places like the recreational Wannsee lake area where "English gramophone records" might be surreptitiously spun by alleged war shirkers, who were to be inducted immediately into punitive Labor Service details. Pianist Fritz Schulze, then still traveling on *Truppenbetreuung* business, in 1941 was hauled out of a train by SS men who had caught him listening to Tommy Dorsey and Benny Goodman sides on a portable. He explained that as a professional he needed this music for practice purposes and, after all, he had no idea that Goodman was a Jew; at any rate, were these not American artists, or was the Reich at war with the United States? This particular excuse, that one had been listening to "American" rather than "English" music, often saved record lovers from more dire consequences.[128]

Things took a turn for the worse after the United States entered into the war in early December 1941. All the previous stereotypical arguments against America and its degenerate Jewish–Negroid culture now were magnified and systematically disseminated by Goebbels's propaganda apparatus, for instance *Das Reich*.[129] Logically, this invective soon targeted "uninhibited jazz sounds" and the rhythmic fever of "swing."[130] The Nazis released a propaganda film called

"Around the Statue of Liberty," which showed generous scenes with American swing bands. These scenes were meant as a deterrent, but ironically, jazz aficionados in all the metropoles rushed to watch this movie, often more than once.[131] And then, in February 1942, the propaganda ministry finally issued the first blanket indictment of all records originating in enemy states or containing compositions or renditions by enemy musicians; this unmistakably included all jazz recordings from the Anglo-American countries. Also forbidden was the performance of all live American music in the Reich.[132]

Threatening the habits of the jazz listener was a much sharper proscription of enemy radio monitoring, with penalties ranging from jail to penitentiary and concentration camp, and ultimately to the death sentence. This proscription manifestly included tuning in to foreign music, not just news, which for jazz fans came mostly from the BBC. Indeed, the BBC surmised that by 1943 there were up to three million Germans who checked out its stations at least some of the time. Transgressors were typically caught by Nazi party block wardens, minions such as apartment building janitors who spied around assigned street blocks and reported anything suspicious to local party headquarters, which would then notify the Gestapo.[133] For the balance of 1939, there were 36 convicted radio offenders, but that annual rate had jumped to 985 for 1942. Although Goebbels did not implement the death sentence until the spring of 1941, most of the population were reportedly already terrified in January 1940.[134]

For the remaining foreigners and non-"Aryans" connected with the jazz culture, life became increasingly hazardous. Probably the last alien jazz musician to leave Nazi Germany was American guitarist Mike Danzi, who was harassed before he and his family could sail for New York, with difficulty, in October 1939.[135] While quarter Jews like Brocksieper and Hans Berry were apprehensive about their safety in the Reich, even though they knew that by the Nuremberg Blood Laws of 1935 they were not in immediate danger, reedman Eugen Henkel was half Jewish and was, in fact, drafted out of Charlie's Orchestra.[136]

Half Jews were treated quite capriciously, according to demand. Singer Margot Friedländer, who had received admission to the RMK sometime in the late 1930s, was evicted again in February 1940, only to be reinvited in August 1941, probably because of the general scarcity of entertainers; she was soon needed for Truppenbetreuung.[137] After his discharge from the army by Christmas 1940, which had been anything but "honorable," record expert Pick briefly returned to Televox, only to be fired because of his non-"Aryan" status. He then worked in a scrap yard to escape from the Organisation Todt, which was wont to requisition half Jews for physical labor toward the armament effort. All the while, his father was still hiding in Berlin-Grunewald as a Jewish "U-boat."[138]

There were even full Jews who performed jazz illegally at great risk to their lives. One was Hanns-Joachim Bessunger, originally from Darmstadt, who moved to the anonymity of Hamburg's St. Pauli red-light district after his father had been murdered in Buchenwald in early 1940. There he played swing piano in various disreputable clubs, such as the Regina, usually protected by prostitutes who warned him whenever Gestapo men in their notorious leather coats approached. Just in case, he had with him a faked RMK license that he had received through his demimonde connections. After the war Bessunger found out that the guitar player he had been working with was also Jewish and had safeguarded himself with false papers as well.[139]

Coco Schumann was working in Berlin. Off and on he played guitar, with the likes of Tullio Mobiglia, Primo Angeli, and Helmut Zacharias, in some of the newer and more clandestine clubs such as Gong and Groschenkeller, in their enforced simplicity a far cry from the secure elegance of a Carlton Club or Sherbini. At times the altruistic Hans Korseck would join him to show him a chord or two. Schumann, who was sixteen in 1942, was a brazen young man; his mother was Jewish, which by the Blood Laws made Coco a full Jew. As a young teenager Coco had always regretted this status; he had been envious of the Hitler Youth and had wanted to be one of them. Now he was working quite recklessly without any RMK legitimation whatsoever, and leaving the obligatory yellow Star of David at home. But he knew that with his blue eyes and regular Berlin street accent no stranger would ever take him for a Jew. Still, in 1942 when the Berlin Jews were already being deported to the death camps, the devil was daring him. One night an SS officer entered his club and walked up to the bandstand. "You should arrest me, Sir, for I am under age and Jewish to boot," the precocious youngster challenged him. The SS man looked at him in disbelief and then laughed heartily. It had been a good joke.[140]

Schumann's and Bessunger's experiences were extreme cases of musicians in concrete danger. Other players were at least potentially threatened. All this happened as a result of the publication of the *Lexikon der Juden in der Musik,* a book that identified Jews in German music in the manner of Hans Brückner's earlier volume, but was much less amateurish and therefore acutely dangerous. Written by the music critics Herbert Gerigk, an SS official working for Alfred Rosenberg's office, and Theo Stengel of the RMK, the book appeared in 1940, officially backed by the Nazi party, and was subsequently reissued in revised editions in 1941 and 1942. The 1942 version claimed to be able to unmask Jewish musicians of all genres who were still active in the Reich—under disguise.[141]

The handbook also mentioned partially Jewish musicians, and if they were linkable to the world of jazz, their careers if not their lives could be in jeopardy. One such professional was the serious-music composer Boris Blacher, who had a Jewish grandparent and was repeatedly accused of proximity to jazz. Thus in December 1940 Fritz Stege wrote in an influential journal that his compositions were lacking in substance. While Blacher was promising, he now should make up his mind what he wanted to do with himself, for he was too much influenced by jazz.[142]

Dance and jazz musicians with Jewish spouses also had to be watchful. Hans Bund, for instance, who was well known around the Berlin studio scene and associated himself with such orchestra leaders as Otto Stenzel, had a Jewish wife and in 1939 had been contemplating emigration to Australia, without success. Thereafter, he was constantly beset by a Nazi colleague who attempted to take advantage of his situation.[143] In the spring of 1942 the Dutch singer Anny Xhofleer was denied a work permit by the RMK because she had briefly been married to the German-Jewish expatriate pianist Martin Roman, before her country's invasion by the Germans. And Berlin's versatile Otto Fuhrmann, whose piano-playing encompassed a variety of styles and who was called upon by many local groups, in July 1942 merited an entry in the Gestapo files to the effect that "he has been married to a Jewess and in Berlin has repeatedly rented rooms from Jews." Fuhrmann was given no particular credit for the fact that he had already divorced his Russian-Jewish spouse, the bar pianist Faina Saponitzkaja, in 1933.[144]

For those followers of jazz who found themselves in some conflict with the regime after September 1939, there was little solace short of emigration, which was impossible now. Yet there existed one small island of refuge to which they could turn on occasion, even though this was occupied, ironically, by a formal member of the SS. Dr. Johann Wolfgang Schottländer was a musicologist at the Berlin conservatory who had joined the Nazi party in 1933, and the SS a year later. At one time his research had been financially supported by the so-called Ahnenerbe foundation, Himmler's pseudoscientific academy. But after the beginning of the war, he and the SS "Ahnenerbe" were quarreling, and it may well be that spiritually Schottländer had already removed himself from the goals of the Nazi movement. Having become a specialist for film music, he was employed by Goebbels's ministry in the early 1940s to help the minister perfect movie technology, for which he so envied the Americans. It was Schottländer's job to screen American films and examine them, for their music or otherwise.[145]

The musicologist became a charismatic figure for the sensitive among Berlin's jazz artists and their admirers, who would meet with him to watch those rare originals; there seems to have developed a consensus in this circle of friends about the rights and wrongs of life. Hans Korseck went there to meet with the half-Jewish Pick and Friedrich Meyer; Helmut Zacharias and his girlfriend Hella, a dancer; and the critical Hans Blüthner. The group that gathered there was not really conspirational, but they were convinced of the genuine quality of American culture that shone through those films, and they all shared a great admiration for jazz. When the obese Schottländer died suddenly in April 1943, at the age of thirty-seven, jazz had one ally less in Hitler's Reich.[146]

Schottländer would not have been able to come to the aid of Otto Stenzel, even if the two had been acquainted, when the bandleader of the Scala found himself on the spot a few weeks after the onset of World War II. Stenzel's dilemma was the consequence of the venal obsession with glamor that surrounded show business, even in the outwardly dour Nazi state, but also of Stenzel's own libertarian proclivities, and in that sense it once again possessed a political dimension.

What happened was that late on 12 October 1939, after the evening's Scala performance, the revue's key crew attended a party at the nearby apartment of singer Gertie Schönfelder's mother. After several drinks Stenzel, who resented the war's interference with his international entertainment routine and who was sure to lose universally famous artists, started grumbling about the turn of events and, according to Mike Danzi (whose German farewell celebration this was), proposed a toast to the "Fourth Reich." Regardless of the degree of seriousness of this remark, during wartime it was treason. Very early the next morning, Gestapo men came for Stenzel and a few of his friends and arrested them. Goebbels, who was immediately notified, after a few days of interrogation and after consultation with police chief Reinhard Heydrich decided on a term in a concentration camp as punishment. Stenzel was sent to Sachsenhausen, north of Berlin, where his head was shorn and he had to perform demeaning tasks such as collecting the camp's garbage for three weeks. As was the SS's custom, he was released only on condition that he never talk about his experience in the camp.[147]

The affair had a prehistory that linked three men to the aura of riches, fame, and sex notoriously associated with the Scala. Stenzel and his friends had been betrayed to the Gestapo by twenty-eight-year-old Wilhelm Fanderl, senior editor at Berlin's *12 Uhr Blatt,* one of the popular tabloids gossiping about the wealthy and the beautiful and their nightly diversions.[148] Fanderl had struck up some kind of a pact with Stenzel, who was interested in a good local press for himself and his acts. Stenzel would allow Fanderl to come to the shows as he liked and to be seated in the Scala's orchestra pit, presumably so that the journalist could eye as closely as possible the beautiful revue girls who would parade up and down the stage.[149] Those he wanted to sleep with he would get to know better behind the stage after the show. Stenzel understood this, for he too, always elegantly attired and considered good-looking, was forever a skirt-chaser.[150] The last member of this trio was none other than Hans Hinkel, the secretary general of the RKK, who constantly attempted to match his boss Goebbels in the seduction of young girls, preferably those from show business. Because of his various affairs, the strappingly handsome Hinkel by 1937 was known, at least to Goebbels, as unhappily married; indeed, in 1938, he succeeded in divorcing his first wife (whom he had married during the party's Time of Struggle), which gave him more freedom than ever to play the field.[151]

Hinkel and Fanderl's friendship began in Berlin. As fervent National Socialists both of them had worked for Gauleiter Goebbels's party press, in particular the aggressive political broadsheet *Der Angriff.* Fanderl first joined the illegal Austrian Nazi party in 1929 and then crossed over to the Reich party in 1932. Having been awarded the Golden Party Badge after 1933 and having received his influential newspaper position in the German capital, which opened many doors for him, this former Austrian in 1939 was a man of some standing in the party and someone to be reckoned with.[152]

Hinkel had risen to even greater heights, all the while on the lookout for opportunities to womanize, which was one of the reasons why he had sought to protect Stenzel and his director Duisberg during the Mohaupt scandal in 1937–38. Preserved correspondence between Fanderl and Hinkel reveals that they had made some type of agreement whereby they would lure young girls into sexual trysts after promising to use their combined influence to help the girls pursue show business careers.[153] As it turned out, certainly with Stenzel's help, Hinkel as well as Fanderl regularly met young starlets at the Scala, two of whom they were later to marry: Hinkel the delicately blond singer Anneliese Kambeck, who was to call herself Anita Spada, and Fanderl the luscious brunette Charlotte

Treml, a Sudeten-German vocalist and actress who adopted the nom de guerre of Kary Barnet.[154]

The cabal enmeshing Stenzel in October 1939 was rendered more complex by the fact that among his colleagues who were arrested was twenty-six-year-old Fräulein Kambeck, who had been seeing Hinkel for a while already. Nonetheless, she, too, was dispatched to the concentration camp of Ravensbrück on the express order of Goebbels, and on the same charge as the one against Stenzel.[155] Why Fanderl, whom Gertie Schönfelder in retrospect describes as "very nice" and who naturally had been a hanger-on at that party, would have wanted to squeal to the Gestapo, in this way compromizing both Stenzel, an accomplice in his love life, and Hinkel, now the all-powerful culture warden, remains something of a mystery. A partial explanation may be that Fanderl was a psychopath. Surviving documents indicate that the journalist had to satisfy a huge ego and was prone to nervous breakdowns.[156]

Significantly, Fanderl's friendship with Hinkel chilled during the last two war years when the journalist intimated to the SS general that in the autumn of 1939 Kary Barnet had been in some kind of antiregime conspiracy with Hinkel's girlfriend Spada. In 1944, Fanderl was filing for divorce from Barnet.[157] At that time, this unpredictable man was justifying his betrayal of Stenzel through hindsight, using the politically opportune formula that "as a National Socialist, I place my belief above everything else."[158]

As for Stenzel, his glorious show business career, which had helped so many jazz musicians develop over the years, was virtually finished by the time Hinkel had managed his (and, assuredly, Kambeck-Spada's) release from the concentration camp.[159] His lips remained sealed from then on, recalls Schönfelder; because he was, after all, a famous personality, he was used by Hinkel and Goebbels for *Truppenbetreuung* well behind enemy lines, while an understudy continued to lead the original Scala orchestra in the Lutherstrasse.[160] This amounted to a punitive demotion for the bon vivant; it was, in any event, humiliating. The Gestapo kept a close watch over Stenzel, finding him politically "unreliable" yet circumspect in his personal bearing.[161] Full-blooded swing apostle that he was, Stenzel provoked the secret police to complain about him musically on occasion, such as in the fall of 1940, when Stenzel, this time conducting on home ground, daringly performed a Jack Hylton arrangement of "Clarinet Marmelade" and black woman pianist Mary Lou Williams's arrangement of "Camel Hop." On tour half a year later he thoroughly jazzed up a simple sailor song, possibly because he knew Hinkel was with him and, for old time's sake, would stand up for him.[162]

But Stenzel also knew that he was past his zenith. After the terrible air raid on Berlin in November 1943, which totally destroyed the Scala building, he was sent on a mission to duplicate Scala acts in the Teatro Madrid in Spain—another Fascist country to be sure, but nothing like the oppressive dictatorship he had just been allowed to leave behind. Opportunistically, Spada stayed on in Germany—her marriage with Hinkel in September 1942 had been attended by Goebbels himself—and reportedly her career was furthered by the Reich culture warden over that of other singers such as Lale Andersen of "Lili Marlen" fame, whom experts thought more talented.[163] Kary Barnet did a stint with Heinz Wehner in Oslo and later also appeared for live shows with several Soldatensender.[164] This was the end of the jazz and the big-band phenomenon called the Scala.

The "war inside" also affected jazz activities in the newly occupied countries, slated to be part of a "Great Germanic Reich," particularly those in Western and Northern Europe. The jazz tradition of those countries had always been superior to that of Germany, because of close ties with England and America. It is true that on the surface, jazz musicians in France, Belgium, Holland, and Denmark continued, after the spring of 1940, to play much as before the German conquest.

In France, virtually all of this music revolved around the Belgian-born Gypsy guitarist Django Reinhardt, the most prolific European jazz musician ever. Reinhardt still had his headquarters in Paris, even though the original Hot Club quintet had been disbanded because of violinist Stephane Grappelly's move to England. After September 1939 French musicians had even more work to do for a jazz-crazed clientele now that the Americans, long the established leaders of the French scene, had hurried out of the country. The Hot Club in the Rue Chaptal, led in the main by Charles Delaunay, was very much in evidence also, lending Reinhardt and his various comusicians—Gus Viseur (accordion), Alix Combelle (tenor), André Ekyan (alto), Hubert Rostaing (clarinet)—what support they needed. In ever-changing combinations, the musicians, including also pianist Eddie Barclay and drummer Pierre Fuoad, who was of Egyptian royalty, performed in certain clubs such as Jane Stick and Le Montecristo, or played at special festivals organized by the Hot Club, as did Reinhardt's own group in the Salle Gaveau in December 1940. There were even sojourns to the South—Lyon and the Côte d'Azur, then under Vichy jurisdiction—and also to neighboring Belgium. German jazz fans in uniform were enthused to hear these bands, and the Latin playboy Porfiro Rubirosa once engaged Reinhardt's combo for a private party in the Paris suburb of Neuilly.[165]

In Belgium, the German-employed orchestras of Fud Candrix, Jean Omer, Stan Brenders, and Eddie Tower were frequently moving in and out of Brussels, Antwerp, and Lüttich to satisfy their native fans. There were other superb Belgian musicians, such as the bandleaders Henry Blum and Chas Dolne, who never went to the Nazi Reich, perhaps because they possessed the patriotism lacking in the Reich's collaborators, such as Candrix. Against the official rules, Wehrmacht soldiers came to Brussels or to Lüttich to dance swing, to the sound of unknown, pseudolegal, and marvelous jazz bands.[166]

Holland's jazz scene was at least equal to Belgium's, for here, as in France, great American soloists such as Benny Carter, Duke Ellington, and Coleman Hawkins had made a lasting impression. Amsterdam was the hub of it all, but The Hague and Rotterdam too featured many good groups. By far the most famous Dutch band was Het Ramblers led by pianist Theo Uden Masman. Then there were De Moochers, the band of trumpeter Boy Edgar, or Boyd Bachmann's often clownish combo. In Amsterdam, typically, the best jazz was offered, usually by totally anonymous musicians, in greasy little joints right in the red-light district near the railway station. Of one such band a visiting German soldier wrote: "One dive especially, the 'Hotel Holland,' had a truly superior band, consisting of three men, on tenor, piano, and drums. . . I could hardly tear myself away. The drummer especially had a terrific rhythm, and the tenor saxophonist, too, had a fabulous style marked by wonderful improvisations. And this in a dump of the worst kind, full of rotten scum, but who should care amidst such music. This band's name happened to be Pim Maas. Incidentally, there is a whole slew of similar establishments around here."[167]

Judged by the small size of the country, Danish jazz was amazingly rich. Like the Dutch and French, the Danes had long had the benefit of visiting American musicians such as Armstrong, Ellington, Carter, Hawkins, and Fats Waller.[168] After 1939 the scene was dominated by the violinist Svend Asmussen, who rivaled Grappelly in expertise (but was himself soon to be rivaled by Helmut Zacharias); the trombonist Peter Rasmussen; and, to a lesser extent, the pianists Leo Mathisen and Kjeld Bonfils, who also played a good set of vibes à la Hampton. Indisputably, reedman Kai Ewans, who had once worked in the German salon orchestra of Bernard Etté and been on tour in the Reich, conducted the most significant big band. From 1940 to 1945 Copenhagen possessed no fewer than twelve clubs in which pure swing could be heard—probably a record for all of occupied Europe.[169]

There are a few solid reasons why the German authorities did not completely clamp down on this. For one, because the Reich wanted to win over those territories for a Germanic federation under Nazi hegemony, it granted a relatively large measure of self-governance, varying with the occupation status of the country. Inasmuch as cultural self-administration was a part of this and native censors turned out to be either lenient or incompetent, art forms such as jazz could flourish.

Second, once again the Nazi regime knew full well that the occupying Wehrmacht had to be courted for the sake of its morale, and hence Nazi leaders not only tolerated but encouraged indulgences that were typically cherished by soldiers on pacified alien ground inhabited by compatible people: casual amours with willing native girls and women, alcoholic consumption often to the point of excess, and, to encourage these activities, agreeable music available in clubs that ideally were licensed, in bordellos, and sometimes also in officers' messes. The letter by Fiddlin' Joe Frommann from France cited earlier ably summarizes these diversions.[170] Now if, in Goebbels's vernacular, "rhythmic dance music" was performed, the borderline between that and swing was always very thin, perhaps regrettably so, but, as in radio policy, it was better to err in favor of the soldiers' contentment than to incur their wrath. This explains why soldiers even found it possible to dance to swing in Belgium or in Holland, although military law forbade it.

The third reason why the Nazi overlords allowed jazz to be played within limits in Western and Northern Europe is that some of it could be recorded there and then sold in those new markets, with the main profits going to the Reich. For when England had to cut off her huge record imports to those markets after the commencement of hostilities, a large void was created, which Germany now proceeded to fill.[171] Most of the prominent jazz groups cut records to their hearts' delight; the records were then freely purchased by their countrymen, often, as Delaunay himself has explained, as replacement for the now prohibited American films. However, the Germans also marketed the records in the Baltics and the Czech Protectorate.[172] Thus in Denmark alone, indigenous record production tripled between 1939 and 1940, reaching its all-time high in 1942, yet falling again below the prewar level in 1945.[173] The catalog for the French swing label of Panassié and Delaunay for 1941 listed 170 titles, including many older recordings by former American residents like Bill Coleman and Hawkins.[174]

For the very same reason, foreign bands in Germany, such as those led by Candrix and van't Hoff and Mobiglia, also produced records in Berlin, and they went to the same markets beyond Germany's borders. Even the German groups of Templin, Brocksieper (on a custom-designed Brocksi label), and Winter recorded their brand of jazz for export purposes, and some of those singles could even be had in German stores.[175] It was ironic, however, that the Belgian or Danish shellacs, including some re-releases of earlier American artists, were just as easily purchased by Wehrmacht personnel of all ranks; they then took them back home on furlough, so that ultimately the Reich became swamped with fine jazz recordings, the best that Europe had to offer at the time, and also older, American specimens. The situation once again closely resembled that of 1933–37, when no restrictions on record sales whatsoever had applied in all of Germany.[176]

And so, on the one hand, jazz in the occupied countries was freer, more ubiquitous, and generally of better quality than in the Reich. On the other hand, however, much of it went on surreptitiously and, despite certain benefits the German occupiers themselves derived from the art, at considerable risk to the performing musicians. Whether these artists would survive to a large extent was up to the capriciousness of the civilian and military administrators and otherwise to Lady Luck. If there were clubs in Paris, for instance, they were secret and hidden away; officially, the old places had been closed down. Officially there was censorship, by the native quislings such as Tobie Goedewagen and Jan Govert Goverts in Holland, or by the Gestapo and even Wehrmacht patrols in France or elsewhere. Censors in France and in Holland authorized repertoires according to the Nazi antijazz catechism of the day, threatening to punish infractions with the concentration camp.

Hence if musicians were playing American standards (which virtually all of them did), they had to be camouflaged—as had already happened, less systematically, in Germany. In Paris, "St. Louis Blues" became "La Tristesse de Saint Louis," and Ella Fitzgerald's "A-Tisket, A-Tasket" turned into "Sans Ticket." Musicians in Paris had to possess official passes to play, though more often than not they performed without them. They arranged benefit concerts for French prisoners of war, and some of them, for example the drummer Arthur Motta, were arrested by the Gestapo and sent to do forced labor in the Reich. Svend Asmussen, too, along with five hundred other prominent Danes from the realm of politics and culture, spent four weeks in a makeshift camp in Copenhagen. Despite their outward vitality, therefore, jazz musicians in Germany's newly dependent territories always had one foot in the organized resistance or the concentration camp, and hence, once again, jazz came close to assuming its original function as protest music.[177]

In important respects, the problems of these artists were rather different, and perhaps potentially more aggravating, than those of their compatriots in the German Reich. Over the years, these artists lacked the attitude of compromise that German jazz musicians had had to adopt—always prepared to retreat to the tamer genre of social-dance music. These non-Germans were hardcore jazz players and had been known and respected for it, even by Americans such as Hawkins and Carter; it was impossible to imagine Django Reinhardt in a slick hotel orchestra, as one could Kurt Hohenberger. On their own home ground these officially conquered men had played on a long-term basis with black musicians such as pianist Freddy Johnson and the Willie Lewis band, musicians who had never dared to approach Germany's boundaries. All of a sudden, those blacks found themselves imperiled. Johnson performed in Amsterdam clubs until, after Pearl Harbor, the Nazis arrested him in December 1941. They kept him in a Bavarian camp until 1944, when he was repatriated to the United States in exchange for some German POWs. Willie Lewis's entirely black band had safely slipped into Switzerland early in 1941. But there also were mulatto musicians of varied nationality hanging on in Paris, and colored ones from the Dutch colonies such as Surinam whom the indigenous racist Nazi party of Anton Adriaan Mussert wanted to silence. Copenhagen throughout its occupation period had its Harlem Kiddies group, including two black brothers, Jonny and Jimmy Campbell, on alto sax and guitar respectively. Because of the Nazis' relatively lenient treatment of Denmark, they seem to have stayed out of harm's way.[178]

This was virtually impossible for the numerous Jewish jazz musicians, particularly in Holland. When the first Nazi pogroms occurred in 1940, the Jews either were arrested right away or managed to stay underground for a while. In Amsterdam, their names were legion: the drummer Maurice van Kleef, the saxophonist Sally Doof, the pianist Leo de la Fuente, to name only the most eminent. To this group must be added refugees from the Reich such as the Reininghaus brothers, pianist Martin Roman, and trumpeter Rolf Goldstein. As it turned out, hardly any of them survived the Holocaust.[179]

Even the giant among these musicians, Django Reinhardt, was potentially at risk because he belonged to the minority of Gypsies, deemed racially inferior by Nazi ideology. In the German Reich, the campaign against Gypsies had begun in earnest in January 1940, before the fall of France. Dr. Robert Ritter, a scientist delegated to look into the matter, rendered the devastating judgment that 90 percent of all known Gypsies were not of the pure "Indo-Germanic" race (which fanatics like Himmler bowed to), but asocial mongrels who deserved to be detained in camps and forced to do an honest day's work. A few weeks after the release of this report certain jurists stated that Gypsies were reminiscent of "African or Asiatic primitive tribes" and that therefore they should be sterilized. Right on cue, the RMK now stepped up the expulsion of its Gypsy members. The next major step came in the winter of 1941–42, when Dr. Ritter attended a conference at which the murder of thirty thousand German Gypsies was discussed: they were to be placed on ships in the Mediterranean and then bombed into the water. Himmler finally commanded the deportation of all impure Gypsies to the Auschwitz death camp in December 1942. By that time, Django Reinhardt was already terrified; he could sense that his association with the jazz culture and his Gypsy origin would be regarded as a nefarious combination. For had not jazz critic Paul Bernhard written as early as 1927 of the special kinship between jazz music and those sounds characteristic of the Gypsies' life? So when Paris fell, in the spring of 1940, Reinhardt quite impulsively fled, "panic-stricken" writes Delaunay, from the capital to the south, "in the hope that a miracle would save France from defeat; but the miracle never happened and after the armistice had been signed came the dreary return towards Paris." There Reinhardt made do as best as he was able.[180]

There were hordes of youngsters, in Belgium and especially in France, who in their life-style as well as in their peculiar mode of appreciating modern jazz resembled the Swings of Hamburg. They were called "Zazous," and, as in Germany, they tended not to be taken seriously by the puristic jazz aficionados. It seems this was a mistake, for from their midst could grow true jazz musicians or impresarios, or simply democratic citizens. Worse, even today as sober a critic of the jazz scene as Eric Hobsbawm is not willing to credit these teenagers, who were obviously defying authority—an authority that represented first and foremost in their minds Hitler's "New Order"—with social and political maturity. But, as Hobsbawm himself concedes, "several of the poor things ended in labor camps." Therefore, did not this very circumstance render these young men and women infinitely more valuable morally than their run-of-the-mill cohorts, not to mention the collaborators, for instance young French girls who would bed down with any Wehrmacht soldier? Mike Zwerin does better justice to this group in his surmise that an appreciable number of the Zazous eventually had their long hair shorn off and exchanged their dandy jackets for a plain old suit, in order to join the Maquis, that intrepid French resistance.[181]

Back in Germany, the first three war years consolidated preexisting loose groupings of amateur jazz fans and musicians, spawned a few new ones, and galvanized them all into shells of defiance that went noticeably beyond the political naïveté of the prewar groups. After all, short of written enactments, jazz had become forbidden fruit closely associated with the regime's outside foes, unless it was channeled and directed by the Goebbels ministry to hand-picked target groups, such as Wehrmacht soldiers. The younger fans not yet inducted into military service or those who successfully had evaded it now consciously tended to ascribe to jazz an oppositional value, which symbolized their quest for individual freedom in a manner that Schulz-Köhn or Michaelis had never felt to be required.

In the greater Frankfurt area, accordionist Emil Mangelsdorff, trumpeter Carlo Bohländer, and pianist Hans Otto Jung found themselves to be kindred spirits and formed the nucleus of what was to become the important Harlem club. In Frankfurt, Mangelsdorff had gotten together with a number of other teenagers, all with aspirations to play jazz. Horst Lippmann was interested in drumming, and his parents owned a restaurant that could be used for practice purposes. Karl

("Charlie") Petry played the clarinet, and there was yet another drummer, Hanns Podehl. By the spring of 1941 they had started to jam, as best they could, in a hidden-away bar called Rokoko-Diele, in Frankfurt's downtown Kyffhäuser hotel; the advantage of this location was that any spies from the Hitler Youth or Gestapo could easily be spotted by special sentries and the players forewarned. Jung, who officially was studying for his doctorate in economics at Frankfurt University, one day met Podehl through a mutual friend at a rowing club, and so he became the pianist of the group. At the same time, Bohländer was still in the army, stationed in nearby Giessen and desperately trying to break away from the service. He was introduced to Petry by a common musician friend. By May 1941 Bohländer was slipping out of the barracks on weekends to join the Harlem combo, whose reputation in the Frankfurt subculture was growing by leaps and bounds. Soon the Rokoko-Diele became a natural meeting place for critical, anti–Hitler Youth boys and girls, several hundred altogether.

The combo's name was taken from the first few bars of "Benny Moten's Swing," which had just been popularized on record by Britain's Eddie Carroll under the title "Harlem." Like the Hamburg Swings, the Frankfurt Harlem clique, if boys, wore their hair longer than Nazi etiquette prescribed, and the girls accentuated their femininity and, surely, their sexuality, in dress and in composure. A later generation's lingo would have used the attributes "cool" or "laid back." After a while, the musically knowledgeable Bohländer, supported by the stunningly proficient pianist Jung, injected technical know-how into the group, so that some of them, like Mangelsdorff, were starting to read music. Mangelsdorff soon switched to clarinet from accordion, which was, after all, an odd tool for the jazzman's art. And now he also attended the conservatory.[182]

The Harlem club developed its own conspirational routines. Members did all the forbidden things, such as listening clandestinely to the BBC, for jazz and also news, and dodging Hitler Youth service, for most were under eighteen. Whenever there were jazzlike performances in Frankfurt for soldiers, such as those by the visiting foreign bands of Ernst van't Hoff and Arne Hülphers, the sworn friends would attend. Some of the better music was being performed in the Regina café, which featured the Dutch bands of John Kristel or van't Hoff or the Belgian one of John Witjes, and it was on those occasions that Emil Mangelsdorff would take along his brother Albert, more than three years his junior. Thus thirteen-year-old Albert Mangelsdorff in 1941 was thoroughly socialized in the quasi-illegal jazz milieu at the height of the Third Reich, and, influenced by Emil and a musician uncle, this young violinist caught the fire of the genre. He soon switched to guitar.[183]

Still, in 1941, pieces that this group was fond of playing were cut in wax by the private Giese & Messerklinger recording studio; for example, "Bugle Call Rag" and "Dinah" were done in July and November respectively, with Emil Mangelsdorff still playing a rigid-sounding harmonica. In 1942, through Jung, the group's connections with the former Berlin circle surrounding Hans Blüthner had solidified, resulting in occasional visits to the capital, chiefly by Jung. The perfect-pitched economics student by this time had impressed Hülphers and van't Hoff with arrangement transcriptions of tunes such as "I'm Comin' Virginia," straight off a Benny Carter record, which both orchestra leaders actually used on the bandstand. On 3 April 1942, Good Friday, Jung was in Berlin with his friend Blüthner. Hans Blüthner and Gerd Peter Pick had rounded up musicians they knew from Melodie-Klub days, and also some of van't Hoff's, whom Jung had just astounded in Frankfurt. A secret, genuine jam session was staged at the Delphi-Palast, which was not in use on that day and which Blüthner and Jung had managed to rent, using as a bribe a rare cognac distilled by Jung's firm—then worth a small fortune. Four musicians from van't Hoff's band as well as Hans Korseck on guitar and his chum, the reed player Herbert Müller, performed the most fiery tunes with Jung himself on piano. Although most of the numbers appear to have been recorded with Pick's expert know-how, only one song has survived, a stomp later entitled "Jam at the Delphi." It was then that Jung finally met Dietrich Schulz-Köhn in person, as he was passing through from the Western front. The next day Dietrich took Hans Otto home with him to Magdeburg to meet his parents, and this sealed a life-long friendship.[184]

The Frankfurt group continued to practice together thereafter, often with visiting Dutch and Belgian musicians such as the bassist Hubert Venesoen and Freddy de Bondt, the tenor player, but also with the German quarter-Jewish trumpeter Hans Berry, who had returned from Belgium and was soon to be drafted. These musicians played for their own pleasure and that of their fans, always in some hideaway; after the Rokoko-Diele folded they inhabited an empty factory hall, where French and Belgian conscript laborers might sneak in. There were one or two personnel changes in that Emil Mangelsdorff was drafted in early 1943, but at that time he was ably replaced by twenty-two-year-old Louis Freichel, a scholarship conservatory student who had been wounded at the front and was at home recovering. He was a trumpeter who could play swing on virtually any instrument he touched.[185]

The concentric circles of the Harlem clique knew they were treading on thin ice, for their antiregime proclivities were blatant. At the time, the brother of a close family friend of the Jungs, a man by the name of Schmidtmann, was in Sachsenhausen concentration camp and eventually murdered there.[186] The club members' physical appearance and apparel were less than what the Wehrmacht, party, or Hitler Youth leadership could allow. Their BBC addiction was endemic. In the choice of their outside friends, they favored the nationals of vanquished countries, musicians or inducted workers, forever suspicious by Nazi standards. Increasingly, they infected other groups of youths who would then whistle the secret signature tune, the first few notes of Carroll's "Harlem," when by chance they would meet in the street.

These young men and their girls were regularly watched by a Gestapo agent by the name of Heinz Baldauf, whom they had nicknamed "Ganjo." Baldauf, born in 1915, was a former printer who had joined the Hitler Youth in 1931 (two years before Hitler became chancellor), the party and the SS in 1933, and the Gestapo as a full-time agent in June 1939. He seems to have understood nothing about jazz, but he was sufficiently indoctrinated to believe, rightly, that among young people it could well be the motor for and the manifestation of an anti-Nazi disposition. Less concerned with the older members of the Harlem clique, because they were either more carefully dressed, like Jung, or de facto members of the Wehrmacht, such as Bohländer, Ganjo took pleasure in singling out the younger ones among the kingpins, namely Emil Mangelsdorff and Horst Lippmann. A police edict "for the protection of youth" of 9 March 1940 had empowered Gestapo personnel such as Baldauf (and others in Hamburg or Berlin) to hunt down, harass, and even arrest youths under the age of eighteen, who were found lingering outside after dark or in public entertainment places such as cinemas or taverns after 9:00 P.M.

Mangelsdorff and Lippmann transgressed those rules many times and were abused for this by Ganjo. On occasion he would haul Mangelsdorff into Gestapo headquarters, forcing him to cut his hair and even slapping him in the face for being a recalcitrant hood. Lippmann suffered similarly. Baldauf relished interrogating his victims about other subversive suspects they might know, rebellious youths who would listen to BBC and seditiously play swing records on portable players in Frankfurt's Forrest Stadium, or in small vessels on the Main river, where the secret police could then chase them with speed boats.[187]

Meanwhile in Leipzig, some five hundred miles to the east, a new generation of young jazz followers was in the process of replacing Kurt Michaelis and his circle, even though they originated within it. Politically, they did not have the nonchalance of Hot-Geyer, Fiddlin' Joe, or Dreamy-Hot; their youth had already been marred by too many years of Nazi rule. In November 1938, Michaelis had introduced to the Leipzig Hot Club Frohwalt ("Teddie") Neubert, who was the son of an erudite Goethe scholar and had ambitions to become a drummer. Although Teddie was only seventeen then, he was soon taking responsibility for some of the club meetings in his father's book-lined apartment. As the older club patrons gradually left for war service, Teddie's younger cohort became larger: Lutz Warschauer, a half Jew; Herbert Becke, who wanted to be an architect; Stefan Kryves; and art academy student Ingfried Henze.

Here the rites of passage between two generations were determined by nothing but the same fundamental love of jazz music. Nonetheless, that the successors were already much more liberated in their outlook, their customs, and almost certainly their political views than the founders had been is indicated by the fact that some of the new boys brought girlfriends to the meetings as equals, even as amateur musicians. Herbert Becke's sweetheart, Maria Rausch, liked to sing jazz, and by 1940 Henze's girl, a young graphic arts student with a talent for the keyboard, had joined the circle.[188]

That young woman's name was Jutta Hipp, and she symbolized everything that was novel and progressive in this new throng of jazz enthusiasts. In retrospect it is fair to say that she was the female alter ego of Emil Mangelsdorff, who was exactly the same age, was socialized in similar family surroundings, and had the same political and ideological sensibilities and a matching concept of aesthetics. As will be shown, both were to find this out when they met much later.

Jutta became Teddie Neubert's girl after Henze had left, presumably for the front. Kryves, too, was conscripted and eventually was listed as missing in Russia. With the situation of the boys in the club in flux, the girls became a more stable element because they could not be drafted. These youngsters not only listened to jazz records and programs on the BBC, but in a makeshift way they also got a band going, with Jutta becoming increasingly interested in swing piano. For four years she took harmony and sight-reading lessons from church organist Fräulein Selle, one of an increasing number of tough, self-determined women professionals during this war who got around on a motorcycle and made Jutta transpose from old church keys. Jutta's idols were Teddy Wilson, Fats Waller, and Art Tatum; her favorite record was "Margie," recorded in January 1938 by Jimmy Lunceford. When she became engaged to Neubert, they exchanged rings, his with the inscription, "It Don't Mean a Thing," and hers with the complement, "If It Ain't Got That Swing."[189]

Jutta and her circle became politicized as the war escalated, with all its ugly, visible side effects. Jutta's father, a former Freemason, had given in to pressure, joining the Nazi party in order to keep his job; he later left the party in disgust. "My father always hated the Nazis." Even at the risk of being caught by an air raid, Jutta routinely sneaked downstairs to the family radio in order to listen to jazz on the enemy stations, copying down the melodies on music paper with the help of a primitive flashlight. In and around Leipzig, she saw prisoners being put to forced factory labor clad in thin, striped suits, and she tried to console them that it would soon be over. But this was not to be for some time, and when the group's members met to listen to their discs and play their own music, for example in Kryves's apartment before his conscription, he would exhort his friends not to tap out the rhythm on the floor, "for neither neighbors nor Nazis liked the sound of jazz." This clique, against the sternest of official rules, congregated even during bombing raids.[190]

It is clear that Jutta Hipp's antiregime awareness interacted with her personal nonconformism, and her behavior, like that of the Frankfurt fans, suggests parallels with the behavior of the Hamburg Swings. "I used to wear blue silk-stockings [sic], with a red seam, red heart on the knee," she writes, "and as teenagers do, wanting to be different, would walk a whole block backwards to see if anyone gets upset and then smile at them."[191]

After 1940 the combination of political skepticism, personal nonconformity, and love of jazz music was not so scarce a phenomenon among certain juveniles in Germany's larger cities and even some smaller ones. Under steadily darkening clouds, jazz signified the growing resentment of Germany's younger generation against the politics of war and oppression, as manifested by party and Wehrmacht, SS and Hitler Youth. The longer the war dragged on, the more potentially lethal this dissident attitude among certain of Germany's youth became, for ultimately, from the rulers' vantage point, personnel recruitment for the Nazi movement and its long-term goals was at stake. In the early 1940s there were groupings in Weimar, in Rostock, and in Breslau, and they were still multiplying elsewhere. The cell in Breslau resembled the Frankfurt group in that its members fraternized with alien workers, and the Leipzig group in their taste for current jazz recordings; members sustained day-to-day clashes with the Hitler Youth. They resembled all the other forbidden groups and cliques, with Hamburg, albeit at a distance, serving as the role model, in that dress and comportment were provocatively unconventional, and girls fulfilled a growing pivotal function.[192] The rebellious spirit became contagious.

Hamburg's Different Drummers

Throughout this period, from September 1939 to August 1942, the critical situation of the Hamburg Swing youth was exacerbated and, perforce, further politicized by the circumstances of war. In that process, various elements intersected. One was a continuation of prewar attempts by Nazi zealots to develop new Germanic dance forms for the nation, coupled with the customary venom against jazz and the swing dance. Even though most of this got stuck in rhetoric and remained as ineffective as ever, the rigid stance of those reformers in the RKK, Nazi party, and Hitler Youth was bound to harm the Hamburg Swings in the long run.[193] Within this scenario, music teacher Max Merz had chosen as his personal mission to travel around the Reich and conduct party-sanctioned public lectures against jazz and the associated swing mannerisms; Merz's bouncers used force to manhandle young hecklers disturbing his harangues.[194]

The inconsistency of official dance prohibitions since September 1939 tended over time to hamper the Swing youths also, for in periods of strict interdiction their carelessness could be caught, and during permissive phases they would throw all caution to the wind. In March 1941, when social dancing was allowed three days a week, Goebbels became exasperated over "excrescences of our dance music," which he felt called upon to chastize. His state of mind at that point contributed to the short-lived ban on dancing during the Balkan campaigns a couple of months later, which, according to the records, was not fully comprehended by the impervious Swings. Whether they paid attention or not, in January of the following year Hamburg Swings were directly affected by the decree forbidding any dancing in semiprivate organizations such as their exclusive sports clubs, which had gone unmolested until that month.[195]

It was, in fact, the activity of the dance itself through which the chief members of this self-selective Hamburg movement slipped up and even marginal ones skidded closer to catastrophe. For their gyrations visibly attracted the attention of the secret police, which then could press further charges and push those adolescents to the outer edge of Nazi society. The key events here were two quasipublic dances in early 1940, the first of which was organized in the Kaiserhof hotel in Hamburg-Altona on 3 February. Gestapo agents found out that approximately five hundred Swings had staged their own fete in a somewhat hidden hall adjacent to the main premises, where a postal sports club was celebrating its annual, and entirely respectable, get-together. "The Swing dance was being executed in a completely hideous fashion. . . English music was played along with English vocals, while our soldiers are engaged in battle against Britain." It was obviously not the first happening of this kind.[196]

Under the eyes of the watchful Gestapo, on 2 March another mass dance was held at the public Curio-Haus on the Rothenbaumchaussee, a wing of which could be rented. The police officials discerned similarly wild scenes; the music, by gifted Hamburg amateurs, was just as compromising. The dance was conducted in style: participants had been invited to attend by printed cards, signed by one Alfred Dreyer; "esteemed acquaintances" were heartily welcomed, but only after prior registration with the organizers. At eleven o'clock sharp—Heinz Beckmann's student band had just intoned "Bei Mir Bist Du Shein"—the police burst in. Whistles blowing, forty agents instantly locked all exits, set up long tables, and fingerprinted the detainees. Incriminating personal effects such as girls' lipsticks were confiscated. All this lasted until the early morning hours. Exactly 408 Swing boys and girls were identified, and hardly any got away unnoticed. The great majority were released the same night, pending further investigation, but a few, thought to be gang leaders, were arrested, among them a nineteen-year-old half Jew by the name of Wolf. Only seventeen of the Swings were over twenty-one.[197] A follow-up party planned for 14 March in the White Hall of the Curio-Haus, for which the invitations were already printed, never came to pass.[198]

If the Gestapo had stopped the custom of semipublic events for the Swings, it had many more problems with private house parties and the still openly beckoning entertainment business. The noted prewar dance establishments such as the Café Heinze, Trocadero, and Faun, which continued without interruption for a while, were still frequented by Swings; also playing there were the better foreign bands such as that of Arne Hülphers from neutral Sweden, or Hohenberger, when he was still on the road.[199]

But a more typical public gathering place for the Swings gradually turned out to be the Alsterpavillon on the expansive river in the town center. A large glass-encased dance casino, it had maliciously been nicknamed "Jewish Aquarium" by Nazis long before. In early 1941 the Dutch Swing band of John Kristel was performing here. He was soon appropriated by the Swings as "their" bandleader; his stage show was one of the highlights of their colorful existence. For a few weeks, John Kristel was the Pied Piper of Hamburg. "The mood at the Alsterpavillon in 1941 was great," remembers one surviving Swing, "and it escalated. People went mad with excitement. What was happening was unbelievable. John Kristel's Dutch band had a fabulous trumpeter. Whenever he stood up to blow his solos, the entire house broke down."[200] Not surprisingly, the Gestapo got news of this and showed up on 28 February, interrupting the evening's performance. Kristel and his comusicians were locked into a basement room and then released from the pavilion through a back door; the assembled Swings were told that the entire orchestra had had to leave Hamburg on very short notice. No one believed the police, and some Swings were able to spot Kristel's bandsmen on the street some two days later.[201]

The thirty-three-year-old Amsterdam musician returned to the Alsterpavillon in August, after its temporary closure, most certainly because Hamburg, like Berlin or Frankfurt, needed musical diversions for the troops on furlough, and ever fewer German players were available. Yet this time around he had been warned both by the RMK and the Gestapo to keep things on the quiet side, while the Hamburg Swings themselves were increasingly cowed into submission. Indeed, the songs were "not all that great," wrote Swing girl Hanne-Lore Evers to a friend in uniform, and as if to vindicate the Gestapo further, a year after Kristel's engagement the pavilion was bombed to bits by the Royal Air Force.[202]

There were other favorite spots for the Swings to meet in, the svelte Café Condi in Hotel Vierjahreszeiten where Stauffer used to room, or the Moritz and the Ex bar, or the cozy Schiff Ahoi, the last two of which the Gestapo closed as a precautionary move in the fall of 1941.[203] As before the war, Swings congregated in the Waterloo cinema near the Dammtor railway station. Here newspaper publisher Axel Springer, who had meanwhile become an optician, acted as projectionist; bad health had prevented his Wehrmacht induction. The Waterloo still showed American films right up to the United States' entry into the war, or halfway acceptable German ones like *Frau Luna,* and Springer would signal to his waiting friends whenever the despised news reel was finished, upon which they all would enter the theater to delight in the feature.[204]

In the autumn of 1942, the authorities concluded in retrospect that the interdiction of semiprivate swing dance celebrations à la Curio-Haus, coupled with the social-dance prohibition of May 1940, had triggered a rise in the number of totally private parties.[205] This judgment was not far off the mark. In the face of mounting persecution by secret police and also the Hitler Youth, Swing juveniles simply felt more protected in the basements of their parents' often sumptuous villas, situated in expensive Hamburg neighborhoods. These comfortable dens were sanctuaries even the Gestapo was reluctant to break into. Inga Madlung remembers that in the intricately laid-out cellar rooms there were "bright-red leather cushions on the floors, warm and inviting." They were enhanced by "murals on the walls, and fitted carpets." The gramophone was handy with many swing records to spin, and wine and perhaps cognac were available, all making for an "erotic ambience" that encouraged sexual intimacies. The degree of such intimacies varied and largely depended on whether parents were in the house or not. Most often they were, and so usually the meetings were relatively harmless. But a few venues had been specifically designed with seduction in mind, as was the apartment of the somewhat older Persian Oromutchi brothers on Bellevue near the Alster river, with its mirrored ceilings.[206]

The last of these assemblies appears to have occurred in June 1942 on an estate in the country north of the city, with cocktails in the garden and uninhibited swing dance on the lawn and patios. By nightfall everybody had moved inside, and after a lavish buffet dinner a cabaret was started with impersonations of Goebbels and the Führer. Kaki Georgiadis accepted the credit for this, and a few days later a spy within the group betrayed him to the Gestapo. This scandal signaled the end of a way of life for the Swings.[207]

The difficulties of this life-style were compounded, as time went on, by the unbending hostility of the Hitler Youth against the Swings, whom they regarded as a danger to their existence. The Gestapo acted in collusion with the Hamburg Hitler Youth leadership whenever it staged a raid on the Swings, as was the case in the Kaiserhof and Curio-Haus situations. For Hitler Youth members could assume the role of coeval pals in Swing crowds, undiscovered at least for short periods of time, and then lead the policemen on.[208] But just as often, the HJ-Streifendienst, an internal patrol unit, swarmed out on its own to catch transgressors against the various youth-restraining laws promulgated by the regime, and of course to catch the misfits in the swing dance.[209] Sometimes, Hitler Youth and Swing youths battled it out in the open; this happened more frequently when middle-class and sometimes even proletarian juveniles sided with the original Swings, aping their manner and their dress in less expensive fashion.[210] In addition, the Hitler Youth played an instrumental role in the Gymnasien, where they informed on pupils and collaborated with the school directors in the expulsion of renegades.[211]

In Hamburg, as perhaps in other towns and cities of the Reich, the Hitler Youth had good reason to fear for its survival as the monopolistic state organization of all teenagers up to eighteen years of age. It was no secret that while most genuine Swing youths had managed, by one trick or another, to avoid joining the Hitler Youth, boys and girls who were in it were gradually infected with the swing virus already during the first months of war. After the Curio-Haus arrests, for instance, it was discovered that of the 408 culprits registered, almost half were nominal members of the Hitler Youth, whereas over 50 had at one time or another been able to leave the state youth without having joined any of the adult regime formations instead.[212]

What exactly did the Swings do that so invoked the frothy rage of their adversaries? After September 1939 their activities fell more clearly than before the war into two separate categories: an unpolitical and a political one, although sometimes the boundary was still blurred. The swing dance itself continued to be a hedonistic exercise, with no political message, notwithstanding its increasing criminalization and, by inference, politicization as far as the regime was concerned. This held true for the provocative dress as well, for example Hanne-Lore Evers's elegant, self-tailored gray suit complemented by a gentleman's vest and an open jacket with shoulder pads ("an absolute knock-out"), or aspiring artist Kurt-Rudolf Hoffmann's soft felt hat, black shirt with bow tie, Stars and Stripes on the coat lapel, and light trench coat slung loosely over the shoulders.[213]

Swing teens played their jazz records, sometimes in inopportune places such as public air raid shelters, or, in the case of several lower-class Swing formations, during nightly air raid watches in essential industries, on which occasions dancing was natural and sexual promiscuity not unheard of.[214] Jazz records were traded and sometimes copied, with special gadgets, to be freely distributed or sold to friends.[215] Somewhat more serious than an immature prank, but still not political, was Andreas Panagopoulos's illegal acquisition of a submachine gun in 1941. He tried it out in his spacious parental home, allowing one bullet to escape through a window onto the neighbor's property, and of course it gave him away.[216]

There were grand capers such as when a group of Swings, all decked out in formal wear, entered a first-class train compartment at Hamburg-Harburg and then emerged at the main station, only to be greeted by a similarly attired throng of other Swings acting like a reception committee. They took the travelers' pictures with many flashbulbs and ceremoniously ushered them into a waiting horse-drawn coach, all for the benefit of gaping onlookers, who were told that this was a "peace maneuver."[217] Hans-Joachim ("Tommie") Scheel and two friends dressed up as hoodlums and faked a robbery in a friendly villa, neatly photographing every step of their "escape." Too bad for them that the Gestapo later took this lark for real![218] Scheel and his Swing gang also went to the Waterloo movies, sitting through the news part booing and making noisy comments until the lights went on and the ushers tried to shove them out: "We did this all the time." Deprecating remarks were passed in cafés, especially when the Gestapo was thought to be present; still, Scheel insists that a distinct political motive was absent. "We were going to tell these dumb bastards that we were different, that was all."[219]

It was decidedly more in cases where National Socialist taboos were touched on or overturned. The impersonations of Hitler and other party greats were neither naive nor without danger; apart from Kaki Georgiadis, the specialist here was a young physician, Heinz Lord, already removed in age from Tommie's cohort and politically accountable.[220] It was popular, and not without risk, to cover up the obligatory Führer portrait that hung in many a semipublic room, for instance in the schools.[221] Associating and especially having affairs with non-"Aryans" of the opposite sex was frequent and condemnable, according to the Nazi code, as "race defilement."[222] Swings listened to the BBC routinely, for news and for the jazz, and a few meticulously copied, multiplied, and distributed among each other British news items or pacifist prose as that by the outlawed writer Erich Kästner.[223]

The raid on the Curio-Haus in early March 1940 had been the first decisive action on the part of the Gestapo to crush the menace of the Swings. Even then a few kingpins had been arrested, but merely momentarily. Thereafter, the secret police began with a more systematic surveillance of the Swing outcasts. This included the establishment of a spy network and direct contact with certain Swings, for purposes of persuasion or deterrence.[224] Hanne-Lore Evers, sized up during the night of the Curio-Haus, was approached by Hamburg's equivalent of Ganjo, thirty-seven-year-old Hans Reinhardt, who wanted to know something about the whereabouts of the Curio musicians. This former goldsmith's apprentice had entered Hamburg's local police force in 1925; he joined the Gestapo in 1935 and became a party member two years later. Whereas Evers was able to elude his queries, professing total ignorance, she was uncomfortably aware that Reinhardt, who had been married for ten years, was interested as much in her attractive physical features as in the misdemeanors of the Swings. Soon "The Fox," as Reinhardt was nicknamed, would earn a reputation as a man excessively concerned with every Swing's love life, about which he could never collect enough detail.[225] Reinhardt's boss was Karl Hintze, swarthy and fortyish, a Nazi Old Fighter and career policeman, who held the rank of Sturmbannführer (major) in the SS. They both commanded Karl-Heinz Kügler, in his early thirties, once a bank clerk, who had joined party and SS a few years before the *Machtergreifung*.[226]

The first real arrests date from October 1940, and Tommie Scheel was among the victims. He and his Belgian friend Maurice Thomas had already been searched by the Gestapo officials in September, just after they had committed compromising materials, such as photographs, to the flames. A few weeks later the police were back to take them to the Stadthaus, Hamburg's feared Gestapo headquarters. Scheel was beaten during interrogations whose purpose was to get him to betray his friends. In between he had to sit—soon joined by other Swings—in a narrow lobby on a bench, facing the wall for hours. "Paul the Tall," one of Reinhardt's henchmen, was the overseer. Each time one turned one's head, he would come and smash it repeatedly against the wall. A bloody nose was certain to result, if not something more serious such as a skull concussion.[227]

Only seventeen at the time, Scheel was charged by the Gestapo (albeit never in a court of law, as was this police state's practice) with having been a leader of the seditious Swings, a veteran of the Curio-Haus disorder, a perpetrator of typically obscene "hot feasts," and, of course, with that staged house robbery. He was then shipped off to the notorious Fuhlsbüttel prison, located in a Hamburg suburb; entirely run by the SS, it was more a concentration camp than a proper legal institution. From here he was marched to outlying areas near the airport for forced labor, which consisted of heavy earth-moving work. Guarded by SS men and in full view of the civilian population, he soon found himself in the company of other Swings. If anyone tried to escape, he was invariably caught and beaten with rifle butts until he collapsed in his own blood. He then had to be carried back to the prison by his comrades.[228]

Among other Swings who entered the Stadthaus over time were Thomas, who was twenty, and B.B., a sixteen-year-old lad characteristically accused by Reinhardt and his crew of sexual relations with a fifteen-year-old Jewess.[229] Altogether sixty-three Swings were picked up that fall, yet only few of them spent more than a week in Gestapo custody; young men over eighteen, however, had to count on fairly immediate service at the front.[230] The next great wave of arrests happened in the autumn of the following year, when Kaki Georgiadis was hauled in and terrified by The Fox.[231] He spent weeks in confinement. So did Kurt-Rudolf Hoffmann, who first was placed in a solitary cell and then shared one with Swing friend Ernst Jürgensen, destined to be a casualty of the Eastern war theater just a few months later.[232]

One of the most despicable aspects of the Gestapo's machinations was its cunning use of stool pigeons. Perhaps not even half the number of Swings would have been captured had there not been means of psychological and physical torture to make those pitiable juveniles speak out against their peers.[233] Undoubtedly, what aided the police was the fact that those young men and women had few resources left for resistance once the pressure was applied, for, leaping from the lap of luxury as many of them were now forced to do, they found that the tribulations of confinement were all the harder to endure.

The school principals who played into the hands of the Hitler Youth and Gestapo by dismissing suspected students represented another example of willful collaboration, this time by the traditionally influential establishment with the omnipotent dictators against the weak. Those series of expulsions constitute an inglorious chapter in the history of that proud Hanseatic city, never before told in full detail.[234] Tommie Scheel became one of the first victims when he was removed from the worthy Gelehrtenschule des Johanneums in November 1940, with the aim of barring him forever from postsecondary education.[235]

In spite of these strenuous efforts, however, by the end of 1941 the question of the Swings was far from resolved; in fact it was becoming an embarrassment to the Hamburg party leadership, all the more so since the regime authorities in the capital were watching the Hamburg scene with mounting consternation. Already in February and then again in August 1941 an official in the propaganda ministry, asking for support, had complained to his boss about "hot and swing demonstrations by juvenile, Anglophile circles in Hamburg." Goebbels was apprehensive about the relative degree of freedom he had accorded exponents of the jazz culture for the sake of the troops and general civilian pacification. Hence he hesitated somewhat to participate in a headlong rush against jazz-crazed Swings or anyone else who might temporarily step over the boundaries of acceptable behavior. But his heart was with the disciplinarians, and to prove it, he had early on cooperated with his cabinet colleagues wherever he found it politic, for example in the drafting of the restrictive youth law of March 1940.[236]

In August 1941, then, State Secretary Leopold Gutterer was finally empowered by the minister to send a letter to police chief Reinhard Heydrich, urging him to try a little harder in coping with the Hamburg conundrum.[237] Half a year later Artur Axmann, the new Reich youth leader, expressed his own well-founded concerns to SS chief Himmler, asking him to prosecute the Swing youth "in the toughest manner." Himmler concurred that in the case of those recalcitrants only brute force would help, and so on 26 January 1942 he instructed Heydrich "to extirpate this evil root and branch" and recommended the concentration camp for all "gang leaders," whether male or female. There they should first of all be beaten, and then exercized and put to work. Their terms of punishment should not be less than two or three years, and never should they be allowed to pursue their studies. Parents were to be examined for complicity; in their case also concentration camp and property confiscation should by no means be ruled out. "Only if we move with brutality, shall we be able to prevent the dangerous spread of such Anglophilic tendencies in a period when Germany is fighting for its very existence."[238]

The Hamburg Gestapo proceeded to implement these extraordinarily cruel directives instantly, ushering in the ultimate phase in the history of those peculiar jazz followers. Already in January 1942 Hintze and Reinhardt were sending youths to camps, among which Moringen, Uckermark, Ravensbrück, and Neuengamme were the most notable.[239]

Moringen was a special work compound south of Hanover for male insurgents between sixteen and eighteen or sometimes even twenty-one years of age, who were already said to be beyond the educational influence of the Hitler Youth. They were grouped as asocial and paracriminal types who might still, after the application of severe penalties, be rescued for the good of Nazi society. Yet before 1945, only 5 percent were ever freed. For the same Dr. Robert Ritter, who was toiling over a finite solution of the "Gypsy problem" that eventually would amount to gassing, was principally in charge of the camp's punitive philosophy and the definition of its captives as worthless social aliens. This site, with up to eight hundred inmates, was guarded by approximately eighty-five SS men, who supervised a formidable day of heavy factory labor lasting eleven hours. Nutrition was minimal, and corporal punishment, punitive sports exercizes, and maximum-degree confinement were additional devices of retribution. The first Swings from Hamburg appear to have been sent there in June 1942.[240]

The complement for girls was Uckermark, which served as a subunit of the infamous Ravensbrück concentration camp for women in Mecklenburg and was tightly connected to its regimen. Life there was comparable to that in Moringen in almost every respect. Two Hamburg Swing girls known to be dispatched there in August 1942 were Eva Rademacher, on account of her Jewish friends, and Helga Rönn, an extremely attractive seventeen-year-old whom the police officials, in their perverse frame of mind, had long regarded as the personification of Swing promiscuity.[241]

Swings who were already around twenty, however, tended to end up in regular concentration camps, for here they could be more severely charged with being political criminals. This would include being members of or in cahoots with the non-"Aryan" minority, but it could also have a purely ideological background.

Ursula Nielsen fell into the latter group. Her father was a well-known Social Democratic trade unionist, and by 1940 she had joined the generally upper-class Swings, along with a few others from the lower social ranks, after having met Alfred Dreyer while skating. Already in March 1941 she had been taken to the Stadthaus and to Fuhlsbüttel; in January 1942, barely eighteen years old, she was in Ravensbrück. Two months later she missed a chance to go to a camp called Auschwitz; the SS had recommended it as a quick way of returning home. Disappointed, she was cheered up after the arrival in Ravensbrück of Jutta and Inga Madlung, twenty and twenty-two, respectively, who, a quarter Jewish, had attempted to assist some Hamburg Jews marked down for evacuation. Half-Jewish Eva Petersen also turned up, albeit not for long: this Protestant with a Jewish mother was sent to Auschwitz and never seen again. Eva became the *mater dolorosa* of the Swing movement. In April Ingeborg Jarms was there, and in November Verena Kerber, both after months in Fuhlsbüttel.[242]

Their more conspicuous male friends—Maurice Thomas, Eva Petersen's brother Uwe, and Günther Koppe, for example—were trucked to other forms of Hades: Buchenwald or Sachsenhausen, and, most usually, the new camp Neuengamme, twenty miles southeast of Hamburg. Hans-Joachim Scheel today is certain that the only reason why the SS left him in Fuhlsbüttel, for eventual service in the Wehrmacht, was that the acting mayor of Altona was rooming in his mother's home and was able to intervene on his behalf.[243]

Anyone attempting to evaluate the phenomenon of the Swings at this stage—(the reader will encounter them again), either in a psychological or political context, will meet with considerable difficulties of categorization, for nothing comparable did exist in Nazi Germany, or either before or after. When Erik Erikson writes about "identity confusion" in the growth process of nonconformist adolescents in America, his examples point to modern society in which youth cohorts have stood up primarily against their parents in symbolic actions of generational revolt that are only secondarily directed against the state.[244] This pattern is of course not new. During earlier phases of German history, for instance in the Weimar Republic, young people's disenchantment with the existing order, including the political system, had found expression in animosity toward parents for failing to change that order. This tension, so it has been argued, even became one of the constituent factors in the rise of National Socialism, which was seen by the young as the harbinger of overall change.[245]

Yet the collective case of the Hamburg Swings proves the very opposite. In their undoubted antagonism to the Nazi order they did not choose to contradict their parents as convenient symbols of the powers that be. Occasional exceptions strike the chronicler as the consequence of parental worry *after* their beloved offspring had elected that hazardous course. Objections in principle to the Swings' way of life seem to have been raised more by mothers and fathers of socially less privileged children, who came to penetrate the Swing ranks after 1939. Such objections were natural because National Socialism was, on the whole, a movement much more compatible with lower-middle-class values, values which also were anathema to jazz.[246] Hence the Hamburg Swings would not have been analogous to those known proletarian youths in Cologne or Leipzig who battled the Hitler Youth in their own mode, for it can safely be assumed that many of their parents, however Marxist they had been before, now were trusty Nazis.[247]

From a more narrow, political perspective and quite apart from the parental issue, a review of the Swings' own post-1945 positions reveals the extremes of either total noncommitment or consciously political, if not to say ideological, dissidence.[248] They had participated in this movement, observed Hans Engel in 1985, "long on hair and short on brains," and the writer Walter Jens, once next to the Swings, has protested the label of "resistance fighter."[249] But Axel Springer has moved closer to a point between the two seemingly irreconcilable opposites when he says that as a product of the Swing subculture he had been no resister, while admitting, in the same breath, that he assisted the oppressed, including Jews.[250]

There was, in fact, a middle ground that opened up as the Swings developed both in age and maturity, so that in 1942 they were noticeably removed from the ingenuous beginnings of only five years earlier. Hanne-Lore Evers wrote to a friend in October 1940 that Günter, one of their mutual Swing friends in uniform, had become "more serious"; perhaps he had a premonition of events to come, including his own death just a few months later at barely twenty-two.[251] Almost one year hence, Hanne-Lore herself displayed more profundity of thought when she mused that perhaps she could stand the absence of Kristel and Hohenberger "if only this wretched war would come to an end and then everything would stop and once again would be as in the olden days or even better." Little did she care to know that the Gestapo could intercept such letters and charge her with defeatism![252] As Uwe Storjohann has suggested, most Swings of his ilk were forcibly politicized by a regime that loathed them because they had withheld their respect, had dissociated themselves from it.[253]

It is true that such politicization became obvious to some only on the day they were put behind bars. In the case of the Hamburg Swings, if not of all the fans in the Reich and certainly the musicians, jazz assumed many a tortuous detour to help a reasonably sensitive group of young Germans toward a responsible understanding of inequality in politics and society, an understanding more closely in keeping with the sentiments of this music's original followers.

4

Near Defeat: Jazz Toward the "Final Victory," September 1942 to May 1945

Compromise and Failure

After the summer of 1942, the tide began to turn against the Nazi Reich. Field Marshal Erwin Rommel was losing out in the North African war arena, and in Russia the Wehrmacht suffered more opprobrium. By May 1945, the denouement had been marked by three or four altogether disastrous developments. First, on 3 February 1943, Hitler had to concede defeat at Stalingrad. The Allied armies then landed on the Normandy coast during D-Day, the sixth of June. Ten weeks later, the Führer withstood the severest assassination attempt of his career thus far. And finally, the Red Army entered Berlin in the last week of April 1945. On the eighth of May, a mere eight days after Hitler's and Goebbels's suicides, the government capitulated unconditionally.[1]

To a large extent the fate of German jazz was tied up with these events. The most immediate and certainly the most evident phenomenon that increasingly affected jazz and dance music, as well as its resilient subculture, was the recurrent bombing raids, especially when they targeted Berlin. The first truly serious attack upset Berlin in January 1943, and then again on 1 March. On that day, there were more than seven hundred deaths, and over sixty thousand people lost their homes. The terrible firebombing of Hamburg in July, when tens of thousands of lives were lost, was a foreboding of tragedies for the capital. Berlin's Black Days were 22 and 23 November. After 776 Royal Air Force bombers attacked, the entire city was enveloped in a ball of fire and asphalt was aflame in the streets. There were nearly four thousand casualties, with almost half a million homeless. Hallmarks of Berlin were hit: the Kaiser Wilhelm Memorial Church near the Kurfürstendamm, the fabulous zoo, and the Romanische Café. And sadly, the Scala went up in flames. In the following months, as the assaults persisted, more and more Berliners left their city for safer places in the Reich.[2]

163

In his capacity as Gauleiter of Greater Berlin, Joseph Goebbels reacted to this with equanimity on the outside and trepidation on the inside. With the Stalingrad disaster looming on the horizon at the end of January 1943, he publicly warned Germans that a new time for belt-tightening lay ahead, when very little could be taken for granted. Goebbels reaffirmed the fundamentally totalitarian nature of the regime when he stated that the "personal freedom" of an individual did not matter at all within the collective of the *Volksgemeinschaft*.[3] Two weeks after the Stalingrad disaster, before fanatic followers in the Sportpalast stadium, he gave a long and intense speech in which he again demanded a lowering of the general standard of living in favor of a redoubled war effort. He also began to draw an artificial line between, on the one side, useless diversions such as sitting around in "bars and night clubs" and frolicking in "luxury restaurants," and, on the other side, quality enlightenment such as that offered by theater, cinemas, and concert halls. And while here he displayed an iron resolve by demanding popular consent for the waging of "total war," he was privately quite worried that Germans, and his Berliners in particular, would become unsettled by events.[4] So, as threatened, Goebbels did close the bars and night clubs in deference to the martyrs of Stalingrad, and he even shut down movie houses and theaters. But he did so only for a few days. Wisened by past experience, he knew that life must go on for the sake of internal stability.[5] Scores of soldiers were coming home on furlough now, wishing to blank out the war, and the general populace would be all the more willing to endure the vicissitudes if they were kept in good spirits—all within certain limits.

Goebbels was in fact hoping that proper doses of show business and high culture alike would help Germans live through this crucible, thereby steeling their resistance to the enemy. His tactic became starkly apparent after the historic air attacks on Berlin of November, when he insisted that popular establishments such as Nollendorftheater and Wintergarten be reactivated immediately, as soon as the air raid rubble had been cleared away. One actress who, beside herself with fear, had fled to more tranquil East Prussia, was immediately punished.[6] It was only after the 20 July 1944 attempt on Hitler's life, after which Goebbels had been appointed "plenipotentiary for the total war effort," that the minister shut down all variety shows, stage theaters, and the last surviving clubs, without, however, trying to affect the Reich's classical concert performances and the propagandistically valuable film business.[7] And to visiting soldiers, many of the old and treasured pastimes were still available.

After fall 1942, then, there was essentially no atmosphere in Berlin or anywhere else in Germany in which such a light-hearted Muse as jazz could flourish as a well-executed art. With a few individual exceptions, the core clientele of aficionados was absent. While Berlin was gradually being depleted of Germans, it was filling up with foreign laborers—Frenchmen and Poles, Belgians and Italians. They frequented their own restaurants where, as far as Germans were concerned, they conversed loudly in the tongues of Babylon. Telephone communication and basic transportation were becoming increasingly hazardous, and early curfews weighed heavily on inhabitants.[8] Famous hotels such as the Eden and the Kaiserhof were getting bombed out, with only the

Adlon holding out almost to the end. The ambience of restaurants and what they insolently offered as meals became intolerable.[9]

Worn down by constant idle air raid sirens and many a true alarm, the population slowly became demoralized, sometimes to the point of not even bothering with shelter, and always at risk of death. Gruesome scenes, such as bodies scattered over the ruined landscape and burning street facades, became normal occurrences, adding to everyone's mood of depression.[10] By 1944 Berlin was no place of entertainment for anybody, jazz lover or not, for by then, contrary to the minister's hopes, no type of distraction was able to compensate for the cruel realities of war. One interesting if seedy novelty available by the spring of 1943, but only for the hardened soldiers passing through the capital for a few hours, were nonstop B-grade movies and cheap, all-night cabarets at the railway stations, some of them offering vaudeville sex against a jazzlike background. Admission to these was free.[11]

Whatever live jazz there was in those final years of the regime took place principally in three forms. A few well-known venues were kept open for prominent combos to play in, exclusively for the benefit of the Wehrmacht and diplomats, though wayward civilians did slip in. Then there were out-of-the-way places, invariably illegitimate, that were obvious only to a few initiates, among them certainly soldiers. Finally, people of sufficient wealth or influence would organize private parties and engage musicians, but more for dancing and background sound than for a connoisseur's delectation. Not unexpectedly, Berlin's record production was stopped sometime in 1943.[12]

In the capital, the original home of German jazz, the most prominent places still were the Patria, Rosita, and Uhlandeck, but also the Swing, Gong, and Groschenkeller, which were relatively recent and somewhat makeshift and intermittently featured recordings. The Bulgarian Lubo D'Orio and the two Italians Tullio Mobiglia and Alfio Grasso performed in their old haunts, playing in changing combinations and offering music of varying quality. By and large, they had now lost their discriminating audience, and with it their enthusiasm; Berlin was being Balkanized. From the Patria, in November 1942, a jazz fan reported after a soldier's night of dissipation: "Loud was the din, sour the wine, and sky-high the price."[13] Kurt Widmann held sway in the Imperator hotel until it was bombed in 1943.[14] The legendary Delphi-Palast featured John Kristel's band, for true fans a rather disappointing show, until the palace was converted to a Wehrmacht provisions depot in the spring of that year.[15]

Those clubs were suffered by the regime as a regimental commander would suffer field brothels.[16] Corresponding establishments in Hamburg were the Faun and Trichter, which had already become disreputable, if not outright raunchy, in ordinary times.[17] Frankfurt had its Regina, Vienna its smoky Steffel-Diele near Stephen's Cathedral. The latter spotlighted excellent swing musicians like the budding local pianist Ernst Landl and the foreigners Vittorio Ducchini and Arthur Motta, the latter deported there from Paris.[18]

These bands and their venues, insofar as they continued to work under some cover, moved deeper and deeper into illegality, especially after Goebbels's proscription of most forms of light entertainment in the summer of 1944. Out of the way of regime leaders, Czech musicians were risking "Tiger Rag," "Harlem," and "Bei Mir Bist Du Shein" in an obscure café in the Bavarian Alps, cheered on by young officers and their teenage girlfriends. Still, rural party headquarters was up in arms about it, and the SS was informed.[19] When Uhlandeck on the Kurfürstendamm was destroyed one day in 1943, D'Orio opened in a place called Café Leon, a few houses further down on Lehnin Square. The Bulgarian now performed behind boarded-up windows and utterly against the law, according to some observers until February 1945, with the Red Army at the gates. Almost certainly this was the last of the professional jazz bands active in the capital.[20]

Privately, jazz was still ingested like a rare liqueur. It was considered chic and apropos to accompany the dance among the ruins, now practiced by friends and foes of the regime alike. Cynical Prussian aristocrats engaged a Czech student band for such a party in January 1944. The festival lasted until the early morning hours when a plate collection netted the musicians hundreds of marks. This feast's motto had been "The Decline of the West." In June of that year Foreign Minister Joachim von Ribbentrop invited foreign diplomats and their companions for drinks and a choice buffet; this time, the swing came from recordings for fitful dancing in the library of the summer villa. "After us, the deluge," murmured those journalists lucky enough to attend. And the Fascist Croat legation quartered in Frau von Pannwitz's Dahlem mansion gave "farewell parties" every night in March 1945, pleasing German and foreign revelers with brandy, a folk choir, and jazz played by "a Croat anti-aircraft battery stationed nearby."[21]

Other than that, opportunities continued to exist for jazz artists within the troop entertainment scheme, but under steadily deteriorating circumstances. Since 1940, when *Truppenbetreuung* had been reasonably popular among German musicians and actors of both genders, changes had set in that tended to render the entire venture an increasingly questionable proposition. On one hand, the relatively high salaries paid to all manner of artists, usually with total disregard for their real abilities, was beginning to irk Wehrmacht soldiers who were, of course, receiving but a fraction of these wages. Yet when Goebbels and Dr. Robert Ley, the two cosponsors of the programs, decided on a much lower fixed stipend, those artists still volunteering their services became dismayed because they could earn considerably more at home in the civilian sector, even if they were censored, at arm's length, by Goebbels, Himmler, or Göring.[22]

On the other hand, *Truppenbetreuung* itself became more precarious by the month, as artists, who would have preferred comfortable routines in the safety of occupied countries like Norway or France, were more often than ever sent perilously close to the lines of combat, especially on the Eastern front, and for weeks at a time. This brought upon much physical hardship as well, especially the danger of pneumonia due to lasting exposure to sub-zero weather. At least one musician was known to have suffered permanent hearing damage.[23]

As a result of these mounting dangers, which became disproportionately related to the psychological and material rewards, artists of higher caliber squeamishly withdrew from the troop entertainment scene, leaving it almost exclusively to second- and third-rate performers. Apart from crude amateur shows that angered all military audiences, their specialty was off-color jokes and sexual innuendo, which were enthusiastically greeted by the majority of soldiers yet flatly rejected by those with education and a bourgeois sense of decency. And just as before, of the approximately eight thousand artists jobbing at the fronts in 1943–44, most were regarded by the military to be grossly overpaid, even at the new reduced rates.[24]

Paradoxically, the low overall quality of troop entertainment helped the few active jazz musicians, for their generally high professional standards were doubly appreciated by the otherwise duped Wehrmacht listeners. This judgment holds true even if one adjusts for the absence at that time of the best of the German players, such as Kurt Hohenberger or Fritz Schulze, who were serving in the military themselves. But some good ones were still making the rounds, Kurt Widmann for instance, or Willi Stech, the pianist, while Heinz Wehner was considered to be in stationary service with his big band at Soldatensender Oslo.[25]

Sometimes such jazz programs unfolded under tragic conditions, sometimes on the edge of catastrophe. In 1943 Evelyn Künneke was sent to entertain a suicide squad billeted near Warsaw, just before the men were dispatched on special mission to Russia under their wiry commander, "Karl Bones." The general permitted the scat singer to vocalize American swing tunes, for "the day after tomorrow they will be leaving, and there won't be any songs for them thereafter."[26] And a dancer named Lieselotte, an admirer of Ellington, was ordered to perform her "Intoxication Dance" for troops near Breslau. As she clambered on stage, she was overwhelmed by a huge portrait of the Führer before which she had to perform. She handed her arrangement of "Sophisticated Lady," done by Hans Rosenfelder, an old and spotless "Aryan" friend of Brocksieper's from Munich, to the bandleader. And then the bandsmen entered, each one of whom was an impeccably composed SS man, perfectly trained and miraculously able to sight-read the score for the "dope dance." The music had been beautiful, said the SS orchester conductor to Lieselotte when it was over, but the name of the arranger on the sheet music did sound more than a trifle Jewish![27]

This involuntary compromise was matched by deliberate ones at higher levels. Lutz Templin's jazz band, Charlie's Orchestra, was ordered to go on performing swing for Goebbels's propaganda purposes. In September 1943, when there was no longer any guarantee that recordings could be made safely in Berlin, Templin's organization was moved to provincial Stuttgart, while singer Karl Schwedler, William "Lord Haw Haw" Joyce, and his female counterpart "Axis Sally"—the latter haranguing the Americans—remained in the capital. From now on, the propaganda recordings, now solely hot jazz, were transported to Berlin and there mixed with other programs. At the radio station in Stuttgart, Templin, Brocksieper, bassist Otto Tittmann, and bandoneonist Max Gursch were the only Germans left in the band, the others being Italians, Belgians, and Dutchmen. Yet even in the hitherto quiet Swabian capital, the air attacks became more terrifying, until one day early in 1945 the city, including the radio station, fell total victim to ferocious firebombs. It was only then that Charlie and His Orchestra, already cut short, stopped their fantastic exploits.[28]

They could have stopped them before had this been up to a few skeptical functionaries at Reich radio central. For it was gradually sinking in to them that Templin's jazz à la dictatorship was not exactly what overseas listeners wished to hear. On the other hand, these officials were finding out that German listeners were able to tune in to the short-wave band for the sake of highly illicit entertainment.[29] Evidently, the distribution of "Charlie's Orchestra" jazz records in Allied POW camps was also halted, again because of ineffectiveness. Instead, entire boxes of records were handed out to certain Wehrmacht units, at the discretion of local commanders. One such set was found in December 1944 by British soldiers at a former Wehrmacht radio station in Greece, after the withdrawal of the German troops.[30]

Fritz Brocksieper survived the final months of the war, hidden by a farmer in the Tübingen hinterland.[31] Members of the sister organization, the Deutsche Tanz- und Unterhaltungsorchester, or DTU, incurred a much more complicated fate. The orchestra's practice hall in Berlin's RTK having been bombed in the summer of 1943, the oversized band, including its arrangers, repaired to Prague, which was being spared by Allied planes, had workable broadcast studios, and offered many of the amenities of a peacetime life-style, including plenty of alcohol. In principle, nothing could have been more welcome to these musicians who wanted to evade the front.[32]

And then, in February 1944, Goebbels suddenly relieved Franz Grothe and Georg Haentzschel of their duties and replaced them in Prague by King of Strings Barnabas von Géczy and pianist Willi Stech. In part, their dismissal was a consequence of the despondency progressively invading the propaganda ministry after the fall of Stalingrad. For just as their jazz had broken all the rules and had become too fervent, the musicians themselves had taken too many liberties and had become unruly.

Until the end of 1943 it had seemed as if the DTU was accomplishing the impossible by broadcasting arrangements that would keep the aficionados of swing happy as well as satisfy the more temperate German consumers. Soldiers, and above all air force personnel, relished the twice-weekly broadcasts of moderate swing, as was duly acknowledged by Werner Daniels's "Musikalische Feldpost" at the end of 1942. A Swiss listener even compared the DTU to the best of the British—Harry Roy or Caroll Gibbons.[33] On the other hand there were complaints, especially from rural areas, about "trumpet and saxophone racket."[34] Hinkel and Goebbels, who personally monitored the productions of Grothe and Haentzschel very closely, were haunted by the mounting suspicion that Haentzschel in particular was slipping in too many full-bodied jazz arrangements. This went against the grain of their original policy, that the DTU become a paragon for all the other dance bands in the land, at least those still extant.[35] For many months Fritz Stege paid lip service to this chimera in the pages of his party tabloid, even late in 1943, because the DTU conductors had been clever enough to add the music critic's indolent composition, the tango "Little Shepherdess," to their less jazz-oriented repertoire.[36] Haentzschel and Grothe became foolhardy; in November 1943 they transmitted "Alles wird gut," by Ernst van't Hoff, which was based on the first four notes of Beethoven's *Eroica* symphony, long a symbol of libertarian Swings in Hamburg, as well as of the German program of the BBC they frequently tuned in to.[37]

Once in Prague, the German jazz musicians were worked overtime, which caused considerable unrest, despite the comparative luxury surrounding them. Their rebellious attitude was encouraged by concert master Kurt Henneberg, who had earlier been prominent as a member of the Peter Kreuder combo but also was a fine classical violinist with high ambitions for a solo concert career once the war was over.[38] Henneberg had been "democratically" elected as the spokesman of these individualistic players, much to the chagrin of Goebbels's administrators, who were painfully aware that their party spy, the violist Hermann Däubner, was failing in his prescribed function. Also failing in the eyes of Hinkel and of Goebbels were the two conductors, who were obviously not able to impose sufficient discipline upon a bunch of thirty musicians, said to be a "source of political danger" since hardly any of them even knew what the SA was![39]

Goebbels was probably not alone in making the decision. He had come under pressure from SS-Brigadeführer Karl Cerff, whom the ever-more powerful Himmler had launched, as his liaison for radio content, in the propaganda ministry in the summer of 1941. Cerff, a Nazi from the very first hour and a former HJ regional chief, had helped Himmler introduce "Germanic" cultural artifacts and rituals into SS ceremonies and resembled his boss in his fanaticism regarding the purity of National Socialist ideology. In this Cerff assuredly was the opposite of the cynical Goebbels, who hated this police stooge, even though the minister realized as well as anyone the surging influence that Himmler and his apparatus had had in all facets of the regime's life since the beginning of the war. Cerff appears to have been paranoic about the effect even of the toned-down version of jazz Goebbels was willing to countenance for the DTU, for, as he remarked, was it not preposterous for SS men to measure skulls during the day and then tango away the night?[40]

After Barnabas von Géczy, that "pioneer of 'German' dance music," and his deputy Willi Stech had taken the spots of Grothe and Haentzschel, the DTU deteriorated audibly.[41] This was entirely the fault of Géczy himself, who had been invested with the title of "Professor" by Hitler in 1939 and now augmented the already bulky orchestra with many of his original strings. The monthly budget for the entire organization grew even larger, with Géczy alone taking an inordinately hefty stipend for himself.[42] Accepting Stech into the band as the working conductor was something of a risk, however, because even though the pianist was known as a party faithful, his dance band, which was anchored at the long-wave station (and staffed by the well-known foreigners or members of Templin's group, as well as of the DTU), had until early 1944 earned the respect of many a German jazz fan.[43]

From now on an extremely tight regimen made the life of the bandsmen less amusing than anything short of their being called up for the colors. Henneberg and a few others were censured for sedition, and everyone's contractual right to a vacation was canceled. Even Stech and Géczy had to watch what they were saying these days, and the music was ever so closely screened.[44] Gone now were the somewhat daring sounds of brass and reeds; violins proliferated.[45] All of this still served the official goal of upholding the ultimate model of a dance band, and upholding it beyond the anticipated Final Victory.[46] The entire concept, however, was endangered by the unspeakable: actual conscriptions into front service that the minister himself could not control. By November 1944 four musicians had been drafted, and in December Serge Matul, the hard-drinking guitarist, went off to the war as well.[47]

Under the circumstances, the end of the DTU was surprisingly benign. Just before the Czechs regained control of their capital early in 1945, the German Volkssturm, that last-ditch defence organization consisting mostly of old men and children, nearly pressed the musicians into service. Subsequently, almost all of them were able to shield themselves in their hotels against the irate Czech masses, and slowly they embarked on arduous journeys west to a war-torn homeland.[48] Perhaps the most gifted of the group, and also the man who deserved his fate the least, did not succeed. When the twenty-nine-year-old Henneberg, in good faith and not knowing any Czech, ventured out into the square, he was quickly surrounded by a mob. They strung him up on a lamp post, simultaneously setting him on fire.[49]

The case of the DTU is as much an example of compromise and failure as any. But ultimately Goebbels was also to fail with his radio policy (for which the DTU was a model), one reason being that the British, soon to be aided by the Americans, were beating him at his own game of propaganda. It is true that at the end of 1942 the BBC German-language broadcasts had stopped transmitting the special program that had contained much swing and older jazz along with anti-Hitler news and commentary, because Goebbels had succeeded in jamming its transmission to the Continent. But the BBC's regular German programming on short-, long-, and medium-wave bands still featured some jazz, as in the series "From the Free World." Contributers to this series included Mischa Spoliansky of Weimar cabaret fame (in April 1943); Spike Hughes, the trusty British jazz pioneer, as author and speaker; and Nobel laureate Thomas Mann and his eccentric daughter Erika, whose exhortative addresses were prerecorded in America. This everyday service, introduced by the "Eroica" signal ("All Will Be Well"), was so powerful that even Himmler was overwhelmed by it on his nightly returns to his command bunker in East Prussia. Many of the announcers for the service were well-known German expatriate Jews, so that one Hamburg Nazi blockhead complained in October 1944 that "dirty kikes" had been placed in front of the microphones with the goal of insulting the beloved Führer and all German womanhood.[50]

For Germans living near the North Sea coast or soldiers stationed in Northwestern Europe, it was frequently possible to follow the BBC's home broadcast schedule and listen to programs in English containing pure news and much jazz by British and American formations.[51] The same German audience could also catch the British Forces Network; on 15 April 1943, for instance, it broadcast records by Earl Hines, the Nat King Cole Trio, and Artie Shaw, and the day before could be heard the trio of blind drummer Carlo Krahmer, Hot-Geyer's old Cockney pal.[52]

Much more insidious than the BBC, however, were Sefton Delmer's British-based special stations: Kurzwellensender Atlantik, transmitting on short wave, and the programmatically linked medium-wave-length station Soldatensender Calais. The Atlantic station, staffed by German POW collaborators and originally conceived as a German-language capacity aimed at Wehrmacht navy crews, began its broadcasting of news, jazz, sundry light music, and propaganda on 5 February 1943. From 24 October on it could also be heard on ever changing medium-wave-band positions, camouflaged as a German soldiers' station allegedly situated in Calais, and directed to other military units and the Reich population alike. With its 600 kilowatt transmitter, Calais was the strongest station on the Continent, able to displace several regional Reich networks because of its wave-band flexibility. For the pungent music alone and some of the cautiously critical commentary, many Germans really did think it a German Wehrmacht station such as Belgrade's, but others soon reasoned that it had to be a British contraption after all, one planted on the French coast after or even before the invasion. Very few people, Goebbels included, knew that it was always lodged on the British Isles, a masterpiece of so-called Black Propaganda, which the Berlin-born Delmer had perfected to a fault and which, as a psychological tool of warfare, was nonpareil in the American or the Nazi German war camps.[53]

Soldatensender Calais provided plenty of "American jazz with a German flavour," meaning some U.S. recordings (including special songs by Marlene Dietrich), but even more of the better German jazz records of the Brocksieper or Zacharias variety, which were obtained via Stockholm or from German prisoners of war. While Brocksieper recalls encountering his own music on Atlantik, still on short wave, Zacharias remembers that he was able to listen to his records during his stay in Holland, most certainly on Calais.[54] For younger interested soldiers such as Frankfurt's Emil Mangelsdorff, then in Russia, these daily broadcasts became a lifeline, even a ritual; in the best of cases they were permitted (on short wave) by understanding officers who could easily pretend that Calais was truly a Wehrmacht institution and therefore cleared by security.[55]

Apparently, in 1943, some of the Reich's subjects, particularly in the south, were still receiving American Armed Forces radio signals, including much jazz, broadcast by Italian-based army stations.[56] But what gave Goebbels even more cause for concern was the radio entertainment program, that was very largely based on swing and intended for British and American GIs through the Allied Expeditionary Forces (AEF) setup. The driving force behind this was U.S. Air Force Captain (later Major) Glenn Miller. The AEF network, an original idea of General Dwight Eisenhower, was hosted by the BBC in London and contained fifty parts American, thirty-five parts British, and fifteen parts Canadian programming, in accordance with the Allied forces personnel ratios. The predominant Americans, over some British protest, made swing the bedrock of the total programming range, and trombonist Miller's forty-piece band, especially imported to England, became the fulcrum. Back in the States, this had been the most prominent dance band, one with unheard-of discipline, uncannily clever arrangements, and enough room for swing solos to offset the sometimes saccharine strings. In fact, the orchestra had become the U.S. Air Force Band before its arrival in Britain at the end of June 1944.[57]

AEF broadcasting actually began one day after D-Day, on 7 June, with many American swing records and some live British performances. On the eighth, for instance, one could listen to recorded selections by Woody Herman, Bert Ambrose, Benny Goodman, and other Anglo-American jazz stars, but also to a live show with Kay Kaiser's British social-dance band. These programs were squarely beamed in the direction of Northern France, where the Allied soldiers could receive them, but naturally also the German Wehrmacht, now in retreat. Captain Miller's band kicked in on Monday, 10 July. Besides that characteristic big-band sound there were the sounds of smaller, and inevitably tangier, groups—led by the formidable Goodman pianist Mel Powell, all of twenty years old, and the experienced drummer Ray McKinley—which jazz fans became glued to. Singer Johnny Desmond, once with the Gene Krupa organization, resembled Frank Sinatra's current open approach to jazz.

A typical example of AEF programming was offered on Friday and Saturday, 4 and 5 August 1944: the early morning program "Rise and Shine," which featured a medly of recorded swing; "The American Band of the Supreme Allied Command" (the Glenn Miller Orchestra); Henry Hall's band; recorded music by trumpeter Harry James; Powell's brilliant Swing Sextet; McKinley's American Dance Band; Mel Powell and Jack Rusin, the piano understudy, on two keyboards; Tommy Dorsey's orchestra on record; and finally, Xavier Cugat's recorded Latin jazz. For the sake of equilibrium, there were also spots for Georges Bizet and Richard Strauss, as well as the Northumbrian Fiddlers, the Royal Canadian Air Force Band, and the British Army Pipes and Drums, not to mention news, commentary, and light comedy. Yet altogether, these forty-eight hours provided a fascinating selection for contemporary jazz lovers, and on a continuous basis at that. The program went on, with only slight changes, after Miller vanished over the Channel on his flight to Paris on 15 December (all of the other bandsmen made it to the French metropolis). The extremely popular venture was stopped only in July 1945.[58]

Because the Allies were well aware of the Wehrmacht's predilection for its AEF programs, Glenn Miller's swing was used for demoralization attempts in a manner essentially not dissimilar to Goebbels's "Charlie" jazz, only this method was much more persuasive, since the music was pristine and the messages rang true. Evidently, sequences were planned in weekly intervals, and if implemented, appear to have been neither archivized nor chronicled; for posterity, only a lone German soldier's private recording has survived.

One day in November 1944, Miller was interviewed before the microphone by a young woman named Ilse, undoubtedly a German émigré in the employ of the Allies. In a pleasant voice, she is heard to say: "Guten Abend, deutsche Soldaten!" She then proceeds to introduce Miller in German, and his band follows through with the signature tune "In the Mood." In between "Star Dust,"

"Tuxedo Junction," and "Now I Know," crooned in butchered German by Sergeant Desmond ("Ik Vursteh"), Miller makes somewhat pathetic attempts at replying to Ilse's comments in the language of the enemy. The intended highlight of the "interview" is a brief sermon by Ilse addressed to the Soldaten, a piece of unmitigated propaganda: "Isn't it wonderful that no restrictions obtain for American musicians of any kind! For they can play the type of music they want, whatever their listeners like, whether it be American, German, Russian, Chinese, or Jewish!" "I know what you mean," rejoins Miller in his American drawl, "America means freedom, and there is no expression of freedom quite so sincere as music!" Ilse replies (in German): "Exactly, Herr Major! I hope that everyone listening to you understood what you have just said." The orchestra lends emphasis with a spirited rendition of the American swing dance standard "Poinciana."[59]

Just how many German soldiers tuned in to these special programs as well as the regular AEF broadcasts, including the English-language news, is not known, but a fairly high percentage may be assumed considering the freer climate of the German forces stationed in France. Lieutenant Schulz-Köhn caught them on his radio when he was surrounded by the enemy in the fortress of St. Nazaire, in the spring of 1945. None of his comrades bothered him as he savored them.[60]

Despite the specter of draconic punishments, ever more Germans were tuning in to those foreign stations, and they did so for a number of reasons. First, as the fortunes of war reversed themselves, as living conditions, especially in the cities, worsened, and as Goebbels continued to withhold the truth from the people, the temptation to listen to the radio, for instance the BBC, grew by the day, no matter what the odds. Second, opportunities for listening increased as more and more Germans were forced to work at night, when fewer supervisors could catch them near the radio set. Third, the radio was rendered inevitable virtually everywhere because sudden air raid alarms came via regional stations. And fourth, as Himmler so shrewdly observed, the regime leaders were once again failing to erect technical barriers that would keep the foreign signals at bay. Dedicated cable service (*Drahtfunk*), which Hitler had demanded years ago, was introduced only toward the end of the war and then was practically useless in the monopolistic control of public opinion. Moreover, the Germans lacked the ability to block out enemy broadcasts permanently by heightening the kilowatt potential of their own stations. Lamented the SS chief: "Even people who have the best of intentions and really do not want to listen to foreign networks end up doing so against their will."[61]

Goebbels received Himmler's written complaint at a time when he himself was finding it excessively difficult to make proper policy decisions concerning radio, especially with regard to the place of jazz. As in previous years, his official stance was governed by five variables: his personal taste, especially insofar as it came under the dictates of the Nazi weltanschauung; the desires of the soldiers at the fronts and, equally important, on home vacations; the run-of-the-mill demands of the masses of civilian listeners; competitive enemy offerings; and finally, extraneous circumstances connected, in one way or another, with the course of the war. More importantly than ever, Goebbels had to find a balance and maintain it, and as it turned out, the events of the war influenced him more than anything else.

There were four events, some protracted, to which he reacted not at all consistently, though his qualified responses were in fair correspondence with his decisions concerning cultural continuity at large. The minister was faced, first, with the defeat at Stalingrad of 3 February 1943, and second, with the ominous air attacks on Berlin in November. In the aftermath of the aborted coup against Hitler of July 1944 he had to adjust again, and finally, for weeks during early 1945, he was called to the task of dealing with the imminence of certain defeat.

Tendencies toward censorship had already existed during the war, conveniently justified by the mediocre tastes of the majority of listeners; but they were reinforced on the occasion of Stalingrad for a period lasting approximately from January to early summer 1943, when, significantly, Kurzwellensender Atlantik had begun to broadcast. On 3 February, after Field Marshal Friedrich Paulus had surrendered to the Soviets, Hinkel permitted only serious classical music for all German stations, including, ironically, the very *Eroica* that the German BBC division and the swing fans had adopted for themselves. Subsequently, in accordance with Goebbels's Sportpalast address of 18 February, any form of dance music in radio, including allusions thereto, was spurned.[62]

Thereafter, the return to more rhythmically accentuated music on the German wave bands was as much owing to the persistent enemy stations as it was to lobbying by the Wehrmacht spokesmen, whose arguments the rational Goebbels found difficult to counter. The memory of Stalingrad had faded somewhat, and the soldiers were demanding their due. Thus in October 1943 Goebbels wanted to hear a blend of popular classics, in deference to prevailing public somberness, and loosened-up entertainment of the kind the DTU could provide.[63] He pursued this policy after the November air raids even though he found them deplorable, for he believed that it wouldn't "do for sadness to be placed on the program on this saddest of all months." Whereas the minister was impelled to fire both Grothe and Haentzschel as conductors of the DTU because they had overstepped their limit, in the interest of equilibrium he was unwilling to let them leave their radio posts as section leaders responsible for dance and light-entertainment music, for alternate experts were nowhere in sight.[64]

In May 1944 Hinkel was replaced as the main functionary overseeing radio by the glib Hans Fritzsche, who henceforth presided over the regular program meetings while Hinkel turned his attention to the equally propaganda-sensitive film industry. It befell Hinkel and Fritzsche both to answer angry letters, which progressively came from dyed-in-the-wool yet disenchanted Nazi hacks, explaining to them why "jazz" still had a place in German radio, and why, contrary to their misguided opinion, it was not the old type of jazz at all.[65]

The attempt on Hitler's life in late July 1944 created a national trauma very similar to that of Stalingrad, and it called for dignity rather than diversion. At the same time Goebbels was realizing a new dilemma, in that the old formula that had justified jazz music in the past did not, on the whole, apply any more: if the Wehrmacht was losing the war, Germany was going to be doomed, and there was no point in rewarding both soldiers and civilians with resources for levity. Yet paradoxically, Wehrmacht representatives, in those grueling times, were advancing the cause of "rhythmic music" more energetically than ever!

In any event, exactly two months after the putsch there was passed down to radio central, for the first time, an unequivocal policy directive from Hitler's East Prussian headquarters. It was impossible for radio to continue working as before, as far as so-called jazz was concerned, in as crucial a period as this! Haentzschel was quick to reply that he was already being as careful in his content planning as was humanly possible. Three weeks later, in a meeting with the minister, he was told that no major changes were envisaged: Goebbels obviously was still affected by the combined impact of military exigency and Allied broadcasting, if not by his private proclivities and the overall mood of despair.[66]

Whether Goebbels, at this point, had genuine optimism left in him or was merely cynical is open to conjecture. According to published fragments of his 1945 diary, he was totally realistic about the Reich's impending defeat on strategic criteria alone, even though he did not miss an opportunity to record, for his own purposes, the slightest detail in Germany's favor. Perhaps it was a function of the overall confusion in early 1945 that absolute censorship did not descend on the entire German landscape. In February of that year, Fritzsche ordered light-entertainment music that was "earnest yet not joyless."[67] This phrase faithfully reflected Goebbels's own cleft vision for Germany: on the first of April, he confided to his diary that the war was as good as lost, while on the same day in *Das Reich*, in his last published essay ever, he excoriated historic precedents of fortuitous reversal in war.[68] In such a twilight zone, and aided by Haentzschel's duplicity, jazz in Nazi radio was not even now extinct.

No doubt the soldiers were aiding Haentzschel, for after the war that once stellar jazz pianist admitted that the presence of licentious music on the Soldatensender could always be used as an excuse to keep vestiges of jazz on the Reich programs.[69] In fact, some of those soldiers' stations were rather daring, and they cared little about directives from Nazi headquarters. Soldatensender Weichsel, for instance, routinely spun Kurt Widmann's maddest platters and also those of another German combo that played in the style of "Benedict Gutmann," as "Musikalische Feldpost" ingeniously camouflaged it—perhaps it was Horst Winter's band. Standards such as "Tiger Rag" and "Dinah" that did not have a chance on civilian radio were Weichsel's daily staple.[70]

The worst possibility feared by the soldiers was a switchover to regular Reich programming, which Goebbels wished to see more of in February 1944, in the interest of centralization and conformity. Such a measure was agreed upon in theory by the Wehrmacht, but chronically ignored in practice, for the generals knew full well that anything but what the soldiers really wanted to hear would be an imposition for the fighting man and bad for the morale. They could back their argument with statistics. For example, 70 percent of all the German soldiers billeted on the Crimean Peninsula wanted "modern dance and entertainment music," and for the Luftwaffe stationed in the center of the war theater, the radio programs "could not be 'hot' enough."[71]

Goebbels, who had no final jurisdiction in matters of the army, was forced to acquiesce; yet he thought that his DTU had solved the problem for the soldiers once and for all, and he abhorred the real excrescences produced by those stations in the direction of genuine American jazz, whether played from records or imitated live. He was confirmed in his attitude by more conservative field commanders and, significantly, by the fully indoctrinated Waffen-SS. A German soldiers' station somewhere in Italy, for instance, stood to be investigated for transmitting "decadent music," but in this case it was not even certain if this was not one of the few mobile German propaganda units especially organized for the Allies, to whom they broadcast Charlie's productions mixed with Haw-Haw's and Axis Sally's diatribes. Against this the Allies were warning their own men.[72]

It was by no means safe for German musicians posted to those stations to attempt to uphold the jazz tradition regardless of the consequences. Rumor has it that in 1944 Heinz Wehner, who managed to remain at Soldatensender Oslo with his big band almost to the end, was ordered into one of the Nazis' infamous punitive battalions and sent to the Eastern front because he had been performing a brand of swing that was certainly too steamy for Goebbels and, in the long run, for all the Nazis. Wehner was last seen on 21 February 1945 in Landsberg-on-Warthe, whence he was trying to make his way back west, but then he vanished without a trace.[73]

Friedrich Meyer, the friend of half-Jewish Gerd Peter Pick and one of the musical directors of Soldatensender Belgrad since June 1942, lived at least as dangerously as Wehner. Meyer arrived in Belgrade about a year after the "Lili Marlen" song, first spun repeatedly by a disc jockey in May 1941 for lack of other items, had already become a daily standard. The song had been recorded by Electrola in 1939, with the moderately well-known Bremerhaven singer Lale Andersen, backed by a combo in which Brocksieper was on drums. Virtually overnight, Andersen had turned into a German celebrity, and the Allies would soon record English-language versions of "Lili Marlen" sung by Vera Lynn and Marlene Dietrich, for their own troops. Toward war's end, Delmer's Soldatensender Calais was broadcasting the ballad every evening.[74]

After February 1943 Meyer systematically built up a jazz big band, embellished with strings and staffed by Serbs and, more importantly, eminently musical Gypsies. Because of his former activities as an arranger for the DTU and his personal friendship with the influential Willi Stech, he was able to secure most modern sheet arrangements for his band. The Belgrade orchestra frequently performed in the city's university, playing such standbys as Harry James's "Backbeat Boogie" to the delight of the native youths. Supported by an exceptionally sympathetic superior, First Lieutenant Karl-Heinz Reintgen, Meyer himself composed jazzlike songs and improvised freely on the station's grand piano, for instance in between the often American jazz records. One Wehrmacht jazz fan who heard him play his "Lullaby" thought it "a mixture of a rhapsody and a hot-piano solo." Moreover, Meyer persuaded some of the Reich's more imaginative artists, such as the scat-singing Evelyn Künneke, Kary Barnet from the old Scala, and clarinetist Horst Winter, to make brief cameo appearances at the station. Meanwhile back in Berlin, Stech made a jazz recording of Meyer's composition "Without Delay," featuring Brocksieper on drums, Primo Angeli on piano, and Kurt Wege on clarinet.[75]

Soldatensender Belgrad became notorious not only for its huge transmitting power, through which it could be heard all over Europe and North Africa by friend and foe alike, but also, in the eyes of the Berlin regime, for its irreverent jazz policy and its conscious affinity with the cabaret culture of the republic. Members of the Kadeko, suspect but still visible, performed at the station at the end of 1943.[76] Meyer fell irreparably out of grace when in early 1944 he was accused of having used "Jewish-American numbers" in one of his piano presentations. They had indeed been variations on themes from *Shall We Dance* and *Broadway Melody,* strictly taboo after February 1942! The matter was brought before the RKK, and Meyer's immediate expulsion from the German corps of musicians was prevented only by the course of the war—because of the general shortage of experts, it was more convenient to wait until after the Final Victory. Still, he was affected by a performance ban applying to all the German civilian stations.[77] At the eleventh hour, someone in high places had decreed that one of the more vocal exponents of jazz in the German Reich must fall victim to disgrace.

The Jazz Victims

Sometime very early in the morning on a day in 1943 there was a knock on the door of pianist Martin Roman's rented room in Amsterdam. Curtly, Gestapo men ordered him to get dressed. Then they shot Roman's dog before his eyes and took the musician with them. Eventually he found himself in the Dutch Westerbork concentration camp where he met other German-Jewish artists who, like himself, had fled to the Netherlands. Because the camp commander, a former policeman from Düsseldorf now in the SS, was fascinated by cabaret, Roman received an opportunity to ply his trade as a jazz musician for several months. The Westerbork Stage Group, as it was called, also employed Kurt Gerron, once famous in Germany as a comedian and operetta singer, who had played "Tiger Brown" in the 1928 premiere of Kurt Weill's *Threepenny Opera* and had starred, alongside Marlene Dietrich, in *The Blue Angel.*[78]

The Nazis had finally caught up with a man who, like all other jazz artists in the occupied countries of Northwestern Europe, had been exposing himself to ever greater risks just for his art. In Amsterdam and while touring before 1940, pianist Roman had had the good fortune to accompany famous American players Coleman Hawkins, Lionel Hampton, and Louis Armstrong. The former Weintraub Syncopator had also played with Django Reinhardt at the Amsterdam Carlton hotel.

After the fall of 1942, the careers of French, Belgian, Dutch, and Danish musicians increasingly hinged as much on indigenous cultural policies in their countries of origin as on inflexible tenets of Nazi ideology. Because nothing was really binding in the administration of those countries and much was left to chance, they often got away unscathed. Thus, although the Hot Clubs of Paris and also Brussels took a quasi-political stand by establishing morale-boosting contacts with jazz-loving prisoners of war in Germany, French and Belgian jazz musicians, as long as they were not Jewish, were generally left alone. Undoubtedly, Berlin intended them to continue providing ready entertainment for scores of fun-starved German soldiers. As Dietrich Schulz-Köhn has explained: "A soldier stationed in France could be transferred to Russia practically any day. And they said: Who knows how long the poor bugger has still got left! Hence there was a certain leeway."[79]

Even the Gypsy guitarist Django Reinhardt was not molested, although in 1943 he almost dug his own grave when trying to escape from southern France to Switzerland because he had heard that Gypsies from the Reich were beginning to be gassed. He was let go by the Wehrmacht frontier commander who happened to be a jazz fan. When Reinhardt tried again a few days later, Swiss customs officials refused him entry and sent him back into Vichy territory, all caked with mud, so that ultimately Django returned to Paris. Here he and his friends kept on playing in various formations, to the delight of many German soldiers who knew just where to find him.[80]

In Brussels, Paris, and Hilversum in Holland even records were cut at a time when this was impossible in the badgered Reich.[81] Dutch musicians continued to be harassed and finally regulated much more sharply because of fanatical quisling censors (who had probably had a hand in Roman's capture), whereas in accordance with overall occupation policy the Danes appear to have been the least molested.[82]

In early January 1944 Gerron and Roman were among hundreds of Westerbork inmates who were entrained for the Czech concentration camp of Terezín, a former self-contained Austro-Hungarian garrison known to its German victims as Theresienstadt. The modest urban site served the Nazis as a model concentration camp in case they had to produce prominent Jewish prisoners to International Red Cross commissions in a hurry, and therefore many formerly well-known artists, but also professionals and eminent leaders of local Jewish communities such as the German Dr. Paul Eppstein—later Terezín's mayor—ended up there. A comfortable stay in Terezín was never guaranteed; periodically, transports were sent to Auschwitz, and they invariably consisted of the sick and elderly.[83]

Roman and Gerron both qualified for entry into this camp under the "artist" rubric. And while Kommandant Karl Rahm, yet another culture-craving SS officer, immediately engaged Gerron to take charge of a cabaret entitled "Karussell," the pianist was at first made to sweep the streets. Subsequently, Roman was discovered by a Czech amateur trumpet player, Eric Vogel, who had organized an orchestra that played mostly Jewish tunes, chiefly for the amusement of the commandant. Vogel immediately asked for and received permission to entrust the leadership of the band to Roman, whose fame had preceded him among musicians. The pianist needed a few weeks until he had reshaped the entire orchestra along the lines of a current American swing band.[84]

The Ghetto Swingers, as that band came to be called, had as their most prolific musician Bedřich Weiss, an already renowned twenty-five-year-old Jewish clarinetist from Prague whom they called Fricek, and who looked and nearly played like Benny Goodman. The distinguished Czech-Canadian novelist Josef

Škvorecký has recently described him as "a musician of rare genius."[85] Yet another musician whom Roman came to meet there was the young Berlin guitarist Coco Schumann, by racial standards a Jew who had, in 1943, been rounded up by the Gestapo and sent to Terezín rather than Auschwitz because his father, an "Aryan," had fought in World War I. When Coco joined the orchestra, there already was a guitarist there, so he took the place of the drummer who had just been sent to Auschwitz. Coco knew some percussion from his earlier days when his uncle, before emigration to America, had left him with a drum set.[86] In the relatively unfettered atmosphere of Terezín, the regular inmates themselves were on rare occasions allowed to visit the café in the central marketplace where the Ghetto Swingers performed, but ordinarily, only the crème of concentration camp society, the capos and block wardens, could attend, that is, apart from the omnipotent SS.[87]

A chance to prove themselves, or so the artists thought, came in the summer of 1944 when the regime leadership had decided to create a propaganda film showing the German public how well cared for the Jews, alleged victims of persecution, really were. This was contemplated in connection with an International Red Cross visit on 22 June. As the expert showman that he was, Gerron was ordered to produce the film, which was intended to give a totally false picture of the camp situation. The planning for it was meticulous. Beforehand, approximately seven thousand aged inmates were moved out to Auschwitz in order to convey the impression of youthfulness. Those who remained cleaned the streets and painted the facades, and even a phony bank was opened to deal in worthless ghetto currency. The central café was splendidly decked out, and there were special rehearsals for several theater productions as well as for the jazz band. Rahm had threatened its leader Roman: "I tell you something, when you conduct, your hair will fly. Because if your hair doesn't fly, I grab you on your tie and then your hair, I promise you, your hair will fly!"[88]

The movie, cynically entitled *The Führer Donates a Town to the Jews*, turned out to be one of the most perfidious lies the National Socialists ever managed to cast in celluloid. As the team was filming, children were seen eating fresh fruit and calling out to Karl Rahm, that philanthropic commandant, "Again sardines, Uncle Rahm, do we have to eat sardines again?" In the newly erected wooden pavilion of the town center Karel Ančerl's string chamber orchestra performed selected classics, and then the Ghetto Swingers sizzled it up with a swing arrangement of "Bugle Call Rag." It has been said that Fricek Weiss had never played his clarinet better. Like his fellow bandsmen, he was dressed in an immaculate blue blazer adorned with the Star of David. Nevertheless, immediately after the filming, these blazers were collected again and matters returned to normal. The film was shipped to Berlin for editing, but was never completed for the German cinemas. Copies of it later reached Czech and Israeli archives.[89]

The "reward" for the participating principals was to be transport to Auschwitz. Schumann arrived there with his friend Fricek Weiss, on 4 September; other musicians, including Roman and Vogel, were brought in a few weeks later. During "selection" on the Auschwitz ramp, sinister SS physician Josef Mengele inquired of the blue-eyed, nineteen-year-old Coco whence he came and what he did. "Berlin, Herr Obersturmbannführer!" shouted Schumann in his best High German, "Occupation: Plumber, Herr Obersturmbannführer!" Mengele, who was quick to acknowledge the straightforward manner, the Berlin origins, and an honest trade at the same time, told Coco to step to the left, which saved the youth's life. Then it was Fricek's turn, and that of his parents. After the old couple had been told to move to the right, Fricek immediately asked Mengele to be allowed to join them. With a diabolic grin, the doctor granted the wish. Within a few hours, the Weiss family was dead.[90]

Eventually, Schumann was able to organize something with Roman and Vogel that could vaguely pass for a band. There was no dearth of instruments, what with thousands of Jews and Gypsies having brought them into the camp for months as part of their baggage. Indeed, Auschwitz already had several orchestras, including the all-woman formation well known from Fania Fénelon's description and The Merry Five, a swing combo. Because for reasons of camp prestige every lowly SS guard wished to maintain an orchestra in his own block, no matter how small, reasonably healthy musicians arriving at the railway station had an excellent chance of saving themselves. Henryk Eisenman, who stemmed from generations of professional musicians in his native Lodz and who had played classical as well as dance music on the saxophone and the piano with Germans, Poles, and Jews, remembers his arrival at the death camp around the time of Schumann's: "We were greeted in Auschwitz by a full, first-class symphony orchestra playing Richard Wagner's 'Lohengrin.' "[91]

While in Auschwitz, Eisenman and other musician inmates conversant with swing and older jazz styles met with a phenomenon that might seem strange but will not surprise anyone who has already encountered the entire spectrum of absurdities and contradictions in the Third Reich: an SS corporal who was bent on intoxicating himself with modern jazz. In the fall of 1944 Pery Broad was twenty-four years old. The son of a German woman and a Brazilian merchant, he had accompanied his mother back to the Reich as a very young child. He had attended school in Berlin, evidently learning several languages, and while there had become an ardent member of the Hitler Youth, as would so many ethnic Germans not wholly sure of their heritage. In 1941 the eccentric young man volunteered for the Waffen-SS and, because of extreme short-sightedness, was posted to Auschwitz for training. And there he stayed, becoming a member of the feared Political Division in June 1942. When Broad was a defendant at the Frankfurt Auschwitz Trials in 1964–65, where I caught more than a glimpse of him from the spectator's gallery, charges of deathly selection on the Auschwitz ramp; multiple murder, especially of Gypsies; and individual killings could not be proved against him, and hence he got off lightly as a mere "accomplice."[92] Yet among Auschwitz inmates his aura was that of a capricious killer; in retrospect, Henryk Eisenmann has called him a "sadist." In his better moods Broad would listen to and join in the performance of modern jazz, swinging, with expert ease, on a multiregister accordion. In the autumn of 1941, already an SS soldier, Broad had attempted to become a member of Werner Daniels's Wehrmacht jazz reporting circle and had, in fact, volunteered a story about the

Jewish musicians Benny Goodman and Artie Shaw. Plausibly, Daniels explains today that Broad participated in the jazz news service only once.[93]

Was it Broad who was responsible for distributing sheet music to certain of the camp musicians? There were fox-trots by the jazz experts Horst Kudritzki and Billy Bartholomew, among others, and even an arrangement for the Andrews Sisters' "Joseph, Joseph," written by four Jews, including Charlie Chaplin, and, in a camouflage version, beloved by swing fans from Breslau to Frankfurt as a vehicle for ridiculing Goebbels.[94] Whatever the case may be, it is clear that Coco Schumann, after he had been reunited with a few of the Terezín musicians, did not play these scores or any other jazz tunes, at least not very frequently. Instead, they mostly had to perform songs popular in Germany, such as "La Paloma"; sometimes operetta standards; and ever again military marches. They did so for the private amusement of their captors, but also for powerful inmate capos. Regularly, they were compelled to work during the obligatory tatooing of new inmates, but often their job was even more gruesome than that. When men were carted by on lorries to be hanged, they had to play, as well as during the actual executions, or processions of entire phalanxes of emaciated inmates to the gas chambers. And they had friends who performed in idle gas chambers for SS men frolicking there with SS women, straight out of Dante's Hell.[95]

The legendary Kurt Gerron was marched to the gas chamber while being forced to sing the tune that had made him famous, the "Canon Song" from *The Threepenny Opera*. Coco Schumann, Martin Roman, and Eric Vogel were the only original members of the Terezín Ghetto Swingers to survive the Holocaust, for they were finally liberated when Allied troops reached Auschwitz and camps further west. Every one of them has maintained ever since that music saved his life; in fact, that it was jazz that saved it, jazz utilized, abused, and debased by representatives of a regime that had become inured to the impact of a universal culture, to the same degree that it had become immune to the sufferings of humankind.[96]

In camps such as Auschwitz or Buchenwald, Jews were permitted and sometimes ordered to perform "Jewish" music as a sport for the SS.[97] In Germany itself, where only a few initiates whispered of concentration camp horrors, a somewhat contradictory, if not to say counterproductive, policy toward jazz music was now being followed. Officially, since the institution of the DTU in the summer of 1942, American-style jazz was extinct in the Reich. The DTU's music was accepted at face value as a competent replacement, and when it had gotten out of line by late 1943, its course was appropriately corrected.

But the position of jazz in the last two years of the Third Reich was somewhat similar to that of whiskey in Saudi Arabia during the 1980s: despite consensus that it was blacklisted it could be had, clandestinely, if one knew where to get it, and obviously for a price. In the greater Nazi Reich, jazz, still broadcast by the Wehrmacht stations, was produced by a specially dedicated short-wave studio and could be purchased on the sly by the Wehrmacht in the form of recordings made in occupied territories. One could tune in to it on Anglo-American broadcasts, even at great risk, and fan groups in Hamburg,

Frankfurt, Leipzig, and Breslau would either jive to it, as it emanated from illicit loudspeakers, or produce it for private consumption themselves.

Against the background of this compromised situation, in which even the SS realized the need for front soldiers to relax with the help of swing, pen-wielding party fanatics of the old order, chief among them Herbert Gerigk and Fritz Stege, had great difficulty in coming to grips in the pages of their pamphlets with the hated, still extant phenomenon. On the one hand they could adopt the official line that Goebbels seemed to suggest, namely that the evil had been excized. Hence deceptive laudations were printed hailing the arrival of a new era, in which jazz as one used to know it had been purged. On the other hand, those critics who were aware that old-style, swinging jazz was still lurking in nooks and crannies and who did not—and with good reason!—trust the DTU model, went on with their old polemics.

In those diatribes it was habitual to associate jazz with blacks, Jews, and degeneracy.[98] Especially vicious now were spokesmen for the Hitler Youth, which had borne its share of troubles in altercations with big-city dissidents and was at pains to go on renewed offensives for what it regarded as its genuine new Teutonic subculture.[99] A particularly hideous example of such invective, clearly focusing on juveniles, appeared after D-Day toward the end of June 1944, when the "Swing Jew" Benny Goodman was depicted in a leading Berlin weekly as the "Pied Piper of New York," with the hands of a criminal, bent on the sexual corruption of America's young.[100] This piece could conceivably have been authored by one Prof. Gotthold Frotscher, who taught at the Berlin State Conservatory for Music Education and also served as a section leader in the Hitler Youth central hierarchy.[101] Another writer capable of producing this was the notorious Max Merz, the inveterate former Austrian public school teacher, whose credibility had lately suffered on account of his inability to prove his "Aryan" pedigree beyond a doubt, even though the party had already issued him a membership card in February 1940.[102]

In the midst of these developments, the position of the RMK, Goebbels's original instrument for the control of music in the land, was gradually being eroded. Its president, Prof. Peter Raabe, would surely have been happy to accept credit for any of the policing measures that had occurred in the past, and certainly for those that were still being enacted. For instance, there were edicts in 1942 and 1943 that set down new regulations for any music to be played by dance musicians, evicted the odd instrumentalist for having performed "Jewish" music, and warned German bands not to play the "U-Bahn-Fox" in an arrangement by the scorching Fud Candrix band.[103] There was even an attempt to put a stop to the racy style in which Fritz Brocksieper was wont to issue some of his better records on the Brunswick label.[104]

Overall, however, Raabe was frustrated by the fact that Goebbels had seen fit, for whatever practical reasons, never to promulgate a cut-and-dry prohibition of jazz, even during Germany's darker hours, and the professor had no illusions about the Wehrmacht stations, German civilian radio, and the role the DTU was playing there. As far as this unctious old man was concerned, the Reich stations were still broadcasting undiluted jazz and, as he unequivocally stated in July

1943, as long as this continued, "an effective fight against it simply is impossible."[105] Raabe was immeasurably irked by his own impotence in the area of radio, whose functionaries were countermanding anything that he was trying to set right through his policies for the RMK. And he must have been insulted by the fact that party leaders at regional levels again and again found it necessary for their own purposes to issue autonomous indictments of jazz (as did Gauleiter Martin Mutschmann for Saxony about the time that Raabe wrote his letter), indictments that had nothing to do with either himself or Minister Goebbels.[106]

Moreover, not only was the party encroaching on Raabe's own prerogative, but the SS and Gestapo were doing it also, as had been painfully demonstrated in the case of the Hamburg Swings. Why, even the social-dance proscription, in whose formulation Raabe had earlier had a hand, was in danger of being lifted in April 1944, reportedly because the Hitler Youth had complained to Goebbels about a lack of communal recreation![107] To complicate matters, the RMK was devalued even further two months later, when Hinkel left his post in the overarching RKK. For his tentative replacement there as general secretary was Dr. Hans-Erich Schrade, a virtual nonentity in the Reich culture administration and a man even less interested in doing Raabe's bidding than the SS general had been.[108]

Whether the hapless RMK was involved or not, from fall 1942 to the end of the regime there certainly was no lack of harassment, even persecution, of active instrumentalists and vocal artists connected with the jazz culture. The targeted men and women now were truly made to feel like outcasts, as Nazi dogma had defined them long ago. It is significant that woman singers suffered for a variety of reasons wholly paradigmatic of the Nazi system of intolerance. These women—none of them a true jazz singer, for this species did not yet exist in Germany—sometimes approximated not a German, but an American composure; they tended to be of foreign origin, or they had Jewish blood or were closely associated with Jews. Above all else, they were independent women often commanding large fees, and as such their professional existence deeply offended this fundamentally misogynist regime. It is telling that one of the malicious charges of the male-elitist SS in July 1944 was that nowadays it had become the custom for woman singers to effect a "beer-barrel bass."[109] This broadside was meant for deep-voiced Zarah Leander, Kirsten Heiberg (Franz Grothe's Norwegian wife), Rosita Serrano, and Lale Andersen, all style-setting divas in show business and song; most of them, alas, had left the Reich by the time it was published, for reasons to be explained below.

In late 1939 Margot Hielscher was an unusually attractive brunette, who at twenty years of age had a job in the costume department of Terra Filmkunst, one of the Berlin movie companies Joseph Goebbels was fond of stalking for suitable starlets to warm his bed with. He happened upon Margot, as she was already cast in a minor role for the Mary Stuart film *Heart of a Queen*. In 1940 she was invited to have dinner with him and, typically, to watch a private showing of *Gone with the Wind*, during which he tried to become intimate. She reminded him of Vivien Leigh, said Goebbels, which displeased Margot, who wished to resemble Katherine Hepburn instead. The starlet resisted several attempts by the minister to seduce her, and finally, in 1942, succeeded in obtaining a larger role in *Women Are No Angels*. In this movie, Margot the swing disciple and solid Stauffer fan played a seductive nightclub singer aboard a huge, luxurious ocean liner; the screen music was by real jazzmen, and on the sound-track, as well as on an Odeon recording simultaneously produced with the jazz band of Benny de Weille, Hielscher sang very much like her American counterparts of the period.[110]

Now a star, the actress was nonetheless censored in May 1943 by Hans Hinkel, after she had reproduced some of her film songs on radio, for having sung too hot. By that time, the post-Stalingrad directives were in effect, which forbade any loosened-up music. This may not be the whole story, however. For already, Margot Hielscher had become the epitomy of the Americanized woman whom the Nazi press eschewed. Goebbels himself—in a gesture of revenge— told her to her face that her mouth was much too large, that it was an American mouth, "not a good German mouth." Hielscher thereupon went on tour as chansonnier with Peter Kreuder and tried to spend more time in Prague than in Berlin, at any rate to stay out of the way of the spiteful lechers in the Goebbels ministry. Indeed, Sefton Delmer's Black Propaganda service had already dropped a leaflet from the sky, conveying the apocryphal message that Margot was the mistress of Hinkel, kept by him in a secret mansion.[111]

The woman who had successfully protected Margot Hielscher at that 1940 film showing with Goebbels was Zarah Leander, the Swedish film star and singer, who throughout much of the Third Reich reigned supreme in German movie studios. Leander, too, claims that Goebbels never succeeded in possessing her. Be that as it may, with her basso contralto, she was perhaps even more removed from the art of jazz than was Hielscher, but she was a friend of the Swedish big-band leader Arne Hülphers, whom she later married. Her private relationship with Goebbels notwithstanding, the tall, dark-haired Leander for years was the absolute darling of the German entertainment world, a superstar who enjoyed the rare privilege of collecting a third of her munificent pay in hard Swedish currency.[112]

Her falling-out with the regime most certainly was a consequence of increased personal fears on her part, especially as the bombs were falling on Berlin, and mounting xenophobia in the Reich: after Stalingrad, any foreigner could be a spy, and so her personal freedom was curtailed. As Werner Daniels's "Musikalische Feldpost" sequels show, hardcore German jazz fans had never particularly liked her singing on the borderline between commercial tunes and jazz—a line that every musician from either camp sooner or later has to contend with, greats like Charlie Parker, Oscar Peterson, or Stan Getz not excluded.[113]

Although Leander had become expert at playing Wehrmacht war widows in morale-boosting movies, her characteristically deep voice was rejected by ordinary radio listeners as "alien" as early as December 1940. In June 1943 Goebbels received a letter from a German doctor stating that "Zarah Leander might croon her tunes to the accompaniment of an American jazz band in the hangout of hookers, but German Radio can have no room for this category of 'art.' "[114] A few weeks before, the star's villa in Berlin-Grunewald had taken a hit and become inhabitable. Goebbels had already tried to move her off her Swedish payroll and now wanted her to assume German citizenship and the status of a "State Actress." Hence in October Leander hurriedly left for Sweden; thereafter, all her films were banned in the Reich and she herself was declared persona non grata.[115]

In her halcyon days, Chilean-born Rosita Serrano was almost as popular as "Die Leander," but her imperfect knowledge of German precluded a career in films, which the admiring Goebbels would otherwise have offered her. She had arrived in Berlin in September 1937 as a twenty-three-year-old to visit her mother, Sophia del Campo, a famous opera singer who had starred in the Paris opera and now had joined her second husband, a German-Chilean businessman based in the Reich. One evening the two ladies visited the show in the Wintergarten, featuring a well-known female singer. Unimpressed, amateur Rosita persuaded the manager in fluent French to allow her to try out a few days later. She then appeared with her Spanish acoustic guitar, accompanying herself as she showed off the immense range of her phenomenal untrained voice, from the deepest bass to coloratura soprano. The Germans, who had never heard such sounds before, applauded frenetically. Thus was launched one of the most picturesque show business careers of the Third Reich.[116]

The exotic-looking descendant of a Chilean Araucanian Indian soon was sought after by composers and arrangers of all popular genres, including the vaunted swing. Within two weeks of her own, much-celebrated premiere in the Wintergarten, the "Chilean Nightingale" was signed on by Telefunken managers, who also had Teddy Stauffer and Peter Kreuder under contract. After Serrano had won first prize at the Berlin Radio Festival of 1938, Telefunken arranged a German concert tour for her as vocalist for Kreuder's well-known group. And so the singer was initiated into the jazz culture, for while Kreuder's music always had the commercial touch, he had at heart remained the jazz pianist he was when he started his career. Serrano, whose primadonna airs often clashed with the excessive vanity of Peter Kreuder, struck up a friendship with Hans Korseck, Kreuder's entirely jazz-oriented guitarist, and from him as well as from reed player Kurt Wege she learned not only a jazz approach to vocalizing, but also several technical tricks for her own guitar-playing. Yet her style always remained inimitably hers; the most jazzlike elements of her performance were that unshakeable sense of rhythm possessed by many Latin Americans and the original timbre of her voice, which often, if not always, blended effectively with the harmonies of the jazz instruments around her. Rosita improvised and used her vocal chords, as she insists today, "like an instrument."[117]

Prompted by Telefunken, Serrano cut a Latin-jazz record with Teddy Stauffer, whom she briefly joined as a singer during a Swiss engagement. Just before the outbreak of the war Serrano teamed up with Kurt Hohenberger's new-formed combo, with Fritz Schulze on piano and Detlef Lais on reeds. Right into 1942, she was with this group on *Truppenbetreuung,* and in between, she sang popular hits, live and on recordings, some written just for her. Hers became a household name, and she was mobbed wherever she greeted soldiers.[118] Among German jazz fans she also met with qualified approval, because her rendition of

swing tunes, even under the necessary disguise, ably complemented the virtuosity of the Hohenberger soloists.[119]

Like Zarah Leander, the Chilean singer began to fall victim to nationalist-
inspired xenophobia by about the end of 1940. In 1942 she embarked on a three-
month tour of Sweden, accompanied by a Swedish orchestra, and gave a special
performance for King Gustav V. After her return to Berlin, she received anonymous telephone calls insinuating that she was the King's mistress and, as a
threat, a postcard from a German concentration camp. The Gestapo visited her
house a couple of times, one night finding her tuned in to Jack Hylton on the
BBC. Imperiously, she frightened away the secret policemen with the help of the
Chilean ambassador, whom she had ordered to arrive at once, in his pyjamas if
necessary. But by year's end—the Stalingrad debacle was imminent—radio
directives had specified that the artist's participation in future programs, while
not exactly censored, was "undesirable."[120]

Serrano's difficulties were exacerbated thereafter. In the spring of 1943, the
intensifying bomb attacks were intimidating her as they intimidated Leander; in
the German sky, the proverbial silver lining had now been replaced by traces of
enemy warplanes. There were more ugly telephone calls. Urged by her ailing
mother, the entertainer left for Sweden in early summer and was instantly suspected as an Allied spy. When she decided to stage special performances for
fugitive Jewish children from Denmark, the Gestapo banned all her recordings
and prepared for her arrest should she ever return to the Reich.[121]

To be sure, the regime's opposition did not weigh all that heavily on those
three singers. Margot Hielscher, never persecuted, was only on the edge of
censorship, and the two foreigners must accept the charge of having taken advantage of material benefits offered to them by a totalitarian regime that remunerated
them handsomely for their show of loyalty and temperamental charm, which was
beneficial to the regime's credibility abroad. It is highly questionable whether
Leander and Serrano would ever have left the Reich had the war not caused a
wave of ill will against foreigners and had they themselves not become physically
inconvenienced. After the war, both singers paid dearly for their obvious opportunism: Leander was shunned by her Swedish cocitizens, and Serrano found it
problematic to make an artistic comeback in a democratic Germany.[122]

Three other women found themselves in much more precarious situations
because, as German citizens, they could not leave the Reich even had they
wanted to, and their offence was not merely an affinity with jazz, but a provable
connection with Jews.

Heading that list is Lale Andersen, who brought "Lili Marlen" to life. This
blond and blue-eyed Frisian German, who personified the "Aryan" notion of
racial superiority like no one else, fell out of grace with the Nazi regime less for
her proximity to jazz, which was marginal, but for more important, albeit jazz-
related, reasons.[123]

First, as a Berlin chansonnier barely over twenty she had been closely
associated with the political cabaret of the republic and had, in fact, participated
in the Berlin performance of *Mahagonny* by Bert Brecht and Kurt Weill in
November 1931. Since then, she remained a reasonably prominent denizen of the

Kadeko, in which she acted as late as 1938. Second, while in Zurich in 1933, she had become the lover of Rolf Liebermann, the young Jewish student of composition and proponent of atonal music who, incidentally, was to act as an important European champion of jazz after 1945. Lale almost married Liebermann, had it not been for her need to pursue an independent artist's career for herself, which was impossible in narrow Switzerland. Early in the Nazi regime, she helped Liebermann smuggle valuables of Jewish émigrés across the German-Swiss border. Back in the Reich in 1933, she remained in correspondence with those émigré friends, in particular Kurt Hirschfeld, the artistic director of Zurich's municipal stage.

Third and most seriously, however, she became the victim of her own success when in 1941–42 she was internationally known as the original "Lili Marlen," after Soldatensender Belgrad's phenomenal venture had taken off. While it has been said that Goebbels himself envied Andersen for her newly won popularity, it is much more likely that it was Anita Spada, then Hinkel's chief mistress, who had become jealous of the singer and wanted her neutralized. This suspicion is fortified by evidence which proves that Hinkel single-handedly planned every step of the campaign against her.[124]

Andersen's ordeal began in November 1941, at the height of her newfound fame, when Hinkel informed Goebbels that the singer was now demanding much higher fees because of the "Lili Marlen" song which, in his opinion, was rendered less than perfect through her art. In December, Hinkel prohibited the production of new recordings by the singer, and six months later, the publication in the media of her portrait had become subject to ministry censure.[125] In September 1942, Andersen's latest letter to Hirschfeld, like all the others intercepted by the Gestapo, was used as a pretext to isolate her from the entertainment business forthwith. A formal charge of treason was considered along with a concentration camp term; her voice disappeared forever from the Belgrade station. By November the desperate Andersen noted in her diary that rumor had it that she had been Hinkel's mistress and now was being booted out by her successor.[126]

When in May 1943, as the post-Stalingrad restrictions were slowly being lifted, she was readmitted to the public realm, the embargo on her signature tune, "Lili Marlen," remained in place. It is likely that Goebbels himself had decided not to make a martyr of a woman whose oldest son, by this time, was serving on the Eastern front and who had transmitted signals of personal naivité rather than political design. Andersen survived yet another nasty affront in October, when a concert she was giving with her Belgian jazz accompanist John Witjes in Sudeten Gablonz was shouted down by a delegation of Hitler Youths specially trucked in for the occasion. By this time she had a Gestapo chaperone.[127]

Two other female singers became victims because of the combination of jazz and a partly Jewish ancestry. Evelyn Künneke had one Jewish grandparent, and Margot Friedländer was a half Jew. In the recollection of jazz fans today, Künneke's scat-singing came close to the real thing; it was definitely swing-oriented. Having done her share of *Truppenbetreuung,* she was loved by the soldiers.[128] In Amsterdam one day in 1944, she dropped a defeatist remark to the effect that the Red Army would soon occupy all of Germany. Back in Berlin, the Gestapo arrested her in December. She was beaten, and on 28 January 1945 she appeared before a special court. The verdict threatened her with execution on a charge of treason, and she was transferred to death row. Fans of hers in the SS managed to get her out on the pretense that her voice was needed to imitate Ella Fitzgerald's for broadcasts against the Allies planned by Charlie and His Orchestra. But matters were already too confounded that late in the war, and Künneke survived, staying with her parents in Berlin.[129]

Margot Friedländer was entrapped in a similar manner, perhaps deliberately so. While on a troop entertainment junket at the front near Leningrad in fall 1943, she befriended a group of local Russian musicians in the employ of the Wehrmacht. Having brought them cigarettes and sweets, she mentioned that as dictators Hitler and Stalin were very comparable. One of these musicians was a Gestapo spy who immediately reported her. Friedländer was taken into custody and interrogated by Major Egon Baron von Wackerbarth of the military police, a party and SA member. However, because he had pity on the singer, the baron had the initial, lethal charge of defeatism replaced by "suspicion of spying." He must have known that no evidence for spying would be found, and so Wackerbarth was able to cause Friedländer to be sent back to Berlin rather than delivered into the hands of the merciless Gestapo. Friedländer returned to the singing business in 1944 but endured more tribulations when her comusician Heinz Sandberg was indicted. Again the Gestapo became interested in her. She was to be conscripted for a chain gain on the permanently endangered railway tracks when one of the Italian resident musicians in Berlin agreed to hide her until the war was over.[130]

Male jazz artists were also treading on much thinner ice after August 1942, when their private and public behavior became more closely scrutinized by the authorities. Peter Kreuder has several times been mentioned in this book as a musician who was normally commercially attuned and whose many original songs were featured on records and in films. In the entire realm, his greed for worldly possessions, his callousness against fellow musicians, and his craving for attention of any kind were legend. Yet at the same time everyone knew that at heart this erstwhile assistant to Weintraub Syncopator Friedrich Hollaender was a jazzman with a unique piano touch, and his prewar group, consisting of Korseck, Klagemann, Wege, Henneberg, and Otto Tittmann on bass became famous throughout continental Europe. In the autumn of 1943 Kreuder, who had earlier, quite credibly, been accused of plagiarizing Robert Schumann's "Träumerei," fell into disgrace because of his refusal to concertize in the industrialized Rhineland, which was threatened by Allied bombing more than any other German region. Charged with cowardice, his military-exempt status came close to being suspended, and he was almost expelled from the RMK. But Goebbels wished to give this popular entertainer, whose regular commercial clichés were great favorites with Hitler, another chance, and he still was needed in the propagandistically viable film business.[131]

Unlike the political ingenue Kreuder, who could easily separate his superb jazz qualities from the rest of his disreputable persona, bar pianist Peter Igelhoff had a consistent political conscience as well as a sharp satirical wit with which he spiced the lyrics of his songs, some of them not so veiled criticisms of the dictatorship.[132] Igelhoff was the musical Werner Finck. For years, he had been in residence at the Uhu-Bar, near the Scala, whose patrons would often come to hear him after the revue performance. Igelhoff worked the keyboard and used his voice very much in the manner of Fats Waller. Billy Bartholomew and Fritz Brocksieper had played with him, and with Hans Korseck he had recorded such jazz standards as "Organ Grinder's Swing" and "Pennies from Heaven."[133]

Just before the Stalingrad catastrophe, Igelhoff, who like Kreuder had performed for *Truppenbetreuung,* was deemed a disrespectful entertainer who could not hold his tongue, and his long-standing association with the Kadeko suddenly was thought unbearable. In mid-January 1943 the pianist was drafted by the army and employed in clerical positions, mostly in France. At the same time, his recordings were deleted from German radio programs. As late as March 1945 the vengeful RMK officials were considering active combat for the forty-year-old pianist, and it was merely the confusion of the last weeks of the regime that prevented this disaster.[134]

Three other jazz musicians fared much worse than either Kreuder or Igelhoff, who were ultimately too prominent to be put out of the way without much ado. One was Heinz Sandberg, a young ex–Hitler Youth piano and accordion player who in the spring of 1944 was working in Hamburg's Faun and Trichter bars with Margot Friedländer and a swing band consisting mostly of Czechs. "We were burning alright," asserts Friedländer, who then would announce such numbers as "Cotton Pickers' Congregation" under the pseudonym "Rhythmic Study, A,B,C." The twenty-three-year-old Sandberg already was under suspicion for having played swing quite unrestrainedly for soldiers stationed in Norway, and his last-known performance in Hamburg openly violated the system of rules carefully constructed since 1939. After his arrest by the Gestapo early in June 1944 he was committed to Wehrmacht authorities, who were looking for him anyhow because of draft evasion. Sandberg's expulsion from the RMK occurred in August. It is a miracle that he came through the war untouched, for Friedländer saw him during 1946 in Berlin, after he had changed his name to Charlie Sanders and opened a small Hamburg concert agency.[135]

Karl Hohenberger, the younger sibling of the much more famous Kurt, had been fortunate enough to gain a trumpet chair in the DTU, whence he had come from the Scala. Like many of these musicians, he drank heavily, but unlike them, he often got thoroughly out of control and then spoke his mind. Despite his enviable position in the DTU, he was obviously smarting under the fetters that kept him from playing the music he was really devoted to, the original jazz from America, not the Nazi-ordered ersatz. On 18 September 1943, just before the DTU's move to Prague, young Hohenberger was arrested after a routine rehearsal with the orchestra. Assuming imminent execution, the DTU's manager Safronow instantly replaced him.[136]

What had happened was that Hohenberger, not quite a week before, had entered the Berlin Cantina tavern in a rather alcoholic state. Lurching toward the piano player he demanded from him that only Jewish songs be played, of the kind that the officers at the front would like. As the proprietor, a party member, attempted to calm him down, Hohenberger pointed to the man's Nazi badge and, using expletives, shouted: "There is no reason to be proud of this thing! One way or the other, Adolf Hitler is finished!"[137]

From Gestapo headquarters Hohenberger was taken to Sachsenhausen concentration camp in December 1943, pending a trial for defeatism and treason. In June 1944 a Berlin special-court judge took his inebriated condition into account when he sentenced him to only two years in penitentiary. Of course, the musician's motive had not been just political; he was already known as a brawler and had been warned by his friends before. There is a double irony to this case. Hohenberger escaped from jail at the end of the war, whereas in Sachsenhausen he would have had a good chance of being killed. Yet just after May 1945, when he had made his way back to the capital, Soviet soldiers on patrol wished to see his papers. Karl reached into his pocket, whereupon the soldiers, thinking that he would pull a gun, shot him dead on the spot.[138]

The fact that Karl Hohenberger had seen fit, for whatever reason, to divorce his first wife, a Jew, in 1938, thereby being in accord with the Nuremberg Blood Laws of 1935, probably inclined the justice even more in his favor, but it is yet another telling comment on the basically apolitical nature of many of these musicians, to whom jazz had suggested vague notions of freedom or even licence without imparting to them a corresponding code of personal or political morality.[139] Had Hohenberger himself been a Jew, he would undoubtedly not even have been tried, but kept in Sachsenhausen to await his doom.

The Jewish pianist Hanns-Joachim Bessunger, still playing illegally on the Hamburg strip under the prostitutes' protection, was caught in 1944 by coincidence, when the Gestapo was looking for his sister. Even by Nazi standards Bessunger had not committed a crime other than "being the son of a person who was killed in Buchenwald," as the Gestapo quaintly put it, and he never had his day in court. He spent the rest of the war in Fuhlsbüttel, on a work detail burying the victims from other concentration camps. Bessunger later learned from captured documents that had the British not liberated the camp one day very early in May 1945, he would have been liquidated seventy-two hours later.[140]

In January 1945 Joseph Goebbels is said to have blamed the general war weariness of German youth on jazz.[141] If true, it would explain why the Swings of Hamburg were so ruthlessly routed after autumn 1942. Himmler, and with him Goebbels, was certain that by casting key Swings into concentration camps, jazz in its least acceptable form could finally be stamped out. After Jutta and Inga Madlung had arrived in Ravensbrück in the summer of 1942, they were especially punished by the SS guards for being fans of swing. They were struck in the face after admitting that they were the notorious Madlung Sisters known to vocalize obscene jazz, and then again after conceding they had been to England. Inga's leg was burned with a heated coin. To augment her agony, she was placed close to where the infamous camp physician Dr. Herta Oberheuser was dispatching the living to their death; she could hear the cries of the victims as they received lethal injections. Like all the other inmates, Inga and Jutta suffered from food deprivation, hunger, and cold. In their monthly letters the sisters had devised code messages to tell their parents of their wants. "Jutta is writing to

Carsten" meant that they were hungry, and "I want cookies from Pils'chen" conveyed their need for warm clothing; but only very little could come in from the outside.

For lack of nutrition, Inga developed open sores on the insides of her legs, which just would not heal. Over and beyond that, she was individually tortured by one of the sadistic camp physicians, whose name has eluded the historians. She was at the beginning stage of what later was diagnosed as scarlet fever, which was affecting her eyes. When she told an SS doctor about it, he made her look straight into the sun for fourteen days in a row, with a German shepherd dog beside her face, so she could neither turn her head nor nod. When this procedure was over, Inga, the Swing who loved life, had lost 90 percent of her vision.[142]

In Ravensbrück, the Madlung sisters came face to face with their old friend Ursula Nielsen, who had to withstand other travails, including the sexual advances of an amorous SS guard. After Ursula had been released at Christmas 1942, Jutta was freed eight months later. Inga was finally dismissed in November 1943. At the age of twenty-three this once beautiful girl had become obese from a combination of malnutrition and daily doses of saltpeter, used to restrain her libido, for Swings had the reputation of libertines. It took months of special care at her parents' home to return her to her normal weight, but both her eyes remained damaged.[143]

Insofar as they were not yet inducted into the army or had still escaped custody, known male Swings suffered a similar fate at the Neuengamme concentration camp. The Belgian Maurice Thomas eventually was trucked from Buchenwald to Bergen-Belsen and liberated by the British there.[144] The native Greek, Andreas Panagopoulos, was arrested in January 1943. Strangely, the Gestapo was aware of all the details regarding his prewar England trip. After some three weeks in Fuhlsbüttel, he was carted off to Neuengamme, of which he knew only the name. Andreas arrived toward nightfall, and as he was driven down center lane, he saw a white mountain ahead of him. Soon he realized that these were corpses. He was put to work in the stone-breaking compound, clad only in a thin jacket and wooden clogs that stuck in the mud with every step, and was beaten by vicious capos. The mountain of corpses was removed each morning, only to grow back at night. This continued until the summer, when Andreas, too, was released. Thereafter the independently wealthy young man vanished from Hamburg to Berlin, hiding out in various places with a half-Jewish girlfriend and frequenting the semi-illicit jazz joints, every night a new gamble.[145]

Meanwhile, half-Jewish Hans Hirschfeld had been coopted for the war effort, for he had become an expert automobile mechanic and was expected to help construct Mercedes engines for Messerschmitt airplanes. By 1943 his father, the garment retailer, was arrested for the second time, and now he was put on a train to Auschwitz—a rare occurrence for a German Jew married to an "Aryan," but a particular Hamburg Gestapo officer wanted it this way, most likely because of their Swing children. The old gentleman never came back. And while Hans with his rare skills was reasonably safe, his younger brother Kurt became another Swing victim of the Nazis.

Kurt had been conscripted to work, through the Organisation Todt, in a boiler firm. He was about to be transferred to a more strenuous job, when in early 1944 he and two other half-Jewish friends, Rolf Berensohn and Werner Möller, decided on a little celebration. They were joined by Kurt's girlfriend, Ursula Herbatz, a full "Aryan." Somehow the group ended up in one of the few hidden taverns of Hamburg's red-light district, the Reeperbahn, where some real wine was still to be had. The friends enjoyed themselves and became tipsy. On the way home, in jolly spirits, they fell into the good old swing tune, "Begin the Beguine," doing a bit of a tap dance. Little did they know that they were being followed by a crusty old policeman who already had observed them in the bar. This was not a Gestapo agent, just a normal off-duty police officer who thought he was a good patriot. Drawing his service revolver, he forced the four to accompany him to a police station, where they were met by the Gestapo.

The secret policemen immediately recognized Kurt Hirschfeld, whose father, the Jew, had just been sent to Auschwitz. And now they had nothing better to do than to torture and then accuse the three young men of sedition; the innocent little swing ditty had suddenly become the "Communist International." The transfer to organized communism ensured for the three non-"Aryan" suspects an indeterminate time in concentration camp, whereas Herbatz came under pressure to act as a spy among Swings. By the inscrutable logic of the SS, Möller and Hirschfeld were delivered to Neuengamme, whereas Berensohn was shipped off to Buchenwald. He and Möller survived, if somewhat incredibly. Hirschfeld, however, was hit on the neck one day with a rifle butt, contracted sepsis, and died, painfully, on 28 January 1945. His mother received one of those typical SS notices to the effect that he had succumbed to diphtheria. To add insult to injury, the SS camp administration offered this bereaved family a legal death certificate in exchange for seventy-two pfennigs, to be paid forthwith.[146]

It has been estimated that anywhere from forty to seventy male and female Swing youths were thrown into concentration camps, including Uckermark and Moringen for juniors, from 1942 to 1944. That the SS classified them all as "political" prisoners indicates the high ideological significance the Nazis attached to jazz in those last years of the war.[147]

Juveniles in Moringen, after good behavior, at least had the opportunity to join the Wehrmacht, that is if they were not sent to a concentration camp for adults after all.[148] Induction into the army was some kind of solution to the dilemma of Swing boys, short of being taken to the camps, because here they entered a jurisdiction that was removed from that of party and ordinary governmental agencies and afforded them greater liberties within the confines of martial law. It was an open secret that this could include the potential for indulging in jazz music, if not in the Swing life-style these adolescents had been accustomed to.

Nonetheless, many Swing boys are known to have fallen at the front, perhaps because they were purposely placed in unsafe positions to expose them as the effeminate cowards they were reputed to be. Indeed, of the surviving Wehrmacht Swings, at least three have testified that they were careful never to fire a shot at a human being, Russian or otherwise. Two of them, Hans Engel and Tommie Scheel, managed to cross over to enemy lines: Engel in 1944 in Italy and

Scheel in 1945 on the outskirts of Hamburg. That it was Americans and Britons with whom they ultimately fraternized corresponded with their fundamental philosophy of life. It is no accident that both settled in North America after the end of hostilities, Scheel in Toronto, and Engel in New York.[149]

The internment or conscription of these young men and women did not, by any means, end the phenomenon of jazz-inspired dissidence among Hamburg's youth. As in Leipzig and Frankfurt, new members were ever so slyly being recruited from the secondary schools and also the Hitler Youth. These younger cohorts—from a distance and through hearsay—had already been attracted by the fascinating Swings. Even though, because of the strong deterrents, there were fewer of them than ever before, they did exist, and some—unlike the older Swings who were sometimes little more than sybarites—had an acutely sharpened sense of justice and democracy, in addition to their adoration of the essential Swing subculture with its flashy accoutrements.

In 1943 fifteen-year-old Thorsten Müller, who, unlike most of his idols, hailed from the lower strata of Hamburg society, was an intelligent, sensitive, aesthetically aware boy who loved poetry, modern art, and classical music, which he placed next in importance to jazz by Benny Goodman or Duke Ellington. Through osmosis or otherwise, he had also developed eclectic tastes in dress and comportment, and if he was not yet a typical Swing—the movement was now in disarray—he would surely have become one earlier had he been old enough.

Müller was more mature than the Swings of 1940, for he was being politically socialized through the addresses of Thomas Mann and similar programs he sought out on the German service of the BBC, and through his friendship with two other Swings, Gerd Spitzbart and Bruno Himpkamp. One or two years older, they were in touch with student representatives of the "White Rose" resistance movement in Munich, namely Hamburg's Heinz Kucharski and Hans Leipelt. The latter was a brilliant half-Jewish student of biology in Munich who sometimes visited Hamburg and wished to fulfill the original goals of Hans and Sophie Scholl and their friends, all of them arrested and executed early in 1943.[150] Müller, Spitzbart, and Himpkamp, all somewhat on the periphery of the Swing movement proper, through this White Rose connection became linked to another free-floating circle of Hamburg university students and young professionals bent on scuttling the Hitler regime. One among these was Dr. Heinz Lord, Kaki Georgiadis's older friend, the sardonic impersonator of Goebbels and Hitler and now the pillar of a political resistance cell at the surgical clinic in the university.[151]

As a Swing, Himpkamp had been in Fuhlsbüttel in 1942 and then been released. Despite stern SS orders, he told his friend Müller about it. Together with Spitzbart and in loose coordination with Kucharski and others like Heinz Lord, the two were planning to blow up a strategic bridge in the city. But in May 1943 Müller, and Himpkamp for the second time, were arrested by the Gestapo. Whereas Himpkamp was kept in Fuhlsbüttel, Müller was briefly released but then rearrested in June and marked for transport to Moringen. In July a throng of several boys, guarded by the SS, made its way on foot to the station from which the train for the concentration camp was scheduled to leave. Just in those hours the terrible air raids occurred, during which tens of thousands of Hamburg's citizens were to perish. In the confusion of the deafening noise and blinding flames, the asphalt starting to burn beneath their feet, Müller and a few others slipped away.

Helped by some relatives and friends, Müller now embarked on a seemingly aimless journey through all of Germany and occupied Poland, riding trains without a ticket, sleeping in the hay or in somebody's attic, always running from the police, not knowing what the next day might bring. There was no jazz in his life then! In December, back in Hamburg and trying to sneak a train ride to the Swiss border, the Gestapo captured him again. This time the police, having meanwhile tortured other young prisoners, was fully aware of Müller's White Rose connection. Back in Fuhlsbüttel concentration camp, he was reunited with his compatriots Himpkamp and Spitzbart.

This was in a phase when almost all members of the Kucharski-Leipelt circle had been rounded up and several were facing a death sentence for treason. Müller was severely beaten and then kept in an isolation cell for fourteen months. Under this pressure, the youth had to admit one charge after another: the predilection for the BBC, the Anglophilia, his love of jazz, premeditated sabotage. It was after the military putsch against Hitler in July 1944 when Gestapo agent Reinhardt, "The Fox," hurled at him: "Anything that starts with Ellington ends with an assassination attempt on the Führer!"[152] Müller found it difficult to disagree.

At this point Spitzbart, Himpkamp, and Lord were in Neuengamme; the former two were liberated by the British army early in April 1945. Lord had been taken by the SS to the *Cap Arcona,* a floating prison anchored on the Baltic coast near Timmendorf, that old playground of Hamburg's jazz-loving crowd. When the ship was bombed by the Royal Air Force, Lord was one of the very few to come out of it alive. Hans Leipelt, not a Swing in the Hamburg sense but a known Ellington fan, was decapitated in Munich's Stadelheim prison on 29 January; his Jewish mother had committed suicide one year earlier. Finally, on the nineteenth of April 1945, Thorsten Müller was forced to stand trial on a variety of charges in the Hamburg People's Court. The state attorney demanded a sentence of ten years in penitentiary, but the verdict was never pronounced, for the city was freed from Nazi terror a few days later.[153] Müller had come to exemplify one of the extremely few cases in which jazz, a music redolent of liberty, in a roundabout way had moved its disciples to genuine political action.

As paradoxical as it may seem, in 1943 and 1944 the situation of the Swings of Hamburg, with its terrifying potential for danger, had become exemplary, a silent model for other groups in the Reich. Even though the mode of communication used by these groups is uncertain, there is evidence that this archetypal movement formed the backbone for opposition to the Hitler Youth, even to the SS. It gave rise to hope for a new kind of German, one who would abhor Hitlerism and embrace humanity instead, a German who would rebuild the country along democratic lines after the Final Defeat. This is significant in light of the fact that, since about 1940, the ancillary organizations of the party, just as the party itself, had gradually dwindled in popularity and were suffering from a recruitment shortage.[154]

There existed, in the last two years of the war, a new species of young soldier, the *Flakhelfer,* which usually consisted of Gymnasium boys between sixteen and nineteen who were seconded from the classrooms to defensive Luftwaffe units in the Reich to help man the antiaircraft guns. Interestingly, these youthful warriors inherited much of the spirit of the once-famous Luftwaffe pilots, above all their sense of elitism. Like these former idols, they hated the uniformity honed in plebeian party formations such as the Hitler Youth, but they had also seen through the vapidly arrogant SS, including its horrible armed divisions, as robotlike products of mindless fanaticism, intellectual deficiency, and downright brutality.

The *Flakhelfer* of 1943 and 1944 sported some of the visible tokens of the air aces of yore to express a sense of individuality that bordered on dissent. They showed off with white scarves and shunned the short military haircuts of the army; their hair was elegantly longer, if never as long as the Swings'. If the air force pilots had always been contemptuous of party zealots and, to a certain extent, the regular Wehrmacht units, auxiliary antiaircraft gunners openly expressed their hostility to the Hitler Youth, to which most of them formally still belonged. These boys also attempted to develop a different, perhaps more chivalrous attitude toward the other sex, eschewing the predatory approach taken by the Hitler Youth as well as SS.

Consequently, as an expression of their ultimate disinterest in the current sociopolitical order that wooed them as future führers, the *Flakhelfer* venerated American jazz. It was easily received from liberal Danish stations and sometimes from the Soldatensender, or it could be heard on records acquired cunningly through relatives or handed down by sympathetic Wehrmacht officers. *Flakhelfer* knew well Sefton Delmer's deceptive Calais station, the BBC programs, and— their favorites—the Allied Expeditionary Forces broadcasts. "Jazz reinforced in me the already latent feeling of opposition," recalls Werner Wunderlich, who, after his term with the stationary artillery on the Northern coast, continued a dubious stretch of training in a Potsdam SS elite school, where he lived for his BBC habits. He was caught in 1944, saving himself only through a fortuitous induction into the regular Wehrmacht. Almost all his classmates, remembers Wunderlich, at about this time opted for service with the navy, the army, or the Luftwaffe instead of volunteering for the Waffen-SS, as had duly been expected of them.[155]

As participants in the jazz culture, these younger fans were not as victimized through jazz as were the older, practicing instrumentalists and singers. First of all, they were considerably younger and enjoyed the optimism that is the privilege of youth, and secondly, as fans, jazz was not their main occupation, the one by which they would be recognized.

Although the older, seasoned fans were like the younger ones in not considering jazz as a profession, they could not share the eternal hope of that often naive crowd. Many of these older fans had actively carried jazz through the tribulations of the dictatorship from the start. At the fronts and in the disrupted city centers, they had learned how to get by and to overcome, for better or for worse, but their sense of optimism had long been replaced by an attitude that was more realistic, not to say resigned. Facing adversity, they found it more difficult to believe that things would ever change.

This was more or less so. Werner Daniels had surrendered his "Musikalische Feldpost" in the spring of 1943, when he was transferred to the Russian front. Whereas the "Post" lingered on for a few months under a less dynamic editor, Daniels eventually was captured by the Soviets.[156] Dieter Zimmerle, still a dissident, continued to fight, confronting punitive battalions in his clash with martial law. For purposes of deterrence, he was forced to witness his own comrades' execution, escaping his own by a hair's breadth. Opportunities for jazz, in such predicaments, were few and far between.[157] Joachim Ernst Berendt, now twenty-one, was a member of the gargantuan German force besieging Leningrad, when in August 1943 he received word that his father, the theologian, had been murdered in Dachau concentration camp by lethal injection. Was it any consolation to him that his commandant allowed him to go home on furlough, bring back his choicest jazz records, and introduce them on Soldatensender Pleskau? If nothing else, this started Berendt's long and distinguished postwar career as a jazz impresario and radio personality.[158]

Only the pair from Leipzig fared palpably better. Kurt Michaelis did a quiet shift with the Wehrmacht in Scandinavia and northernmost Germany and sampled all manner of live and recorded jazz; Frommann still "occupied" France in his carefree way, traveling to and fro between Paris and Lyon, eating well, consorting with Schulz-Köhn and Delaunay, and always seducing women. One of Fiddlin' Joe's newer affectations now was to speak French, which he knew fluently, with an American accent; it was a practice that enabled him to move around even more comfortably, for, as he remarked sarcastically, "absolutely nobody can tell that I am a Great German."[159]

Back in the Reich, the old fans who by hook or by crook had managed not to be drafted carried on as best they could, and not always to their advantage. By far the greatest problem they had to contend with these days was concealing their unabated predilection for Anglo-American broadcasts, in a time when death sentences for that offence were ever more common.[160] Günter Boas had moved from Berlin to Jena, perfunctorily to continue his medical studies there. A small clique of the like-minded was gathering at the local Café Mankel to play jazz records. This was risky enough as it was. But in September 1944 he was denounced to the Gestapo by his landlady for having tuned in to AEF broadcasts. Boas was sent to the Kalag concentration camp, where captured Europeans of all origins were working on the Reich's virgin jet planes. Belgian SS men acted as guards; American GIs served as liberators in April 1945.[161]

The members of the informal Frankfurt-Berlin connection clung together with all their might. Economics student Hans Otto Jung in Frankfurt preserved what had remained of the Harlem group, staging sessions with Horst Lippmann playing drums, Carlo Bohländer on trumpet, and Charlie Petry on clarinet. Conservatory student Louis Freichel, the multi-instrumentalist, replaced the drafted Emil Mangelsdorff in the spring of 1943. Records were cut privately and expertly by Heiner Merkel, the last one on 22 March 1944, the very day Frankfurt was destroyed by bombs. In the summer of 1943, between air raids, Jung traveled to visit his friend Hans Blüthner in Berlin, and they went to listen to Alfio Grasso's band in order to hear Primo Angeli play his much-vaunted piano swing. Angeli, however, was sick that night, and so Jung himself sat in for him, jazzing, thoroughly professionally, with the group that featured Fritz Brocksieper on drums.[162]

The circle in Frankfurt had every reason to be cautious, for "Ganjo" Baldauf, the Gestapo man, was keeping a close watch. Early in 1943 he pulled Emil Mangelsdorff in on suspicion of defeatism, because Mangelsdorff had warned a friend not to enlist for a nearby training camp that had a reputation for undue harshness. Baldauf kept Mangelsdorff in a solitary cell for twenty days, and again it was the army that saved him, or so it seemed, for in April the now eighteen-year-old musician was conscripted and sent to Russia. Wherever he went at the front, however, his superiors had possession of his personal file stating that he was "politically unreliable."[163]

In order to keep him and other friends abreast of what was transpiring, drummer Horst Lippmann had commenced an informal news service of the kind Daniels used to sustain. Lippmann gleaned international information from the Swedish journal *Orkester Journalen* and some Allied broadcasts, but also reported local events and observations of a more private scope. He gave the circulars the suspiciously English title "News for Friends of Modern Dance Music." Even while in Soviet prisoner-of-war camps Mangelsdorff kept a copy, in this case a shrewd comparison of Teddy Wilson's piano style with patterns of the classics done by Jung, in his breast pocket unmolested. But Lippmann himself was discovered. In the winter of 1943–44 Baldauf had him imprisoned at Gestapo headquarters, where for several weeks he inhabited an unheated cell with insufficient clothing. He was charged with having listened to the BBC and AEF, which was true enough; spreading antiregime propaganda in his newsletters; and of course, actively indulging in jazz. After he had become critically ill, his father managed to get him discharged, but not without Baldauf's trying to press the youth into the Waffen-SS. In the last few months of the war Horst hid in the basement of a friend until, in the spring of 1945, American troops liberated him as well.[164]

As early as 1944, the Frankfurt group had been decimated noticeably, with Mangelsdorff, Podehl, Petry, and Freichel (now recovered from his wounds) in the Wehrmacht, and Lippmann out of commission.[165] Jam sessions were all but impossible, yet were sometimes still attempted between Jung and Bohländer, with whoever was available. Mostly, these were either young men afflicted with health problems like themselves, or, ironically, draft-exempt non-"Aryans." One of their friends was sometime drummer Hans Gräf, the nephew of a former Frankfurt mayor. But Gräf and his Jewish mother spent a term in concentration camp and therefore could not always be relied upon. Yet another half-Jewish drummer was Willi ("Atatürk") Berk, who was part of the group until in early 1945 Organisation Todt shipped him to Thuringia for forced labor in the armaments industry. His mother already was in Terezín, and three uncles had been liquidated.[166]

It stands to reason, then, that the musical and spiritual rector of this loosely organized jazz colony had to be on the lookout for his own safety. Jung had managed to get further deferments from the army for his lung condition, but such luck could run out at any time. He himself came under pressure when his father, the wine entrepreneur and Catholic dignitary of Rüdesheim-on-Rhine, was betrayed to the Gestapo by a spiteful maid, on the by now familiar charge—having listened to BBC news. The secret police came to fetch the senior Jung on that greatest of German holidays, the Führer's birthday, 20 April 1943. The problem was a most delicate one: Because no regular court could convict him of the crime for lack of solid evidence and he would therefore get off lightly, it was virtually certain, what with his long-standing reputation as a regime opponent, that the regional SS would pick him up at the courthouse gate for an indefinite stay in concentration camp. When the sixty-five-year-old grandseigneur did contract a sentence of a few months in prison in the end, it was the urgent task of family friends to use their influence with the SS and ensure a proper release. With great difficulty this was done by August. The incident did not bode well for Hans Otto's own future. With his health in reasonable shape and currently without an excuse for exemption, it took fifty bottles of select house wine to bribe the authorities into letting him stay at the helm of the family enterprise, which, after generous interpretation, was classifiable as "conducive to the war effort."[167]

In Berlin meanwhile, Hans Blüthner and Gerd Peter Pick were trying to get by. Pick was in danger of being conscripted for forced labor by Organisation Todt, and to avert that, Blüthner attempted to offer him employment in his uncle's firm. That having failed, Pick found shelter in some other Berlin "war-conducive" business that looked after him acceptably, while his father, the Jew, was still in hiding in Berlin-Grunewald. How easy it would have been for the Gestapo to get the son to tell about it![168]

Blüthner himself courted disaster late in 1944 when he, too, was charged with having listened to the BBC for years. His uncle's business partner had been spying on him and had, in fact, goaded him on with constant questions about how the war was going. The Gestapo labeled the by now familiar charges against the young man: shirking active war service (Blüthner still suffered from that vital arm injury and osteomyelitis), consorting with foreigners, being beholden to jazz and, not least, being a friend of the Jews. In this context, Pick was specifically mentioned, and the secret police counted it against Hans that he had tried to help Pick out. However, since it was so late in the war and there was total confusion in the capital and absolutely no room for additional political prisoners, Blüthner luckily was let go by Christmas 1944.[169]

It had escaped the Gestapo that both Pick and Blüthner up to this time had been involved in a clandestine activity that could have brought them charges of high treason or defeatism, or at the very least the sort of trouble that Horst Lippmann got himself into with his informal jazz newsletter. For in conjunction with Dietrich Schulz-Köhn, who irregularly dropped in from occupied France, they wrote, edited, and sent out a jazz newsletter of their own, but with considerably more risk than Daniels and even Lippmann. Blüthner explains why: They used consignments of paper that were intended for the war effort and hence were conflicting with war-resources prohibitions, particularly after the defeat of Stalingrad; they openly composed stories about condemned people and undesirables such as Jews (Artie Shaw and Benny Goodman), blacks (Benny Carter), and degenerate Frenchmen and Gypsies (Eddy Barclay and Django Reinhardt); they unashamedly lauded American jazz and its subculture; and, worst of all perhaps, they sent these full-featured "letters," four in all, to soldiers at the fronts and into neutral countries such as Sweden without any official authorization.

Unlike Daniels's circulars, which had been stopped before some of the tougher war restrictions had descended, there was no attempt at camouflage in these pages, and whereas Daniels had sent his missives more or less properly as from one soldier to another, trying to comply with the rules of military censorship, it was Blüthner, not Lieutenant Schulz-Köhn, who was in charge of the posting from Berlin. Some of the news items were indeed hair-raising, because they were treated as classified information back in the Reich. One of these was the story that the black expatriate American trumpeter Harry Cooper had been performing somewhere in Paris just after having returned "fresh from the concentration camp, into which he had been clapped because he is an American." Even more incriminating was the fact that the half Jew Pick, who would have had every reason to keep a low profile, had signed for at least one article (the story on Carter, with a clear-cut drawing of the black man). In a way, it was a continuation of the outlawed Berlin Magische Note club, and hence, by extension, itself illegal. "We could have been hanged seven times," Hans Blüthner has mused in retrospect.[170]

Schulz-Köhn and Blüthner agree that it was Schulz-Köhn, the Luftwaffe lieutenant, who provided the list of mostly military addressees and placed his own portrait, in full military regalia, on the cover of the first issue in late 1942, the latter intended as a protective shield, whatever good that may have done them.[171] In any event, there is no doubt that despite his Wehrmacht status, or perhaps even because of it, Schulz-Köhn was assuming a considerable risk for his own person, because of the form in which the questionable content was presented, because of his collaboration with those two highly suspect Berliners, and because of the unauthorized mode of distribution.

As it happens, the example of Schulz-Köhn provides the final enigma in this history of jazz during the Third Reich. That may not be surprising after what the reader has learned about this highly individualistic activist on behalf of jazz in the period before the war. Until May 1945, Dietrich Schulz-Köhn remained the good German officer who had sworn his oath to the fatherland several years earlier, and at the same time, he virtually risked his life for jazz. He kept in close contact with Hugues Panassié and Charles Delaunay, the latter of whom after 1942 was deeply involved in the French resistance, using the Hot Club de France as a decoy. Undoubtedly, Dietrich knew this, and he helped him in efforts to republish, illegally, his 1938 *Discography*.

In late 1942, the Luftwaffe officer once again traveled to Paris to listen to his most favorite Gypsy guitarist, with whom he had his picture taken, outside the club near the Place Pigalle where Reinhardt was showcased at the time. In this memorable photograph, Schulz-Köhn is flanked by the Gypsy and four colonial black musicians; at the very far left stands Henri Battut, a French Jew, who was actually in hiding and whom Dietrich was helping out with food stamps.[172]

In June 1943 Schulz-Köhn, dressed in his officer's uniform, also gave a radio lecture at Nîmes, in fluent French, in which he extolled the virtues and played the records of Django Reinhardt. In the Hot Club de Marseille, in Vichy France, the lieutenant spun the latest American discs that he had just received from Stockholm, in return for his collaboration as a correspondent for the Swedish tabloid *Orkester Journalen*.[173]

And yet he also, around that time, traveled to Frankfurt on his way to Berlin or Magdeburg and met his friends, Jung, Bohländer, and now Charlie Petry. Until the early hours of the morning they had an argument in Hans Otto's student quarters during which the Frankfurters voiced their qualms, their doubts, their fears about the Third Reich and, in particular, what it was doing to jazz. Not to worry, retorted Schulz-Köhn, after the Final Victory jazz in Germany, and the entire Germanic realm, would become much stronger; it wasn't doing that badly right now. Although both Bohländer and Jung vouch for the contents of this conversation, Schulz-Köhn has not the slightest recollection of it; but neither does he deny that it actually took place.[174]

Was this an attempt to square the circle once again? If one attaches mere thoughtlessness to the lieutenant's remarks about the future of jazz in Germany, then his involvement in the newsletter venture with Blüthner and Pick could be judged equally ingenuous; the political acumen disappears in both cases. Yet that might perhaps be too simple an equation. It is more likely that Schulz-Köhn was as serious about the newsletter business as a conscious activity with possible political consequences as he was about the future of a Nazi-ruled Germany. He was beguiled by Germany's military strength and his own role in it as an officer. It bolstered his personal authority, which had always been important to him. At the same time he felt deeply that jazz simply was not the evil the Nazis had made it out to be and that one might be able to convince them of this eventually. Hence a lot of clarification, of demonstration, was called for, even at some personal risk. And this was precisely what Schulz-Köhn was righteously engaged in, in Germany or France. Therefore a genuine jazz victim Schulz-Köhn was not (although he could have slipped up badly several times in the last remaining years), but neither was he on the persecuting side. To this day the enigma of the man remains impenetrable.

The end of Dietrich Schulz-Köhn's jazz and military careers in the Third Reich was nothing short of spectacular. His company had been locked in by Allied troops for months since the summer of 1944, at St. Nazaire on the Loire River, near Rennes. There were captured Frenchmen, some wounded, held by the German troops in that pocket. An attempt to negotiate their release through the International Red Cross was made several times, the last one early in 1945. Schulz-Köhn, fluent in both French and English, was chosen by the German side to meet the Allies as its representative. Under the protection of a white flag, he approached the American officer in the enemy camp. The American looked at the

Nazi lieutenant's Rolleiflex camera, slung about the Wehrmacht leather coat. He wanted to have this camera and offered to exchange it for Lucky Strikes ciga-rettes. Schulz-Köhn declined, saying that he happened to be interested in jazz records. His counterpart's offer to give him recordings by the Budapest String Quartet or Leopold Stokowski resulted in the following exchange, recounted later by Schulz-Köhn: "'No, I would like to know what Count Basie, Benny Goodman, and Lionel Hampton sound like right now.' He was flabbergasted. He looked at me and said: 'Have you ever heard of Panassié? You know Delaunay?' I said: 'Man, you are a cat!' " With this the ice was broken, an armistice was soon arranged, and prisoners from both sides were exchanged. The story sur-faced in various American media, including the U.S. Army's *Stars and Stripes,* in which Schulz-Köhn, in March 1945, was introduced, somewhat unkindly, as "tall, bespectacled Oberleutnant Schulz-Kroehn [*sic*], a high-voiced nervous Jazz fan from Berlin, whose passion is hot records."[175]

On 8 May 1945, the day of the Third Reich's capitulation, Lieutenant First-Class Dr. Dietrich Schulz-Köhn was taken prisoner by the Americans. In the POW camp it was Hugues Panassié and Charles Delaunay from whom he re-ceived morale-boosting letters and care packages.[176] Both men had inspired the German jazz fan decisively nearly fifteen years earlier. Jazz had conquered.

Epilogue
The Final Victory
Postwar Jazz Triumphant

In the area of popular culture in the Third Reich, the history of jazz, with its inherent contradictions, inconsistencies, and paradoxes, well illustrates the improvised nature of a dictatorial regime whose alleged totalitarianism was neither seamless nor inevitable. It was punctured by compromise and accommodation, evident primarily in the executive organs of the Reich propaganda ministry and Joseph Goebbels himself, who was ridden with duplicity and often inertia. Throughout the duration of the Nazi regime, Goebbels's original blind faith in National Socialism was unrelentingly challenged by his probing intellect, and as a private person he appears to have suffered from the constant adjustments he had to undertake in his capacity as public servant. In the case of jazz, Goebbels the politician was compelled by a never-ending series of circumstances to allow for the continued existence of a phenomenon which he personally found contemptible as much from an aesthetic vantage point as from the perspective of the racial purist.

And there were other examples of disjointedness and paradox, emphasizing the heteromorphic nature of the Nazi state and its administration in the widest sense: a culture secretary who sold his principles for sexual gratification, or ideologically fortified SS officers who gave the lie to the Nazi weltanschauung by indulging Jewish swing. On the side of jazz, too, the territory was not so carefully staked out as one might have expected of an ideologically condemned music that was nonetheless capable of self-reliance: some very creditable jazz musicians such as Willi Stech or Fritz Schulze thought nothing of joining the Nazi party or Himmler's Black Order; a non-"Aryan" such as Fritz Brocksieper unreflectively offered his soul to the enemy for a well-stocked larder and the opportunity to indulge his passion in perpetuity. Dietrich Schulz-Köhn, the most distinguished promoter of jazz in the Third Reich from 1933 to 1945 (and also one of the most altruistic as far as the musicians themselves were concerned), at

Joseph Goebbels distributing gifts to German airmen on Christmas Eve, 1940. Goebbels is assisted by Hans Hinkel. (Ullstein Bilderdienst, Berlin)

Georg Haentzschel examining a band arrangement in 1942. (Ullstein Bilderdienst, Berlin)

Fritz (later "Freddie") Brocksieper at his drum set, Munich, 1958–59. (Ullstein Bilderdienst, Berlin)

Singer Kary Barnet with bandleader Heinz Wehner entertaining soldiers in a military hospital, November 1942. (Ullstein Bilderdienst, Berlin)

Maurice Thomas, left in the picture, and Hans-Joachim ("Tommie") Scheel at an exclusive Hamburg tennis club, August 1939, just before the start of World War II. (Private Archive of Hans-Joachim Scheel, Mississauga)

Christmas concert by big band of Soldatensender Belgrad with singer Kary Barnet, December 1943. Bandleader Friedrich Meyer is sitting, in Wehrmacht uniform, to the right of the grand piano. (Ullstein Bilderdienst, Berlin)

Margot Hielscher as nightclub singer Lola in the 1942 motion picture, "Women Are No Angels." Director was Willy Forst. Almost certainly, the musicians in the picture, who cannot be identified, are faking their performance. (Ullstein Bilderdienst, Berlin)

Albert Mangelsdorff (trombone) and his older brother Emil (saxophone) during a live performance in 1956. (Ullstein Bilderdienst, Berlin)

The Peter Kreuder Group in concert, ca. 1940. From left: Hans Klagemann (drums), Otto Tittmann (bass), Kreuder, Hans Korseck (guitar), Kurt Henneberg (violin), Kurt Wege (clarinet). (Ullstein Bilderdienst, Berlin)

Joachim Ernst Berendt as jazz radio host at Südwestfunk Baden-Baden in 1959. (Ullstein Bilderdienst, Berlin)

Pianist Jutta Hipp in performance during a German jazz club date, in 1955, just before her arrival in New York. (Ullstein Bilderdienst, Berlin)

Wehrmacht Lieutenant Dietrich Schulz-Köhn outside Paris club, near Place Pigalle, featuring Django Reinhardt's group, in late 1942. Reinhardt is standing on Schulz-Köhn's right. On his left are four French colonial black musicians and Henri Battut, a French Jew. (Private Archive of Dr. Hans Otto Jung, Rüdesheim)

the climax of an aggressive war assured his trembling friends that the National Socialist state would propel the genre to the greatest heights after the Final Victory!

Ironically, it was jazz and not the Third Reich that saw the Final Victory so often conjured up by the Nazi leaders. This victory was possible because enough genuine musicians and true believers in jazz had managed to stay alive, quietly treasuring the music in their hearts. When the aura of freedom returned, players and fans alike were suddenly overwhelmed, moved to tears of gratitude for a recaptured privilege. For a precious few weeks, jazz was again experienced as a highly potent symbol of liberty. Hanne-Lore Evers of Hamburg exulted in listening openly to "Sentimental Journey" on the novel British Forces Network; it was not even performed by a regular jazz band, but by some pop-chart players. "I started to cry uncontrollably and had goose bumps all over."[1] Kurt Wege's clarinet improvisations, long restrained, were felt to be "a surprise to everyone who now hears him playing 'freely' for the first time," as Horst Lippmann observed in the fall of 1945.[2]

To be sure, German jazz musicians had all but forgotten how to perform this art; forced to play the substitutes, they had been out of practice as well as out of touch for much too long. Even in the best of times, between 1932 and 1939, jazz in Germany had been anything but trailblazing; on the contrary, it had been insular and later, during wartime, virtually stagnant. How could the German musicians, even if they were willing, catch up with American developments, of which, in 1945–46, bebop was the most auspicious?

Hence, during the first few years after the Third Reich's capitulation jazz in Germany did not exactly rise like a phoenix from the ashes. Instead, there first descended on the land an aura of commercialism that was contingent on the fact that leading DTU musicians, now also somewhat older and more staid, were entering a few key radio stations on subventions and there continued to play very much in the vein of the former model orchestra. The presence of American and British forces in Germany did not necessarily help, because they had their own bands, nightclubs, radio stations, and recordings.

Nowhere was this more obvious than in Berlin, where DTU musicians such as Walter Dobschinski and Horst Kudritzki came to staff a Radio Berlin Tanzorchester (RBT), which, in extremely difficult economic times, paid handsomely for well-rendered commercial dance music, so that pure jazz—now ever more difficult to master—was regarded as gratuitous. Pianist Fritz Schulze and trumpeter Kurt Hohenberger, both returned from the war theater, made such a comfortable living in this and similar radio ventures, that for them, parallel attempts to play swing lasted a couple of years, at the most. Through a variety of circumstances, money not excluded, both Schulze and Hohenberger in the early 1950s got lost to jazz, the former eventually changing his name to Schulz-Reichel and adopting for himself the comical persona of "Crazy Otto," the out-of-tune piano man, and the latter leaving the music scene for the sake of a textile business. In private life, the financially successful "Crazy Otto" became a down-and-out playboy who immersed himself in the dolce vita that was a hallmark of Germany's Economic Miracle. Eventually he crashed his sports car, and as a result succumbed to gradual paralysis. When I visited him in 1987, the wheelchaired pianist could still talk in his charming Berlin dialect, but he could hardly hold a cigarette between his fingers, with his Steinway grand piano a mere yard away from the once prodigious limbs. Whereas Hohenberger had died an alcoholic several years earlier, Schulze passed away only in February 1990.

Enthralled by commercial opportunities, and not backed by a true jazz vocalist tradition, singers Evelyn Künneke and Margot Friedländer both joined the RBT on a fairly regular basis. All too soon, however, they fell into oblivion. The orchestra itself remained undistinguished in the history of West German jazz, an embarrassing reminder of the perversion Goebbels once had intended for the genuine product.

There were a few temporary exceptions to this barren situation, notably Hans Berry, who came back from Russian POW camp to rejoin Kurt Widmann's swing band, which was around in the former capital for a while and then also disappeared, probably for lack of a profitable radio contract. Hot violinist Helmut Zacharias, too, kept some small groups going and himself was young enough to adapt to the exciting bebop quite credibly. He produced a few interesting records and even published a jazz violin method book. But the financial lure for this extraordinarily gifted violinist was so strong that sometime in the 1950s he decided to leave modern jazz altogether, in favor of popular light music. Internationally, he became known as the "Magician Fiddler," with fourteen million commercial records to his credit, several villas (one of which was in the Swiss Alps), and an unfathomable fortune in the bank by the late 1980s. He went the way of the accomplished Nat King Cole in the United States.

Munich had always been much more provincial in matters of German jazz. But with postwar Berlin torn asunder, it eventually became the "secret capital" of democratic Germany, with a flourishing art and music scene and a university attracting the largest number of students in the land. Also, unlike Berlin, Munich was surrounded by several American military bases, where the demand for nightly jazz entertainment was large enough to sustain a few good local jazz combos. This was a chance for Fritz (now "Freddie") Brocksieper, who along with old friends like trumpeter Charly Tabor was soon performing in American clubs, indulging in the best of swing, and never missing a beat. The currency in those years before financial restabilization in 1948 was American cigarettes and nylon stockings, easy for the GIs to afford, and potent tender indeed for native musicians in the Black Market.

Sometime in the 1950s, with the money he had saved, Freddie Brocksieper was able to open two superb nightclubs of his own in fashionable Munich-Schwabing, the Studio 15 and the Klub Reitschule, where the legends of America—Harry James, Dizzie Gillespie, Oscar Peterson, and, not least, drummers Gene Krupa and Buddy Rich—came visiting. In his Schwabing apartment in 1987, Brocksieper showed me a book containing photographs and signatures of virtually all the American jazz giants, who had appreciated Freddie's style. In the four decades after the war, the drummer was able to keep up his stunning technique, somehow managing never to compromise himself and staying true to the jazz idiom. Apart from the Munich club and radio scene, he also played widely in the rest of Germany, and thus, by 1955, had become the best-known German jazz musician of the early postwar period. While never able to change his essential swing mold, he was nevertheless capable of adapting himself to more modern bebop musicians—another reason why the visiting Americans loved to perform with him. Unlike his Munich comusicians Tabor and Hans Klagemann, who intermittently became Munich studio employees, Brocksieper free-lanced, never compromising his personal independence, even though he suffered financially for it in old age. Churning out his drum rolls until the end, he died in January 1990 after having collapsed on stage from a chronic stomach ulcer. He was seventy-seven years old. Klagemann had preceded him by almost three years, two weeks after having granted me an interview in connection with the writing of this book.

Other former German jazz greats either took the commercial route or, like Kurt Hohenberger, dropped out of the music business altogether. Georg Haentzschel and Franz Grothe continued their astonishingly successful film music careers, Haentzschel winning, after Grothe's death, the West German equivalent of the Oscar. By that time Haentzschel had become something of a legend in that metier, what with having composed the music for the stunning color film production *Baron Münchhausen* in 1943! Both Haentzschel and Grothe also led radio orchestras under generous contracts, but after 1945, nobody would have know that the pair had once been Germany's two leading jazz pianists.

Friedrich Meyer safely made his way back from Belgrade to join Radio Bremen, where he led a dance orchestra in which a young musician by the name of Hansi Last played bass. This was the professionally decisive start for the commercially successful James Last, whose relationship with jazz always proved to be tenuous. Meyer himself eventually retired to Munich, where he became a free-lancing composer and arranger of light music, with only the slightest of jazz touches. But it reflects well on his past that today he is married to the actress and former swing singer Margot Hielscher. The screen star had been with Gene Hammer's big band, entertaining American GIs in Germany for several years before settling back into the movie business.

Otto Stenzel, once of the Berlin Scala, eventually left Madrid for Germany. There were plans to reconstruct the Scala in Berlin, but with its originator, Jules Marx, having been captured in France and murdered in Sachsenhausen and with popular culture changing under the impact of television, nothing ever came of them. Stenzel soon went with the "Holiday on Ice" revue as its musical director, constantly traveling around the world. All but forgotten, he died of a prostate disorder in Baden-Baden, in March 1989.

One who was never a member of the German jazz scene proper and yet had such an immense influence on its swing phase was Teddy Stauffer. After the war broke out, the Swiss saxophonist did not have much success in his native country with the remnants of his band, including the German clarinetist Ernst Höllerhagen. Down on his luck, he decided to leave Europe for California in 1941. After torrid affairs with various Hollywood starlets and eventually aided by his newfound friends Frank Sinatra and Errol Flynn, he began another life in Mexico. As a suspected enemy alien, America had refused him permanent residency.

Eventually, Stauffer married film star Hedy Lamarr and, almost, Rita Hayworth, after her disastrous union with Orson Welles. With his acute sense for business, Stauffer then turned the little fishing village of Acapulco into one of the world's great resorts, himself becoming "Mr. Acapulco," a millionaire many times over. Some time before his death in August 1991, the old man was seen and heard playing a violin in the vicinity of swimming pools, inevitably surrounded by young beauties. In 1976, at the age of sixty-seven, he made an astonishing if perhaps typical statement when he wrote: "Should I, Teddy Ernest Stauffer, die in the course of making love to any young lady, said young lady will receive from my attorneys the sum of fifty thousand dollars, unless foul play is discovered by my doctors via an autopsy."[3] Would this not have been a fitting ending for a man who based his life-long success not just on the allures of swing but on adulation by the fairer sex as well?

Like Kurt Henneberg and Karl Hohenberger, several other musicians fell victim to the postwar turbulence, while others never recovered from the blows they had received from their Fascist tormentors. Trumpeter Rolf Goldstein had survived the Nazi onslaught after his escape to Holland, and in 1945 immigrated to the United States, where he changed over to piano. But he never got accepted there, especially since his essentially swing way of playing was fast being out-moded. A broken man, he then went to Switzerland and eked out a meager living as a tired solo entertainer in hotel bars.

Something similar happened to both Coco Schumann and Martin Roman, who escaped with their lives from Auschwitz. Schumann played for a while with various swing groups around Berlin, especially those of his old pal Zacharias, but then, disenchanted with Germany, he decided to embark for Australia. After years in Melbourne, where the jazz scene was not exactly overwhelming, home-sickness drove him back to Berlin. He worked on several cruise ships, and today can still be heard in some of the lesser known Berlin nightclubs, his guitar oddly out of tune with the times.

Roman came to the United States to settle in the New York area. A much more seasoned musician than Schumann ever was, he did well for a while in commercial groups, mostly playing the lounge and supper club circuit. Yet no one active in the jazz world today has ever heard his name.

Three veterans of the old Berlin jazz set perished unpredictably. Waldi Luczkowski, once a drummer with the Golden Seven and the DTU, after 1945 had a falling-out with the music business and became a postcard vendor near a famous Rhine resort. Suffering from severe depression, one day he had a nervous breakdown and threw himself into the river. He was dead when they found him downstream.

Ingenious clarinetist Ernst Höllerhagen, too, cracked under the postwar strain. After Stauffer had left Switzerland, Höllerhagen had been playing with various Swiss successor groups and once, in Sweden, even met his paragon, Benny Goodman. The King of Swing was so impressed that he let the German try his instrument, something never heard of, before or after! Yet in the 1950s Höllerhagen, who had been successful neither as a group leader nor with women, drank heavily and ran up huge debts. A very sick man, he killed himself in a Swiss hotel room in July 1956.

Erhard "Funny" Bauschke had come through the Nazi period with much of his big band intact and, as always, in good spirits. Like fellow German musicians, he was jobbing for American clubs in the Frankfurt area as early as the summer of 1945. But in the hustle and bustle of such a life many a thing could go wrong. On 9 October 1945, as he was standing behind a U.S. military truck loaded with instruments, he was crushed by an oncoming jeep driven by a drunken soldier. The saxophonist was dead on the spot.

Nonetheless, the combination of a heavy U.S. army contingent in and near Frankfurt, with U.S. headquarters in Heidelberg nearby, and the existence of a core group of younger jazz players in no way prostituted by Nazi impositions, made the Hessian metropolis the natural place for a rebirth of jazz as an art. Carlo Bohländer, Hans Otto Jung, and their younger associates, some of them still in POW camps, were the artistic midwives. Whereas Jung, with a freshly earned doctorate, soon had to look after the family wine business and therefore always played on the side, Bohländer became instrumental in several important ways. As a well-trained trumpet expert, he authored method books on swing and acted as a patient teacher for his younger friends. He founded jazz clubs and, not least, became the leader of several seminal Frankfurt-based combos. These groups got to perform not only in American service clubs, as was the custom into the 1950s, but also for German audiences and, soon, for refreshingly open-minded directors of the newly founded Radio Hesse.

At the turn of the decade, most of Gestapo-Ganjo's enemies had returned to an exciting Frankfurt jazz scene, one that was not bounded by the dictates of the once-popular swing style. The old and formerly clandestine Harlem clique was becoming a catalyst for the development of more modern jazz throughout Germany, with several of the younger musicians, such as Louis Freichel, now entering into secure radio and studio engagements. When Emil Mangelsdorff, the clarinetist, was released from Russian POW camp in 1949, he found that his friends were performing in a new vein called bebop that he had never heard of before. The player most promising in this style happened to be his younger brother, Albert, who in 1948 had switched from guitar to trombone, prompting Emil himself to take up the more up-to-date saxophone.

Right into the 1960s, the "Frankfurt Sound" set the pace for modern jazz in all of Germany. By that time Albert Mangelsdorff, the kid whom Emil had taken to hear Ernst van't Hoff and other wartime greats in local hotels, already was arguably one of the three best trombone players in the world, and certainly Germany's most internationally known musician, having won several listener polls. At the time this book was written, Albert was being rated as the top trombonist anywhere, while his brother Emil remains virtually the only musician from the Third Reich scene who not only is still playing jazz professionally, but is playing it in the ever-changing postbebop styles, not excluding the latest avant-garde ones.

Frankfurt's initial postwar success attracted other players, fans, and impresarios; it gave a boost to jazz programming on radio, and spawned the organization of a West German Jazz Federation. The most promising new musician to arrive in Frankfurt was the idiosyncratic pianist Jutta Hipp from Leipzig. Having fled East Germany as soon as the Russians had taken over that city from the Americans, her once amateurish playing had blossomed into full professional form by the early 1950s, so that German polls in 1954 chose her as the best piano player in the country. By this time she was sounding very much in the "cool" West Coast vein of her idol Lennie Tristano. Her own group then included, at various times, the brothers Mangelsdorff, but also newer musicians such as tenor man Joki Freund and guitarist Attila Zoller, a Gypsy like Django Reinhardt.

The story goes that in 1955, during a performance in Cologne with American guests Billie Holiday and Buddy De Franco, impresario Leonard Feather heard Hipp perform. Deciding that she was world-class, he urged her to come to America in November of that year. For a brief while, Jutta Hipp was the rage of the East Coast jazz scene, playing for months at New York's Hickory House with the likes of tenor man Zoot Sims, drummer Ed Thigpen (of Oscar Peterson Trio fame), and Paul Motian, who later became Bill Evans's drummer. She toured the continent and was recorded on Franz Wolf's Blue Note label. But suddenly, with "hard bop" ushered in by players such as pianist Horace Silver, the "cool" jazz approach she had preferred was out of fashion and the pianist found it difficult to adjust. In 1958 Jutta Hipp reverted to her original vocation, that of a graphic artist, and today she lives modestly in New York among painters, factory workers, and social critics.

Werner Wunderlich, once of the SS elite school, elected Frankfurt as his home after lengthy internment by the Poles. Along with former members of the Berlin Melodie and Magische Note clubs, notably Hans Blüthner and Olaf Hudtwalcker, he organized a national jazz federation that supported jazz concerts, an active club life, and the publication of various journals. Soon Günter Boas from Jena joined this circle, and so did Gerd Peter Pick from Berlin, who was engaged as a Frankfurt radio impresario before he accepted an offer to direct the German-language service of the Canadian Broadcasting Corporation in Montreal.

The jazz federation was actively supported by Horst Lippmann, who had founded a concert agency specializing in bringing to Germany leading American players, for instance the Modern Jazz Quartet. Blüthner, now a partner in his uncle's former firm, together with onetime Melodie-Klub member Günter von Drenkmann, became the federation's chief representative in the Western sector of Berlin. Regrettably, Drenkmann, a high-placed justice, was to be the victim of another kind of fanaticism as the first person assassinated (in 1974) by the terrorist Baader-Meinhof Gang.

In Baden-Baden to the south of Frankfurt, the French were in control. Their intention being the establishment of a new, democratic radio service there, they asked Joachim Ernst Berendt, repatriated from the Russian front, to help them out. Berendt did it with jazz, founding pioneering programs and inviting American musicians of stature such as bassist Oscar Pettiford for longer periods of tenure. The establishment of the most successful German big band ever, that of Kurt Edelhagen, was Berendt's work. Like Radio Hesse, Südwestfunk Baden-

Baden was able to educate a new generation of democratic-minded Germans in the appreciation of modern jazz. Berendt took his own political commitment so seriously that in the 1950s, with jazz blaring from mobile loudspeakers, he helped a young, unknown Social Democratic politician campaign for an electoral foothold in Berlin. That man was Willy Brandt. After Berendt had authored his *Jazzbuch,* an authoritative introduction to the subject based on substantive research, it became the most widely distributed music book in the world, selling well over a million copies in a plethora of languages. Berendt topped his success as a West German jazz impresario with more books and the establishment and leadership of the now classic Berlin Jazz Festival.

Although within a much smaller format, freedom-loving Dieter Zimmerle was to do something similar at Radio Stuttgart, further east. Dr. Schulz-Köhn, on the other hand, became Berendt's counterpart at West German Radio in Cologne, and the two have been friendly rivals for the title of doyen of German jazz ever since 1950. Schulz-Köhn also authored several books. When "Dr. Jazz," as he is still popularly called, retired from his permanent position as jazz radio host in the mid-1980s, the station invited Benny Carter to play at a huge farewell party for him. Both Berendt and Schulz-Köhn, no strangers to the American jazz scene, received honorary professorships toward the end of their careers, functions which have helped the rather specialized but very necessary jazz education at the academies.

The younger Leipzig jazz denizens, Jutta Hipp's old friends, were scattered, most of them settling into respectable positions in the Western zones, such as Herbert Becke, now a retired architect in Düsseldorf. Some had been lost in the war; others, like Lutz Warschauer, the half Jew, were arrested by the Soviets and disappeared without a trace. Hipp's vicarious mentors, Kurt "Hot-Geyer" Michaelis and Joachim-Ernst "Fiddlin' Joe" Frommann, left their beloved hometown, where infatuation with the jazz culture soon was persecuted by the Communist East German regime in a similar manner as under the Nazis. Whereas Michaelis became a Lufthansa employee in Frankfurt, Frommann, having gracefully survived the German occupation of France, was a piano lounge entertainer in the Hessian jazz capital until he succumbed to a heart ailment in the 1960s.

Insofar as they survived, virtually all the aficionados once surrounding Düsseldorf's Werner Daniels returned from the fronts into well-ordered bourgeois lives, with one exception: like Frommann, hobby pianist Theo Hoeren turned professional, playing for American holiday crowds on the West Coast. Daniels himself became an influential business executive.

The final victory that jazz achieved in a democratic Germany, although belated and not without vicissitudes, was an experience that totally eluded the once active Nazis on the scene. Goebbels's right-hand man Hans Hinkel was initially interned by the Americans in Dachau. Thereafter delivered to the Poles, he was almost fatally beaten, as some had mistaken him for the defected Martin Bormann, whom he somewhat resembled in appearance. Hinkel was tried on war crimes charges, yet acquitted. Eventually he was returned to Germany in a wheelchair, physically and spiritually a cripple.

Nazi party member Willi Stech, the last conductor of the German Dance and

Entertainment Orchestra, was in a Russian labor camp until he could make his escape. Ultimately he was posted at Berendt's Südwestfunk Baden-Baden, leading thoroughly mediocre dance bands until his death. Nazi music critics Fritz Stege and Herbert Gerigk both were perfunctorily "denazified." Gerigk continued his journalistic career at a provincial newspaper, to the shame of the new republic. Stege—perhaps even more heavily compromised—professionally seems to have vanished into thin air. Turncoat Alfred Baresel suddenly remembered his democratic heritage, along with his former penchant for jazz, and forthwith began publishing on that subject once more, as if nothing at all had happened.

Heinz "Ganjo" Baldauf of the Frankfurt Gestapo was accused by a German civilian court prosecuting Nazi misdemeanors some ten years after the war. Again, as was then typical in such procedures, he received a very mild sentence to begin with, which later was further reduced. Unmolested, Baldauf died a few years ago, undoubtedly enjoying his state pension as a former policeman until the end. Expecting that worse things were in store for him, Hamburg's Hans Reinhardt, the hangman of the Swings, committed suicide. But his aide Karl-Heinz Kügler met with only light punishment and was sighted repeatedly by one-time Swings, an experience apt to produce nightmares for them. It is vital that historians finally write the definitive history of the incomplete denazification in West Germany.

Nothing could haven proven Himmler and his Gestapo more wrong about the paracriminal disposition of the Swings than the conspicuous success almost all of the surviving ones experienced in their private and business lives. This survey must restrict itself merely to a few chosen few. Hans-Joachim Scheel and Hans Engel built important careers for themselves in North America, Scheel as an architect and mining engineer, and Engel as a corporate travel consultant. Axel Springer, of course, became the media czar of Western Europe. It is said that until his death in 1985, he kept his tailor on London's Savile Row very busy.

The Cypriot, Demitrius "Kaki" Georgiadis, soon moved to England, changed his name to Harry Stephens, and became a high-level airline executive. He died suddenly, of cardiac arrest, while vacationing in Cyprus during February 1991. Hajo Hartwig, too, founded a lucrative business in New York. In the 1960s, he visited his old sweetheart, Inga Madlung, in London, and was shocked to find her playing a game of cards under extremely powerful lights, the cards as large as shoe soles.

Indeed, Inga Madlung was still suffering from virtual blindness, but fate could have been more unkind to her than it actually was. In 1945, her father, the half Jew, was the first lawyer to be readmitted to the bar by the British military government in Hamburg. His business it became to assist in the prosecution of former concentration camp guards, such as those of Neuengamme and Fuhlsbüttel. One evening Derek Shelton, a young British occupation official, originally an Austro-Jewish refugee, came for dinner. Having fallen in love with the beautiful young woman, he married her and took her to London in 1948. While he looked after a profitable transport business, Inga Shelton raised a daughter, an excruciating task with the inadequate vision she was left with. It was in 1971 that a skillful London ophthalmologist was able to restore almost all of her former eyesight, which subsequently has enabled her to read voraciously, though she has never stopped listening to jazz. As for going back to Hamburg, where her younger sister Jutta is comfortably settled with her own family, Inga Shelton has said, "Quite frankly I don't think I could."[4] Not everyone was able simply to forget.

Occasionally Inga Shelton receives a visit from Helga Rönn, once of Uckermark concentration camp, who also married an Englishman while he was stationed in Hamburg. Helga Rönn, with striking physical features, became a model and had roles in British films and television. She now lives, retired, in London.

Her sister-in-law Ursula Nielsen-Rönn, who escaped from Ravensbrück alive, still is haunted by the gruesome scenes she witnessed, for example the death of a young girl named Edith, the daughter of a Danzig justice, accused of currency infractions. Edith had always comforted the even younger Ursula but then was slowly killed by constant drops of ice-cold water on her head. Ursula Rönn also remembers the scene with Eva Petersen, as she quite innocently was getting ready for the death transport to Auschwitz. It was Eva's mother, the Jew, who saw Gestapo's Kügler enter a Hamburg bank without the slightest qualm one day after the war. West Germany had reached a state of high prosperity; Frau Petersen's complaints had no effect.

In fact, what these jazz victims received in compensation for their suffering from the West German authorities was next to nothing, and their experience remains an unerasable black spot on the history of that otherwise admirable postwar democracy. In the worst of cases, those victims were irrevocably ruined, and some died early as a consequence of their ordeals. This is what happened to Heiner Fey, who was in Moringen camp as a Swing. Günter Discher, also once in Moringen, permanently damaged his health to the detriment of his career: he endured one stomach operation, one hernia operation, and two eye operations. Dr. Heinz Lord, who had escaped the traumatic sinking of the *Cap Arcona,* in 1954 immigrated to the United States, where he became an Ohio small-town surgeon. Elected president of the World Medical Association, he died of a heart ailment at age forty-three, a medical casualty after terms of captivity and torture.

Nor can the immeasurable psychological damage be overlooked today. Thorsten Müller, who was loosely associated with Heinz Lord via the White Rose connection, not only suffered from cavernous tuberculosis but also from psychic shock, which prevented this sensitive, creative young man from ever completing a full course of studies in university, where he belonged. That much injury notwithstanding, Müller has had a prolific career as one of West Germany's preeminent journalists, and he is productive in this area to this day. His most rewarding experience has been to act as a keeper of the records as well as an eloquent spokesman for the dispersed Swings. Moreover, Thorsten Müller has done much to recover and patch together various pieces that contribute significantly to the history of jazz in the Third Reich. This book owes him a great debt.

Notes

Introduction

1. Josephine Baker and Jo Bouillon, *Josephine* (New York, 1977), 58; Eugen Szatmari, *Das Buch von Berlin* (Munich, 1927), 11.

2. Willy Fritsch, . . . *das kommt nicht wieder: Erinnerungen eines Filmschauspielers* (Zurich and Stuttgart, 1963), 60–62; Hermann Behr, *Die Goldenen Zwanziger Jahre: Das fesselnde Panorama einer entfesselten Zeit* (Hamburg, 1964), 112–14; Felix Gilbert, *A European Past: Memoirs, 1905–1945* (New York and London, 1988), 57–58.

3. Friedrich Hollaender, *Von Kopf bis Fuss: Mein Leben mit Text und Musik* (Munich, 1965), 82–83; Lothar Fischer, *Tanz zwischen Rausch und Tod: Anita Berber, 1918–1928 in Berlin* (Berlin, 1984), esp. 60, 66–67, 90.

4. Klaus Budzinski, *Die Muse mit der scharfen Zunge: Vom Cabaret zum Kabarett* (Munich, 1961), 162–65; Walter Rösler, *Das Chanson im deutschen Kabarett, 1901–1933* ([East] Berlin, 1980), 173–75; Nico Dostal, *Ans Ende deiner Träume kommst du nie: Berichte, Bekenntnisse, Betrachtungen* (Innsbruck and Frankfurt am Main, 1982), 126.

5. Maurus Pacher, *Sehn Sie, das war Berlin: Weltstadt nach Noten* (Frankfurt am Main and Berlin, 1987), 254–56; Michael Danzi, *American Musician in Germany, 1924–1939: Memoirs of the Jazz, Entertainment, and Movie World of Berlin during the Weimar Republic and the Nazi Era—and in the United States,* as told to Rainer E. Lotz (Schmitten, 1986), 52, 230.

6. *Musik* 21 (1929), 833–34; Monika Sperr, ed., *Schlager: Das Grosse Schlager-Buch: Deutscher Schlager, 1800–Heute* (Munich, 1978), 117.

7. Pacher, *Berlin,* 209–10.

8. Behr, *Jahre,* 91–94; Rösler, *Chanson,* 177–79.

9. Szatmari, *Berlin,* 78–85; Pacher, *Berlin,* 206.

10. Szatmari, *Berlin,* 84, 151; Axel Eggebrecht, *Der halbe Weg: Zwischenbilanz einer Epoche* (Hamburg, 1975), 247–48.

11. Fischer, *Tanz*, 70, 85; Szatmari, *Berlin*, 153–54; Danzi, *American Musician*, 52; Günter Boas, *Rudi Anhang: Ein Musiker im Hintergrund* (Menden, 1986), 6.

12. Rösler, *Chanson*, 174; Budzinski, *Muse*, 164.

13. Danzi, *American Musician*, 230; Hollaender, *Von Kopf bis Fuss*, 118; *Artist*, 6 September 1929.

14. Behr, *Jahre*, 92, 94.

15. Chris Goddard, *Jazz away from Home* (New York and London, 1979), 14; bassist Otto Tittmann's information in Christian Kellersmann, "Jazz in Deutschland von 1933–1945," Master's thesis, University of Hamburg, 1989, 8; Ekkehard Jost, "Jazz in Deutschland: Von der Weimarer Republik bis zur Adenauer-Ära," in *That's Jazz: Der Sound des 20. Jahrhunderts: Eine Ausstellung der Stadt Darmstadt . . . 29. Mai bis 28. August 1988* (Darmstadt, 1988), 357.

16. Bärbel Schrader and Jürgen Schebera, *The "Golden" Twenties: Art and Literature in the Weimar Republik* (New Haven and London, 1988), 136.

17. *Artist*, 24 April 1925; Franz Born, *Berliner Luft: Eine Weltstadt und ihr Komponist Paul Lincke* (Berlin, 1966), 160.

18. *Tanz*, no. 2 (November 1927), 14–15; Danzi, *American Musician*, 21.

19. Hedda Adlon, *Hotel Adlon*, 2nd ed. (Munich, 1979), 169–80; Haentzschel interview.

20. Horst H. Lange, *Jazz in Deutschland: Die deutsche Jazz-Chronik, 1900–1960* (Berlin, 1966), 44; Danzi, *American Musician*, 19; Blüthner diary of broadcasts, 5 December 1931, PA Blüthner.

21. Horst J. P. Bergmeier and Rainer E. Lotz, *Eric Borchard Story* (Menden, 1988), 24, 33, 48, 53–55, 64; *Neue Leipziger Zeitung*, 13 June 1931. Cited in Szatmari, *Berlin*, 147.

22. Horst J. P. Bergmeier, *The Weintraub Story incorporated The Ady Rosner Story* (Menden, 1982), esp. 5, 7, 9; Hollaender, *Von Kopf bis Fuss*, 118; Blüthner diary of broadcasts, 2 June 1930, PA Blüthner.

23. Whitney Balliett, *American Musicians: Fifty-Six Portraits in Jazz* (New York and Oxford, 1986), 122; Jim Godbolt, *A History of Jazz in Britain, 1919–50* (London, 1984), 66, 71; Danzi, *American Musician*, 24.

24. Bergmeier and Lotz, *Borchard Story*, 28; Danzi, *American Musician*.

25. Horst J. P. Bergmeier and Rainer E. Lotz, *Billy Bartholomew: Bio-Discography* (Menden, 1985); Danzi, *American Musician*, 36; *Artist*, 6 September 1929.

26. Bergmeier and Lotz, *Bartholomew*, 23; Haentzschel interview.

27. Bergmeier and Lotz, *Borchard Story*, 20; Danzi, *American Musician*, 35; *Artist*, 5 July 1934.

28. Like the Boston "Zwei, so wie wir," performed by the Béla band in February 1930 (Blüthner diary of broadcasts, 3 February 1930, PA Blüthner). Also Danzi, *American Musician*, 22, 32; Bergmeier and Lotz, *Borchard Story*, 42.

29. Danzi, *American Musician*, 47; Bergmeier, *Weintraub Story*, 25, 27; Haentzschel interview.

30. Gerhard Conrad, *Posaunen-Dob: Kleine Biographie Walter Dobschinskis* (Menden, 1983), 7–11 (quotation 9); Dobschinski interview.

31. Wolfgang Muth, *Ernst Höllerhagen: Ein deutscher Jazzmusiker* (Magdeburg, 1964), 6; *Artist*, 27 January 1933.

32. *Artist*, 18 November 1932; Teddy Stauffer, *Forever Is a Hell of a Long Time: An Autobiography* (Chicago, 1976), 64; Haentzschel interview.

33. Michaelis to author, 6 February 1989.

34. Brocksieper interview; Peter Kreuder, *Schön war die Zeit: Musik ist mein Leben*

(Munich, 1955), 214–15; Ernst Höchstötter, "Als der Jatz nach München kam . . . ," *Fox auf 78*, no. 4 (Fall 1987), 54–57.

35. Albert McCarthy, *Big Band Jazz* (New York, 1974), 310; Egino Biagioni, *Herb Flemming: A Jazz Pioneer Around the World* (Alphen aan de Rijn, [1977]), 15–25.

36. *Neue Leipziger Zeitung*, 18 August 1928; Goddard, *Jazz Away*, 111; S. Frederick Starr, *Red and Hot: The Fate of Jazz in the Soviet Union, 1917–1980* (New York and Oxford, 1983), 57; Gunther Schuller, *Early Jazz: Its Roots and Musical Development* (New York and Oxford), 325, n. 8.

37. McCarthy, *Big Band Jazz*, 310; Cheatham, cited in Goddard, *Jazz Away*, 292, 296, and in Balliett, *Musicians*, 70; Muth, *Höllerhagen*, 7.

38. Schuller, *Early Jazz*, 325, n. 8.

39. McCarthy, *Big Band Jazz*, 187; Goddard, *Jazz Away*, 76–78; Hodes, cited in Balliett, *Musicians*, 149.

40. Danzi, *American Musician*, 23; Neil Leonard, *Jazz and the White Americans: The Acceptance of a New Art Form* (Chicago and London, 1962), 13, 75–84.

41. Schuller, *Early Jazz*, 192, n. 21; also Starr, *Red and Hot*, 67.

42. Fritsch, *Erinnerungen*, 111; Jack de Graef, *De Swingperiode (1935–1947): Jazz in België* (Wettelijk, 1980), 73.

43. *Artist*, 27 January 1928.

44. Ibid.; *Artist*, 16 November 1928; Joachim Ernst Berendt, *Das Jazzbuch: Entwicklung und Bedeutung der Jazzmusik* (Frankfurt am Main and Hamburg, 1953), 10.

45. *Artist*, 28 October 1932; *Neue Leipziger Zeitung*, 10 December 1931; *Skizzen*, no. 4 (April 1934), 15; Blüthner diary of broadcasts, 27 September 1930, PA Blüthner.

46. Sidney Bechet, *Treat It Gentle* (New York, 1975), 147, 157; Hopkins, cited in Goddard, *Jazz Away*, 289–90; Balliett, *Musicians*, 28.

47. Danzi, *American Musician*, 50–51; Rainer E. Lotz, "A True Jazz Hound: Die Geschichte des Trompeters Nick Casti," *Fox auf 78*, no. 5 (Spring 1988), 61.

48. Kurt Michaelis, "A Historic Milestone—Louis Armstrong's Debut in Europe," *The Second Line* 24 (Summer 1982), 11–14; Michaelis to author, 6 February 1989; Michaelis "Reminiszenzen," 12 February 1989, PA Michaelis; Michaelis and Schulz-Köhn interviews; Blüthner diary of bands, 8 April 1931 and 28 October 1932, PA Blüthner.

49. Rolf Goldstein to Werner Daniels, 3 July 1977, PA Daniels; interviews with Schulz-Reichel, Schulz-Köhn, and Jung.

50. Franz Wolfgang Koebner, ed., *Jazz and Shimmy: Brevier der neuesten Tänze* (Berlin, 1921), 89.

51. Horst J. P. Bergmeier and Rainer E. Lotz, *Alex Hyde: Bio-Discography* (Menden, 1985), 21; Danzi, *American Musician*, 14.

52. Dietrich Schulz-Köhn, *Die Schallplatte auf dem Weltmarkt* (Berlin, 1940), 91; "Gesamtkatalog Brunswick: Elektrische Aufnahmen bis einschl. Oktober 1930," 17 (PA Jung). Quotation in *Melos* 9 (1930), 482.

53. Schulz-Köhn interview; Charles Delaunay, *New Hot Discography: The Standard Directory of Recorded Jazz*, ed. Walter E. Schaap and George Avakian (New York, 1948), 85; *Statistisches Jahrbuch für das Deutsche Reich 1932* (Berlin, 1932), 255.

54. Michaelis, "Milestone," 13; Boas interview; Delaunay, *New Hot Discography*, 36. An excellent assessment of Armstrong's 1928 work is in Schuller, *Early Jazz*, 89, 115–19; also Berendt, *Jazzbuch*, 35–40, 207.

55. Michaelis interview; Michaelis to author, 6 February 1989; Schuller, *Early Jazz*, 144, 180, 346.

56. Franz Heinrich, *"Swing-Generation": Selbsterlebtes* (Menden, 1988), 9.

57. Advertisement in Koebner, *Jazz and Shimmy,* 124; *Musik* 21 (1929), 359–60; facsimiles in *Fox auf 78,* no. 5 (Spring 1988), 32; Schrader and Schebera, *Twenties,* 117; interviews with Michaelis, Schulz-Köhn, and Blüthner.

58. Schulz-Köhn, *Schallplatte,* 108, 111–13, 137.

59. Heinz Pohle, *Der Rundfunk als Instrument der Politik: Zur Geschichte des deutschen Rundfunks von 1923/38* (Hamburg, 1955), 245–46, 250; Winfried B. Lerg, *Die Entstehung des Rundfunks in Deutschland: Herkunft und Entwicklung eines publizistischen Mittels* (Frankfurt am Main, 1965), 213, 272–73; Max Butting, "Rundfunkmusik—wie wir sie brauchen," *Musik* 21 (1929), 444.

60. Interviews with Michaelis, Blüthner, Schulz-Köhn; Lerg, *Entstehung,* 185–87; Gerhard Eckert, *Der Rundfunk als Führungsmittel: Studien zum Weltrundfunk und zum Fernsehrundfunk* (Heidelberg, 1941), 218–19.

61. Joachim Ernst Berendt, *Ein Fenster aus Jazz: Essays, Portraits, Reflexionen* (Frankfurt am Main, 1977), 290; Kellersmann, "Jazz," 10.

62. Blüthner diary of broadcasts, PA Blüthner. On Bird see also John Kolda in "Musikalische Feldpost," 1 and 15 May 1943, PA Daniels.

63. Michaelis to author, 6 February 1989; Jung interview; Ansgar Diller, *Rundfunkpolitik im Dritten Reich* (Munich, 1980), 272–73.

64. Schuller, *Early Jazz,* 6; idem, *The Swing Era: The Development of Jazz, 1930–1945* (New York and Oxford, 1989), 79.

65. Balliett, *Musicians,* 108.

66. Schuller, *Early Jazz,* 124.

67. Goddard, *Jazz Away,* 103–6; Arthur Briggs, cited in Goddard, 287; Godbolt, *History,* 268; Danzi, *American Musician,* 25; Boas interview.

68. *Artist,* 12 February 1926, 16 November 1928; Haentzschel interview.

69. In broadcast series "Jazz in Germany: A Survey of Hot Dance, Swing and Traditional Jazz in Germany, 1924 to Present," produced for and broadcast on KALW FM, San Francisco, by Dave Radlauer and Ray Taubert, n.d., courtesy of the Goethe Institute, Toronto (program 5).

70. See advertisements, "'The joyful brothers' Jazz-Dancing-Band," *Artist,* 30 January 1925; "Der heitere Fridolin mit seinem Jazz-Stimmungs-Trio! Kanonen," *Artist,* 30 January 1925; "The buffoon Orig. American Jazz-Trio," *Artist,* 8 May 1925; "The Bobby Stanlay Jazz-Band das vielseitige und vornehme Stimmungs-Trio," *Artist,* 26 May 1925.

71. Leonard, *White Americans,* 13.

72. Haentzschel interview. Drummer Fritz Brocksieper's opinion, stated in interview, was: "A model for jazz they were not."

73. *Artist,* 26 March 1926; Paul Bernhard, *Jazz: Eine musikalische Zeitfrage* (Munich, 1927), 53–54; Astrid Eichstedt and Bernd Polster, *Wie die Wilden: Tänzer auf der Höhe ihrer Zeit* (Berlin, 1985), 49; Leonard, *White Americans,* 119–20.

74. The latter was played by The Ding's Jazz Company in Altenburg, Sachsen-Anhalt, in early 1925 (*Artist,* 6 February 1925). On musicians' traditional training see *Artist,* 21 May 1926.

75. The first was performed by Billy Bartholomew's band at the Delphi-Palast on 20 August 1931 (Blüthner diary of broadcasts, same date, PA Blüthner). The hit tune "Wo sind deine Haare, August?" was copyrighted by Richard Fall (music) and Beda (text) in 1926 (Sperr, *Schlager,* 133).

76. See *Artist,* 20 May 1927.

77. Michael H. Kater, "The Jazz Experience in Weimar Germany," *German History* 6 (1988), 152. The sweet violin sound can be heard intermittently in Dajos Béla's

rendition of "Dear Henderson" (1927), which is included in Radlauer and Taubert's broadcast series "Jazz in Germany," program 5 (see n. 69).

78. *Artist*, 18 March 1927.

79. John Kolda in "Musikalische Feldpost," beginning of March 1942, PA Daniels; Haentzschel interview; McCarthy, *Big Band Jazz*, 316; Dostal, *Ende*, 110–11; Danzi, *American Musician*, 24; Jost, "Jazz," 360.

80. Haentzschel and Brocksieper interviews; Goldstein to Daniels, 13 June 1977, PA Daniels; Danzi, *American Musician*, 28; Jost, "Jazz," 357–58. In 1929 Curry Wehner, leader of a six-piece *Jazzensemble* whose members played thirty (!) different instruments among themselves, presented the song "a Miste" ["In a Mist"] by "Biggs-Büderlegg" [Bix Beiderbecke] on the piano (*Artist*, 8 November 1929).

81. "Deep Henderson" (1927), "Crazy Rhythm" (1928) in the broadcast series "Jazz in Germany" (as in n. 69).

82. *Artist*, 18 November 1927; Rainer E. Lotz, "Amerikaner in Europa," in *That's Jazz*, 294; *Artist*, 13 March 1925 (quotations).

83. *Deutsches Musiker-Lexikon*, ed. Erich H. Müller (Dresden, 1929), 50; "Lebenslauf" Alfred Baresel, n.d., BDC, RKK Baresel; *Neue Leipziger Zeitung*, 19 July 1931.

84. Alfred Baresel, *Instruktive Jazz-Etüden für Klavier* (Leipzig, 1928); idem, *Das neue Jazzbuch: Ein praktisches Handbuch für Musiker, Komponisten, Arrangeure, Tänzer und Freunde der Jazzmusik* (Leipzig, 1929), 6 (quotation), 62.

85. Alfred Baresel, ". . . and his Boys: Das moderne Orchester und seine Musik," *Musik* 24 (1932), 580–83; idem, "Jazz als Rettung," *Auftakt* 6 (1928), 213–16; idem, "Kunst-Jazz," *Melos* 7 (1928), 354–57.

86. See Eberhard Preussner in *Musik* 20 (1927), 136–37; Hans Heinz Stuckenschmidt in *Vossische Zeitung*, Berlin, 15 December 1928. Also E. J. Müller, "Jazz als Karikatur," *Auftakt* 6 (1928), 216–18; Manfred Bukofzer, "Soziologie des Jazz," *Melos* 8 (1929), 387–91.

87. Adolf Aber, "Ernst Krenek: 'Jonny spielt auf': Uraufführung in Leipzig," *Anbruch* 9 (1927), 127–32; Geoffrey Skelton, *Paul Hindemith: The Man Behind the Music: A Biography* (London, 1975), 59–60; Starr, *Red and Hot*, 94; Kater, "Jazz Experience," 149–50.

88. See Sekles's *vita* in *Deutsches Musiker-Lexikon*, 1334, and Sekles's proclamation as reprinted in *Zeitschrift für Musik* 94 (1927), 706.

89. Matyas Seiber, *Schule für Jazz-Schlagzeug* (Mainz, 1929); idem, "Jazz als Erziehungsmittel," *Melos* 7 (1928), 281–86; idem, "Jazz-Instrumente, Jazz-Klang und neue Musik," *Melos* 9 (1930), 122–26; *Frankfurter Zeitung*, 18 November 1932; Schulz-Köhn interview.

90. Matyas Seiber, "Jugend und Jazz," *Zeitschrift für Schulmusik* 3 (1930), 29–32.

91. *Anbruch* 9 (1927), 193; *Deutsche Kultur-Wacht*, no. 6 (1933), 14.

92. *Wille und Werk* 2, no. 9 (1927), 70–71; *Deutsche Turn-Zeitung* 75 (1930), 76; Walter Kiefner, "Singbewegung und Jazz," *Singgemeinde* 8, no. 6 (1932), 162–69.

93. Hans M. Wingler, *The Bauhaus: Weimar, Dessau, Berlin, Chicago* (Cambridge, Mass., 1986), 485. See also Otto Alfred Palitzsch, "Jazz," *Kreis* 4 (1927), 288–90; Egon Larsen, "Das Geheimnis der Jazzmusik," *Zwiebelfisch* 22 (1930), 259–63.

94. Koebner, *Jazz und Shimmy*, 17; *Singgemeinde* 9, no. 1 (1932), 26; M. Kay Flavell, *George Grosz: A Biography* (New Haven and London, 1988), 83.

95. Cited in Hans-Ulrich Wehler, *Historische Sozialwissenschaft und Geschichtsschreibung: Studien zu Aufgaben und Traditionen deutscher Geschichtswissenschaft* (Göttingen, 1980), 235.

96. See Fritz Giese, *Girlkultur: Vergleiche zwischen amerikanischem und europäischem*

Rhythmus und Lebensgefühl (Munich, 1925), 19, 29, 32, 35–36. Also *Anbruch* 7 (1925), 426; Bernhard, *Jazz,* 90; Karl Schaetzler, "Jazz," *Hochland* 25 (1927/28), 441.

97. Hermann Hesse, *Steppenwolf,* trans. Basil Creighton (New York, 1970), 132. Also see Modris Eksteins, *Rites of Spring: The Great War and the Birth of the Modern Age* (Toronto, 1989), 271.

98. R. G. S. Weber, *The German Student Corps in the Third Reich* (Basingstoke and London, 1986), 50–51; Margret Boveri, *Verzweigungen: Eine Autobiographie,* ed. Uwe Johnson (Munich, 1982), 193–94; Eggebrecht, *Weg,* 230–31.

99. See *Artist,* 9 November 1928.

100. Cheatham cited in Goddard, *Jazz Away,* 296; Samuel Wooding, "Eight Years Abroad with a Jazz Band," *Etudes* 57, no. 1 (April 1939), 233–34.

101. Wiser, *Years,* 157–65; Robert Goffin, *Jazz from the Congo to the Metroplitan* (New York, 1975), 68–84; Goddard, *Jazz Away,* 14–16, 114–33, 139–41.

102. Bergmeier and Lotz, *Borchard Story,* 48–49.

103. *Artist,* 11 February 1927; 23 March 1928; 18 October 1929; 7 August 1931; 22 January 1932.

104. *Artist,* 28 May 1926.

105. Eichstedt and Polster, *Wilden,* 71.

106. Johann Kull in *Artist,* 16 April 1926; Richard H. Stein, "Auslandspropaganda," *Musik* 19 (1927), 642.

107. See Paul Schwers, "Die Frankfurter Jazz-Akademie im Spiegel der Kritik," *Allgemeine Musikzeitung* 54 (1927), 1246–48 (quoting Hausegger and Pfitzner).

108. Ibid.; *Zeitschrift für Musik* 94 (1927), 706–7; *Artist,* 2 December 1927; *Vossische Zeitung,* Berlin, 10 December 1927.

109. Cf. [Julius] Steinhardt, *"Ehombo"* (Neudamm, 1922), 22–27, 49, 154, 161, 225, 234, 280–83, 290–91; and Dietrich Schäfer, *Kolonialgeschichte,* 4th ed., vol. 2, (Berlin and Leipzig, 1921), 117–18.

110. Eugen Fischer, "Spezielle Anthropologie: Rassenlehre," in Eugen Fisher et al., *Anthropologie* (Leipzig and Berlin, 1923), 189–90; Fritz Lenz quotation from "Die krankhaften Erbanlagen," in Erwin Baur et al., *Menschliche Erblichkeitslehre,* 3rd ed., vol. 1 (Munich, 1927), 530. Also see Alfred Ploetz, *Die Tüchtigkeit unsrer Rasse und der Schutz der Schwachen* (Berlin, 1895), 132–33.

111. Sally Marks, "Black Watch on the Rhine: A Study in Propaganda, Prejudice and Prurience," *European Studies Review* 13 (1983), 297–333; George L. Mosse, *Toward the Final Solution: A History of European Racism* (New York, 1978), 175–76; Giese, *Girlkultur,* 64.

112. Richard Thurnwald in *Archiv für Rassen- und Gesellschaftsbiologie* 15 (1923/24), 99; Fischer, "Anthropologie," 193–94; Lenz, "Erbanlagen," 529 (quotation). For a dispassionate analysis of the undeniable connection between jazz and sexuality, see Neil Leonard, *Jazz: Myth and Religion* (New York and Oxford, 1987), 58–61. Also see idem, *White Americans,* 38–39.

113. Regina Bruss, *Die Bremer Juden unter dem Nationalsozialismus* (Bremen, 1983), 13; Mosse, *Final Solution,* 176.

114. Bukofzer, "Soziologie," 387; George E. Sokolsky, *We Jews* (London, 1935), 280; John Katz, "Chasidism in Jazz," *Journal of Synagogue Music* 2, no. 4 (1970), 28–33; Heinrich August Winkler, "Die deutsche Gesellschaft der Weimarer Republik und der Antisemitismus," in Bernd Martin and Ernst Schulin, eds., *Die Juden als Minderheit in der Geschichte,* 2nd ed. (Munich 1982), 277.

115. Klagemann interview; Danzi, *American Musician*, 55.

116. *Song-Magazin* (November/December 1946), 14; Lange, *Jazz in Deutschland*, 60; Goldstein to Daniels, 15 October 1977, PA Daniels; Starr, *Red and Hot*, 196.

117. Blüthner and Daniels interviews.

118. Hans Pfitzner, *Gesammelte Schriften*, vol. 3 (Augsburg, 1929), 256; Paul Schwers, "Die Frankfurter Jazz-Akademie im Spiegel der Kritik," *Allgemeine Musikzeitung* 54 (1927), 1246–48; *Zeitschrift für Musik* 94 (1927), 706–7; Ernst Klein in *Vossische Zeitung*, Berlin, 10 December 1927; A. von Gizycki-Arkadjew, "Jazz-Hetze," *Artist*, 1 February 1929.

119. Hans Pfitzner, *Gesammelte Schriften*, vol. 1 (Augsburg, 1926), 113–20 (quotation from 115); ibid., vol. 3, 309–10.

120. Doc. 307 in *Der Strom der Töne trug mich fort: Die Welt um Richard Strauss in Briefen*, ed. Franz Grasberger (Tutzing, 1967), 298–99; Muck to Matthes, 10 March 1929, BDC, RMK Wilhelm Matthes.

121. Wagner as cited in Starr, *Red and Hot*, 95; Palitzsch, "Jazz," 288.

122. For *Jonny*, see the partially still benevolent critique by Heinrich Kralik in *Musik* 20 (1928), 386. For Antheil, *Musik* 19 (1927), 530 (quotation); George Antheil, *Bad Boy of Music* (New York, 1981), 59–65.

123. Joel Sachs, "Some Aspects of Musical Politics in Pre-Nazi Germany," *Perspectives of New Music* 9 (Fall–Winter 1970), 84–85.

124. Alfred Einstein, *Geschichte der Musik*, 3rd ed. (Leipzig and Berlin, 1927), 130.

125. For America, see Leonard, *White Americans*, 30–46.

126. Günther Dehn, *Proletarische Jugend: Lebensgestaltung und Gedankenwelt der grossstädtischen Proletarierjugend* (Berlin, [1929]), 39; handbill of Jungstahlhelm, n.d. [1930], SAB, 4, 65, II E 3a 1.1; Eichstedt and Polster, *Wilden*, 71. See also Walter Laqueur, *Weimar: Die Kultur der Republik* (Frankfurt am Main, 1977), 106–7.

127. Hermann Reichenbach, "Jugend und Musik," *Junge Deutschland* 24 (1930), 229–30; Kurt Westphal, "Voraussetzungen des Musikunterrichts in grossstädtischen Oberklassen," *Zeitschrift für Schulmusik* 5 (1932), 174; Erwin Liek, *Der Arzt und seine Sendung: Gedanken eines Ketzers*, 4th ed. (Munich, 1927), 72; Liek, *Krebsverbreitung, Krebsbekämpfung, Krebsverhütung* (Munich, 1932), 237; Otto Lubarsch, *Ein bewegtes Gelehrtenleben: Erinnerungen und Erlebnisse: Kämpfe und Gedanken* (Berlin, 1931), 419; Oswald Bumke, *Erinnerungen und Betrachtungen: Der Weg eines deutschen Psychiaters* (Munich, 1952), 156–57.

128. Kater, "Jazz Experience," 154.

129. Kurt Blome, *Arzt im Kampf: Erlebnisse und Gedanken* (Leipzig, 1942), 23–25; Ernst von Salomon, *Die Geächteten: Roman* (1929; rpt. Reinbek, 1968), 32 (quotation); Kurt Hutten, *Kulturbolschewismus: Eine deutsche Schicksalsfrage* (Stuttgart, 1932), 12–15, 29, 82–91.

130. Edwin Erich Dwinger, *Wir rufen Deutschland: Heimkehr und Vermächtnis* (1932; rpt. Jena, 1941), 350; Gerhard Schumann, *Entscheidung* [written 1931] (1943; rpt. Bodmann, 1980), 71–73, 82–85, 136–37. On young Schumann's *völkisch* socialization, see Jay W. Baird, *To Die for Germany: Heroes in the Nazi Pantheon* (Bloomington and Indianapolis, 1990), 131–36.

131. Martin Green, *Mountain of Truth: The Counterculture Begins: Ascona, 1900–1920* (Hanover, N.H., and London, 1986), 153; G. R. Halkett, *The Dear Monster* (London, 1939), 202–9.

132. Berger to Snaga, 27 January 1939, BDC, RMK Snaga (quotation).

133. Heuss quoted in Fritz Stege, *Bilder aus der deutschen Musikkritik: Kämpfe in zwei Jahrhunderten* (Regensburg, 1936), 93; also see ibid., 94–99, and Sachs, "Aspects."

134. "König Jazz," *Allgemeine Musikzeitung* 57 (1930), 929–32.

135. F. Woweries, "Wir rechnen ab mit euch," *H. = J. = Z.*, no. 1/2 (Hartung/Hornung 1928), 5; Werner Müller, "Begegnung mit der Hitler-Jugend," *Die Kommenden*, 10 May 1929, 218.

136. *Studierstube* (1927), 252–55; tenets of Deutscher Frauenorden, [2 May 1929], SAB, 4, 65, II A 9a 13; memorandum police president Hanover, 27 January 1930, NHSA, Hann. 122a, XI, 79; *Nordwestdeutscher Freiheitskämpfer*, 25 November 1931; Benedikt Lochmüller, *Hans Schemm*, vol. 2 (Munich, 1940), 128; Guida Diehl, *Die Deutsche Frau und der Nationalsozialismus* (Eisenach, 1933), 66; Stauffer, *Forever*, 63.

137. *Ziel und Weg* 2 (1932), 23.

138. Point 23 of the program as printed in Gerd Rühle, *Das Dritte Reich: Dokumentarische Darstellung des Aufbaues der Nation: Die Kampfjahre, 1918–1933* (Berlin, [1933]), 51; Hitler's public speeches in Munich (May 1921–November 1923), docs. 232, 264, 313, 355, 436, and 598 in *Hitler: Sämtliche Aufzeichnungen, 1905–1924*, ed. Eberhard Jäckel (Stuttgart, 1980), 380, 444, 531, 565–66, 753, 1057.

139. Michael H. Kater, "Inside Nazis: The Goebbels Diaries, 1924–1941," *Canadian Journal of History* 25 (1990), 238.

140. *Die Tagebücher von Joseph Goebbels: Sämtliche Fragmente*, ed. Elke Fröhlich (Munich, 1987), vol. 1, 144.

141. Ibid., 33–34, 159–60, 236, 277, 417, 488, 490, 524, 586.

142. See ibid., vol. 1, 356, 458; vol. 2 (Munich, 1987), 113, 218. Also Alfred Rosenberg, *Letzte Aufzeichnungen: Ideale und Idole der nationalsozialistischen Revolution* (Göttingen, 1955), 188–92; Helmut Heiber, *Joseph Goebbels* (Munich, 1965), 111.

143. Alfred Rosenberg, *Der Sumpf: Querschnitte durch das "Geistes"-Leben der November-Demokratie* (Munich, 1930), 23–36, 87–89.

144. [Proclamation by Alfred Rosenberg], "Kampfbund für deutsche Kultur, München, im Januar 1929," near p. 4 in *Mitteilungen des Kampfbundes für deutsche Kultur* 1 (1929).

145. *Die Tagebücher . . . Goebbels*, vol. 2, 313.

146. See Hans Hinkel, *Einer unter Hunderttausend*, 9th ed. (Munich, 1942). Goebbels rightly suspected in Hinkel a schemer like himself, which made the relations between the two men complicated. See *Die Tagebücher . . . Goebbels*, vol. 1, 550; vol. 2, 47, 57, 60, 66, 72–73, 76, 89, 100.

147. *Mitteilungen des Kampfbundes für deutsche Kultur* 1 (1929), 29 (quotation); Kater, "Jazz Experience," 156–157.

148. *Mitteilungen des Kampfbundes für deutsche Kultur* 2 (1930), 36 (quotation): Kater, "Jazz Experience," 157.

149. *Artist*, 6 and 20 February, 13 March, 15 May, 12 June 1925; 12 and 26 March 1926; 7 January, 20 May, 16 December 1927.

150. *Artist*, 23 April 1926; 7 January, 18 February, 25 November 1927; 11 January 1929 (quotation).

151. *Artist*, 20 December 1929; 12 September 1930; 4 December 1931; 23 September 1932; 13 January 1933.

152. Haentzschel interview; *Artist,* 3 April 1925 and 26 February 1926; Fritsch, *Erinnerungen,* 28–29.

153. Curt Riess, *Das gab's nur einmal: Die grosse Zeit des deutschen Films* (Vienna and Munich, 1977), vol. 2, 80–83; *Fox auf 78,* no. 6 (Fall 1988), 18–19.

154. *Artist,* 15 March and 6 September 1929; 8 August and 17 October 1930; 15 January 1932; 21 July 1933; Jost, "Jazz," 361.

155. *Artist,* 15 May and 1 August 1930; 2 January 1931.

156. Lange, *Jazz in Deutschland,* 58; idem, "Zwischen Optik und Hot-Takt: Max Rumpf," *Fox auf 78,* no. 5 (Spring 1988), 4; *Artist,* 7 February 1930; Eichstedt and Polster, *Wilden,* 72; Bernd Polster, "Es zittern die morschen Knochen: Orchestrierung der Macht," in Bernd Polster, ed., *"Swing Heil": Jazz im Nationalsozialismus* (Berlin, 1989), 10.

157. Electrola Gesellschaft M. B. H. to Schulz, 8 November 1932, PA Schulz-Köhn; Danzi, *American Musician,* 62–63; Schulz-Köhn, *Schallplatte,* 111.

158. Haentzschel and Klagemann interviews; author's telephone conversation with Schulz-Reichel, Berlin, 14 May 1987; Goldstein to Daniels, 13 June 1977, PA Daniels.

159. *Artist,* 6 February, 20 March, 12 June, 10 July 1925; 12 March 1926; 11 October 1929.

160. *Artist,* 7 February, 15 May, 1 August, 7 November 1930; 31 July, 20 and 27 November, 4 December 1931; Haentzschel interview.

161. Danzi, *American Musician,* 62, 69–70, 73–74, 77; Lange, *Jazz in Deutschland,* 58–59.

162. Etté as paraphrased in *Musik* 22 (1929), 230; Hans T. David, "Abschied vom Jazz," *Melos* 9 (1930), 416; Wilhelm Twittenhoff, "Musikalische Jugendbewegung und Jazz," *Zeitschrift für Schulmusik* 4 (1931), 9; *Artist,* 22 January and 9 September 1932; Sperr, *Schlager,* 104; Eichstedt and Polster, *Wilden,* 72; Polster, "Knochen," 11.

163. Schuller, *Early Jazz,* 203, 241, 292, 356–57.

164. See Michael H. Kater, "The Revenge of the Fathers: The Demise of Modern Music at the End of the Weimar Republic," *German Studies Review* (forthcoming).

165. Karol Rathaus, "Jazzdämmerung?" *Musik* 19 (1927), 336; Matyas Seiber, "Jazz-Instrumente, Jazz-Klang und neue Musik," *Melos* 9 (1930), 126; Josef Robert Harrer, Joe Charles Fischer, and Gerhard Winkler in *Artist,* 1 March 1929, 11 September 1931, 18 November 1932; Eberhard Preussner in *Musik* 20 (1928), 362; David, "Abschied," 413–17; Heinrich Strobel and Frank Warschauer in *Melos* 9 (1930), 482; Richard Baum in *Singgemeinde* 9, no. 1 (1932), 26.

166. *Zeitschrift für Instrumentenbau* 50 (1930), 708; *Artist,* 15 January 1932; István Deák, *Weimar Germany's Left-Wing Intellectuals: A Political History of the Weltbühne and Its Circle* (Berkeley and Los Angeles, 1968), 189–228; Modris Eksteins, *The Limits of Reason: The German Democratic Press and the Collapse of Weimar Democracy* (London, 1975), 194–263; Laqueur, *Weimar,* 322–38.

167. *Musiker-Lexikon,* 1574; Adorno in *Musik* 21 (1929), 625; Theodor Wiesengrund-Adorno, "Kleiner Zitatenschatz," *Musik* 24 (1932), 738. See also Anthony Heilbut, *Exiled in Paradise: German Refugee Artists and Intellectuals in America, from the 1930s to the Present* (Boston, 1984), 163, 167–68.

Chapter 1

1. *Deutsche Podium,* 31 July 1936, 4.

2. BDC, RMK Stein; Fritz Stein, "Chorwesen und Volksmusik im neuen Deutschland," *Zeitschrift für Musik* 101 (1934), 285–86.

3. Friedrich Hussong, *"Kurfürstendamm": Zur Kulturgeschichte des Zwischenreichs* (Berlin, [1933]), 7.

4. For examples of the latter, see Walter Kempowski, *Tadellöser & Wolff: Ein bürgerlicher Roman* (Munich, 1975), 68; Franz Heinrich, *"Swing-Generation": Selbsterlebtes* (Menden, 1988), 34.

5. *Die Tagebücher von Joseph Goebbels: Sämtliche Fragmente,* ed. Elke Fröhlich (Munich, 1987), vol. 2, 564; vol. 3, 155, 426. Fritz Wiedemann, *Der Mann der Feldherr werden wollte: Erlebnisse und Erfahrungen des Vorgesetzten Hitlers im 1. Weltkrieg und seines späteren persönlichen Adjutanten* (Velbert and Kettwig, 1964), 214–15; Gerhard L. Weinberg, "Hitler's Image of the United States," *American Historical Review* 69 (1964), 1010–13; Fritz Stege in *Unterhaltungsmusik,* 22 June 1939, 852.

6. Joseph Goebbels, "Der neue Stil," unidentified newspaper fragment [June 1939], PA Jung. See also Ludwig Altmann, "Untergang der Jazzmusik," *Musik* 25 (1933), 749; *Ziel und Weg* 6 (1936), 317.

7. Quotation from *Skizzen,* May 1934, 17. Typically, also see ibid. June/July 1934, 18–19; *Allgemeine Musikzeitung* 61 (1934), 448–49.

8. See Amadou Booker Sadji, *Das Bild des Negro-Afrikaners in der Deutschen Kolonialliteratur (1884–1945): Ein Beitrag zur literarischen Imagologie Schwarzafrikas* (Berlin, 1985), 57–58, 113–16.

9. Kapitän Alfred Schneider to Lucht, 11 December 1936, BA, R 56I/90. Also see *Schwarze Korps,* 18 March 1937; Reiner Pommerin, *"Sterilisierung der Rheinlandbastarde": Das Schicksal einer farbigen deutschen Minderheit, 1918–1937* (Düsseldorf, 1979), 63.

10. Martha Dodd, *Through Embassy Eyes* (New York, 1940), 211–12; *Die Tagebücher . . . Goebbels,* vol. 2, 655; Arnd Krüger, *Die Olympischen Spiele 1936 und die Weltmeinung: Ihre aussenpolitische Bedeutung unter Berücksichtigung der USA* (Berlin, 1972), 197, 208.

11. Klaus to Konzertdirektion C. Ebner, 9 April 1936, BA, R 55/1177. See also the adjoining tirade in the musicians' trade journal *Deutsche Podium,* 13 December 1935, 9; 3 April 1936, 4.

12. Joachim Mrugowsky, ed., *Das ärztliche Ethos: Christoph Wilhelm Hufelands Vermächtnis einer fünfzigjährigen Erfahrung* (Munich and Berlin, 1939), 9; Theodor Mollison, "Rassenkunde und Rassenhygiene," in Ernst Rüdin, ed., *Erblehre und Rassenhygiene im völkischen Staat* (Munich, 1934), 36–37; Ernst Rodenwaldt, "Die Rückwirkung der Rassenmischung in den Kolonialländern auf Europa," *Archiv für Rassen- und Gesellschaftsbiologie* 32 (1938), 388–89, 391–95.

13. First quotation from Prof. Heinrich Wilhelm Kranz, Giessen (1934), cited in doc. 164, in Walter Wuttke-Groneberg, ed., *Medizin im Nationalsozialismus: Ein Arbeitsbuch* (Tübingen, 1980), 283; second quotation from *Musik* 28 (1936), 432.

14. Arthur Gütt, *Dienst an der Rasse als Aufgabe der Staatspolitik* (Berlin, 1935), 11; Gerd Rühle, *Das Dritte Reich: Dokumentarische Darstellung des Aufbaues der Nation,* vol. 3 (Berlin, 1935), 282; Rodenwaldt, "Rückwirkung," 393.

15. Hans Macco, *Rasseprobleme im Dritten Reich* (Berlin, [1933]), 13–14; Pommerin, *Sterilisierung,* 71–84.

16. Quotation from Dietz Degen, "Warnung und Vorschlag," *Musik in Jugend und Volk* 2 (1939), 259.

17. See Max Merz, "Der volkstumszersetzende Einfluss des Jazz," *Studentische Kameradschaft* (special issue), no. 10 [1937]; idem, "Der Jazz und wir," *Volkstum und Heimat* 48 (1939), 151–53, 182–85, 206–10; *Deutsche Podium,* 5 September 1935, 5, and 20 December 1935, 7–8; Hans Brückner, "Rund um den Hot," *Deutsche Podium,* 15 July 1937, 1–3; *Artist,* 19 May and 21 July 1933; ibid., 9 January 1936, 3; ibid., 26 March 1936, 354; ibid., 14 May 1936, 555–56; *Unterhaltungsmusik,* 9 June 1938, 713; ibid., 14 July 1938, 850; ibid., 24 November 1938, 1548–49; ibid., 25 May 1939, 739; *Zeitschrift für Musik* 100 (1933), 491; Walter Hochschild, "Was ist Niggerjazz?," *Königsberger Allgemeine Zeitung* [after 12 October 1935], facsimile in *That's Jazz: Der Sound des 20. Jahrhunderts: Eine Ausstellung der Stadt Darmstadt . . . 29. Mai bis 28. August 1988* (Darmstadt, 1988), 391; Hermann Blume (1936) as quoted in Joseph Wulf, ed., *Musik im Dritten Reich: Eine Dokumentation* (Reinbek, 1966), 387; Horst H. Lange, *Jazz in Deutschland: Die deutsche Jazz-Chronik, 1900–1960* (Berlin, 1966), 64–65. For an objective account of Sax see *The Grove Dictionary of Music and Musicians,* ed. Stanley Sadie, vol. 16 (London, 1980), 530–31.

18. Hans F. K. Günther, *Kleine Rassenkunde des deutschen Volkes,* 3rd ed. (Munich, 1933), 52, 56; Eugen Fischer as quoted in Benno Müller-Hill, *Tödliche Wissenschaft: Die Aussonderung von Juden, Zigeunern und Geisteskranken, 1933–1945* (Reinbek, 1984), 16; *Deutsche Podium,* 16 October 1936, 2.

19. In mentioning "Jewish physics," Lenard noted sarcastically: "As yet nothing is known about Negro physics" (*Deutsche Physik,* vol. 1 [Munich, 1936], ix). Also see Fritz von Borries in *Zeitschrift für Musik* 199 (1933), 839–40; Georg Gräner, "Kunst und Künstler von heute: Tagebuchblätter," *Allgemeine Musikzeitung* 60 (1933), 165–67; Friedrich Welter, "Um die deutsche Musik—Ein Bekenntnis," *Musik* 25 (1933), 727–30.

20. Hans Severus Ziegler, *Entartete Musik: Eine Abrechnung* (Düsseldorf, [1938]), esp. 26; Albrecht Dümling and Peter Girth, eds., *Entartete Musik: Eine kommentierte Rekonstruktion* (Düsseldorf, [1988]).

21. *Unterhaltungsmusik,* 12 August 1937, 961; ibid., 15 December 1938, 1630; Hans Brückner, "Und unsere Antwort," *Deutsche Podium,* 31 July 1936, 6; *Schwarze Korps,* 25 November 1937.

22. Quotation from Ludwig K. Mayer, "Unterhaltungsmusik," *Musik* 31 (1938), 163. Also see Richard Litterscheid, "Nachruf auf den Jazz," *Musik* 28 (1936), 824; Hans Brückner, "'Jazz' und 'Jazz,'" *Deutsche Podium,* 19 June 1936, 2; *Unterhaltungsmusik,* 3 November 1938, 1443; *Stuttgarter NS-Kurier,* 7 January 1939; Merz, "Der Jazz," 185.

23. Quoted in *Deutsche Podium,* 14 August 1936, 2.

24. Breuers to Goebbels, March 1933, BDC, RMK Breuers.

25. Reinmar von Zweter [Fritz Stege] in *Artist,* 29 July 1936, 872. See also *Unterhaltungsmusik,* 15 December 1938, 1635; and the biomedical imagery of Friedrich Bartels, "Die berufstätige Frau," *Ziel und Weg* 3 (1933), 15.

26. First under the nom de plume Reinmar von Zweter, then under his own name. *Artist* was changed to *Unterhaltungsmusik* in the autumn of 1936.

27. Stege to Hinkel, 16 August 1933, BDC, RKK Stege; *Deutsches Musiker-Lexikon,* ed. Erich H. Müller (Dresden, 1929), 1387.

28. BDC, RKK and SS Gerigk; *Musiker-Lexikon,* 403.

29. See p. 16.

30. BDC, RKK and MF Baresel; Alfred Baresel, "Detektiv und Musikkritiker," *Deutsche Kultur-Wacht,* no. 32 (1933), 9–10; Baresel in *Artist,* 9 January 1936, 4; Merz, "Einfluss," 13; Michael H. Kater, "Forbidden Fruit? Jazz in the Third Reich," *American Historical Review* 94 (1989), 15.

31. Theodor Wiesengrund-Adorno, "Abschied vom Jazz," *Europäische Revue* 9 (1933), 315. See also his polemics-in-exile: Hektor Rottweiler [Adorno], "Über Jazz," *Zeitschrift für Sozialforschung* 5 (1936), 235–59; Kater, "Forbidden Fruit," 14.

32. *Deutsche Kultur-Wacht,* no. 3 (1933), 12, and no. 11 (1933), 18; "Reichs-kulturkammergesetz," 22 September 1933, in Karl-Friedrich Schrieber and Karl-Heinz Wachenfeld, eds., *Musikrecht: Sammlung der für die Reichsmusikkammer geltenden Gesetze.* . . (Berlin, 1936), 1–2; Heinz Ihlert, *Die Reichsmusikkammer: Ziele, Leistungen und Organisation* (Berlin, 1935).

33. BDC, SS Hinkel.

34. Background in Fred K. Prieberg, *Musik im NS-Staat* (Frankfurt am Main, 1982), 203–11. See also p. 44.

35. *Zeitschrift für Musik* 101 (1934), 255–73, quotation from 269. Also see Ihlert, *Reichsmusikkammer,* 6–8, 11, 27–28; Martin Thrun, "Die Errichtung der Reichs-musikkammer," in Hanns-Werner Heister and Hans-Günther Klein, eds., *Musik und Musikpolitik im faschistischen Deutschland* (Frankfurt am Main, 1984), 75–81; Prieberg, *Musik,* 176–78.

36. *Berufszählung: Die berufliche und soziale Gliederung des Deutschen Volkes: Text-liche Darstellung der Ergebnisse (Statistik des Deutschen Reichs: Volks-, Berufs-und Betriebszählung vom 16. Juni 1933, vol. 458)* (Berlin, 1937), 49.

37. Michael H. Kater, *Doctors Under Hitler* (Chapel Hill and London, 1989), 19–25, 35–40; Konrad H. Jarausch, *The Unfree Professions: German Lawyers, Teachers, and Engineers, 1900–1950* (New York and Oxford, 1990).

38. Prieberg, *Musik,* 179. See as a representative sample the RMK membership card for Hans Klagemann, BDC, RMK Klagemann.

39. *Die Tagebücher* . . . *Goebbels,* vol. 3, 438. Most musicians' questionnaires today are in BDC, RMK.

40. Ihlert, *Reichsmusikkammer,* 8–9; Horst H. Lange, "Zwischen Optik und Hot-Takt: Max Rumpf," *Fox auf 78,* no. 5 (Spring 1988), 5.

41. BDC, RMK Klagemann; Klagemann interview.

42. Michael Danzi, *American Musician in Germany, 1924–1939: Memoirs of the Jazz, Entertainment, and Movie World of Berlin during the Weimar Republic and the Nazi Era—and in the United States,* as told to Rainer E. Lotz (Schmitten, 1986), 83; Brocksieper interview.

43. *Daily Mirror,* 13 March 1937; *Artist,* 9 February 1939, 164–65; Arthur Maria Rabenalt, *Joseph Goebbels und der "Grossdeutsche" Film,* ed. Herbert Holba (Munich and Berlin, 1985), 80–83; *Die Tagebücher* . . . *Goebbels,* vols. 2 and 3, from 2 March 1933 to 4 August 1938; Michael H. Kater, "Inside Nazis: The Goebbels Diaries, 1924–1941," *Canadian Journal of History* 25 (1990), 237–38. The jazz-oriented musicians Hans Klagemann and Friedrich Meyer both said in interviews that their bands had performed regularly for Goebbels's social functions. On one such occasion Magda Goebbels told Meyer that she liked his piano im-provisations on the theme of "Everything I Have Is You." Also see p. 101.

44. Quotation from Goebbels, "Zehn Grundsätze deutschen Musikschaffens" (28 May 1938), in Fred K. Prieberg, *Kraftprobe: Wilhelm Furtwängler im Dritten Reich* (Wiesbaden, 1986), 41. Also see *Artist,* 9 June 1937, 712.

45. Rumors according to Zimmerle and Brocksieper interviews. Plausibly, Georg Haentzschel (interview) affirms: "Goebbels had no ear for jazz."

46. *Artist*, 13 February 1936, 154; *Deutsche Podium*, 11 December 1936, 8; *Unterhaltungsmusik*, 7 April 1938, 421; Rabenalt, *Goebbels*, 82; Johannes Heesters, *Es kommt auf die Sekunde an: Erinnerungen an ein Leben im Frack* (Munich, 1978), 125–28.

47. *Allgemeine Musikzeitung* 60 (1933), 237; *Artist*, 4 and 18 May 1934; ibid., 13 September 1934; ibid., 15 November 1934, 147.

48. See *Artist*, 13 December 1934, 242, and 14 November 1935, 1275; *Statistisches Handbuch von Deutschland, 1928–1944* (Munich, 1949), 468–69.

49. *Zeitschrift für Musik* 101 (1934), 255, 261; Ihlert, *Reichsmusikkammer*, 9, 15.

50. *Artist*, 25 April 1935, 424; Ihlert, *Reichsmusikkammer*, 15, 18, 23.

51. *Artist*, 16 April 1936, 427–30; ibid., 17 September 1936, 1166–67; ibid., 1 October 1936, 1144–46; *Deutsche Podium*, 7 August 1936, 10.

52. See *Artist*, 12 August 1937, 994–95.

53. Para. 6 of "Erste Verordnung zur Durchführung des Reichskulturkammergesetzes," 1 November 1933, in Schrieber and Wachenfeld, *Musikrecht*, 3–4; *Unterhaltungsmusik*, 10 March 1938, 285; questionnaire for Italian (sometime jazz) guitarist Athos Micheli, Berlin, 14 April 1937, BDC, RMK Micheli.

54. Schrieber and Wachenfeld, *Musikrecht*, 23–24; *Deutsche Podium*, 24 July 1936, 9; *Unterhaltungsmusik*, 24 February 1938, 231.

55. *Unterhaltungsmusik*, 7 October 1937, 1216; *Amtliche Mitteilungen der Reichsmusikkammer*, 15 January 1938, BA, RD 33/1–2.

56. *Amtliche Mitteilungen. . .* , 12 May and 21 July 1933.

57. Ibid., 7 February 1935, 110, and 10 September 1936, 1127; *Unterhaltungsmusik*, 1 December 1938, 1581; Danzi, *American Musician*, 90.

58. *Deutsche Podium*, 3 September 1937, 3.

59. *Artist*, 28 May 1936, 628.

60. Danzi, *American Musician*, 83, 99, 125; Horst J. P. Bergmeier and Rainer E. Lotz, *Billy Bartholomew: Bio-Discography* (Menden, 1985), 45–46, 52.

61. *Deutsche Podium*, 24 September 1937, 3, and 8 October 1937, 5–6; *Unterhaltungsmusik*, 7 October 1937, 1217, and 26 January 1939, 109.

62. *Deutsche Podium*, 25 September 1936, 13; ibid., 27 November 1936, 8; ibid., 14 August 1937, 26; ibid., 24 September 1937, 6–7; Teddy Stauffer, *Forever Is a Hell of a Long Time: An Autobiography* (Chicago, 1976), 104–5, 112–18; Stauffer's story in video "Heisse Ware Swing" (ARD 1983), televised ARD on 4 January 1984; Hirschfeld interview; Becke to author, 8 February 1990.

63. *Deutsche Podium*, 10 April 1936, 9, and 15 October 1937, 1; Stauffer, *Forever*, 103.

64. Rühle, *Das Dritte Reich*, 282; *Deutsche Podium*, 20 August 1937, 1–5, and 3 September 1937, 1–2; *Unterhaltungsmusik*, 27 April 1939, 595, and 4 May 1939, 619.

65. Joseph Walk, ed., *Das Sonderrecht für die Juden im NS-Staat: Eine Sammlung der gesetzlichen Massnahmen und Richtlinien—Inhalt und Bedeutung* (Karlsruhe, 1981), 70.

66. *Die Tagebücher . . . Goebbels*, vol. 2, 509, 515, 529, 540, 753; vol. 3, 32, 64, 134, 165, 189, 272, 294, 343, 354, 399, 437–38, 445, 562; Goebbels quoted in *Deutsche Podium*, 3 December 1937, 1.

67. *Wer ist's?*, 10th ed., ed. Herrmann A. L. Degener (Berlin, 1935), 683.

68. BDC, SS Hinkel; *Artist,* 14 April 1933; *Deutsche Kultur-Wacht,* no. 8 (1933), 5–6.

69. BDC, SS Hinkel; *Wer ist's?,* 683.

70. Prieberg, *Musik,* 179–80; RMK membership card for (half-Jewish jazz musician) Eugen Henkel, BDC, RMK Henkel; *Amtliche Mitteilungen der Reichsmusikkammer,* 14 August 1935, BA, RD 33/2-1; RMK questionnaire for (Jewish drummer) Günter Heilborn, 8 November 1934, BDC, RMK Heilborn.

71. *Amtliche Mitteilungen der Reichsmusikkammer,* 25 May 1937, BA, RD 33/2-1; *Deutsche Podium,* 22 August 1935, 6.

72. Para. 10 of "Erste Verordnung zur Durchführung des Reichskulturkammergesetzes," 1 November 1933, in Schrieber and Wachenfeld, *Musikrecht,* 4; Raabe to (one-quarter Jewish jazz trumpeter) Hans Berry, 19 August 1935, BDC, RKK Berry (quotation); case of Felix Sztal in *Deutsche Podium,* 12 September 1935, 9–10.

73. Eberhard Fechner, *Die Comedian Harmonists: Sechs Lebensläufe* (Weinheim and Berlin, 1988), 240–69.

74. Pettack to Amtsvorsteher, 8 November 1937, BDC, RMK Fritz Wellnitz; Friedländer-Reimann interview.

75. Uwe Dietrich Adam, *Judenpolitik im Dritten Reich* (Düsseldorf, 1979), 46–232.

76. Hans-Joachim Teichler, "1936—ein olympisches Trauma: Als die Spiele ihre Unschuld verloren," in Manfred Blödorn, ed., *Sport und Olympische Spiele* (Reinbek, 1984), 64, 66; Krüger, *Spiele,* 198, 229.

77. Publicity brochure, "Sid Kay's Fellows" [1929], PA Petrushka [Petruschka]; Petrushka to author, 28 June 1990; Horst J. P. Bergmeier and Jürgen W. Susat, "Spitzenband im Hintergrund: Sid Kay Fellows," *Fox auf 78,* no. 9 (Winter 1990/91), 34–39.

78. Petrushka [Petruschka] to author, 28 June 1990.

79. Ibid.; also "'Lukraphon' Schallplatten," Berlin, n.d., PA Eike Geisel; quotation from Susat to author, 24 June 1990. On the Kulturbund see Prieberg, *Musik,* 79–104. A sample recording of the Fellows is on cassette tape supplied with Christian Kellersmann, "Jazz in Deutschland von 1933–1945," Master's thesis, University of Hamburg, 1989 (see p. 131).

80. *Artist,* 31 March 1933; Stietz to NSDAP-Landtagsfraktion, 11 April 1933, BDC, RMK Marek Weber; Danzi, *American Musician,* 78–79; *Fox auf 78,* no. 3 (Spring 1987), 12.

81. Günter Boas, *Rudi Anhang: Ein Musiker im Hintergrund* (Menden, 1986), 12; Boas interview.

82. Horst J. P. Bergmeier, *The Weintraub Story incorporated The Ady Rosner Story* (Menden, 1982), 13, 23, 31–51; Stauffer, *Forever,* 84–85; S. Frederick Starr, *Red and Hot: The Fate of Jazz in the Soviet Union, 1917–1980* (New York and Oxford, 1983), 122, 194–225; Erik Wiedemann, *Jazz i Danmark: Ityverne, trediverne og fyrrerne* (Copenhagen, 1982), vol. 2, 79; Schulz-Köhn interview.

83. Bernd Polster, "Es zittern die morschen Knochen: Orchestrierung der Macht," in Polster, ed., *"Swing Heil": Jazz im Nationalsozialismus* (Berlin, 1989), 21–22; *Fox auf 78,* no. 3 (Spring 1987), 4.

84. Danzi, *American Musician,* 55–56; Boas, *Anhang,* 13; Polster, "Knochen," 25. See p. 93.

85. Haentzschel interview.

86. Starr, *Red and Hot,* 196.

87. Goldstein to Werner Daniels, 3 July and 22 November 1977.

88. Bergmeier, *Weintraub Story,* 25; transcript of Roman interview for British video series, "Swing under the Swastika," Yorkshire Television, London, 1988.

89. Advertisement in *Artist,* 15 January 1932; Lange, *Jazz in Deutschland,* 67.

90. Quotation from Schulz-Reichel interview.

91. Ibid.; Kok as interviewed by Inge Klaus (place and date unknown), cassette tape kindly supplied by Werner Daniels; *Artist,* 14 February 1935, 129–30; ibid., 14 March 1935, 243; ibid., 11 April 1935, 349; ibid., 18 April 1935, 392–93; ibid., 9 May 1935, 469; ibid., 16 May 1935, 492; ibid., 6 June 1935, 581; *Deutsche Podium,* 17 April 1935, 5 and 16 May 1935, 7; Hans Brückner, "Wie sie lügen!," *Deutsche Podium,* June 1935, 1–3; *Melody Maker,* 1 June 1935; Lange, *Jazz in Deutschland,* 68; Petrushka [Petruschka] to author, 28 June 1990.

92. Robert König, "Wir gratulieren!," *Deutsche Podium,* 8 October 1937, 2.

93. *Deutsche Podium,* 17 April 1935, 4; ibid., 22 August 1935, 7; ibid., 12 September 1935, 9–10; ibid., 8 November 1935, 2.

94. *Deutsche Podium,* 23 March 1935, 8; ibid., 17 April 1935, 4; ibid., 24 April 1935, 6–7; ibid., 16 May 1935, 6; ibid., 30 May 1935, 8 (quotation); Schulz-Reichel interview.

95. *Deutsche Podium,* 15 August 1935, 4, and 24 January 1936, 8 (quotation).

96. *Artist,* 22 May 1936, 595; *Unterhaltungsmusik,* 15 October 1936, 1293; Danzi, *American Musician,* 110; Haentzschel interview.

97. *Deutsche Podium,* 25 September 1936, 8; ibid., 18 December 1936, 3; ibid., 8 January 1937, 5; ibid., 12 February 1937, 6; ibid., 24 September 1937, 3; *Artist,* 17 September 1936), 1169; *Unterhaltungsmusik,* 21 January 1937, 66–67.

98. *Deutsche Podium,* 18 September 1936, 13; ibid., 20 November 1936, 3; ibid., 26 March 1937, 6; *Unterhaltungsmusik,* 19 November 1937, 1402.

99. *Deutsche Podium,* 12 November 1937, 5.

100. *Deutsche Podium,* 23 February 1935, 3; ibid., 15 August 1935, 1–2; ibid., 29 August 1935, 11; ibid., 11 June 1937, 1. Also see *Unterhaltungsmusik,* 15 October 1936, 1291, and 20 November 1936, 1470.

101. See p. 38; *Unterhaltungsmusik,* 10 February 1938, 155.

102. *Deutsche Podium,* 26 March 1937, 4–5, and 21 May 1937, 20. See Christa Maria Rock and Hans Brückner, eds., *Judentum und Musik: Mit dem ABC jüdischer und nichtarischer Musikbeflissener,* 2nd ed. (Munich, 1936), 57, 128, 230–31.

103. Brückner in Rock and Brückner, *Judentum,* 18.

104. Mayor of Essen to Hinkel, 25 September 1933, BDC, RMK Ralph Benatzky; Rock and Brückner, *Judentum,* 88; *Deutsche Podium,* 16 May 1935, 3, and 12 February 1937, 7–8; Leonard Feather, *The Encyclopedia of Jazz* (New York, 1960), 229–31, 416; Zimmerle interview. Goebbels venerated G. B. Shaw.

105. *Deutsche Podium,* 10 March 1935, 2; ibid., 9 May 1935, 1; ibid., 12 September 1935, 8; ibid., 8 October 1937, 3; ibid., 19 November 1937, 4; Theo Stengel and Herbert Gerigk, *Lexikon der Juden in der Musik: Mit einem Titelverzeichnis jüdischer Werke* (Berlin, 1941); transcript of radio broadcast by Fred Prieberg, "Das Musikalische Juden-ABC," produced 21 June 1988, Deutschlandfunk, Cologne.

106. *Die Tagebücher . . . Goebbels,* vol. 2, 540; Prieberg, *Musik,* 179–81. Case of Berry: Berry-RMK corr., August 1935–October 1937, BDC, RKK Berry. Contemporary accolades for Berry appear in *Artist,* 6 December 1934, 225, and 18 April 1935, 393. Lange, *Jazz in Deutschland,* 91, wrongly characterizes Berry as "half-Aryan."

107. RMK membership card for Eugen Henkel, BDC, RMK Henkel; Brocksieper interview; Lange, *Jazz in Deutschland,* 83.

108. Brocksieper interview; Leiter der Reichsstelle für Sippenforschung, "Abstammungsbescheid" for Bruno Hans Friedrich (Fritz) Brocksieper, 24 July 1939, PA Brocksieper.

109. Reichs-Rundfunk-GmbH to Reichsrundfunkkammer, 22 February 1938, BA, R 78/1162; *Amtliche Mitteilungen der Reichsmusikkammer,* 19 June 1935, BA, RD 33/2-1; Prieberg, *Musik,* 57; Evelyn Künneke, *Sing, Evelyn, Sing: Revue eines Lebens* (Reinbek, 1985), 42.

110. Raabe as paraphrased in *Deutsche Podium,* 8 July 1937, 3. Also see Raabe's statement, *Deutsche Podium,* 27 March 1936, 1; Peter Raabe, *Die Musik im Dritten Reich,* 16th–20th eds. (Regensburg, 1935), esp. 33, 48, 56; *Musiker-Lexikon,* 1103. On Strauss's antijazz attitude, see Gerhard Splitt, *Richard Strauss, 1933–1935: Ästhetik und Musikpolitik zu Beginn der nationalsozialistischen Herrschaft* (Pfaffenweiler, 1987), 117–19.

111. Thon as quoted in Kellersmann, "Jazz," 28; Tabor interview.

112. *Deutsche Kultur-Wacht,* no. 24 (1933), 14; *Musik* 25 (1933), 672; *Artist,* 19 May 1933; Schulz-Köhn interview.

113. *Pommersche Zeitung,* Stettin, 6 November 1938; *Unterhaltungsmusik,* 18 November 1938, 1507–8.

114. *Unterhaltungsmusik,* 16 March 1939, 367, and 19 May 1939, 689.

115. *Unterhaltungsmusik,* 19 January 1939, 74–75, and 13 April 1939, 510–11; Uwe Dietrich Adam, *Hochschule und Nationalsozialismus: Die Universität Tübingen im Dritten Reich* (Tübingen, 1977), 114; *Frankfurter Zeitung,* 23 August 1933.

116. For the latter, see *Artist,* 28 April, 5 and 19 May 1933; Wilhelm Hartseil, "Rassestimmen und Hörerbriefe zur Sendereihe 'Rundfunkball des Reichssenders Leipzig' (Reichssender Leipzig, Neue Wege zum Deutschen Tanzstil)," mimeographed ms., [Leipzig, 1938], 45, 78 (BDC, Library, Rundfunk 62).

117. See *Die Tagebücher . . . Goebbels,* vol. 2, 728; vol. 3, 7.

118. Raabe quoted in *Unterhaltungsmusik,* 15 May 1939, 738.

119. *Amtliche Mitteilungen der Reichsmusikkammer,* 29 May 1935, BA, RD 33/2-1; *Deutsche Podium,* 7 May 1937, 4.

120. Goebbels's edict of 5 September 1938 in *Unterhaltungsmusik,* 8 September 1938, 1187.

121. *Allgemeine Musikzeitung* 66 (1939), 268; *Amtliche Mitteilungen der Reichsmusikkammer,* 1 July 1939, BA, RD 33/2-2; *Unterhaltungsmusik,* 10 August 1939, 1169.

122. Kurt Pabst, "Nazi-'Kultur': Dokumente über Kunstpflege im Dritten Reich," unpublished ms., Erfurt, [1946], 38 (BDC, RKK Pabst); *Artist,* 15 November 1934, 148.

123. "Musikalische Feldpost," beginning of May 1942, PA Daniels; Bessunger to author, 26 April 1989.

124. Interviews with Klagemann, Brocksieper, Haentzschel, and Tabor; BDC, RKK Woschke, Research Föhl, MF Föhl; *Deutsche Podium,* 27 September 1935, 1–2; ibid., 6 December 1935, 3–4; ibid., 11 September 1936, 5–6; *Fox auf 78,* no. 4 (Fall 1987), 11.

125. *Unterhaltungsmusik,* 15 June 1939, 822; Gestapo entry of 15 December 1941 in personal file, BDC, RMK Leschetitzky; Gerhard Conrad, *Heinz Wehner: Eine Bio-Discographie* (Menden, 1989), 41–42; Klaus Krüger, "Wir machen Musik: Tanzorchester im Dritten Reich," in Polster, *"Swing Heil,"* 55.

126. *Die Tagebücher . . . Goebbels,* vol. 2, 398; Heinz Pohle, *Der Rundfunk als Instrument der Politik: Zur Geschichte des deutschen Rundfunks von 1923/38* (Hamburg, 1955), 172–78, 188–90, 213–16; Ansgar Diller, *Rundfunkpolitik im Dritten Reich* (Munich, 1980), 9, 111, 142, 155.

127. Pohle, *Rundfunk*, 186; Gerhard Eckert, *Der Rundfunk als Führungsmittel: Studien zum Weltrundfunk und Fernsehrundfunk* (Heidelberg, 1941), 219; Hans-Joachim Weinbrenner, ed., *Handbuch des Deutschen Rundfunks 1938* (Heidelberg and Berlin, 1938), 284.

128. Jochen Klepper, *Unter dem Schatten deiner Flügel: Aus den Tagebüchern, 1932–1942* (Munich, 1976), 46; corr. Reichssendeleitung of Reichs-Rundfunk-Gesellschaft, November 1933–August 1936, BA, R 78/902, 909, 192, and 913.

129. *Artist*, 13 August 1936, 1011; *Zeitschrift für Musik* 103 (1936), 774.

130. *Die Tagebücher . . . Goebbels*, vol. 2, 417, 545, 706, and vol. 3, 11–12; Eugen Hadamovsky, *Der Rundfunk im Dienste der Volksführung* (Leipzig, [1934]), 21; Kurt Wagenführ, *Rundfunk dem Hörer vorgestellt* (Leipzig, 1938), 14; Wolfgang von Bartels, "Verpflichtung des Rundfunks zur musikalischen Kultur," *Zeitschrift für Musik* 102 (1935), 1112; Diller, *Rundfunkpolitik*, 147.

131. See *Die Tagebücher . . . Goebbels*, vol. 3, 121; Werner Bergold, "Das Problem der Jazzmusik im Rundfunk," *Preussische Zeitung*, Königsberg, [Fall 1934], PA Schulz-Köhn; Pohle, *Rundfunk*, 282–83, 343–44.

132. The profusion of marches is mentioned in Wolfgang Hallgarten to Eckart Kehr, 24 March 1933, in Joachim Radkau and Imanuel Geiss, eds., *Imperialismus im 20. Jahrhundert: Gedenkschrift für George W. F. Hallgarten* (Munich, 1976), 278; *Melos* 12 (1933), 130. Also see Goebbels on 25 March 1933 as quoted in Diller, *Rundfunkpolitik*, 144, and Pohle, *Rundfunk*, 319.

133. On the abolition, see *Deutsche Kultur-Wacht*, no. 37 (1933), 10; *Artist*, 31 March 1933; "Anhang zu Bericht über die Personalveränderungen beim Süddeutschen Rundfunk Stuttgart," 15 March 1933, BA, R 78/622; Pohle, *Rundfunk*, 321.

134. RMK membership card for Willi Stech, BDC, RMK Stech; *Artist*, 28 December 1934, 310; ibid., 14 March 1935, 242; ibid., 18 April 1935, 392; ibid., 25 April 1935, 425; Haentzschel interview.

135. Haentzschel interview; review of Golden Seven swing arrangement of "Jawohl, meine Herr'n," Electrola 3970, ORA 1964-2, May 1937, in *Fox auf 78*, no. 4 (Fall 1987), 41.

136. *Musik* 27 (1935), 466; Helmut Klare as quoted in Kellersmann, "Jazz," 36; *Melody Maker*, 16 October 1937.

137. Thanks to Dr. Rainer E. Lotz of Bonn, Germany, who sent me a cassette tape, I have been able to examine several tunes, all passable as jazz, if by no means overwhelming. My judgment is complicated by the fact that the selections are undated.

138. Haentzschel interview.

139. *Völkischer Beobachter*, 13 October 1935; Reichssendeleitung A 2 to Reichssendeleitung A 3 b, 4 September 1936, BA, R 78/912. According to the Haentzschel interview, the radio official opposing the Golden Seven was the composer Dr. Willy Richartz.

140. *Deutsche Podium*, 25 October 1935, 3–4; *Artist*, 29 January 1936, 107; *Zeitschrift für Musik* 103 (1936), 774.

141. Detailed transcript of broadcast by Fricke on 9 December 1935, "Vom Cake-Walk zum Hot: Ein Stück Sittengeschichte unserer Zeit," made by Schulz-Köhn, PA Schulz-Köhn. Also see Bessunger (who listened to this in the Frankfurt area) to author, 25 April 1989; *Musik* 28 (1936), 292; Pohle, *Rundfunk*, 325.

142. Reichssendeleitung A 2 b, circular A 2 b no. 127, 5 February 1936; circular A 2 B no. 135, 13 March 1936, BA, R 78/694.

143. Klagemann as reported in Krüger, "Musik," 60.

144. On these connections, see Dietrich Schulz-Köhn, *Die Schallplatte auf dem Weltmarkt* (Berlin, 1940), 64–94; Lange, *Jazz in Deutschland*, 62–63.

145. *Deutsche Kultur-Wacht*, no. 8 (1933), 17–18; *Deutsche Podium*, 30 April 1937, 3, and 15 July 1937, 7.

146. *Artist*, 15 October 1936, 1290; transcript of Schulz-Köhn interview for British video series, "Swing under the Swastika" (see n. 88 above).

147. *Artist*, 16 May 1935, 492; Hinrich Schlüter, "Neue Schallplatten," *Musik* 28 (1936), 377–80.

148. Interviews with Blüthner, Hielscher, Jung, and Vogel; Bessunger to author, 25 April 1989.

149. *Die Tagebücher . . . Goebbels*, vol. 3, 361.

150. Ibid., 373; Deutsche Grammophon, Berlin-Tempelhof, record number list, "Achtung! Achtung! Nur dieses numerische Verzeichnis . . . hat Geltung!," n.d., PA Jung (quotation).

151. Hitler quoted in Max Domarus, *Hitler: Reden und Proklamationen, 1932–1945*, vol. 2 (Wiesbaden, 1973), 730. Also see ibid., 717, 727–29; Ian Kershaw, *The "Hitler Myth": Image and Reality in the Third Reich* (Oxford, 1987), 237–38.

152. Goodman's benefit concert role is vouched for by Lange, *Jazz in Deutschland*, 86, but unfortunately, like all of Lange's statements, it is not documented. Still, the counterargument by Hamburg jazz expert Thorsten Müller in *Deutsches Allgemeines Sonntagsblatt*, 6 December 1981, is not convincing. Also see James Lincoln Collier, *Benny Goodman and the Swing Era* (New York, 1989), 205–6.

153. "Swing Music auf Electrola," [1937], PA Jung. For Goodman record ads on the Electrola label, see *Skizzen*, April 1936, 22; ibid., December 1936, 18; ibid., January 1937, 20; ibid., November 1937, 21. For Goodman on the Brunswick label, see Brunswick minibrochures for February, October, and December 1937, PA Jung.

154. Lange, *Jazz in Deutschland*, 87.

155. See p. 45.

156. Schulz-Köhn interview.

157. Ibid.; Kleindin as quoted in Conrad, *Wehner*, 58.

158. Dieter Zimmerle, "Jazz im Nationalsozialismus," PA Zimmerle.

159. Jung interview; Jung to Electrola, 7 June 1938 (quotation); Deutsche Grammophon to Jung, 13 June 1938; Kristall-Schallplatten to Jung, 20 June 1939. Also see catalog, "Brunswick Platten 1937," 13, 21. All documents PA Jung.

160. *Schwarze Korps*, 25 November 1937.

161. "Brunswick Platten-Verzeichnis," up to and including March 1939, 10, 24–25 (PA Jung); Reginald Rudorf, *Jazz in der Zone* (Cologne and Berlin, 1964), 19.

162. Boas interview; Hans Blüthner, "Plattensammeln und was sonst noch so war," *Fox auf 78*, no. 7 (Summer 1989), 18; Brunswick record catalog, "Swing-Musik," [1936], 15 (quotation) (PA Schulz-Köhn); "Brunswick Platten 1937," 19 (PA Jung). "Brunswick Platten-Verzeichnis," until March 1939 (PA Jung), does not contain an entry for Trumbauer. Trumbauer's German descent is not corroborated by Feather, *Encyclopedia*, 445–46.

163. *Artist*, 12 March 1936, 272; ibid., 19 March 1936, 304; ibid., 29 July 1936, 872; Peter Raabe, "Die Musik im Dritten Reich," *Zeitschrift für Musik* 101 (1934), 729; *Deutsche Podium*, 8 October 1937, 6; Oskar Joost, "Denkschrift zur Kultivierung der Tanzmusik in Deutschland," enclosed with Joost to Hinkel, 16 November 1936, BDC, RMK Joost.

164. For the connection between the two events, see *Deutsche Podium*, 8 November 1935, 3; Pohle, *Rundfunk*, 322–23.

165. *Artist*, 14 November 1935, 1279.

166. *Deutsche Podium*, 20 March 1936, 3.

167. Interviews with Vogel, Blüthner, Bohländer, Madlung-Shelton.

168. Keudell to Hinkel, 7 October 1935, BA, R 56I/87; Reichssendeleitung A 2 to Reichssendeleiter, 28 December 1937, BA, R 78/913; Schlüter, "Neue Schallplatten," 377; *Deutsche Podium,* 9 May 1935, 3, and 29 July 1937, 8; *Skizzen,* December 1935, 19; ibid., February 1937, 16; ibid., April 1937, 11–12; *Artist,* 26 May 1933; Hans Schnoor, *Barnabás von Géczy: Aufstieg einer Kunst: Rhapsodie in zehn Sätzen* (Dresden, [1937]); *Schwarze Korps,* 25 November 1937. Géczy's "Vieni, Vieni" (July 1938) is on cassette tape, *Wir tanzen wieder Swing Time,* no. 2, Bob's Music, Hamburg, 1989.

169. Joost was *NSDAP-Amtswalter,* below the post of *NS-Ortsgruppenleiter.* See "Fragebogen" Joost and postscript, 10 June 1933, RMK Joost; and Reichssendeleitung A 2 to Reichssendeleiter, 28 December 1937, BA, R 78/913; Schlüter, "Neue Schallplatten," 377; *Deutsche Podium,* 23 February 1935, 5, and 31 October 1935, 7; Danzi, *American Musician,* 82; interview with his brother and fellow musician Albert Joost in Polster, *"Swing Heil",* 95–98; Boas, *Anhang,* 12–13; Krüger, "Musik," 47–48; *Fox auf 78,* no. 4 (Fall 1987), 40. Listen to Joost's "Oh Muki Muki oh" (May 1935) on *Wir tanzen* (see n. 168).

170. *Deutsche Podium,* 14 November 1935, 1280; Fritz Stege, "Gibt es eine 'deutsche Jazzkapelle'?" *Zeitschrift für Instrumentenbau* 56 (1936), 251.

171. Quotation from *Artist,* 19 March 1936, 303. Also see *Artist,* 6 February 1936, 129; ibid., 26 February 1936, 228; ibid., 5 March 1936, 244; *Deutsche Podium,* 14 February 1936, 3.

172. Fred Malige, "Was ist Tanzmusik—und was 'Wettbewerb'?," *Deutsche Podium,* 7 February 1936, 1–2, and 24 January 1936, 4; *Artist,* 13 February 1936, 156.

173. Pohle, *Rundfunk,* 322; *Artist,* 20 February 1936, 189.

174. Interview Zimmerle; *Artist,* 13 September 1934, and 28 August 1935, 961. Weber's "Ich tanz mit Fräulein Dolly Swing" (June 1938), a timely concession to the swing dance fad of the period (see p. 103), features relatively well-swinging section-playing but is too tightly arranged, drags tempo, and has mediocre solos (cassette tape, *Wir tanzen* [as in n. 168]).

175. *Artist,* 19 March 1936, 304–5, and 4 June 1936, 651–52; *Deutsche Podium,* 3 April 1936, 1–2; Heinrich, *"Swing-Generation,"* 14–15.

176. *Deutsche Podium,* 25 September 1936, 13, and 22 January 1937, 3; *Unterhaltungsmusik,* 25 May 1938, 674.

177. Stege, "Gibt es," 252.

178. Joost to Hinkel, 12 June 1936, BDC, RMK Joost; *Deutsche Podium,* 28 February 1936, 5, and 22 May 1936, 7.

179. Joost to Hinkel, 19 September 1936, BDC, RMK Joost.

180. Reichssendeleitung A 2, "Aktennotiz über die Schaffung eines mustergültigen Rundfunk-Tanzorchesters," signed by Joost, Richartz et al., 6 November 1936, BDC, RMK Joost.

181. Oskar Joost, "Denkschrift zur Kultivierung der Tanzmusik in Deutschland," enclosed with Joost to Hinkel, 16 November 1936, BDC, RMK Joost.

182. Joost to Hinkel 17 March 1937 (quotation), Joost to Glasmeier 22 March 1937, Joost to Hinkel 5 April 1937, BDC, RMK Joost; Diller, *Rundfunkpolitik,* 198.

183. BDC, personal files Hartseil; Diller, *Rundfunkpolitik,* 204.

184. "Rassestimmen und Hörerbriefe" (see n. 116), esp. 1, 3, 5–6, 10–15, 18, 24, 35, 79, 102, 123; *Unterhaltungsmusik,* 6 January 1938, 4.

185. *Unterhaltungsmusik,* 14 April 1938, 451, and 11 August 1938, 1054–55; *Musik in Jugend und Volk* 2 (1939), 33.

Chapter 2

1. Joachim Ernst Berendt, *Ein Fenster aus Jazz: Essays, Portraits, Reflexionen* (Frankfurt am Main, 1977), 300; Ray Taubert in the broadcast series "Jazz in Germany: A Survey of Hot Dance, Swing and Traditional Jazz in Germany, 1924 to Present," produced for and broadcast on KALW FM, San Francisco, by Dave Radlauer and R. Taubert, n.d., courtesy of the Goethe Institute, Toronto (program 1).

2. Quotations in order of occurrence: *Artist,* 11 March 1937, 260; *SA-Mann,* 19 February 1938, 10; *Bewegung,* 6 December 1938; Joachim-Ernst ["Fiddlin' Joe"] Frommann to Kurt ["Hot-Geyer"] Michaelis, 17 December 1935, PA Michaelis; transcript of radio broadcast by Hajo Steinert, "Und Abends in die Scala: Girls, Bonzen und die Partei," produced 25 August 1987, Deutschlandfunk, Cologne.

3. Gunther Schuller, *The Swing Era: The Development of Jazz, 1930–1945* (New York and Oxford, 1989), 3–45; see p. 28. See also Neil Leonard, *Jazz and the White Americans: The Acceptance of a New Art Form* (Chicago, 1970), 119–27; Carlo Bohländer, *Jazz-Geschichte und Rhythmus* (Mainz, 1960), 42–48; James Lincoln Collier, *Benny Goodman and the Swing Era* (New York, 1989), 122–229.

4. Schuller, *Swing Era,* 4. Also see Albert McCarthy, *Big Band Jazz* (New York, 1974), 321.

5. *Deutsche Podium,* 21 August 1936), 36–37, and 4 September 1936, 4–5.

6. *Artist,* 21 April 1933.

7. Zacharias interview.

8. Interviews with Panagopoulos, Berendt, Bohländer, and Mangelsdorff; Franz Heinrich, *"Swing-Generation": Selbsterlebtes* (Menden, 1988), 29–30; Blüthner interview in transcript of radio broadcast by Astrid Eichstedt, "'Swing Heil!': Jazzcliquen im nationalsozialistischen Deutschland," produced 17 March 1989, Westdeutscher Rundfunk I.

9. Michael Danzi, *American Musician in Germany, 1924–1939: Memoirs of the Jazz, Entertainment, and Movie World of Berlin during the Weimar Republic and the Nazi Era—and in the United States,* as told to Rainer E. Lotz (Schmitten, 1986), 102.

10. Martha Dodd, *Through Embassy Eyes* (New York, 1940), 291.

11. Henry H. Sklow to Kurt Michaelis, 6 August 1938, PA Michaelis.

12. Charles Delaunay, *Hot Discography: 1938 Edition* (New York, 1943), 211, 250, 252, 257–58.

13. S. Frederick Starr, *Red and Hot: The Fate of Jazz in the Soviet Union, 1917–1980* (New York and Oxford, 1983), e.g. 115; Jim Godbolt, *A History of Jazz in Britain, 1919–50* (London, 1984), e.g. 212.

14. Hawkins as quoted in Whitney Balliett, *American Musicians: Fifty-Six Portraits in Jazz* (New York and Oxford, 1986), 109.

15. Lehn interview.

16. Transcript of radio broadcast by Lutz Adam, "Swingstadt Berlin: Die Stauffer-Zeit," produced 1 May 1986, RIAS Berlin I; Kurt Hohenberger orchestra, recorded 23 December 1937, reissued on *Swing tanzen verboten,* Telefunken 6.28360 DP, 1976. Also see Wolfgang Muth, *Ernst Höllerhagen: Ein deutscher Jazzmusiker* (Magdeburg, 1964), e.g., 8–10.

17. Schulz-Reichel interview.

18. In broadcast series "Jazz in Germany," program 5 (see n. 1 above).

19. Klagemann and Schulz-Reichel interviews.

20. *Down Beat,* December 1937, 15.

21. Schulz-Reichel interview. Also Schulz-Köhn, Meyer, and Haentzschel interviews; *Unterhaltungsmusik,* 10 August 1939, 1169.

22. Cf. Tatum's August 1939 solo piano rendition of "It Had to Be You."

23. Korseck to author, 15 November 1988; *Unterhaltungsmusik,* 28 February 1940, 177.

24. Cf. "What Will I Tell My Heart" (Hohenberger's combo, 23 December 1937), "Rücksichtslos," and "Evelyn" (both by Peter Kreuder und seine Tanzrhythmiker, 4 January 1938), *Swing tanzen verboten* (see n. 16). But see the positive critique of "Cherokesenfox," recorded for Kristall (3629 C 9770) in August 1936 by Kurt Engel's Tanzrhythmiker, in *Fox auf 78,* no. 6 (Fall 1988), 14.

25. Hans Korseck, hand-written inventory of private jazz record collection [1939/40], PA Hilde Korseck.

26. Brocksieper interview.

27. See Schuller, *Swing Era,* 21, 27–28.

28. Klagemann interview. Klagemann's clipped, restrained approach may be discerned in the Hohenberger group's "What Will I Tell My Heart" as well as Kreuder's "Rücksichtslos" (see nn. 16, 24).

29. Muth, *Höllerhagen,* 8; Haentzschel interview.

30. On "San Francisco," recorded in 1936 and not yet classically swing-influenced, Engel plays a competent albeit not very inspired xylophone, with Haentzschel swinging along impressively, if not anywhere near Schulze (broadcast series "Jazz in Germany," program 3 [see n. 1]). Further see *Artist,* 14 February 1935, 130; *Deutsche Podium,* 8 October 1937, 16; Muth, *Höllerhagen,* 8–9; Haentzschel interview. Also see the critique of Engel in n. 24.

31. Gerhard Conrad, *Posaunen-Dob: Kleine Biographie Walter Dobschinskis* (Menden, 1983), 15.

32. *Artist,* 10 September 1936, 1139; Willy Fritsch, . . . *das kommt nicht wieder: Erinnerungen eines Filmschauspielers* (Zurich and Stuttgart, 1963), 128–29. A moderately swinging "Caravan" (Ellington) of 1938 can be heard on cassette tape provided with Christian Kellersmann, "Jazz in Deutschland von 1933–1945," Master's thesis, University of Hamburg, 1989 (see p. 130).

33. *Deutsche Podium,* 15 July 1977, 8; Gunter and Lissy Lust, . . . *und sie drehen sich immer noch!* (Menden, 1984), 33; Daniels interview; Heinrich, *"Swing-Generation,"* 30. Also Muth, *Höllerhagen,* 9–10; Gunther Schuller, *Early Jazz: Its Roots and Musical Development* (New York and Oxford, 1986), 194, n. 23.

34. See n. 16.

35. Hans Blüthner, "Jazz i Berlin," *Orkester Journalen,* December 1947, 33; *Artist,* 6 December 1934, 225, and 14 March 1935, 242.

36. The pianist for that group was Otto Fuhrmann, never known as a core jazz musician (Tabor interview). On Abriani, who frequently visited Germany in those years, see Horst J. P. Bergmeier and Rainer E. Lotz, "Weltenbummler mit Koffer in Berlin— John Abriani," *Fox auf 78,* no. 7 (Summer 1989), 38–44; *Deutsche Podium,* 15 October 1937, 9, and 29 October 1937, 9.

37. *Down Beat,* December 1937, 15. Also see the Belgian E. van Gils's description in *Music* [Brussels], December 1937, 147; interviews with Schulz-Reichel, Klagemann, Brocksieper, and Schulz-Köhn.

38. *Down Beat,* December 1937, 15; Schulz-Reichel interview. Also Klagemann interview; *Deutsche Podium,* 13 March 1936, 10; Luis Trenker, *Alles gut gegangen: Geschichten aus meinem Leben* (Munich, 1975), 349.

39. Hubert von Meyerinck, *Meine berühmten Freundinnen* (Düsseldorf and Vienna, 1967), 111–14.

40. *Deutsche Podium,* 15 October 1937, 9.

41. Schulz-Köhn interview (quotation). Also Femina program, 1 November 1938, PA Jung; Marko Paysan, "Zauber der Nacht: Tanz- und Vergnügungsbetriebe im Berlin der Dreissiger Jahre," in Bernd Polster, ed., *"Swing Heil": Jazz im Nationalsozialismus* (Berlin, 1989), 87; Michaelis interview.

42. *Artist,* 13 September 1934, and 25 October 1934, 82; *Deutsche Podium,* 10 March 1935, 9. Kok's rendition of "Tiger Rag" (1935) reveals disciplined section-playing, well-improvised clarinet runs apparently by Bauschke, and a nice, dense-chord solo by Schulze; however, it also has a disappointing, "noodled" alto sax solo (broadcast series "Jazz in Germany," program 3 [see n. 1]).

43. *Artist,* 8 August 1935, 805, and 15 August 1935, 874.

44. *Artist,* 23 January 1936, 77, and 16 July 1936, 821; Horst H. Lange, *Jazz in Deutschland: Die deutsche Jazz-Chronik: 1900–1960* (Berlin, 1966), 68; Lehn interview.

45. Quotations in order of occurrence: *Unterhaltungsmusik,* 24 December 1936, 1660; *Deutsche Podium,* 24 September 1937, 3; Schulz-Köhn, "Programm eines Abends im 'Moka Efti' bei Erhard Bauschke," [1937], PA Schulz-Köhn. Also see Horst Lippmann in "Jazz-Club News," October–November 1945, PA Jung.

46. RMK membership card for Heinz Wehner, BDC, RMK Wehner; *Artist,* 13 September 1934, and 25 October 1934, 82; *Deutsche Podium,* 25 October 1935, 16; ibid., 6 November 1936, 18; ibid., 12 March 1937, 7; *Unterhaltungsmusik,* 1 April 1937, 379; ibid., 3 February 1938, 142; ibid., 29 March 1939, 461–62; Lange, *Jazz in Deutschland,* 75; Gerhard Conrad, *Heinz Wehner: Eine Bio-Discographie* (Menden, 1989), 5–64.

47. *Orkester Journalen* as quoted in Conrad, *Wehner,* 37; *Down Beat,* December 1937, 15; Schulz-Köhn, "Programm eines Abends im 'Moka Efti' bei Erhard Bauschke," [1937], PA Schulz-Köhn; "Das Fräulein Gerda," recorded 2 September 1938, featuring Berking, Müller, Wernicke, reissued on *Swing tanzen verboten* (see n. 16). Very similar in texture are Wehner's "Cherokesen-Fox," 29 September 1936, ibid., and the 1937 recording of "Bugle Call Rag," broadcast series "Jazz in Germany," program 1 (see n. 1).

48. *Artist,* 8 August 1935, 806; 5 September 1935, 982; and 27 November 1935, 1358; *Unterhaltungsmusik,* 24 December 1936, 1659, and 25 May 1938, 673; *Deutsche Podium,* 23 March 1935, 12; ibid., 20 June 1935, 8; ibid., 27 September 1935, 13–14; ibid., 7 August 1936, 10; ibid., 11 December 1936, 11; ibid., 18 December 1936, 8; Horst H. Lange, "Zwischen Optik und Hot-Takt: Max Rumpf," *Fox auf 78,* no. 5 (Spring 1988), 4–9; idem, *Jazz in Deutschland,* 83; Otto Stenzel as interviewed by Hajo Steinert, "Und Abends in die Scala" (see n. 2).

49. *Artist,* 28 December 1934, and 14 February 1935, 129–30; *Skizzen,* March 1937, 16; Lange, *Jazz in Deutschland,* 82; Fred K. Prieberg, *Musik im NS-Staat* (Frankfurt am Main, 1982), 293; "Club der Schellackfreunde Hessen e.V.," Frankfurt am Main, September 1987, 41; Pointon to author, 25 April 1989; Daniels interview.

50. Lange, *Jazz in Deutschland,* 93; Danzi, *American Musician,* 122; Heinrich, *"Swing-Generation,"* 32.

51. Personal communication to author by Roy Ackerman of Yorkshire Television, in London, 8 May 1988.

52. Henry Hall, "I Played in Nazi Germany," *Rhythm,* April 1939, 3–6.

53. Ibid., 4; unidentified fragment, "Besuch aus London: Henry Hall in Berlin,"

[1939], PA Jung; Charles Fox, "Jazz in England," in *That's Jazz: Der Sound des 20. Jahrhunderts: Eine Ausstellung der Stadt Darmstadt . . . 29. Mai bis 28. August 1988* (Darmstadt, 1988), 437; *Unterhaltungsmusik*, 5 September 1940, 829.

54. Teddy Stauffer, *Forever Is a Hell of a Long Time: An Autobiography* (Chicago, 1976), 101–18; *Deutsche Podium*, 17 April 1935, 7; *Melody Maker*, 16 October 1937; Femina program, 1 November 1938, PA Jung; Conrad, *Posaunen-Dob*, 11–25; Lange, *Jazz in Deutschland*, 78. The first two tunes may be heard on *Swing tanzen verboten* (as in n. 16); the last one is included in Radlauer and Taubert's broadcast series "Jazz in Germany," program 1 (see n. 1). Cf. Lutz Adam, "Swingstadt Berlin" (see n. 16).

55. *Deutsche Podium*, 11 December 1936, 8; ibid., 18 December 1936, 7; ibid., 29 October 1937, 8; *Unterhaltungsmusik*, 2 February 1939, inner cover; Lange, *Jazz in Deutschland*, 81. Listen to Hülphers's rendition of "Don't be that Way" (1937) in definite swing style. It is marred only by a somewhat amateurish tenor saxophone solo (broadcast series "Jazz in Germany," program 3 [see n. 1]).

56. Zimmerle interview.

57. See *Artist*, 27 November 1935, 1358.

58. Zacharias interview; Heinrich, *"Swing-Generation,"* 27–29.

59. Egino Biagioni, *Herb Flemming: A Jazz Pioneer around the World* (Alphen aan de Rijn, [1977]), 5–7, 49–53; Schulz-Reichel interview; Hans Blüthner, "Sweet and Hot: Blick in die Vergangenheit," *Jazz-Podium* 35 (September 1986), 9.

60. Vogel interview; Heinrich, *"Swing-Generation,"* 31.

61. Dietrich Schulz, "Lebenslauf," 30 April 1936, BDC, RSK Schulz; Dietrich Schulz-Köhn, "Lebenslauf," on back of *Die Schallplatte auf dem Weltmarkt* (Berlin, 1940).

62. Quotation from transcript of Schulz-Köhn interview for British video series, "Swing under the Swastika," Yorkshire Television, London, 1988.

63. Milton "Mezz" Mezzrow and Bernard Wolfe, *Really the Blues* (New York, 1949), 194–95; Alfred A. Goodman, *Musik im Blut: Amerikanische Rhythmen erobern die Welt* (Munich, 1968), 118; Chris Goddard, *Jazz Away from Home* (New York and London, 1979), 138–60; Schuller, *Swing Era*, 245; Dietrich Schulz-Köhn, *Django Reinhardt: Ein Portrait* (Wetzlar, 1960), 29–31; Schulz-Köhn interview.

64. Quotation from letter of D. Schulz to W. Schulz, 23 September 1936; Hot Club, "carte de membre" for Dietrich Schulz, signed by President Panassié, November 1935, PA Schulz-Köhn. Also Schulz-Köhn, *Reinhardt*, 7–8; interview with Schulz-Köhn by Annette Hauber, in *That's Jazz*, 335, 339; Schulz-Köhn interview; Charles Delaunay, "Introduction," in idem, *Hot Discography: 1938 Edition;* Balliett, *Musicians*, 5–10.

65. Schulz-Köhn interview; Goddard, *Jazz Away*, 174–79; Godbolt, *History*, 73–76.

66. Schulz-Köhn and Schulz-Reichel interviews.

67. Schulz-Köhn interview; Paesike to Schulz, 23 September 1935, PA Schulz-Köhn (quotation).

68. Quotation from transcript of Schulz-Köhn interview (see n. 62); programs of "Brunswick-Schallplatten-Abend," by Deutsche Grammophon-Aktiengesellschaft Berlin, for 20 January, 5 March, 2 April 1936, PA Schulz-Köhn; "Einführung in die Swing-Musik: Vortrag von Dietrich Schulz," 20 January 1936, PA Schulz-Köhn; "Einteilung der Swing-Musik," in *Händlernachrichten* [Deutsche Grammophon], summer 1936, PA Schulz-Köhn; Schulz-Köhn interview.

69. Brunswick record catalog, "Swing-Musik," [1936], esp. p. 19 (PA Schulz-Köhn).

70. *Metronome*, August 1936, 41.

71. Reinmar von Zweter [Stege] in *Artist,* 17 September 1936, 1169; idem, *Unterhaltungsmusik,* 22 October 1936, 1335 (quotation).
72. *Tempo,* March 1937, 12.
73. Moser to author, 2 February and 14 March 1990.
74. For bands advertised in Königsberg, see *Deutsche Podium,* 23 March 1935, 11; *Artist,* 28 December 1935, 1478. On Börschel, see Jan Grundmann, "Erich Börschel und sein Orchester," *Fox auf 78,* no. 3 (Spring 1987), 4–7.
75. "Programm No. 50 zum Sonntag d. 2.2.1936," PA Schulz-Köhn; Ekkehard Jost, "Jazz in Europa—Die frühen Jahre," in *That's Jazz,* 321.
76. Hans Blüthner, "Plattensammeln und was sonst noch so war," *Fox auf 78,* no. 7 (Summer 1989), 20; Blüthner interview. See p. 10.
77. Michaelis interview; Schulz-Köhn to author, 10 September 1990; see the photograph in this book, dated 19 January 1936, showing Schulz, Michaelis, Flemming, Frommann, and Schulze in the Sherbini club at 3:00 A.M.
78. Michaelis and Jung interviews; "Programm No. 179 (1. Septemberwoche 1938)" and similar programs (nos. 181, 182, 190, 196) for the balance of September and for November and December 1938, PA Jung; enclosure with letter from Michaelis to author, 6 February 1989.
79. Quotation from Blüthner interview. The original German is *Schlagermann.*
80. Blüthner diary of bands, PA Blüthner.
81. Heinrich, *"Swing-Generation,"* 19–20, 26, 32–34; Hielscher interview; Moser to author, 14 March 1990.
82. Hans Blüthner, "Plattensammeln und was sonst noch so war," *Fox auf 78,* no. 6 (Fall 1988), 37; Lange, *Jazz in Deutschland,* 69–70; Blüthner interview.
83. Blüthner and Pick interviews; Schulz-Köhn to author, [August 1990].
84. Interviews with Blüthner, Pick, and Jung; Blüthner, "Plattensammeln" (1988), 36–39; ibid. (1989), 18–21; Blüthner to Jung, 22 May 1938; Magische Note membership card for Jung dated Berlin, 7 March 1939, both PA Jung; Delaunay, *Hot Discography: 1938 Edition,* x. Also see the advertisement for Blue Note, New York, "faithful to the tradition of hot jazz and genuine improvisation," ibid.; Michael Cuscuna, "The Blue Note Story," Manhattan Records Liner Notes (1984), PA Schulz-Köhn.
85. Jung interview; Geoffrey Skelton, *Paul Hindemith: The Man behind the Music: A Biography* (London, 1975), 45, 74–75.
86. Also see Deutsche Grammophon to Jung, 20 August 1936; Jung to Electrola and to Disques Swing (Paris), both 7 June 1938, and to "Werte Firma," 10 November 1938, all PA Jung.
87. Originals of these brochures, 1935–38, PA Jung.
88. Jung to *Melody Maker,* 2 October (quotation) and 11 November 1937, PA Jung.
89. Jung interview.
90. See *Deutsche Podium,* 17 April 1935, 6, and 15 January 1937, 16; also Schulz-Köhn and Bohländer interviews.
91. Bohländer interview; photograph of Schulz, Bohländer, et al. (Frankfurt, 1934), PA Jung.
92. Bohländer interview.
93. Mangelsdorff interview; RCA Victor recording 22938 of "Dinah" as noted in Charles Delaunay, *New Hot Discography: The Standard Directory of Recorded Jazz,* ed. Walter E. Schaap and George Avakian (New York, 1948), 87.
94. *Deutsche Podium,* 13 November 1936, 8–9, and 20 November 1936, 3–4; *Artist,* 27 November 1935, 1358; *Unterhaltungsmusik,* 22 December 1938, 1687–88; program, "1. Gastspiel der Kapelle Karl Ballaban: Wiener Tanzsymphoniker, August–

September 1936," PA Michaelis; enclosure with letter from Michaelis to author, 6 February 1989; Becke to author, 8 February 1990; Michaelis interview.

95. Michaelis interview; Michaelis to author, 1 January 1990; Fox, "Jazz in England," 437–38. See also Geoffrey Butcher, *Next to a Letter from Home: Major Glenn Miller's Wartime Band* (Edinburgh, 1986), 150; Godbolt, *History*, 192, 219, 234.

96. *Tempo*, September 1937, 26.

97. *Melody Maker*, 15 April 1939.

98. *Tempo*, March 1937, 12; Sklow to Michaelis, 2 October 1937 (quotations) and 30 October 1937, PA Michaelis.

99. Sklow to Michaelis, 10 December 1937, PA Michaelis.

100. Ibid.

101. Quotation from Sklow to Michaelis, 28 January 1938; also letters dated 10 December 1937, 6 August 1938, 15 February 1939, all PA Michaelis. See also the interesting testimony by another contemporary New York Goodman fan, Edward Pessen, "The Kingdom of Swing: New York City in the Late 1930s," *New York History* (July 1989), esp. 278–79, 281; and Collier, *Benny Goodman*, 216–19.

102. Ross Russell to Michaelis, 1 May 1937, PA Michaelis.

103. Russell to Michaelis, 20 April 1937, PA Michaelis.

104. Russell to Michaelis, 19 July [1937], 10 November 1937, 16 December [1937], PA Michaelis. See Leonard Feather, *The Encyclopedia of Jazz* (New York, 1960), 406.

105. Russell to Michaelis, 22 January 1938, PA Michaelis; Ross Russell, *Bird Lives! The High Life and Hard Times of Charlie (Yardbird) Parker* (New York, 1973), 376; James M. Ethridge and Barbara Kopala, eds., *Contemporary Authors: A Bio-Bibliographical Guide to Current Authors and Their Works* (Detroit, 1967), 822; Michaelis to author, 26 April 1989. See also Delaunay, *New Hot Discography*, x; Schuller, *Swing Era*, 367, n. 31.

106. Dietrich Schulz in *Tempo*, March 1937, 12; Walter Kempowski, *Tadellöser & Wolff: Ein bürgerlicher Roman*, 2nd ed. (Munich, 1975), 62; Bernd Polster, "Treudeutsch, treudeutsch: Swingheinis unterwandern den Kolonnenzwang," in Polster, *"Swing Heil,"* 130; Boas and Pick interviews; Bessunger to author, 25 April 1989.

107. *Artist*, 15 September 1933 and 27 November 1935, 1357; *Deutsche Podium*, 20 June 1935, 6; ibid., 18 October 1935, 11; ibid., 20 March 1936, 20; ibid., 10 April 1936, 15; ibid., 21 August 1936, 40–41; *Unterhaltungsmusik*, 24 August 1939, 1248; Daniels interview.

108. "ISRC: The International Swing Rhythm Club Germany at Dusseldorf," membership card for Werner Daniels; "Oliver" to "James," [1937], both PA Daniels; Daniels interview.

109. Typewritten carbon copy, sample page, "Mitteilungsblatt des Internationalen Swing Rhythm Club," [1937]; [Swing Rhythm Club] to [newspaper editor] Heiling, [March 1938]; "Reminiszenzen"; private tape of Theo Hoeren, enclosed with letter from Daniels to author, 15 June 1990, all PA Daniels; Daniels to author, 2 February 1989; Daniels interview.

110. *Unterhaltungsmusik*, 29 September 1937, 1203, and 3 March 1938, 272; *Deutsche Podium*, 18 December 1936, 14; Dieter Zimmerle, "Jazz im Nationalsozialismus," PA Zimmerle; Pick and Zimmerle interviews; Schulz-Köhn to author, 10 September 1990.

111. Francis Newton [Eric J. Hobsbawm], *The Jazz Scene* (New York, 1975), 235, 238, 247.

112. Schulz-Köhn to Reichsschrifttumskammer, 8 December 1938, BDC, RSK Schulz; Schulz-Köhn interview.

113. Interviews with Blüthner, Michaelis, and Bohländer.

114. Interviews with Daniels, Zimmerle, Michaelis, and Boas.
115. Interviews with Mangelsdorff, Jung, and Blüthner.
116. This point was well stated both by Blüthner and Daniels (interviews).
117. "Reminiszenzen," PA Daniels.
118. Interviews with Blüthner, Pick, and Michaelis. See the "tea-party" photo in this book, showing the Leipzig fans.
119. Ibid.; "Wichtige Mitteilung" [for Melodie-Klub, Königsberg], 3 April 1935, PA Schulz-Köhn. See the photo mentioned in note 188; another photo, dated 7 March 1937 (PA Michaelis), shows four well-groomed young men attired in suits and ties.
120. Schulz-Köhn, *Reinhardt,* 7 (quotation); Michaelis interview.
121. Zimmerle and Daniels interviews.
122. In my interviews of fans and musicians, I always pointedly asked about their relationships with their parents. Not once did I encounter anyone who had rebelled against a father or mother—quite the contrary.
123. See Newton [Hobsbawm], *Jazz Scene,* 230, 232, 237, 238 (quotation). Also Leonard, *White Americans,* 147.
124. Pick and Blüthner interviews.
125. Blüthner interview. Cf. Michaelis interview: "[The girls] did not understand anything, they only distracted us . . . were only interested in dancing . . . we told them: 'This is for men only, one speaks English here'. . ." Daniels made similar remarks about Düsseldorf in his interview with me.
126. Kurt Michaelis, "Rückblende zum Jahre 1938," PA Michaelis; Michaelis interview.
127. Blüthner interview.
128. Zimmerle interview.
129. Blüthner and Pick interviews; Magische Note circulars of 3 May and 28 June 1938, PA Jung; Lange, *Jazz in Deutschland,* 70; Delaunay, *New Hot Discography,* 435; Rudi Blesh, "This is Jazz," *Arts and Architecture* 66 (March 1944), 20; Newton [Hobsbawm], *Jazz Scene,* 231, 250.
130. Michaelis interview; Russell to Michaelis, 10 November 1937, [late November 1937] (quotation), 22 January 1938, PA Michaelis; Schuller, *Swing Era,* 192.
131. Newton [Hobsbawm], *Jazz Scene,* 233.
132. *Artist,* 16 May 1935, 492; *Unterhaltungsmusik,* 14 January 1937, 39; *Skizzen,* June/July 1938, 23; Femina program, 1 November 1938, PA Jung; Muth, *Höllerhagen,* 20; Lange, *Jazz in Deutschland,* 84; Stauffer, *Forever,* 111; Horst J. P. Bergmeier and Rainer E. Lotz, *Billy Bartholomew: Bio-Discography* (Menden, 1985), 47; Conrad, *Wehner,* 51.
133. Lange, *Jazz in Deutschland,* 87; Starr, *Red and Hot,* 118; Meyer interview.
134. *Skizzen,* April 1935, 15; ibid., January 1936, 20; ibid., March 1936, 19; ibid., December 1938, 22; *Deutsche Podium,* 12 February 1937, 8.
135. *Artist,* 11 April 1935, 349, and 16 May 1935, 493; *Deutsche Podium,* 29 January 1937, 9, and 22 July 1937, 4.
136. *Skizzen,* December 1935, 22, and February 1938, 12; *Deutsche Podium,* 11 December 1936, 13; German Brunswick minibrochure, September 1937, PA Jung; McCarthy, *Big Band Jazz,* 317–18; Godbolt, *History,* 187, 222.
137. German Brunswick minibrochures for February 1938, January and May 1939; "Brunswick Platten-Verzeichnis," up to and including March 1939; Alberti record catalog, [December 1938], all PA Jung; *Skizzen,* December 1938, 21, and March 1939, 22.
138. Russell to Michaelis, 20 April, 23 October, 16 December 1937, 22 January 1938,

PA Michaelis; German Brunswick minibrochure, December 1936, PA Jung; Dietrich Schulz, "Classic Swing Album," [November 1936], PA Schulz-Köhn.

139. German Brunswick minibrochures for March and April 1939; "Brunswick Platten-Verzeichnis" up to and including March 1939, esp. 6, 32, PA Jung; Feather, *Encyclopedia*, 215; Joachim Ernst Berendt, *Das Jazzbuch: Entwicklung und Bedeutung der Jazzmusik* (Frankfurt am Main and Hamburg, 1953), 58–61; Schuller, *Swing Era*, 293.

140. Kurt Michaelis, "Das Swing & Hot-Rhythm Jahr 1938," PA Michaelis; Russell to Michaelis, 10 November 1937, both PA Michaelis; Michaelis to author, 12 February and 26 April 1989, 1 January 1990; Michaelis interview.

141. Blüthner interview; Blüthner to author, 29 March 1989; Blüthner, "Plattensammeln" (1989), 18, 20; ibid. (1988), 39; E. van Gils in *Music*, December 1937, 211 (quotation); *Orkester Journalen* (August 1938), 5; Godbolt, *History*, 175–77.

142. Quotation from Zimmerle interview; also Jung and Daniels interviews.

143. Kurt Michaelis, "Rückblende zum Jahre 1938," PA Michaelis; Michaelis interview.

144. Blüthner and Pick interviews.

145. Michael H. Kater, "Inside Nazis: The Goebbels Diaries, 1924–1941," *Canadian Journal of History* 25 (1990), 239–40.

146. *Skizzen*, January 1935, 19; ibid., February 1937, 21; ibid., March 1937, 18; ibid., February 1938, 15–16; ibid., April 1938, 22.

147. Hielscher and Leonore Boas interviews; Friedländer-Reimann interview. Also see Heinrich, *"Swing-Generation,"* 20; *Skizzen*, February 1936, title page; ibid., August/September 1937, 21; Lange, *Jazz in Deutschland*, 95; Karsten Witte, "Gehemmte Schaulust: Momente des deutschen Revuefilms," in Helga Belach, ed., *Wir tanzen um die Welt: Deutsche Revuefilme, 1933–1945* (Munich and Vienna, 1979), 24; Astrid Eichstedt and Bernd Polster, *Wie die Wilden: Tänze auf der Höhe ihrer Zeit* (Berlin, 1985), 80; *Fox auf 78*, no. 6 (Fall 1988), 9.

148. Quotations from Frommann to Michaelis, 6 April 1936; Kurt Michaelis, "Rückblende zum Jahre 1938"; both PA Michaelis. Also Magische Note circular of 26 April 1938, PA Jung; Blüthner, "Plattensammeln" (1989), 18.

149. Heinz Pohle, *Der Rundfunk als Instrument der Politik: Zur Geschichte des deutschen Rundfunks von 1923/38* (Hamburg, 1955), 251; Magische Note circular of 7 June 1938, PA Jung; interviews with Jung, Pick, and Daniels.

150. Pohle, *Rundfunk*, 247, 251; interviews with Jung, Pick, and Bohländer.

151. Pohle, *Rundfunk*, 251; Muth, *Höllerhagen*, 10; interviews with Pick, Daniels, and Jung.

152. Regarding the performer phenomenon among jazz fans, cf. Newton [Hobsbawm], *Jazz Scene*, 234. Also Kurt Michaelis, "Rückblende aus dem Jahre 1938," PA Michaelis; Michaelis and Blüthner interviews; Heinrich, *"Swing-Generation,"* 32, 34.

153. Quotation from Newton [Hobsbawm], *Jazz Scene*, 232. Also Zimmerle interview; enclosure with letter from Michaelis to author, 6 February 1989; postcard of Leipzig Felsenkeller, Stauffer's venue in 1938, the back of which bears the signatures, among others, of Stauffer, Höllerhagen, and Herbert Müller, enclosed with letter from Becke to author, 6 February 1990.

154. Zimmerle interview.

155. Pick and Blüthner interviews; Magische Note circular of 26 April 1938, PA Jung.

156. Memorandum, 4 July 1947; excerpt from letter of Richard to Hanns Mohaupt, n.d., BDC, RMK Siegfried Muchow.

157. Muchow was a party member as of 1 February 1933. See BDC, MF Siegfried

Muchow; "Fragebogen" Muchow, 12 December 1933, BDC, RMK Muchow; protocol from RMK hearing for Muchow, 25 May 1937, BDC, RMK Mohaupt. Georg Haentzschel, who knew him well, personally confirms Muchow's fanatical Nazi attitude (Haentzschel interview). On Stenzel, see *Berliner Morgenpost*, 10 April 1983.

158. Danzi, *American Musician*, 119; Haentzschel interview.

159. Memorandum from Muchow, 7 April 1937; protocol from RMK hearings for Stenzel, 13 May 1937, and Muchow, 25 May 1937, BDC, RMK Mohaupt; *Stürmer*, May 1937. Haentzschel corroborates Muchow's guilt (interview).

160. Protocols from RMK hearing for Stenzel, 13 May, and Muchow, 25 May 1937; report by Woschke, 31 May 1937; Andress to RMK president, 18 June 1937, BDC, RMK Mohaupt.

161. *Die Tagebücher von Joseph Goebbels: Sämtliche Fragmente*, ed. Elke Fröhlich, vol. 2 (Munich 1987), 500, 527, 539, 542, 546, 595, 731; memorandum Woschke, 1 March 1938, BDC, RMK Mohaupt; testimonies of former Scala singer Gertie Schönfelder and Stenzel in broadcast series, "Und Abends in die Scala" (see n. 2).

162. *Stürmer*, May 1937 (first quotation); *Die Tagebücher . . . Goebbels*, vol. 3, 161–62, 165–66 (second quotation), 293, 326, 346 (third quotation), 393 (fourth quotation), 428; Joseph Walk, ed., *Das Sonderrecht für die Juden im NS-Staat: Eine Sammlung der gesetzlichen Massnahmen und Richtlinien—Inhalt und Bedeutung* (Karlsruhe, 1981), 255.

163. Corr. of August 1937–October 1938, BDC, RMK Mohaupt; *Skizzen*, November 1937, 23; Prieberg, *Musik*, 286–87; Danzi, *American Musician*, 119. Also *Artist*, 17 October 1935, 1163.

164. Protocol of RMK hearing Stenzel, 13 May 1937, BDC, RMK Mohaupt; Fritsch, *Erinnerungen*, 126; Danzi, *American Musician*, 94; Stenzel as interviewed by Götz Kronburger, transcript of radio broadcast, "Funkbesuch bei Otto Stenzel," produced 24 August 1983, Sender Freies Berlin II.

165. Woschke report, 31 May 1937, BDC, RMK Mohaupt.

166. Danzi, *American Musician*, 90.

167. *Artist*, 25 October 1934, 81; speaker in transcript of radio broadcast by Helmut Miesner, "Und Abends in die Scala" (Poppenhusen, 1986), PA Molkenbur-Schönfelder; entry for 30 October 1935 in Blüthner diary of bands, PA Blüthner.

168. Bernd Ruland, *Das war Berlin: Erinnerungen an die Reichshauptstadt* (Bayreuth, 1972), 118; Bergmeier and Lotz, *Bartholomew*, 49.

169. Stenzel died in a Baden-Baden hospital just before I had a chance to interview him.

170. Danzi, *American Musician*, 119; Schönfelder as interviewed by Hajo Steinert, "Und Abends in the Scala" (see n. 2); *Deutsche Podium*, 4 December 1936, 12; *Unterhaltungsmusik* 10 November 1938, 1470; "Lebenslauf" Horst Kudritzki, "Club der Schellackfreunde Hessen e.V.," Frankfurt am Main, September 1987, 65.

171. Protocols of RMK hearings Stenzel and Weiland, both 13 May 1937; report by Woschke, 31 May 1937, BDC, RMK Mohaupt.

172. *Die Tagebücher . . . Goebbels*, vol. 2, 539; *Berliner Morgenpost*, 10 April 1983; Stenzel as interviewed by Hajo Steinert, "Und Abends in die Scala" (see n. 2); Haentzschel interview.

173. Haentzschel interview; Evelyn Künneke, *Sing, Evelyn, Sing: Revue eines Lebens* (Reinbek, 1985), 37; Stenzel as interviewed by Fritz Köhler, transcript of radio broadcast, "Zu Gast bei Otto Stenzel in Poppenhusen," Norddeutscher Rundfunk Welle Nord (1986), PA Molkenbur-Schönfelder.

174. *Die Tagebücher . . . Goebbels*, vol. 3, 293; Danzi, *American Musician*, 120.

175. Eugen Kurt Fischer, *Dramaturgie des Rundfunks* (Heidelberg, 1942), 63.

176. Helga Bemmann, *Berliner Musenkinder-Memoiren: Eine heitere Chronik von 1900–1930* ([East] Berlin, 1981), 131–46; Klaus Budzinski, *Die Muse mit der scharfen Zunge: Vom Cabaret zum Kabarett* (Munich, 1961), 162–85; see p. 4. I am grateful to Prof. Peter Jelavich of the University of Texas at Austin for providing me with information on the Kadeko's political conflation after 1930 (Jelavich to author, 19 May 1991). Jelavich's book, *Berlin Cabaret,* will be published shortly.

177. Transcript of radio broadcast, "Und Abends in die Scala" (see n. 167); Stenzel as interviewed by Hajo Steinert, "Und Abends in die Scala" (see n. 2).

178. Haentzschel interview; Bemmann, *Musenkinder-Memoiren,* 146.

179. Ruland, *Berlin,* 113–14; Helga Bemmann, *Wer schmeisst denn da mit Lehm? Eine Claire-Waldoff-Biographie* ([East] Berlin, 1982), 129–30, 142–44, 153.

180. *Angriff,* 13 November 1936; Wintergarten management to Hinkel, with enclosure, 20 November 1936, BDC, RKK Heuser.

181. *Völkischer Beobachter,* 4 February 1939; *Unterhaltungsmusik,* 9 February 1939, 163; Werner Finck, *Alter Narr—was nun? Die Geschichte meiner Zeit* (Munich and Berlin, 1972), 73–75, 11–15; Frauke Deissner-Jenssen, ed., *Die zehnte Muse: Kabarettisten erzählen* ([East] Berlin, 1982), 345–69; Budzinski, *Muse,* 227; Maurus Pacher, *Sehn Sie, das war Berlin: Weltstadt nach Noten* (Frankfurt am Main and Berlin, 1987), 307 (quotation); Axel Eggebrecht, *Der halbe Weg: Zwischenbilanz einer Epoche* (Hamburg, 1975), 292–93; Bemmann, *Musenkinder-Memoiren,* 157–69.

182. *Die Tagebücher . . . Goebbels,* vol. 3, 108, 113, 117, 302, 565–68.

183. Newton [Hobsbawm], *Jazz Scene,* 260–77.

184. See my letter exchange with Edward Pessen in *American Historical Review* 94 (1989), 932–34; Starr, *Red and Hot,* 204–34; *New York Times,* 4 January 1987; H. Gordon Skilling's letter in *Globe and Mail* (Toronto), 13 September 1986; ibid., 12 and 14 March 1987.

185. Berendt interview; Michael H. Kater, "Forbidden Fruit? Jazz in the Third Reich," *American Historical Review* 94 (1989), 42.

186. Interviews with Jung, Daniels, Mangelsdorff, Boas, Zimmerle, and Bohländer.

187. Berendt interview.

188. Michael H. Kater, "Bürgerliche Jugendbewegung und Hitlerjugend in Deutschland von 1926 bis 1939," *Archiv für Sozialgeschichte* 17 (1977), 171; Jung interview.

189. Schulz-Reichel and Haentzschel interviews.

190. F. Scott Fitzgerald as quoted by Starr, *Red and Hot,* 16.

191. Korseck interview; Korseck to author, 15 November 1988.

192. Quotation from Hans Blüthner, "Berlin und Jazz," 22 September 1950, PA Blüthner; also Blüthner interview; Blüthner as quoted in Mike Zwerin, *La Tristesse de Saint Louis: Swing under the Nazis* (New York, 1985), 24.

193. Pick and Blüthner interviews.

194. Brocksieper interview.

195. Lange, *Jazz in Deutschland,* 70.

196. Dieter Zimmerle, "Jazz im Nationalsozialismus," PA Zimmerle; Zimmerle interview.

197. See p. 35.

198. Klagemann interview.

199. Zacharias interview.

200. Michaelis interview; Michael H. Kater, *The Nazi Party: A Social Profile of Members and Leaders, 1919–1945* (Cambridge, Mass., 1983), 158.

201. See pp. 78–79.

202. Haentzschel and Brocksieper interviews.

203. Peter Kreuder, *Schön war die Zeit: Musik ist mein Leben* (Munich, 1955), 254–55, 292–95; BDC, MF Kreuder.

204. Quotation from SS-Gruppenführer Moser to SS-Mann Schulze, 24 January 1938, BDC, RMK Schulze. See also entire SS file Schulze, BDC, RMK Schulze; Schulz-Reichel interview.

205. Schulz-Reichel interview.

206. "Lebenslauf" Schulz-Köhn, on back of *Schallplatte*.

207. Manfred Franze, *Die Erlanger Studentenschaft, 1918–1945* (Würzburg, 1972), 214–15; Geoffrey J. Giles, *Students and National Socialism in Germany* (Princeton, 1985), 139–40; table 5.2 in Michael H. Kater, *Doctors Under Hitler* (Chapel Hill and London, 1989), 254.

208. Schulz-Köhn to author, 10 September 1990.

209. On the principle of such behavior by ordinary Germans to get by on a day-to-day basis, see Ian Kershaw's enlightening study, *Popular Opinion and Political Dissent in the Third Reich: Bavaria, 1933–1945* (Oxford, 1983).

210. Jung interview; Schulz-Köhn to author, 3 July 1987.

211. Dietrich Schulz, "Lebenslauf," 30 April 1936, BDC, RSK Schulz.

212. In his 20 January 1936 lecture Schulz-Köhn spouts the Nazi myth of Adolphe Sax's German origins, calls for the creation of a "new dance music" (almost echoing Oskar Joost), and talks about orchestra "führers" whom instrumentalists would follow ("Einführung in die Swing-Musik: Vortrag von Dietrich Schulz," 20 January 1936, PA Schulz-Köhn).

213. *Schwarze Korps,* 16 July 1936.

214. *Unterhaltungsmusik,* 28 October 1936, 1377.

215. Because by special regulation, in 1938 only Hitler Youth members could be inducted into the NSDAP. See Kater, *Nazi Party,* 146; BDC, MF Schulz-Köhn.

216. Schulz-Köhn to author, 3 July 1987.

217. Meyerinck, *Freundinnen,* 113; interviews with Schulz-Reichel, Schulz-Köhn, and Friedländer-Reimann.

218. Moser to author, 2 February and 14 March 1990.

219. Hans-Otto Meissner, *Magda Goebbels: A Biography* (London, 1980), 201.

220. Friedländer-Reimann interview. Mrs. Friedländer-Reimann assured me that she escaped Wedel's physical advances. Wedel, born in 1910 on a Pomeranian estate, had been a party and SA member since 1929. Wounded in a street brawl with Communists in 1930, he was a dropout in civilian life, but a full-time SA leader when Goebbels chose him as adjutant in November 1934. He served until early 1939 (BDC, personal files Wedel).

221. Eberhard Fechner, *Die Comedian Harmonists: Sechs Lebensläufe* (Weinheim and Berlin, 1988), 250–51.

222. See p. 69.

223. Brocksieper interview.

224. Kurt Grosskopf, "Gesellschafts-Tanz und kulturelle Erziehung der Jugend," [December 1932], appended to letter from Grosskopf to Hinkel, 24 May 1935, BA, R 56I/85.

225. Grosskopf to Hinkel, 24 May 1935, BA, R 56I/85; Joseph Wulf, ed., *Theater und Film im Dritten Reich: Eine Dokumentation* (Reinbek, 1966), 38–39.

226. *Artist,* 21 July 1933, and 17 October 1935, 2600; *BZ am Mittag,* 13 March 1936; K. Hennemeyer in Joseph Wulf, ed., *Musik im Dritten Reich: Eine Dokumentation* (Reinbek, 1966), 293–94; Alfred Müller-Hennig, "Deutscher Tanz," *Musik* 29

(1937), 776–78; *Unterhaltungsmusik*, 5 August 1937, 883–84, and 2 September 1937, 1058; Wilhelm Stauder, "Tanzmusik," in Joseph Müller-Blattau, ed., *Hohe Schule der Musik: Handbuch der gesamten Musikpraxis* (Potsdam, 1938), 273–315. For a critical view: Astrid Eichstedt, "Wir tanzen ins Chaos: Swing als Bewegung," in Polster, *"Swing Heil,"* 99–108.

227. *Unterhaltungsmusik*, 28 October 1937, 1316–17.

228. *Unterhaltungsmusik*, 23 September 1937, 1163; ibid., 29 September 1937, 1200; ibid., 18 August 1938, 1093; ibid., 27 October 1938, 1408; ibid., 10 November 1938, 1469; *Musik in Jugend und Volk* 2 (1939), 16–20; Eichstedt, "Wir tanzen," 109–10. See also *Jahrbuch der deutschen Musik 1943*, 62.

229. This criticism was still expressed to author in Blüthner and Daniels interviews; Daniels's letter to author, 2 February 1989; Bessunger's letter to author, 1 February 1990. Cf. Lange, *Jazz in Deutschland*, 76; Berendt, *Jazzbuch*, 203–5.

230. Fachschaft Tanz to Weinhaus Bei Toni, 24 November 1937, facsimile in "Reminiszenzen," PA Daniels; *Unterhaltungsmusik*, 9 June 1938, 713; ibid., 8 December 1938, 1600.

231. *Unterhaltungsmusik*, 5 January 1939, 3–4; ibid., 19 January 1939, 75, 81; ibid., 26 January 1939, 111; ibid., 9 February 1939, 165; ibid., 16 March 1939, 367; ibid., 25 May 1939, 738–39; ibid., 1 June 1939, 764–65.

232. *Unterhaltungsmusik*, 28 April 1938, 521; ibid., 19 May 1939, 689; *Bewegung*, 6 December 1938; Uwe Dietrich Adam, *Hochschule und Nationalsozialismus: Die Universität Tübingen im Dritten Reich* (Tübingen, 1977), 114.

233. See above and *Unterhaltungsmusik*, 19 January 1939, 74–75.

234. Heinrich, *"Swing-Generation,"* 30; Lange, *Jazz in Deutschland*, 91; Blüthner interview.

235. Eichstedt and Polster, *Wilden*, 81; Werner Daniels, "Als Swingtanzen verboten war," PA Daniels.

236. *Unterhaltungsmusik*, 18 November 1938, 1507; ibid., 24 November 1938, 1550; ibid., 9 March 1939, 323; ibid., 25 May 1939, 738; *Die Tagebücher . . . Goebbels*, vol. 3, 566, 578; declaration by Raabe and Körner, 13 May 1939, in *Amtliche Mitteilungen der Reichsmusikkammer*, 1 July 1939, BA, RD 33/2-2.

237. *Hamburger Fremdenblatt*, 7 January 1938 (first quotation); *Unterhaltungsmusik*, 6 July 1939, 906 (second quotation).

238. "Einzelbeispiele für die Cliquen- und Bandenbildung neuerer Zeit," appended to: "Reichsjugendführung—Personalamt—Überwachung, 'Cliquen- und Bandenbildung unter Jugendlichen,' " September 1942, BA, R 22/1177.

239. Thorsten Müller in *Hamburger Abendblatt*, 2/3 February 1985.

240. *Deutsche Podium*, 20 June 1935, 7; ibid., 27 September 1935, 10; ibid., 17 September 1937, 19; ibid., 17 December 1937, 7; *Unterhaltungsmusik*, 4 August 1938, 995; ibid., 22 December 1938, 1691–92; ibid., 10 August 1939, 1169; *Artist*, 6 June 1935, 581; Lange, "Optik," 5; Conrad, *Wehner*, 13; Bergmeier and Lotz, *Bartholomew*, 43.

241. Advertisement in *Unterhaltungsmusik*, 12 November 1936; ibid., 13 July 1939, 946–47; *Deutsche Podium*, 17 April 1935, 7; Stauffer, *Forever*, 70.

242. Interviews with Madlung-Shelton, Vogel, Panagopoulos, Hartwig, Engel, and Hirschfeld; Thorsten Müller in *Deutsches Allgemeines Sonntagsblatt*, 27 February 1983.

243. Panagopoulos interview; Harry [Georgiadis] Stephens, "Swing Threatens Third Reich," unpublished ms. (Beccles [Suffolk], 1988), 1–40; author's telephone conversation with Stephens, London-Beccles, 10 May 1988; Stauffer, *Forever*, 113;

Axel Springer, *An meine Kinder und Kindeskinder: Auszüge aus einer Niederschrift* (Berlin, 1985), 9–12; Erik Blumenfeld in Friede Springer, ed., *Axel Springer: Die Freunde dem Freund* (Frankfurt am Main and Berlin, 1986), 18.

244. Stephens, "Swing Threatens Third Reich," 1–40; Hartwig and Madlung-Shelton interviews; Gerd Bucerius in *Zeit,* 27 September 1985.

245. Madlung-Shelton interview (quotations); interviews with Vogel, Panagopoulos, Engel, Hartwig; Stephens, "Swing Threatens Third Reich," 12–13, 16–18, 23–26, 30–31, 38–39.

246. Interviews with Madlung-Shelton, Vogel, Engel, Hartwig, Scheel, Panagopoulos, Hirschfeld; Stephens, "Swing Threatens Third Reich," 12–13, 19, 22.

247. Krogmann eventually became mayor under Hamburg's Gauleiter Karl Kaufmann, originally from the Rhineland. See Carl Vinzent Krogmann, *Es ging um Deutschlands Zukunft, 1932–1939: Erlebtes täglich diktiert von dem früheren Regierenden Bürgermeister von Hamburg,* 2nd ed. (Leoni, 1977); Stephens, "Swing Threatens Third Reich," 158. Significantly enough, Krogmann's daughter was a Swing (Hirschfeld interview).

248. Kater, "Bürgerliche Jugendbewegung," 169.

249. Arno Klönne, *Jugend im Dritten Reich: Die Hitler-Jugend und ihre Gegner* (Düsseldorf and Cologne, 1982), 242; interviews with Hirschfeld (quotation), Vogel, Engel, Panagopoulos, Evers-Frauboes.

250. Engel interview.

251. Springer, *Kinder,* 28.

252. Panagopoulos interview.

253. Scheel interview; Scheel to author, 9 January 1991.

254. Hartwig interview; Stephens, "Swing Threatens Third Reich," 39.

255. Hirschfeld interview.

Chapter 3

1. Ernst Schliepe, "Musik, die wir nicht wünschen," *Musik* 32 (1939), 9; Ilse Deyk, "Der Jazz ist tot—es lebe die Jazzband!," *Zeitschrift für Musik* 109 (1942), 12 (quotation).

2. Quotations in order: *Reich,* 2 June 1940, 19 January 1941, 25 January 1942. Also see ibid., 25 August and 27 October 1940, 26 October 1941.

3. *Amtliche Mitteilungen der Reichsmusikkammer,* 1 October 1939, BA, RD 33/2-2; *Unterhaltungsmusik,* 7 December 1939, 1513; ibid., 23 May 1940, 484; *Reich,* 20 July 1941.

4. Marie Vassiltchikov, *Berlin Diaries, 1940–1945* (New York, 1987), 3; Hans Dieter Schäfer, *Berlin im Zweiten Weltkrieg: Der Untergang der Reichshauptstadt in Augenzeugenberichten* (Munich, 1985), 14; Howard K. Smith, *Feind schreibt mit: Ein amerikanischer Korrespondent erlebt Nazi-Deutschland* (Frankfurt am Main, 1986), 102, 112–13, 130–33.

5. *Unterhaltungsmusik,* 14 December 1939, 1528; ibid., 18 January 1940, 50; *Reich,* 2 June and 29 September 1940; 19 January 1941; Schäfer, *Berlin,* 82–83.

6. Brocksieper interview; Vassiltchikov, *Berlin Diaries,* 32–33. Also see ibid., 28; *Reich,* 27 October 1940; Schäfer, *Berlin,* 34.

7. *Reich,* 25 May 1941; Smith, *Feind,* 56–57; Schäfer, *Berlin,* 34–35.

8. It was as a function of the emerging professionalization of musicians during the Third Reich that by force of law they had to be quickly reinstated. See RMK files of

Kettel and Henkel in BDC; *Unterhaltungsmusik,* 28 September 1939, 1348; Brocksieper interview. On the dance ban, see p. 136.

9. Michael Danzi, *American Musician in Germany, 1924–1939: Memoirs of the Jazz, Entertainment, and Movie World of Berlin during the Weimar Republic and the Nazi Era—and in the United States,* as told to Rainer E. Lotz (Schmitten, 1986), 132; Horst H. Lange, "Zwischen Optik und Hot-Takt: Max Rumpf," *Fox auf 78,* no. 5 (Spring 1988), 6; Jan Grundmann, "Erich Börschel und sein Orchester," *Fox auf 78,* no. 3 (Spring 1987), 5.

10. Teddy Stauffer, *Forever Is a Hell of a Long Time: An Autobiography* (Chicago, 1976), 119; Hans Blüthner, "Jazz i Berlin," *Orkester Journalen,* December 1947, 33.

11. Gerhard Conrad, *Heinz Wehner: Eine Bio-Discographie* (Menden, 1989), 65–69.

12. Tabor and Zacharias interviews.

13. Case of jazz drummer Jens Kröger in Bernt Engelmann, *In Hitler's Germany: Daily Life in the Third Reich* (New York, 1986), 204; interviews with Scheel, Tabor, Engel, and Michaelis.

14. Stengel to RMK-Landesleiter, 24 February 1940, BDC, RMK Karl Hohenberger; "Musikalische Feldpost," beginning of February 1942, PA Daniels; Gerhard Conrad, *Posaunen-Dob: Kleine Biographie Walter Dobschinskis* (Menden, 1983), 27–29; Schulz-Reichel interview.

15. Korseck to author, 15 November 1988; author's telephone conversation with Korseck, Berlin, 24 May 1988. See also "Musikalische Feldpost," September and 7 November 1941, beginning of February and mid-May 1942, PA Daniels; interviews with Meyer, Brocksieper, and Molkenbur-Schönfelder.

16. Meyer and Angeli interviews; Horst J. P. Bergmeier and Rainer E. Lotz, "Rudi Rischbeck—der singende Geiger," *Fox auf 78,* no. 6 (Fall 1988), 45. Angeli can be heard on "Klarinetten-Zauber," with Brocksieper on drums and Teddy Kleindin on clarinet, recorded in Berlin 12 June 1941 (reissued on *Swing tanzen verboten,* Telefunken 6.28360 DP, 1976). By the spring of 1942 at least one-quarter of all bandleaders and one-third of all band musicians were foreigners (*Jahrbuch der deutschen Musik 1943,* 37–38).

17. Knud Wolffram, "Ein Bulgare in Berlin: Die Geschichte des Lubo D'Orio," *Fox auf 78,* no. 8 (Spring 1990), 9.

18. "Musikalische Feldpost," September, 7 November and mid-December 1941, beginning of July 1942, PA Daniels; Horst H. Lange, *Jazz in Deutschland: Die deutsche Jazz-Chronik, 1900–1960* (Berlin, 1966), 112–13.

19. "Musikalische Feldpost," beginning of February, mid-April, beginning of and mid-May, beginning of July and beginning of August 1942, PA Daniels.

20. Inside cover of *Unterhaltungsmusik,* 9 October 1941; *Meldungen aus dem Reich: Die geheimen Lageberichte des Sicherheitsdienstes der SS, 1938–1945* ed., Heinz Boberach (Herrsching, 1984), vol. 6, 2076, 2151–52; RMK file card van't Hoff, BDC, RMK van't Hoff (quotation); "Musikalische Feldpost," 17 October 1941 and April 1942, PA Daniels; Gerhard Rückert cited in Wolfgang Muth, "Wir hotten weiter: Erlebtes, Überliefertes, Hinterlassenes," in Bernd Polster, ed., *"Swing Heil": Jazz im Nationalsozialismus* (Berlin, 1989), 202.

21. *Meldungen aus dem Reich,* vol. 11, pp. 4054–57; "Musikalische Feldpost," beginning of and mid-May 1942, PA Daniels; Franz Heinrich, *"Swing-Generation": Selbsterlebtes* (Menden, 1988), 41–42; Günter Boas cited in Muth, "Wir," 203.

22. "Musikalische Feldpost," September and mid-December 1941, mid-January 1942, PA Daniels; Heinrich, *"Swing-Generation,"* 35; Klagemann interview.

23. Zacharias interview (quotation); Brocksieper and Meyer interviews; Margarete Zacharias to Rückert, 18 March 1942, BDC, RMK Zacharias; Wolffram, "Bulgare," 9; Bergmeier and Lotz, "Rischbeck," 43. The famous record, also with Alfio Grasso and Meg Tevelian, is Od 0-31689; the hit tune is "Bei dir war es immer so schön" (according to Zacharias's recollection, this was the "first German, harmonically interesting song").

24. Gunther Schuller, *The Swing Era: The Development of Jazz, 1930–1945* (New York and Oxford, 1989), 703. Three representative samples of Zacharias's work (early 1942) are included in the broadcast series "Jazz in Germany: A Survey of Hot Dance, Swing, and Traditional Jazz in Germany, 1924 to Present," produced for and broadcast on KALW FM, San Francisco, by Dave Radlauer and Ray Taubert, n.d., courtesy of the Goethe Institute, Toronto (program 5).

25. I am judging from samples by Fud Candrix, "Introducing Mr. Basie," Berlin, 22 November 1940, and "Tiger Rag," Berlin, 28 April 1941; Jean Omer, "Star Dust," Berlin, 1 May 1941; Stan Brenders, "Fascination," Berlin, 18 November 1941; Eddie Tower, "Temptation Rag," Berlin, 22 November 1941 (reissued on *Swing tanzen verboten* [see n. 16]). Also Ernst van't Hoff, "In the Mood," Berlin 1942 (broadcast series "Jazz in Germany," program 1 [see n. 24]).

26. Friedrich Meyer, "Mich hat noch nie ein Mädel angelacht," December 1940; Horst Winter, "Ich mache alles mit Musik," "Carlton-Bar," Berlin, March 1941; Albert Vossen, "Am Montag fängt die Woche an," 26 April 1941; Lutz Templin, "Die Männer sind schon die Liebe wert," August 1942 (cassette tape, *Wir tanzen wieder Swing Time*, no. 1 and 2, Bob's Music, Hamburg, 1989); Kurt Hohenberger, "Ich mache alles mit Musik," 5 February 1941, and "Improvisation," 8 November 1941 (*Swing tanzen verboten* [see n. 16]); Kurt Widmann, "Wenn der weisse Flieder," 16 November 1941 (cassette tape supplied with Christian Kellersmann, "Jazz in Deutschland von 1933–1945," Master's thesis, University of Hamburg, 1989 [see p. 129]).

27. Candrix in broadcast series, "Jazz in Germany," program 6 (see n. 24); Widmann's "Heisse Tage" on cassette tape, *Wir tanzen*, no. 2 (see n. 26). Also see Jim Godbolt, *A History of Jazz in Britain, 1919–50* (London, 1984), 217; Schuller, *Swing Era,* 133–40, 441–45, 703–5, 817–18.

28. See *Reich,* 25 August 1940, 17 August and 26 October 1941.

29. Heinrich, *"Swing-Generation,"* 41–42; "Musikalische Feldpost," mid-February 1942, PA Daniels.

30. Michael H. Kater, "Forbidden Fruit? Jazz in the Third Reich," *American Historical Review* 94 (1989), 30; idem, "Inside Nazis: The Goebbels Diaries, 1924–1941," *Canadian Journal of History* 25 (1990), 240–41.

31. Goebbels's speech from 27 November 1939 printed in Gerd Albrecht, ed., *Der Film im 3. Reich* (Karlsruhe, 1979), 65–69; decrees in: *Unterhaltungsmusik,* 29 August 1940, 813; *Zeitschrift für Musik* 109 (1942), 233; *Podium der Unterhaltungsmusik,* 23 April 1942, 130.

32. Rudolf Sonner, "Kriegsauftrag von 'Kraft und Freude,'" *Musik* 33 (1940), 9–13; K. B. Metzmacher, *Wir sind bei euch, ihr seid bei uns: Ein Buch schlägt eine Brücke* (Kaiserslautern, 1941); Reimer memorandum, 5 March 1942, BA, R 55/129.

33. Hinkel to Johst, 3 July 1940, BA, R 56I/93; Molkenbur-Schönfelder interview; Lale Andersen, *Leben mit einem Lied,* 5th ed. (Munich, 1981), 138–39, 160–66; Evelyn Künneke, *Sing, Evelyn, Sing: Revue eines Lebens* (Reinbek, 1985), 59–60; Hildegard Knef, *Der geschenkte Gaul: Bericht aus meinem Leben,* 8th ed. (Vienna, 1970), 51.

34. "Musikalische Feldpost," 24 September and 17 October 1941, mid-July 1942, PA Daniels; Siegfried Scheffler, "Deutsche Unterhaltungsmusik," *Musik* 33 (1941), 230; interviews with Lehn, Molkenbur-Schönfelder, Tabor, Schulz-Köhn, and Brocksieper; Günther Lust as interviewed in Polster, *"Swing Heil,"* 170; Künneke, *Sing,* 57–58.

35. Interviews with Klagemann, Schulz-Reichel, and Brocksieper; "Musikalische Feldpost," beginning of February 1942, PA Daniels; Bergmeier and Lotz, "Rischbeck," 43.

36. Schulz-Köhn to author, 10 September 1990; Schulz-Köhn interview; quotation from transcript of Schulz-Köhn interview for British video series, "Swing under the Swastika," Yorkshire Television, London, 1988.

37. Schulz-Köhn to author, 10 September 1990.

38. Sklow to Michaelis, 21 August 1939, PA Michaelis; Michaelis interview; Michaelis to author, 26 April 1989.

39. Frommann to Michaelis, 28 September 1940 (first quotation) and 22 June 1941 (second quotation); also Frommann to Michaelis (Paris postcard of May 1941), all PA Michaelis; Michaelis to author, 1 August 1990; Schulz-Köhn interview.

40. Michaelis to author, 1 August 1990.

41. As an example, Daniels paraphrased news printed in the official musician's organ *Unterhaltungsmusik* to the effect that Swedish cows which had listened to jazz over time had diminished their milk output. Commented Daniels: "Bravo, *Unterhaltungsmusik,* this was after my own heart. Your characterization of people who *dis*like Jazz, is apt" ("Musikalische Feldpost," beginning of February 1942, PA Daniels). Also Daniels interview; "Reminiszenzen," PA Daniels.

42. Daniels to author, 18 January 1990 (quotation); "Musikalische Feldpost," beginning of December 1941, PA Daniels; Daniels interview.

43. Quotations in order: "Musikalische Feldpost," beginning of April 1942; 24 September 1942; mid-December 1941; mid-February 1942 (PA Daniels).

44. Interviews with Bohländer, Jung, Boas, and Blüthner.

45. Interviews with Berendt, Pick, and Zimmerle.

46. *Die Tagebücher von Joseph Goebbels: Sämtliche Fragmente,* ed. Elke Fröhlich (Munich, 1987), vol. 3, 665, 668, 670 (1939); Joseph Goebbels, *Das eherne Herz: Reden und Aufsätze aus den Jahren 1941/42,* ed. M. A. von Schirmeister (Munich, 1943), 32 (1941); *The Goebbels Diaries,* ed., Louis P. Lochner, (London, 1948), 58 (1942).

47. DIA, BEF Program as Broadcast, 11 January 1940.

48. Charles J. Rolo, *Radio Goes to War: The "Fourth Front"* (New York, 1942), 161–67; Carl Brinitzer, *Hier spricht London: Von einem der dabei war* (Hamburg, 1969), 163–64; Ellic Howe, *The Black Game: British Subversive Operations against the Germans during the Second World War* (London, 1982), 102–32, 267, 270.

49. Ansgar Diller, *Rundfunkpolitik im Dritten Reich* (Munich, 1980), 304–12, 378–82; *Meldungen aus dem Reich,* vol. 3, 845–46; ibid., vol. 5, 1691–92, 1740; ibid., vol. 6, 1789; ibid., vol. 8, 3077–78.

50. Listener's notes by Hans, [1940–42], PA Evers-Frauboes; Pick and Freichel interviews; Becke to author, 11 September 1989; Willi A. Boelcke, *Die Macht des Radios: Weltpolitik und Auslandsrundfunk, 1924–1976* (Frankfurt am Main, 1977), 445–46; Kristina Söderbaum, *Nichts bleibt immer so: Rückblenden auf ein Leben vor und hinter der Kamera* (Bayreuth, 1983), 169–70.

51. Diller, *Rundfunkpolitik,* 316. Also see Jay W. Baird, *The Mythical World of Nazi War Propaganda, 1939–1945* (Minneapolis, 1974), 38, 79, 133.

52. Diller, *Rundfunkpolitik,* 309, 426; Michael Crone, *Hilversum unter dem*

Hakenkreuz: Die Rundfunkpolitik der Nationalsozialisten in den besetzten Niederlanden, 1940–1945 (Munich, 1983), 69–71, 125–26, 199–200; "Musikalische Feldpost," beginning of December 1941, 15 December 1942, PA Daniels: Freichel and Evers-Frauboes interviews.

53. Heinz Pohle, *Der Rundfunk als Instrument der Politik: Zur Geschichte des deutschen Rundfunks von 1923/38* (Hamburg, 1955), 186; Daniel Lerner, *Psychological Warfare against Nazi Germany: The Sykewar Campaign, D-Day to VE-Day* (Cambridge, Mass., and London, 1971), 137.

54. Pohle, *Rundfunk,* 284; *Die Tagebücher . . . Goebbels,* vol. 4, 149, 165; *Meldungen aus dem Reich,* vol. 5, 1626.

55. Diller, *Rundfunkpolitik,* 312; *Die Tagebücher . . . Goebbels,* vol. 4, 516, 650 (first quotation), 653–57, 685; Goebbels as paraphrased in Willi A. Boelcke, ed., *Kriegspropaganda, 1939–1941: Geheime Ministerkonferenzen im Reichspropagandaministerium* (Stuttgart, 1966), 610 (second quotation).

56. "Der Rundfunk im Kriege," *Reich,* 15 June 1941.

57. Minutes of broadcast planning meeting of 14 October 1941, 7 January 1942 (quotation), 16 February 1942, BA, R 55/695; Hinkel to Goebbels, 17 October 1941, BA, R 55/1254; Goebbels, "Anordnung zur Neugestaltung des Rundfunkprogramms," 15 February 1942, BA, R 78/1000a; Haentzschel interview.

58. See *Meldungen aus dem Reich,* vol. 8, 2931–32, 2950, 2976, 3076; ibid., vol. 9, 3225, 3266. Corroborating the jazz content, which, not surprisingly, was deemed insufficient, was Hanns J. Maassen of "Musikalische Feldpost," 17 October 1941, PA Daniels (mention of Winter and Candrix). Also, minutes of broadcast planning meeting of 2 December 1941 and 29 April 1942, BA, R 55/695; Haentzschel interview.

59. "Musikalische Feldpost," mid-January 1942, PA Daniels; *Meldungen aus dem Reich,* vol. 9, 3229, 3369; Bade to Hinkel, 25 April 1942, BA, R 56I/82; Brocksieper interview.

60. In lead article "Der treue Helfer," *Reich,* 1 March 1942.

61. *Die Tagebücher . . . Goebbels,* vol. 3, 611, 623, 649; ibid., vol. 4, 61, 458.

62. *Reich,* 8 December 1940; Eugen Kurt Fischer, *Dramaturgie des Rundfunks* (Heidelberg, 1942), 135–36; Diller, *Rundfunkpolitik,* 341–43; Maurus Pacher, *Sehn Sie, das war Berlin: Weltstadt nach Noten* (Frankfurt am Main and Berlin, 1987), 319–21.

63. For the survey, see Gerhard Eckert, *Der Rundfunk als Führungsmittel: Studien zum Weltrundfunk und Fernsehrundfunk* (Heidelberg, 1941), 192–201 and chart near p. 204.

64. "Musikalische Feldpost," 17 October 1941, mid-February, mid-July, and beginning of August 1942, PA Daniels; *Meldungen aus dem Reich,* vol. 8, 2750; ibid., vol. 9, 3137; Boelcke, *Macht,* 265; Conrad, *Wehner,* 70.

65. *Die Tagebücher . . . Goebbels,* vol. 1, 592; ibid., vol. 3, 32; ibid., vol. 4, 27, 29, 336, 339, 374, 436; *Reich,* 8 and 21 July, 1 September, 6 and 13 October, 3 November, 8 and 22 December 1940; Kater, "Inside Nazis," 240–41.

66. For Mölders's air force career, see the contemporary [auto-]biography edited by Fritz von Forell, *Mölders und seine Männer* (Graz, 1941).

67. Kurt Pabst, "Nazi-'Kultur': Dokumente über Kunstpflege im Dritten Reich," unpublished ms., Erfurt, [1946], 138 (BDC, RKK Pabst); Heinz Schröter, *Unterhaltung für Millionen: Vom Wunschkonzert zur Schlagerparade* (Düsseldorf and Vienna, 1973), 113; Werner Burkhardt, "Musik der Stunde Null," *Zeitmagazin,* 11 November 1983, 50; Gerhard Conrad, *Posaunen-Dob: Kleine Biographie Walter*

Dobschinskis (Menden, 1983), 31; Molkenbur-Schönfelder and Haentzschel interviews.

68. Quotation according to Boelcke, *Kriegspropaganda,* 730–31. On the turn of campaigns, see Lothar Gruchmann, *Der Zweite Weltkrieg: Kriegführung und Politik* (Munich, 1967), 76–87.

69. Gutterer to Hinkel, 29 September 1941, BA, R 55/200; Pauli, "Tanzmusik im Rundfunk," 3 October 1941, BA, R 55/695; Lucerna memoranda, 7 and 9 October 1941; Ott and Drewes to Goebbels, 18 October 1941, BA, R 55/242/1; Haentzschel interview.

70. Klagemann interview.

71. Enclosure with letter from Hinkel to Goebbels, 10 March 1942, BA, R 56I/34; [RMK] Leiter BV to Abteilung Pro et al., 1 June 1942, BDC, Research Vossen.

72. Margarete Zacharias to Rückert, 18 March 1942, BDC, RMK Helmut Zacharias.

73. See RMK memorandum, 14 March 1942, BA, R 56I/34.

74. See enclosure with letter from Hinkel to Goebbels, 10 March 1942, BA, R 56I/34; Haentzschel DTU contract, signed by Kunitz and Haentzschel, 27 March 1942, BDC, RMK Haentzschel; "Liste 1," n.d., BDC, Research Friedrich Meyer; Haentzschel interview.

75. Haentzschel and Klagemann interviews.

76. Personal file Däubner, BDC, MF and RMK Däubner; BDC, MF Wegener; Klagemann and Meyer interviews.

77. Lucerna Memoranda, 2 and 9 October 1941, BA, R 55/242/1; Haentzschel DTU contract, signed by Kunitz and Haentzschel, 27 March 1942, BDC, RMK Haentzschel; Haentzschel interview.

78. *Statistisches Handbuch für Deutschland, 1928–1944* (Munich, 1948), 469.

79. Staatssekretär to Hinkel, 29 September 1941, BA, R 55/242/1; Bückert to Intendant and to Universum Film AG, both 10 March 1942, BA, R 56I/34; Haentzschel interview; S. Frederick Starr, *Red and Hot: The Fate of Jazz in the Soviet Union, 1917–1980* (New York and Oxford, 1983), 175–89.

80. Joost-Hinkel corr. (September 1940), BDC, RMK Joost.

81. Personal file Safronow, BDC, RMK Safronow; *Unterhaltungsmusik,* 8 May 1941, 460.

82. Safronow to propaganda ministry, 8 July 1942, BA, R 55/242/1; "Musikalische Feldpost," mid-August 1942, PA Daniels; Schröter, *Unterhaltung,* 114.

83. Pabst, "Nazi-'Kultur'," 113.

84. Werner Burkhardt, "Musik der Stunde Null," *Zeitmagazin,* 11 November 1983, 50 (first quotation); Daniels interview (second quotation). See also Lange, *Jazz in Deutschland,* 99; Joachim Ernst Berendt, *Ein Fenster aus Jazz: Essays, Portraits, Reflexionen* (Frankfurt am Main, 1977), 302; Kellersmann, "Jazz," 52.

85. Pick interview.

86. Dobschinski and Haentzschel interviews. After an analysis of twenty-one DTU tunes recently reissued on long-playing records and generously made available to me on cassette tape by Bonn jazz impresario Dr. Rainer E. Lotz (with letter to me dated 15 August 1990), I found a combination of straight melodic playing, often by a reed or brass horn or a unisono section; jazzily arranged section-playing in an unadulterated swing vein; and, ever again, the sweetly adumbrating strings. Rhythmically, the pieces are well executed, in a disciplined Teutonic manner and certainly not without syncopes, but with upbeats and downbeats missing. The instrumental intonation is clean, perhaps sometimes too much so (there is a lack of microtonal "blue notes"). Every once in a while, there are hints of real jazz: in "Auf dem Dach

der Welt," Mück plays snippets of improvisational piano runs behind a pedestrian tenor's melody line. Mück's scanty swing-style runs, in their flashiness reminiscent of the best by Fritz Schulze, are also audible in "Grossstadtlied," one of the more successful authentic German tunes. The same is true in "Schönes Wetter," which also features a jazz-attuned Vossen on accordion throughout. There are several good, if all too brief, drum breaks, as in "Grossstadtlied." The best piece as jazz is "Ganz leis erklingt Musik," with a beautiful introduction, a superior arrangement, and smidges of clarinet solo work. Its melody reminds one of "Blue Moon," but is more intricate.

87. Stege in *Freiburger Zeitung,* 5 August 1942, and *Podium der Unterhaltungsmusik,* 20 August 1942, 256.

88. Haentzschel interview.

89. Brocksieper and Haentzschel interviews.

90. John Alfred Cole, *Lord Haw-Haw—and William Joyce* (London, 1964), 111, 113; Winfried B. Lerg, "Deutscher Auslandsrundfunk im zweiten Weltkrieg: Bemerkungen zu einer William Joyce-Biographie," *Rundfunk und Fernsehen* 14, no. 1 (1966), 25–27; Normal Baillie-Stewart, *The Officer in the Tower* (London, 1967), 148–58; Zacharias interview.

91. *Die Tagebücher . . . Goebbels,* vol. 4, 4, 8, 27, 32–33, 72, 75, 80, 144, 290, 318, 335, 556; *Goebbels Diaries,* 263; William L. Shirer, *Berlin Diary: The Journal of a Foreign Correspondent, 1934–1941* (Toronto, 1961), 390 (quotation); Lerg, "Auslandsrundfunk," 25. Also *Reich,* 29 September 1940.

92. Herbert Schroeder, *Ein Sender erobert die Herzen der Welt: Das Buch vom deutschen Kurzwellenrundfunk* (Essen, 1940), 218 (quotation; original is *Jazzerei*), 223, 227. Also Cole, *Lord Haw-Haw,* 166; Brocksieper interview.

93. Personal file Lutz Templin, BDC, RMK Templin; also *Deutsche Podium,* 16 May 1935, 6; *Unterhaltungsmusik,* 1 April 1937, 378. Brocksieper as interviewed by Michael Pointon, transcript [1987], PA Pointon; Brocksieper as interviewed for broadcast "Swingtime for Hitler," by Michael Pointon, transmitted BBC London 16 August 1987, transcript PA Pointon (quotation); interviews with Brocksieper, Friedländer-Reimann, and Zacharias; Kellersmann, "Jazz," 54–56. On 22 June 1941 Frommann wrote to Hot-Geyer from Paris that he had heard Vossen play on a "hot harmonica platter" as part of a program entitled "Germany Calling" (letter PA Michaelis).

94. Brocksieper as interviewed by Pointon [1987] (see n. 93); liner notes for Discophilia long-play reissue *Charlie and His Orchestra,* 2 vols., DIS 13/UT-C-1/2; *Spiegel,* 18 April 1988, 229. See also Robert Pernet, *Jazz in Little Belgium: Discography (1895–1966)* (Brussels, 1966), 60–62.

95. Brocksieper as interviewed by Pointon [1987] (see n. 93); Brocksieper and Meyer interviews; Smith, *Feind,* 101, 117.

96. "Musikalische Feldpost," mid-March 1942, PA Daniels.

97. The first song was recorded in Berlin ca. November 1940 (*Charlie and His Orchestra,* vol. 1), the second song around April 1942 (ibid., vol. 2) (see n. 94). See also *Spiegel,* 18 April 1988, 236.

98. Brocksieper as interviewed by Pointon for "Swingtime for Hitler" (see n. 93).

99. Friedländer-Reimann and Tabor interviews; Brocksieper as interviewed by Pointon [1987] (see n. 93).

100. Transcript of Boas interview for "Swing under the Swastika" (see n. 36); "Musikalische Feldpost," beginning of June 1942, PA Daniels (quotation); Wolfgang

Muth in *Sonntag*, no. 26 (1984), 8; minutes of broadcast planning meeting of 13 May 1942, BA, R 55/695; Boas interview.

101. Brocksieper as quoted in interview with Pointon [1987] (see n. 93). Above all else it has to be considered that the band played dyed-in-the-wool jazz standards, such as "Dinah," "Night and Day," "St. Louis Blues," "Bye, Bye, Blackbird," and "Avalon." *Charlie and His Orchestra*, 2 vols. (see n. 94).

102. Mangelsdorff as interviewed in Polster, *"Swing Heil,"* 150; Daniels interview. Angeli is most certainly the pianist for "You're the Top," "Boom, Why Did My Heart Go Boom," and "Night and Day," for which trombonist Tischelaar is falsely mentioned as pianist in the liner notes: *Charlie and His Orchestra*, vol. 1 (see n. 94). Listen to Angeli's superb piano-playing in recordings of Brocksieper's Solisten-Orchester, an offshoot from the Templin group for the drummer's own recording purposes (early 1943), reissued as *Freddie Brocksieper*, Deutsche Grammophon 2664208 (n.d.).

103. Minutes of broadcast planning meeting of 22 April 1942, BA, R 55/695.

104. See *Die Tagebücher . . . Goebbels*, vol. 4, 75; Brocksieper as interviewed by Pointon [1987] (see n. 93).

105. Cole, *Lord Haw-Haw*, 166; Pointon's and Martin Esslin's astute observations in "Swingtime for Hitler" (see n. 93).

106. Wolfgang Muth as told to Kellersmann, "Jazz," 58. Also see Künneke, *Sing*, 75; she claims (though she has no proof) that the records were dropped over England by parachute.

107. Transcript of Brocksieper interview (see n. 36); Brocksieper as interviewed by Pointon [1987] and for "Swingtime for Hitler" (see n. 93).

108. In my interview with him, Angeli also advanced the argument that he did not know English. He, for one, was acutely sensitive about being labeled a collaborator, as suggested by *Spiegel*, 18 April 1988, 231. This contrasts with a statement by Friedrich Meyer, who had an early hand in the programs, that Schwedler was attacked by the musicians for his "inane texts" (cited in Kellersmann, "Jazz," 56).

109. See Konrad H. Jarausch, *The Unfree Professions: German Lawyers, Teachers, and Engineers, 1900–1950* (New York and Oxford, 1990); Geoffrey Cocks and Konrad H. Jarausch, eds., *German Professions, 1800–1950* (New York and Oxford, 1990); Michael H. Kater, *Doctors Under Hitler* (Chapel Hill and London, 1989).

110. Here I agree with the judgment of Ekkehard Jost, "Jazz in Deutschland: Von der Weimarer Republik bis zur Adenauer-Ära," in *That's Jazz: Der Sound des 20. Jahrhunderts: Eine Ausstellung der Stadt Darmstadt . . . 29. Mai bis 28. August 1988* (Darmstadt, 1988), 365–66.

111. "Aus Gottes eigenem Land," *Reich*, 9 August 1942.

112. See Hans Dieter Schäfer, *Das gespaltene Bewusstsein: Über deutsche Kultur und Lebenswirklichkeit, 1933–1945*, 2nd ed. (Munich and Vienna, 1982), esp. 132–40, and my earlier criticism of this view in *Archiv für Sozialgeschichte* 22 (1982), 668–71.

113. Ordinances regarding public dancing of 4 and 27 September 1939, 25 July 1940, *Amtliche Mitteilungen der Reichsmusikkammer*, BA, RD 33/2-2; *Die Tagebücher . . . Goebbels*, vol. 4, 154; *Unterhaltungsmusik*, 6 June 1940, 526; *Meldungen aus dem Reich*, vol. 5, 1413, 1425. See also p. 112.

114. Ordinances of 15 August and 18 December 1940, *Amtliche Mitteilungen der Reichsmusikkammer*, BA, RD 33/2-2; *Die Tagebücher . . . Goebbels*, vol. 4, 281, 439; *Reich*, 9 March 1941 (quotation).

115. Ordinances of 6 April, 10 and 23 June 1941, *Amtliche Mitteilungen der Reichs-musikkammer,* BA, RD 33/2-2; *Die Tagebücher* . . . *Goebbels,* vol. 4, 575, 681, 685; *Meldungen aus dem Reich,* vol. 7, 2394.

116. *Podium der Unterhaltungsmusik,* 6 February 1942, 41; minutes of broadcast planning meeting of 20 May 1942, BA, R 55/695; Schäfer, *Berlin,* 24; Haentzschel interview.

117. Ordinances of 19 December 1939 and 25 April 1940, *Amtliche Mitteilungen der Reichsmusikkammer,* BA, RD 33/2-2; *Unterhaltungsmusik,* 19 October 1939, 1388; ibid., 9 November 1939, 1434; ibid., 4 April 1940, 301; Raabe in *Zeitschrift für Musik* 107 (1940), 454; Molkenbur-Schönfelder interview.

118. Ordinance of 9 August 1941, *Amtliche Mitteilungen der Reichskulturkammer,* BA, RD 33/2-2 (quotation); Brocksieper interview.

119. One Frankfurt spy at the time was called Daniel (Mangelsdorff interview).

120. "Musikalische Feldpost," 15 January 1943, PA Daniels.

121. "Musikalische Feldpost," beginning of April 1942, PA Daniels; Heinrich, *"Swing-Generation,"* 44; Pick interview.

122. Wolffram, "Bulgare," 9; Baldauf as cited in Mike Zwerin (who rightly equates the Gestapo with the SS), *La Tristesse de Saint Louis: Swing under the Nazis* (New York, 1985), 90; case of van't Hoff in Stuttgart, BDC, RMK van't Hoff; case of Otto Fuhrmann in Oslo, BDC, RMK Fuhrmann.

123. *Skizzen,* August/September 1939, 22; German Brunswick minibrochure, September 1939, PA Jung.

124. Lange's (*Jazz in Deutschland,* 98) and Kellersmann's ("Jazz," 64) contention that an express prohibition against the sale of English records was based on a Goebbels edict dated 2 September 1939 is mistaken. The edict had mentioned only live performances, not records. See *Allgemeine Musikzeitung* 67 (1940), 32; *Amtliche Mitteilungen der Reichsmusikkammer,* 15 September 1939, BA, RD 33/2-2.

125. "Erste Liste unerwünschter musikalischer Werke," *Unterhaltungsmusik,* 14 September 1939, 1306–7.

126. *Unterhaltungsmusik,* 25 January 1940, 70, reprinting the *Völkischer Beobachter* statement of 12 January; Waldemar Rosen, "Bilder aus dem englischen Musikleben," *Musik in Jugend und Volk* 3 (1940), 2–4; "Zweite Liste . . . ," *Beilage zu den Amtlichen Mitteilungen der Reichsmusikkammer,* 15 April 1940, BA, RD 33/2-2.

127. Haentzschel interview; Korseck to author, 15 November 1988.

128. Hans Petsch, "Der Jazzbazillus," *Zeitschrift für Musik* 107 (1940), 455–57; protocol of Goebbels directive (July 1940) reprinted in Boelcke, *Kriegspropaganda,* 418–19 (quotation); Schulz-Reichel interview; Kellersmann, "Jazz," 22.

129. See, for instance, *Reich,* 10 May and 9 August 1942.

130. *Podium der Unterhaltungsmusik,* 8 January 1942, 9 (quotation); "Der neueste Modeirrsinn Anglo-Amerikas: Sind Sie nicht entzückend 'swing'!?" *Mittag,* 17 August 1942.

131. Lange, *Jazz in Deutschland,* 103; Werner Burkhardt, "Musik der Stunde Null," *Zeitmagazin,* 18 November 1983, 42.

132. Von Borries to RMK president, 4 February 1942, BDC, RMK Fritz von Borries; *Podium der Unterhaltungsmusik,* 6 March 1942, 75–76.

133. *Unterhaltungsmusik,* 14 December 1939, 1529; transcript of Schulz-Köhn interview (see n. 36); Boelcke, *Macht,* 451; Diller, *Rundfunkpolitik,* 316; Smith, *Feind,* 96–97.

134. *Meldungen aus dem Reich,* vol. 3, 630; Boelcke, *Macht,* 454.

135. Danzi, *American Musician*, 133–39.

136. Oral communication to me by Gertie Molkenbur-Schönfelder, Lindau, 2 June 1988.

137. *Amtliche Mitteilungen der Reichsmusikkammer*, 15 February 1940, BA, RD 33/2-2; RMK licence for Friedländer, no. 75124, dated 22 August 1941, PA Friedländer-Reimann.

138. Pick interview.

139. Bessunger to author, 1 August and 25 April 1989, 1 February 1990.

140. Schumann interview; transcript of Schumann interview for "Swing under the Swastika" (see n. 36). Professional musicians under the age of eighteen without special RMK permission were illegal (*Amtliche Mitteilungen der Reichsmusikkammer*, 15 May 1942, BA, RD 33/2-2).

141. Theo Stengel and Herbert Gerigk, *Lexikon der Juden in der Musik: Mit einem Titelverzeichnis jüdischer Werke* (Berlin, 1941); *Amtliche Mitteilungen der Reichsmusikkammer*, 15 January 1941, BA, RD 33/2-2; Wolfgang Sachse's rave review in *Musik* 34 (1942), 167–68.

142. *Zeitschrift für Musik* 107 (1940), 766. Also see Fred K. Prieberg, *Musik im NS-Staat* (Frankfurt am Main, 1982), 127, 275–76, 285–86. I first learned of Blacher's precarious situation from my uncle, the pianist Helmut Roloff, who was rector of the Berlin Hochschule der Künste after the war. He was a close friend of Blacher and was himself persecuted by the Nazis for resistance activities.

143. Danzi, *American Musician*, 124; Sely memorandum, 23 February 1946, BDC, RMK Bund.

144. "Musikalische Feldpost," beginning of April 1942, PA Daniels; Reichssicherheitshauptamt memorandum, 6 July 1942, BDC, RMK Fuhrmann; certificate Kammergericht Berlin, 18 September 1947, PA Molkenbur-Schönfelder; Horst J. P. Bergmeier, *The Weintraub Story incorporated The Ady Rosner Story* (Menden, 1982), 25.

145. See *Die Tagebücher . . . Goebbels*, vol. 3, 599; ibid., vol. 4, 634–35; Kater, "Inside Nazis," 239–40; personal file Schottländer, BDC.

146. Interviews with Blüthner, Pick, Zacharias, Hielscher, and Korseck; Hans Blüthner, "Plattensammeln und was sonst noch so war," *Fox auf 78*, no. 7 (Summer 1989), 21; *Podium der Unterhaltungsmusik*, 13 May 1943, 116.

147. Molkenbur-Schönfelder interview; Molkenbur-Schönfelder to author, 24 June 1989; Stenzel in transcript of radio broadcast by Hajo Steinert, "Und Abends in die Scala: Girls, Bonzen und die Partei," produced 25 August 1987, Deutschlandfunk, Cologne; *Die Tagebücher . . . Goebbels*, vol. 3, 612–15; Danzi, *American Musician*, 137; Reichssicherheitshauptamt memorandum, 14 October 1942, BDC, RMK Stenzel.

148. Stenzel according to "Und Abends in die Scala," (see n. 147); Fanderl to Hinkel, 17 June 1944, BDC, personal file Fanderl.

149. See Danzi, *American Musician*, 137; Stenzel according to "Und Abends in die Scala" (see n. 147).

150. See the photograph of Stenzel fronting his band on the cover of *American Historical Review* 94 (1989) and the photograph in this book showing him on the Berlin Scala stage; *Berliner Morgenpost*, 10 April 1983; Haentzschel interview. Stenzel's often multiple pursuit of the young women he worked with has been attested to by Gertie Molkenbur-Schönfelder, then herself an object of his attention (author's telephone conversation with her, Munich-Lindau, 11 December 1990).

151. *Das Tagebuch . . . Goebbels*, vol. 3, 76; divorce certificate for Hinkel, 1 December 1938, BDC, SS Hinkel; Geza von Cziffra, *Kauf dir einen bunten Luftballon: Erin-*

nerungen an Götter und Halbgötter (Munich and Berlin, 1975), 252; Curt Riess, *Das gab's nur einmal: Die grosse Zeit des deutschen Films* (Vienna and Munich, 1977), vol. 3, 42; Kellersmann, "Jazz," 33. Hinkel had married his first wife, Anny Danzer, a pharmacist's daughter from Neuötting, in 1927 (Hans Hinkel, *Einer unter Hunderttausend*, 9th ed. [Munich, 1942], 174, 207).

152. Personal file Fanderl, BDC; BDC, SS Hinkel.
153. See Fanderl to Hinkel, 28 November 1939 and 9 October 1940, and Hinkel to Fanderl, 30 November 1939, BDC, personal file Fanderl.
154. *Artist*, 17 October 1935, 1163; vita of Anneliese Kambeck [Spada], n.d., BDC, SS Hinkel; Molkenbur-Schönfelder to author, 24 June 1989; BDC, RMK Charlotte Fanderl, née Treml.
155. Haentzschel interview; chief of Sipo and SD to SS-Rasse- und Siedlungshauptamt, 14 November 1942, BDC, SS Hinkel.
156. Molkenbur-Schönfelder to author, 3 February 1989; personal file Fanderl, BDC.
157. Personal file Fanderl, BDC.
158. Fanderl to Hinkel, 17 June 1944, BDC, personal file Fanderl.
159. The latter has been confirmed by Haentzschel (interview).
160. Molkenbur-Schönfelder interview; Metzmacher, *Wir sind bei euch*, 74, 106–7; Hinkel to Terboven, 18 June 1940, BA, R 56I/93; Heilig to Hinkel, 1 September 1941, BDC, RKK Hinkel; Stenzel contract, 1 February 1942, BDC, RMK Stenzel; Stenzel according to "Und Abends in die Scala" (see n. 147).
161. Reichssicherheitshauptamt memorandum, 14 October 1942, BDC, RMK Stenzel.
162. Fischer to Berlin Gauleitung, 20 September 1940; Ohlendorf to Hinkel, 26 May 1941, BDC, RMK Stenzel. See also Schmidt memorandum, 21 August 1940, BDC, RMK Stenzel; "Musikalische Feldpost," 7 November 1941, PA Daniels.
163. Chief of Sipo and SD to SS-Rasse- und Siedlungshauptamt, 14 November 1942, BDC, SS Hinkel; Stenzel according to "Und Abends in die Scala" (see n. 147); Andersen, *Leben*, 163.
164. Fanderl to Hinkel, 17 October 1942, BDC, personal file Fanderl; Conrad, *Wehner*, 72, 101. See also Chapter Four, p. 187.
165. Charles Delaunay, *Django Reinhardt* (New York, 1981), 100–103, 108–11; "Musikalische Feldpost," mid-August 1942, PA Daniels; Ekkehard Jost, "Jazz in Europe—Die frühen Jahre," in *That's Jazz*, 322.
166. Jack de Graef, *De Swingperiode (1935–1947): Jazz in België* (Wettelijk, 1980), 21–32, 43–50, 58–59, 63–68; Robert Pernet, *Jazz in Little Belgium: History (1881–1966)* (Brussels, 1966), 103–15; "Musikalische Feldpost," 24 September 1941 and beginning of June 1942, PA Daniels; Engel interview.
167. "Musikalische Feldpost," beginning of January, mid-April, and mid-July 1942 (quotation), PA Daniels; Kees Wouters, "Krieg dem Jazz! Holland vor und während der Nazi-Besetzung," in Polster, *"Swing Heil,"* 179.
168. A cassette tape kindly supplied to me by Werner Daniels, featuring groups led by Kai Ewans, Kjeld Bonfils, Leo Mathisen, and Bjorge Roger Henrichsen (1940–44) demonstrates European-style jazz of the highest order.
169. Erik Wiedemann, *Jazz i Danmark: Ityverne, trediverne og fyrrerne* (Copenhagen, 1982), vol. 1, 64, 24–56, 268–92; vol. 2, 12–13, 18–19, 34, 44–45, 48–50, 62, 79–80, 83–84.
170. See n. 39 above.
171. Lange, *Jazz in Deutschland*, 101–2; Wouters, "Krieg," 191.
172. Dietrich Schulz-Köhn, *Django Reinhardt: Ein Portrait* (Wetzlar, 1960), 45–47; Pernet, *Jazz . . . Discography;* Wiedemann, *Jazz*, vol. 2; Delaunay, *Django*, 101–2, 111; Jost, "Jazz in Europe," 324.

173. Wiedemann, *Jazz,* vol. 1, 262.

174. "Swing: Catalogue Général 1941 Disques," PA Jung.

175. Lange, *Jazz in Deutschland,* 110, 112, 114, 116; idem in *Jazz-Podium,* no. 6 (1957), 21; "Musikalische Feldpost," mid-March and beginning of June 1942, PA Daniels; Pernet, *Jazz . . . Discography,* 54, 172, 337, 317; Haentzschel and Brocksieper interviews; Brocksieper band (1942–43) reissues on Polydor 2459032 and 2664208, n.d.

176. "Musikalische Feldpost," 24 September 1941; ibid., beginning of January, beginning of February, beginning of August 1942, PA Daniels; transcript of Schulz-Köhn interview (see n. 36); Gunter Lust and Lissy Lust, . . . *und sie drehen sich immer noch!* (Menden, 1984), 30; Lange, *Jazz in Deutschland,* 103; Becke to author, 11 September 1989.

177. Jost, "Jazz in Europe," 323; Schulz-Köhn as interviewed in ibid., 337; "Musikalische Feldpost," 24 September 1941 and mid-April 1942, PA Daniels; Schulz-Köhn, *Reinhardt,* 39; Alfred A. Goodman, *Musik im Blut: Amerikanische Rhythmen erobern die Welt* (Munich, 1968), 118–19; Delaunay, *Django,* 104, 109; Zwerin, *La Tristesse,* 179; Muth, "Wir," 207; Wouters, "Krieg," 181–96.

178. "Musikalische Feldpost," August 1942, PA Daniels; Henk Niesen, Jr., "Occupation Blues," *Jazz Forum* (1946), 15–16; Delaunay, *Django,* 99; Albert McCarthy, *Big Band Jazz* (New York, 1974), 312–13; Wiedemann, *Jazz,* vol. 1, 284–85; ibid., vol. 2, 52; Wouters, "Krieg," 191, 194, 197.

179. Niesen, Jr., "Occupation Blues," 15; "Musikalische Feldpost," 10 December 1941, PA Daniels; Wouters, "Krieg," 182–87.

180. Benno Müller-Hill, *Tödliche Wissenschaft: Die Aussonderung von Juden, Zigeunern und Geisteskranken, 1933–1945* (Reinbek, 1984), 17–18, 20–21; statement of Graz state attorney of 5 February 1940 as quoted in Klaus Oldenhage, "Justizverwaltung und Lenkung der Rechtsprechung im Zweiten Weltkrieg," in Dieter Rebentisch and Karl Teppe, eds., *Verwaltung contra Menschenführung im Staat Hitlers: Studien zum politisch-administrativen System* (Göttingen, 1986), 110 (first quotation); *Amtliche Mitteilungen der Reichsmusikkammer,* 15 February and 25 April 1940, BA, RD 33/2-2; Paul Bernhard, *Jazz: Eine musikalische Zeitfrage* (Munich, 1927), 77; Delaunay, *Django,* 100 (second quotation).

181. Francis Newton [Eric J. Hobsbawm], *The Jazz Scene* (New York, 1975), 261 (quotation); "Musikalische Feldpost," mid-April and beginning of August 1942, PA Daniels; de Graef, *Swingperiode,* 27–29; Jost, "Jazz in Europe," 324; Zwerin, *La Tristesse,* 147–49.

182. Interviews with Bohländer, Jung, and Mangelsdorff; transcript of Lippmann interview for "Swing under the Swastika" (see n. 36); Mangelsdorff as interviewed in Polster, *"Swing Heil,"* 15–46, 151; Carlo Bohländer, *Jazz-Geschichte und Rhythmus* (Mainz, 1960), 67.

183. Bohländer, *Jazz-Geschichte,* 67; *Unterhaltungsmusik,* 17 July 1941, 646; "Musikalische Feldpost," beginning of August 1942, PA Daniels.

184. Hans Otto Jung's liner notes for *Swing under the Nazis* (1986), Harlequin HQ 2051; interviews with Blüthner, Pick, and Jung.

185. Freichel interview; Jung's liner notes (see n. 184).

186. Jung and Mangelsdorff interviews.

187. *Reichsgesetzblatt Teil I* (1940), 499–500; BDC, SS Baldauf; interviews with Bohländer, Freichel, Jung, and Mangelsdorff.

188. Michaelis to author, 26 April 1989; Hipp to author, 17 March and 22 April 1989; Becke to author, 11 September 1989.

189. Hipp to author, 17 March, 29 March (post-stamped), and 22 April 1989; Hipp as

quoted in Richard W. Fogg, "Jazz under the Nazis," in *Down Beat Music '66: 11th Yearbook* (Chicago, 1966), 98; Charles Delaunay, *New Hot Discography: The Standard Directory of Recorded Jazz,* ed. Walter E. Schaap and George Avakian (New York, 1948), 436.

190. Hipp to author, 17 March 1989 (first quotation); Becke to author, 11 September 1989 (second quotation); Hipp as quoted in Fogg, "Jazz under the Nazis," 98.

191. Hipp to author, 22 April 1989.

192. For Weimar, see Muth, "Wir," 204–5; for Rostock, see Walter Kempowski, *Tadellöser & Wolff: Ein bürgerlicher Roman,* 2nd ed. (Munich, 1975), 151–56; Werner Burkhardt, "Musik der Stunde Null," *Zeitmagazin,* 18 November 1983, 42; for Breslau, Koleczek interview.

193. Ludwig Kelbetz, "Vom Gesellschaftstanz in unserer Zeit," *Musik in Jugend und Volk* 3 (1940), 58–60; Hans Frucht, "Tanz und Musik im nationalsozialistischen Staat," *Zeitschrift für Musik* 107 (1940), 261–65; Reinhold Sommer, "Neugestaltung des Gesellschaftstanzes," *Musik* 34 (1942), 253–55; Raabe's pronouncements in *Unterhaltungsmusik,* 26 October 1939, 1405, and *Zeitschrift für Musik* 109 (1942), 410.

194. Max Merz, "Deutsches Volkstum und der Jazz," *Musik in Jugend und Volk* 3 (1940), 51–58; idem, "Wir und der Jazz," *Westermann's Monatshefte* 85 (1940), 3–6; *Unterhaltungsmusik,* 28 December 1940, 1225; *Meldungen aus dem Reich,* vol. 5, 1657; "Musikalische Feldpost," mid-January 1942, PA Daniels.

195. See p. 136; *Unterhaltungsmusik,* 2 November 1939, 1421; *Die Tagebücher . . . Goebbels,* vol. 4, 533 (quotation).

196. Schult to Kohlmeyer, 8 February 1940, SAH, Jugendbehörde I, 343 c.

197. Documents of March 1940 in SAH, Jugendbehörde I, 343 c; interviews with Scheel, Hirschfeld, and Evers-Frauboes.

198. "Einladung zum Tanzabend am Donnerstag, 14. März," SAH, Jugendbehörde I, 343 c. See also "Einzelbeispiele für die Cliquen- und Bandenbildung in neuerer Zeit," appended to "Reichsjugendführung—Personalamt—Überwachung, 'Cliquen- und Bandenbildung unter Jugendlichen,' " September 1942, BA, R 22/1177.

199. Thorsten Müller in *Hamburger Abendblatt,* 1 February 1985.

200. Uwe Storjohann as quoted in Ursula Prückner, "Wilde Jahre: Begegnungen mit Hamburger Swings," in Polster, *"Swing Heil,"* 224–25.

201. Thorsten Müller in *Hamburger Abendblatt,* 30 January 1985; Hanne-Lore Evers to Hans, 11 August 1941, PA Evers-Frauboes; Nielsen-Rönn interview.

202. Evers to Hans, 13 August 1941 (quotation); also letter dated 20 August 1941, both PA Evers-Frauboes; *Unterhaltungsmusik,* 11 September 1941, inside cover; Thorsten Müller in *Hamburger Abendblatt,* 31 January 1985.

203. Thorsten Müller in *Hamburger Abendblatt,* 1 February 1985; Evers to Hans, 21 September 1941, PA Evers-Frauboes.

204. Axel Springer, *An meine Kinder und Kindeskinder: Auszüge aus einer Niederschrift,* 2nd ed. (Berlin, 1985), 36; Harry [Georgiadis] Stephens, "Swing Threatens Third Reich," unpublished ms., Beccles (Suffolk), 1988, 64; interviews with Evers-Frauboes, Vogel, Scheel, and Müller.

205. "Einzelbeispiele" (see n. 198).

206. Madlung-Shelton interview, and transcript of Madlung-Shelton interview for "Swing under the Swastika" (see n. 36); Scheel interview; testimony of A.v.d.E. in Gestapo protocol, 16 October 1941, SAH, Oberschulbehörde VI, 2 F VIII a 2/40/1.

207. Stephens, "Swing Threatens Third Reich," 92–93.

208. Schult to Kohlmeyer, 8 February 1940, SAH, Jugendbehörde I, 343 c; Lust, *drehen,*

36; Rainer Pohl, "'Das gesunde Volksempfinden ist gegen Dad und Jo': Zur Verfolgung der Hamburger 'Swing-Jugend' im Zweiten Weltkrieg," in *Verachtet—verfolgt—vernichtet: Zu den "vergessenen" Opfern des NS-Regimes* (Hamburg, 1986), 16, 28–29.

209. Uwe Storjohann, "In Hinkeformation hinterher: Swing-Jugend an der Bismarck-Schule," in Reiner Lehberger and Hans-Peter de Lorent, eds., *"Die Fahne hoch": Schulpolitik und Schulalltag in Hamburg unterm Hakenkreuz* (Hamburg, 1986), 404; Günther Lust as interviewed in Polster, *"Swing Heil,"* 167; Pohl, "Volksempfinden," 29; Engel interview.

210. Oberschule für Jungen am Stadtpark to Schulverwaltung Hamburg, 9 January 1942, SAH, Oberschulbehörde VI, 2 F VIII a 2/3/1; Günther Lust as interviewed in Polster, *"Swing Heil,"* 167–68; Bernd Polster, "Treudeutsch, treudeutsch: Swingheinis unterwandern den Kolonnenzwang," in ibid., 142; Pohl, "Volksempfinden," 23.

211. Pohl, "Volksempfinden," 29.

212. HJ memorandum, 12 March 1940, SAH, Jugendbehörde I, 343 c. See also testimony of H. P. in Gestapo protocol, 18 October 1941, SAH, Oberschulbehörde VI, 2 F VIII a 2/40/1; "Einzelbeispiele" (see n. 198).

213. Evers-Frauboes interview (quotation); Prückner, "Jahre," 227. Hoffmann affected the special name "K. R. H. Sonderburg." "Sonder" connotes "special" in German.

214. "Einzelbeispiele" (see n. 198); Günther Lust and Günter Discher as interviewed in Polster, *"Swing Heil,"* 161–62, 166–67; Prückner, "Jahre," 224, 226.

215. Testimonies of W. D. and W. J., 18 and 21 October 1941, SAH, Oberschulbehörde VI, 2 F VIII a 2/40/1.

216. Panagopoulos interview.

217. Scheel interview (quotation); Pohl, "Volksempfinden," 23–24.

218. "The Alligators 'Hot' Club," English-language documentation and photographs, n.d., PA Scheel; Scheel interview.

219. Scheel interview.

220. Stephens, "Swing Threatens Third Reich," 67–68.

221. Author's telephone conversation with Volker Jürgen Seitz, Hamburg, 20 June 1988; Scheel interview.

222. "Einzelbeispiele" (see n. 198); interviews with Scheel, Engel, and Madlung-Shelton.

223. Testimony of O. K. S. in Gestapo protocol, 18 October 1941, SAH, Oberschulbehörde VI, 2 F VIII a 2/40/1; Storjohann, "Hinkeformation," 399–400; Springer, *Kinder,* 39; Pohl, "Volksempfinden," 25; Evers-Frauboes interview.

224. Scheel interview; Pohl, "Volksempfinden," 36.

225. Evers-Frauboes interview; BDC, MF and SS Reinhardt; Pohl, "Volksempfinden," 39; Stephens, "Swing Threatens Third Reich," 98.

226. BDC, MF and SS Hintze; ibid., SS Kügler. Also see Pohl, "Volksempfinden," 37.

227. Scheel interview; Scheel to author, 7 April 1988.

228. Scheel interview; Scheel to author, 7 April 1988; Gestapo Hamburg to Schulverwaltung Hamburg, 13 November 1940, PA Scheel.

229. Scheel to author, 7 May 1940; SD Hamburg to Züge, 3 December 1940, SAH, Oberschulbehörde VI, F VIII a 2/3/2.

230. See the document in Pohl, "Volksempfinden," 32.

231. Thorsten Müller, "Synopsis aus 'Veränderungsberichte (Zu- und Abgänge) des Polizeigefängnisses Fuhlsbüttel' für die Zeit vom 2.1.1941 bis zum 7. Mai 1943," PA Scheel; Stephens, "Swing Threatens Third Reich," 75–77, 94–95.

232. Müller, "Synopsis"; Prückner, "Jahre," 229; Pohl, "Volksempfinden," 24.

233. See testimony of H. F. in Gestapo protocol, 13 October 1941, SAH, Oberschulbehörde VI, 2 F VIII a 2/40/1; Panagopoulos interview; author's telephone conversation with Volker Jürgen Seitz, Hamburg, 20 June 1988; Stephens, "Swing Threatens Third Reich," 94.

234. I plan to deal with this in a subsequent study about youth and women in the Third Reich; see Pohl, "Volksempfinden."

235. Oberschule für Jungen an der Armgardstrasse to Schulverwaltung Hamburg, 4 April 1942, SAH, Oberschulbehörde VI, 2 F VIII a 2/3/1; documents regarding Hans-Joachim Scheel's dismissal from Gelehrtenschule des Johanneums (November 1940), PA Scheel; Schulverwaltung Hamburg to Hintze, 29 June 1942, including list of penalized pupils, PA Scheel; Scheel interview; Scheel to author, 7 April 1988.

236. Abteilung Musik, Reichspropagandaministerium, to Goebbels, 18 August 1941, reprinted in *Deutsches Allgemeines Sonntagsblatt,* 8 November 1981; *Die Tagebücher . . . Goebbels,* vol. 4, 30.

237. Gutterer to Heydrich, 20 August 1941, IfZ, Ma 667/5484201–02.

238. Axmann to Himmler, 8 January 1942; Himmler to Axmann, 26 January 1942; Himmler to Heydrich, 26 January 1942, BA, NS 19/neu 219.

239. See Pohl, "Volksempfinden," 41.

240. Documents concerning Moringen (1941–42) in BA, R 22/1176; Detlev Peukert, "Arbeitslager und Jugend-KZ: Die 'Behandlung Gemeinschaftsfremder' im Dritten Reich," in Peukert and Jürgen Reulecke, eds., *Die Reihen fast geschlossen: Beiträge zur Geschichte des Alltags unterm Nationalsozialismus* (Wuppertal, 1981), 422–25; Wolf-Dieter Haardt, "'Was denn, hier—in Moringen?!': Die Suche nach einem vergessenen KZ," in Detlef Garbe, ed., *Die vergessenen KZs? Gedenkstätten für die Opfer des NS-Terrors in der Bundesrepublik* (Bornheim-Merten, 1983), 97–107. See also Pohl, "Volksempfinden," 25; Thorsten Müller, "Feindliche Bewegung," in *That's Jazz,* 386.

241. Michael Hepp, "Vorhof zur Hölle: Mädchen im 'Jugendschutzlager' Uckermark," in Angelika Ebbinghaus, ed., *Opfer und Täterinnen: Frauenbiographien des Nationalsozialismus* (Nördlingen, 1987), 191–216. I received a rare opportunity to review the complete file on Helga Rönn (SAH, Amtsgericht Hamburg, Abtlg. Vormundschaftswesen, 115 XI, R 1886, 1653 Rönn) in the company of her brother, Herbert Rönn, and his wife, Ursula Nielsen-Rönn, who were themselves persecuted ex-Swings. According to their testimonies, Helga's alleged promiscuity and other "asocial" transgressions were hugely exaggerated by the authorities to suit their own purposes.

242. Nielsen-Rönn and Madlung-Shelton interviews; Müller, "Synopsis."

243. Müller, "Synopsis"; Scheel interview.

244. Erik H. Erikson, *Identity: Youth and Crisis* (New York, 1968), quotation 165, and passim.

245. Peter Loewenberg, "The Psychohistorical Origins of the Nazi Youth Cohort," *American Historical Review* 76 (1971), 1457–502; Michael H. Kater, "Generationskonflikt als Entwicklungsfaktor in der NS-Bewegung vor 1933," *Geschichte und Gesellschaft* 11 (1985), 217–43.

246. Testimonies of H. F. and H. P. in Gestapo protocols, 13 and 18 October 1941, SAH, Oberschulbehörde VI, 2 F VIII a 2/40/1; Storjohann, "Hinkeformation," 401; Günther Lust as interviewed in Polster, *"Swing Heil,"* 167; Scheel and Engel interviews; Michael H. Kater, *The Nazi Party: A Social Profile of Members and Leaders, 1919–1945* (Cambridge, Mass., 1983).

247. See Arno Klönne, *Jugend im Dritten Reich: Die Hitler-Jugend und ihre Gegner* (Düsseldorf and Cologne, 1982); Detlev J. K. Peukert, *Inside Nazi Germany: Conformity, Opposition and Racism in Everyday Life* (London, 1982); Detlef Mühlberger, *Hitler's Followers: Studies in the Sociology of the Nazi Movement* (London, 1991).

248. The former position was defended by almost all the Hamburg Swings I interviewed. The latter position is expressed in letter by [Georgiadis] Stephens to author, 18 July 1990. Also see his ms., "Swing Threatens Third Reich."

249. Engel to editors of *Hamburger Abendblatt,* 26 September 1985, PA Engels; Walter Jens as interviewed in Polster, *"Swing Heil,"* 157.

250. Springer, *Kinder,* 41.

251. Evers to Hans, 21 October 1940, PA Evers-Frauboes (her hand-written remark about Günter's death on my copy).

252. Evers to Hans, 11 August 1941, PA Evers-Frauboes; Evers-Frauboes interview.

253. Storjohann as quoted in Prückner, "Jahre," 228.

Chapter 4

1. Lothar Gruchmann, *Der Zweite Weltkrieg: Kriegführung und Politik* (Munich, 1967), 216–450.

2. Hans Dieter Schäfer, *Berlin im Zweiten Weltkrieg: Der Untergang der Reichshauptstadt in Augenzeugenberichten* (Munich, 1985), 36–41; Ursula von Kardorff, *Berliner Aufzeichnungen: Aus den Jahren 1942–1945* (Munich, 1964), 78–79; Kristina Söderbaum, *Nichts bleibt immer so: Rückblenden auf ein Leben vor und hinter der Kamera* (Bayreuth, 1983), 197–98.

3. Goebbels in *Reich,* 17 January 1943 and 31 January 1943 (quotation).

4. Speech of 18 February 1943 printed in Joseph Goebbels, *Der steile Aufstieg: Reden und Aufsätze aus den Jahren 1942/43,* ed. M. A. von Schirmeister (Munich, 1943), 167–204, quotations 186; *The Goebbels Diaries* ed., Louis P. Lochner, (London, 1948), 310–11, 354.

5. Goebbels, *Aufstieg,* 186; *Podium der Unterhaltungsmusik,* 11 March 1943, 64; Evelyn Künneke, *Sing, Evelyn, Sing: Revue eines Lebens* (Reinbek, 1985), 61.

6. *Podium der Unterhaltungsmusik,* 14 October 1943, 178; Schönicke to Fritzsche, 17 July 1944, BA, R 55/557; Konrad Warner, *Schicksalswende Europas: Ich sprach mit dem deutschen Volk . . . Ein Tatsachenbericht* (Rheinfelden, 1944), 210; Schäfer, *Berlin,* 42–43.

7. Helmut Heiber, *Joseph Goebbels* (Munich, 1965), 315–16; *Jahrbuch der deutschen Musik 1944,* 39–41, 75–103; Maurus Pacher, *Sehn Sie, das war Berlin: Weltstadt nach Noten* (Frankfurt am Main and Berlin, 1987), 338.

8. *Reich,* 5 December 1943; Kardorff, *Aufzeichnungen,* 193–94; Matthias Menzel, *Die Stadt ohne Tod: Berliner Tagebuch 1943/45* (Berlin, 1946), 96, 153; Haentzschel interview.

9. Menzel, *Stadt,* 93–94, 124; Hedda Adlon, *Hotel Adlon,* 2nd ed. (Munich, 1979), 306–8.

10. Friedländer-Reimann interview; *Reich,* 30 July 1944.

11. "Musikalische Feldpost," 1 April 1943, PA Daniels; *Reich,* 16 May 1943; Walter Kempowski, *Tadellöser & Wolff: Ein bürgerlicher Roman,* 2nd ed. (Munich, 1975), 453.

12. On this, see liner notes for *Helmy's Swing,* EMI Electrola 1 C134-45 361/62M; Horst H. Lange, *Jazz in Deutschland: Die deutsche Jazz-Chronik, 1900–1960*

(Berlin, 1966), 110, 117; Robert Pernet, *Jazz in Little Belgium: Discography (1895–1966)* (Brussels, 1966), 102–3, 315–16; *Fox auf 78*, no. 3 (Spring 1987), 21.

13. "Musikalische Feldpost," beginning of September and 1 October 1942, 1 November 1942 (quotation), 1 March, 15 April, 1 and 15 June 1943, PA Daniels; interviews with Pick, Blüthner, and Daniels.

14. Klaus Krüger, "Wir machen Musik: Tanzorchester im Dritten Reich," in Bernd Polster, ed., *"Swing Heil": Jazz im Nationalsozialismus* (Berlin, 1989), 58.

15. "Musikalische Feldpost," 15 November and 1 December 1942, 1 April 1943, PA Daniels.

16. Cf. the contemptuous SS remarks in *Meldungen aus dem Reich: Die geheimen Lageberichte des Sicherheitsdienstes der SS, 1938–1945* ed. Heinz Boberach (Herrsching, 1984), vol. 13, 5066. The "Café Melodie" mentioned here is really D'Orio's Uhlandeck.

17. Evers to Hans, 30 December 1943, PA Evers-Frauboes; Lola Rolfs's reminiscence in *Hamburger Abendblatt*, 22 February 1985.

18. Dietrich Heinz Kraner and Klaus Schulz, *Jazz in Austria: Historische Entwicklung und Diskographie des Jazz in Österreich* (Graz, 1972), 13–14; Jandl as interviewed in Polster, *"Swing Heil,"* 155; chap. 3, p. 146.

19. Report, SD-Leitabschnitt München, 11 April 1944; Schiede to Press, 18 May 1944, SAM, NSDAP/31.

20. Lange, *Jazz in Deutschland,* 117; Künneke, *Sing,* 64; Wunderlich interview. In contradiction to these testimonials, Knud Wolffram's second-hand account maintains that D'Orio played there only until mid-1944 ("Ein Bulgare in Berlin: Die Geschichte des Lubo D'Orio," *Fox auf 78*, no. 8 [Spring 1990], 9).

21. Quotations in order: Kardorff, *Aufzeichnungen,* 97–98; Theo Findahl, *Letzter Akt— Berlin, 1939–1945* (Hamburg, 1946), 15–16; *While Berlin Burns: The Diary of Hans-Georg von Studnitz, 1943–1945* (London, 1964), 254–55.

22. "Auszug aus dem Tätigkeitsbericht für Monat Februar Gau Pommern," 10 March 1944; Stemmer to Hinkel, 20 March 1944; Ley to Goebbels, 8 May 1944, BA, R 56I/37.

23. Hinkel to Reinecke, 11 January 1943; Stemmer to Hinkel, 20 March 1944, BA, R 56I/37; case of bandleader Walter Graf in Herrmann to Rückert, 4 January 1945, BDC, RMK Graf; Friedländer-Reimann interview.

24. Cammer to Ehlers, 9 March 1943, BA, R 56I/83; excerpt from Balzer report of 1 July 1943 regarding journey to Eastern front, BA, R 56I/82; Kramer to Feldpostnummer 12 111, 20 March 1944; "Abschrift," [July 1944]; Heinrichsdorff to Schrade, 1 July 1944, BA, R 56I/37; Uebelhör to Goebbels, 15 January 1945, BDC, RMK Uebelhör.

25. Minutes of broadcast planning meeting of 30 June 1943, BA, R 55/696; List "Fronttheater," 1 November 1943, BA, R 56I/84; Lorey to Abteilung Rfk., 9 August 1944, BA, R 55/559; "Musikalische Feldpost," 15 October 1942, PA Daniels.

26. Künneke, *Sing,* 61–62.

27. Werner Burkhardt, "Musik der Stunde Null," *Zeitmagazin,* 11 November 1983, 48; Brocksieper interview.

28. Brocksieper (interview) maintains, plausibly, that the station was bombed out in January and February, while *Spiegel* (18 April 1988, 236) writes that programming continued until early April 1945. See also "Kapelle Lutz Templin," enclosed with letter of Schönicke to Fritzsche, 18 September 1944, BDC, RMK, Rundfunk-Liste;

John Alfred Cole, *Lord Haw-Haw—and William Joyce* (London, 1964), 223–24; Heinz Bardua, *Stuttgart im Luftkrieg, 1939–1945: Mit Dokumentenanhang und 67 Abbildungen* (Stuttgart, n.d.).

29. Winkelnkemper memorandum, 24 January 1943, BDC, RSK Toni Winkelnkemper; Schönicke to Fritzsche, 24 May 1944; "Vorschläge, Wünsche, Kritiken," Juli 1944; Fritzsche to Roddewicz, 21 September 1944; Fritzsche to Goebbels, 11 December 1944, BA, R 55/557.

30. Franz Heinrich, *"Swing-Generation": Selbsterlebtes* (Menden, 1988), 64, 66; Leslie Perowne as interviewed for broadcast "Swingtime for Hitler," by Michael Pointon, transmitted BBC London 16 August 1987, transcript PA Pointon.

31. Brocksieper interview.

32. Haentzschel interview; RKK to Haushaltsabteilung, 3 August 1943, BA, R 56I/34. The Prague life-style is documented in Geza von Cziffra, *Kauf dir einen bunten Luftballon: Erinnerungen an Götter und Halbgötter* (Munich and Berlin, 1975), 296, 310; Gustav Fröhlich, *Waren das Zeiten: Mein Film-Heldenleben* (Munich and Berlin, 1983), 316; Johannes Heesters, *Es kommt auf die Sekunde an: Erinnerungen an ein Leben in Frack* (Munich, 1978), 160, 162.

33. Hinkel to Goebbels, 9 December 1942, BA, R 55/1254; Kainersdorfer to Schwerkolt, 26 November 1942, BA, R 56I/41; "Musikalische Feldpost," mid-September and 15 December 1942, PA Daniels.

34. *Meldungen aus dem Reich*, vol. 11, 4333.

35. Hinkel to Goebbels, 9 December 1942, BA, R 55/1254; minutes of broadcast planning meeting of 9 December 1942, 21 January and 19 May 1943, BA, R 55/696; *Podium der Unterhaltungsmusik*, 15 July 1943, 135; Haentzschel interview.

36. *Podium der Unterhaltungsmusik*, 22 October 1942, 316; ibid., 4 December 1942, 362; ibid., 25 March 1943, 83; ibid., 14 October 1943, 179; ibid., 18 November 1943, 203.

37. *Podium der Unterhaltungsmusik*, 18 November 1943, 203; Blüthner interview; transcript of Müller interview for British video series, "Swing under the Swastika," Yorkshire Television, London, 1988; Müller interview.

38. Personal file Henneberg, BDC, RMK Henneberg, esp. corr. with Hinkel.

39. Rückert memorandum, 1 April 1943 (quotation); Safronow to Tackmann, 30 March 1944, BA, R 56I/34.

40. BDC, personal papers Cerff; *Goebbels Diaries*, ed. Lochner, 445; Kurt Pabst, "Nazi-'Kultur': Dokumente über Kunstpflege im Dritten Reich," unpublished ms., Erfurt, [1946], 110 (BDC, RKK Pabst); Haentzschel interview.

41. Quotation from Stege in *Unterhaltungsmusik*, 17 February 1938, 194.

42. Corr. in BA, R 55/242/1 and R 56I/34.

43. Interviews with Klagemann, Haentzschel, and Brocksieper; "Musikalische Feldpost," 1 October 1942 and 15 January 1943, PA Daniels; "Jazz-Mitteilungen," [1943], PA Schulz-Köhn.

44. Safronow to Tackmann, 30 March 1944; Rückert to DTU, 20 April 1944; RKK president to Safronow, 14 June 1944, BA, R 56I/34; "Bemerkungen zur Aufführung 'Schräge Musik,' " [1944]; Schönicke to Stech and Géczy, 6 November 1944, BA, R 55/557.

45. No certified samples of that sound are extant. But it is easy to imagine it after having listened to pieces by the earlier Grothe-Haentzschel band. One can imagine the contrast with a contemporary U.S. orchestra, such as Woody Herman's, as it was playing the blues "Red Top" in 1944 (air check), featuring Herman on clarinet, Flip Phillips on tenor sax, Bill Harris on trombone, and Pete Condoli on trumpet!

46. Schönicke to Fritzsche, 18 September 1944, and enclosed list, BDC, RMK, Rundfunk-Liste; Haentzschel interview.
47. Rückert to DTU, 9 November 1944, BA, R 56I/34; Hildegard Matul to RMK Berlin, 30 November 1944, BDC, RMK Serge Matul.
48. Jähnert to Rückert, 30 November 1944; Rückert to Jähnert, 6 December 1944, BA, R 56I/34; Dobschinski and Klagemann interviews.
49. Haentzschel interview.
50. Schlegel to Goebbels, 19 October 1944, BA, R 55/532 (quotation); Bernhard Wittek, *Der britische Ätherkrieg gegen das Dritte Reich: Die deutschsprachigen Kriegssendungen der British Broadcasting Corporation* (Münster, 1962), 127; Conrad Pütter, *Rundfunk gegen das "Dritte Reich": Deutschsprachige Rundfunkaktivitäten im Exil, 1933–1945: Ein Handbuch* (Munich, 1986), 84–91; Himmler to Goebbels, 11 August 1943, doc. 8 in Conrad F. Latour, "Goebbels' 'Ausserordentliche Rundfunkmassnahmen,' 1939–1942," *Vierteljahrshefte für Zeitgeschichte* 11 (1963), 435; Thorsten Müller in *Deutsches Allgemeines Sonntagsblatt*, 4 September 1988.
51. Zacharias interview.
52. DIA, [British] Forces Program as Broadcast, 14 and 15 April 1943.
53. Sefton Delmer, *Black Boomerang: An Autobiography* (London, 1962), 81, 108–10; Ellic Howe, *The Black Game: British Subversive Operations against the Germans during the Second World War* (London, 1982), 174–91, 240–41, 259; Pütter, *Rundfunk*, 125–27; *Goebbels Diaries*, ed. Lochner, 358, 606.
54. Quotation from Howe, *Black Game*, 175, 250; Delmer, *Black Boomerang*, 84–85; Brocksieper and Zacharias interviews; *New Yorker*, 13 October 1945, 21–22.
55. Minutes of broadcast planning meeting of 6 September 1944, BA, R 55/556; Werner Burkhardt, "Musik des Stunde Null," *Zeitmagazin*, 18 November 1983, 42; Rolf Schörken, *Luftwaffenhelfer und Drittes Reich: Die Entstehung eines politischen Bewusstseins*, 2nd ed. (Stuttgart, 1985), 156; Mangelsdorff as interviewed in Polster, *"Swing Heil,"* 150.
56. Viera interview.
57. Geoffrey Butcher, *Next to a Letter from Home: Major Glenn Miller's Wartime Band* (Edinburgh, 1986), 43–47, 57–58.
58. Ibid., 60–75, 195–210; DIA, AEF Program as Broadcast, 8 June 1944; [BBC] *Radio Times*, 23 June 1944, 1; ibid., 14 July 1944, 1; ibid., 18 July 1944, 20; ibid., 12 January 1945, 2, 4; *Melody Maker*, 10 June 1944; ibid., 25 May 1945. On Powell, also see Gunther Schuller, *The Swing Era: The Development of Jazz, 1930–1945* (New York and Oxford, 1989), 38–39.
59. *Glenn Miller and His AAF* [*sic!*] *Orchestra*, Soundcraft Records, Kingston, Jamaica, n.d. I owe my knowledge of this re-release to Professor Clark Reynolds, College of Charleston, whose assistance is gratefully acknowledged (Reynolds to author, 23 June 1989).
60. Schulz-Köhn interview.
61. Himmler to Goebbels, 11 August 1943 (see n. 50) (quotation); Hinkel to Goebbels, 19 November 1942, BA, R 56I/27; Bade to Scharping, 2 October 1944, BA, R 55/557; *Meldungen aus dem Reich*, vol. 14, 5447, 5602; *Goebbels Diaries*, ed. Lochner, 452; Daniel Lerner, *Psychological Warfare against Nazi Germany: The Sykewar Campaign, D-Day to VE-Day* (Cambridge, Mass., and London, 1971), 132–33; Ansgar Diller, *Rundfunkpolitik im Dritten Reich* (Munich, 1980), 383–84.
62. "Programmwoche vom 13.–19. Dezember 1942"; minutes of broadcast planning meetings of 6 January, 4 and 11 February, 17 June 1943, BA, R 55/696; Hinkel to

Goebbels, 25 January and 3 February 1943, BA, R 55/1254. See also Jay W. Baird, *The Mythical World of Nazi War Propaganda, 1939–1945* (Minneapolis, 1974), 175–90.

63. *Goebbels Diaries,* ed. Lochner, 358; *Podium der Unterhaltungsmusik,* 15 July 1943, 135; "Neuordnung der Sendegruppen zum 1. Oktober [1943]"; "Protokoll über die Zusammenberufung der Gruppenleiter beim Herrn Staatssekretär," 6 October 1943, BA, R 56I/41.

64. *Goebbels Diaries,* ed. Lochner, 589–90 (quotation); Haentzschel interview.

65. Naumann to Hinkel, 26 May 1944, BA, R 55/559; Diller, *Rundfunkpolitik,* 370; Haentzschel interview; and corr. BA, R 55/532, R 55/557, and R 56I/27 (1943–44).

66. Minutes of broadcast planning meeting of 20 September and 11 October 1944, BA, R 55/556; Fritzsche as quoted in Willi A. Boelcke, *Die Macht des Radios: Weltpolitik und Auslandsrundfunk, 1924–1976* (Frankfurt am Main, 1977), 509–10.

67. Minutes of broadcast planning meeting of 21 February 1945, BA, R 55/556.

68. Joseph Goebbels, *Tagebücher 1945: Die letzten Aufzeichnungen* (Hamburg, 1977), 479–91; idem, "Die Geschichte als Lehrmeisterin," *Reich,* 1 April 1945.

69. Haentzschel interview.

70. "Musikalische Feldpost," 15 November, 1 and 15 December 1942, 1 January 1943, PA Daniels; Hinkel to Fritzsche, 28 June 1943, BA, R 56I/41; Viera interview.

71. "Musikalische Feldpost," 1 June 1943, PA Daniels; Hinkel to Leiter Rundfunk, 18 February 1944; Chef vom Dienst, memorandum, 23 February 1944, BA, R 56I/41 (quotations); "Stellungnahme zu unserem Rundbrief vom 8.6.1944 an die bei der Wehrmacht stehenden Gefolgschaftsmitglieder der Reichsrundfunkgesellschaft," BA, R 55/557.

72. Minutes of broadcast planning meeting of 2 August 1944, BA, R 55/556 (quotation); Boelcke, *Macht,* 162, 167; [BBC] *Radio Times,* 12 January 1945, 1.

73. Leiter Rundfunk to Leiter M., 12 August 1944, BA, R 55/559; Gerhard Conrad, *Heinz Wehner: Eine Bio-Discographie* (Menden, 1989), 76–77; Conrad to author, 22 June 1990.

74. Litta Magnus-Andersen, *Lale Andersen—die Lili Marleen: Das Lebensbild einer Künstlerin* (Munich, 1981), 107–11; 137–40, 212–13, 233; Brocksieper interview; Boelcke, *Macht,* 234.

75. "Musikalische Feldpost," 15 November 1942, PA Daniels; Künneke, *Sing,* 69; Meyer and Haentzschel interviews; Heinz Schröter, *Unterhaltung für Millionen: Vom Wunschkonzert zur Schlagerparade* (Düsseldorf and Vienna, 1973), 116–18; private tape recording of remarks by Friedrich Meyer and Margot Hielscher, Munich, n.d., PA Meyer; memorandum regarding "Sender Belgrad mit Kurzwellensender Belgrad II," 20 June 1944, BA, R 55/559.

76. Hinkel to Goebbels, 10 January 1944, BA, R 55/1254; Boelcke, *Macht,* 230–31.

77. Passavant memorandum, 10 May 1944; Hinkel to OKW, 30 May 1944; OKW to Kommandeur der Prop. Abteilung Südost, 26 June 1944, all PA Meyer; Safronow to Rückert, 1 February 1945, BDC, RMK Meyer; private tape recording of remarks by Friedrich Meyer and Margot Hielscher, Munich, n.d., PA Meyer; Meyer interview.

78. Transcript of Roman interview for "Swing under the Swastika" (see n. 37); *Connecticut Jewish Ledger,* 20 June 1985; Horst J. P. Bergmeier, "Sie spielten um ihr Leben . . . ," in *Fox auf 78,* no. 3 (Spring 1987), 17.

79. "Musikalische Feldpost," 1 October 1942, 15 March 1943, PA Daniels; "Jazz-Mitteilungen" [1942–43], PA Schulz-Köhn; Jack de Graef, *De Swingperiode (1935–1947): Jazz in België* (Wettelijk, 1980), 31–32, 49, 59; Wolfgang Muth,

"Musik hinter Stacheldraht: Swing im Ghetto und KZ," in Polster, *"Swing Heil,"* 212; Schulz-Köhn as interviewed in *That's Jazz: Der Sound des 20. Jahrhunderts: Eine Ausstellung der Stadt Darmstadt . . . 29. Mai bis 28. August 1988* (Darmstadt, 1988), 339 (quotation); Al Livat as quoted in Mike Zwerin, *La Tristesse de Saint Louis: Swing under the Nazis* (New York, 1985), 40.

80. Charles Delaunay, *Django Reinhardt* (New York, 1981), 114–21; Zwerin, *La Tristesse,* 186–87.

81. Pernet, *Jazz . . . Discography,* 8, 143, 234–35, 243, 269, 318–19, 327, 335–36.

82. Kees Wouters, "Krieg dem Jazz! Holland vor und während der Nazi-Besetzung," in Polster, *"Swing Heil,"* 199–200; "Musikalische Feldpost," 1 December 1942, 15 January 1943, PA Daniels.

83. István Deák, *Beyond Nationalism: A Social and Political History of the Habsburg Officer Corps, 1848–1918* (New York and Oxford, 1990), 143; H. G. Adler, *Theresienstadt, 1941–1945: Das Antlitz einer Zwangsgemeinschaft* (Tübingen, 1955); *Connecticut Jewish Ledger,* 18 January 1979.

84. Eric T. Vogel, "Jazz in a Nazi Concentration Camp: Part 2," *Down Beat,* 21 December 1961, 16–17; transcript of Roman interview for "Swing under the Swastika" (see n. 37); Joža Karas, *Music in Terezín, 1941–1945* (New York, 1985), 147–52.

85. Josef Škvorecký, "I Like to Sing Hot: The Fate of Jazz in the *Protektorat Böhmen und Mähren,*" paper delivered at the Annual Meeting of the American Historical Association, Washington, D.C., December 1987 (quotation); Karas, *Music,* 149.

86. Schumann interview.

87. Video series, "Swing under the Swastika" (see n. 37).

88. Transcript of Roman interview for "Swing under the Swastika" (see n. 37).

89. Ibid., *Aufbau,* New York, 4 April 1947; Karas, *Music,* 154–56; Adler, *Theresienstadt,* 179–81; Schumann interview.

90. Schumann interview. Also see Antonin Truhlar, "Dem Vergessen geweiht: Czechoslowak Jazz Story," *Jazz-Podium* 4, no. 2 (1955), 12; he mentions only the father.

91. Eisenman to author, 1 October 1990 (quotation); Fania Fénelon, *Das Mädchenorchester in Auschwitz,* 4th ed. (Munich, 1984); enclosures with letters from Bozena Markiewicz to Yorkshire Television, (1987–88), PA Ackerman.

92. Bernd Naumann, *Auschwitz: Bericht über die Strafsache gegen Mulka und andere vor dem Schwurgericht Frankfurt* (Frankfurt am Main and Bonn, 1965), 24, 530.

93. "Musikalische Feldpost," 24 September 1941, PA Daniels; Daniels interview; Eisenman to author, 1 October 1990; enclosure with letter from Markiewicz to Yorkshire Television, 25 January 1988, PA Ackerman; Szymon Laks, *Music of Another World* (Evanstown, Ill., 1989), 79–82. Author's telephone conversation with Eisenman, Toronto, 27 March 1991.

94. "Piles of scores found by mr Wiktor Zielinski in Auschwitz just after the war, after liberation of the camp," appended to letter from Markiewicz to Yorkshire Television, 6 December 1987, PA Ackerman.

95. Schumann interview; transcript of Roman interview for "Swing under the Swastika" (see n. 37).

96. Transcript of Roman interview for "Swing under the Swastika" (see n. 37); Bergmeier, "Sie spielten," 19; Eric T. Vogel, "Jazz in a Nazi Concentration Camp: Part 3," *Down Beat,* 4 January 1962, 20–21.

97. For attempts at jazz in Buchenwald, see Wolfgang Schneider, *Kunst hinter*

Stacheldraht: Ein Beitrag zur Geschichte des antifaschistischen Widerstandskampfes (Weimar, 1973), 92, 96, 98–102.

98. *Schwarze Korps,* 16 March and 27 July 1944; Karl Blessinger, "Zur Frage der Unterhaltungsmusik," *Musik* 35 (1942), 67–68; *Podium der Unterhaltungsmusik,* 30 December 1942, 393–94; ibid., 15 February 1944, 263; *Musik im Kriege* 1 (1943), 105; Herbert Gerigk, "Die Jazzfrage als eine Rassenfrage," ibid. 2 (1944), 41–45; *Koralle,* 20 August 1944.

99. Carl Hannemann, "Der Jazz als Kampfmittel des Judentums and des Amerikanismus," *Musik in Jugend und Volk* 6 (1943), 57–59; HJ music chief Wolfgang Stumme's statements of 1944 reprinted in Joseph Wulf, ed., *Musik im Dritten Reich: Eine Dokumentation* (Reinbek, 1966), 395–96.

100. *Illustrierter Beobachter,* no. 26 (1944). See Thorsten Müller's trenchant analysis of this in *Deutsches Allgemeines Sonntagsblatt,* 6 December 1981.

101. Personal files Frotscher, BDC, RMK Frotscher; Gotthold Frotscher, "Amerikanismus in der Musik," *Musik in Jugend und Volk* 6 (1943), 94–97. Frotscher's pre-1933 biography is in *Deutsches Musiker-Lexikon,* ed. Erich H. Müller (Dresden, 1929), 374.

102. BDC, MF Merz; corr. (February–March 1944), BDC, RKK Merz.

103. *Amtliche Mitteilungen der Reichsmusikkammer,* 15 November 1942, 15 January 1943, 15 October 1943, BA, RD 33/2-2; *Podium der Unterhaltungsmusik,* 25 March 1943, 80; ibid., 19 August 1943, 144; *Musik im Kriege* 1 (1943), 37.

104. Elschlepp to Brocksieper, 15 September 1943; Brocksieper to Elschlepp, 17 September 1943, PA Brocksieper. See also "Musikalische Feldpost," 15 June 1943, PA Daniels; *Podium der Unterhaltungsmusik,* 19 August 1943, 145; *Musik im Kriege* 1 (1943), 74.

105. Raabe to Salb, 15 July 1943, BA, R 56I/41.

106. *Chemnitzer Zeitung,* 5 July 1943; *Musik im Kriege* 1 (1943), 75.

107. Hamel to Hadamovsky et al., 25 April 1944, BA, R 56I/92. See p. 104.

108. *Musik im Kriege* 2 (1944), 116.

109. *Schwarze Korps,* 27 July 1944. Also see Eric J. Hobsbawm's more general comments about women jazz singers as "underdogs," Francis Newton [Eric J. Hobsbawm], *The Jazz Scene* (New York, 1975), 275.

110. Personal file Hielscher (1939–42), BDC, RFK Hielscher; Söderbaum, *Nichts,* 180; *Fox auf 78,* no. 6 (Fall 1988), 10–11; Michael H. Kater, "Inside Nazis: The Goebbels Diaries, 1924–1941," *Canadian Journal of History* 25 (1990), 237; Hielscher interview; author's telephone conversation with Hielscher, Berlin, 25 May 1988.

111. Author's telephone conversation with Hielscher, Berlin, 25 May 1988 (quotation); Hinkel to Goebbels, 25 January 1943, BA, R 55/1254; minutes of broadcast planning meeting of 5 May 1943, BA, R 55/696; Peter Kreuder, *Schön war die Zeit: Musik ist mein Leben* (Munich, 1955), 311; Curt Riess, *Das gab's nur einmal: Die grosse Zeit des deutschen Films* (Vienna and Munich, 1977), vol. 4, 276; Hielscher interview.

112. Pfennig to Göring, 12 January 1938, BDC, RKK Leander; *Unterhaltungsmusik,* 9 February 1939, 164; Zarah Leander, *Es war so wunderbar! Mein Leben* (Hamburg, 1973), 164–72; Dietrich Schulz-Köhn, *Die Schallplatte auf dem Weltmarkt* (Berlin, 1940), 114–15; Francis Courtade and Pierre Cadars, *Geschichte des Films im Dritten Reich* (Munich and Vienna, 1975), 229–33.

113. See, e.g., "Musikalische Feldpost," 1 June 1943, PA Daniels.

114. *Meldungen aus dem Reich,* vol. 6, 1849, 2105; minutes of broadcast planning of 29 April 1942, BA, R 55/695; Peter to Goebbels, 17 June 1943, BA, R 56I/27 (quotation).

115. Hinkel to Schaub, 22 March 1943, BA, R 56I/93; Richartz to Hinkel, 31 December 1944 (and enclosure), BDC, RKK Leander; Leander, *Es war,* 173–75, 185–88, 208–9, 214–15.

116. RKK file card Serrano, BDC, RKK Serrano; Serrano interview; *Frankfurter Allgemeine Zeitung,* 14 August 1989. Goebbels mentions Serrano very positively in his diary of 13 December 1940: *Die Tagebücher von Joseph Goebbels: Sämtliche Fragmente,* ed. Elke Fröhlich (Munich, 1987), vol. 4, 431.

117. Serrano interview (quotation); Haentzschel interview; Kreuder, *Schön war die Zeit,* 280–81.

118. *Unterhaltungsmusik,* 6 February 1941, 119, 122; ibid., 20 February 1941, 186; Monika Sperr, ed., *Schlager: Das Grosse Schlager-Buch: Deutsche Schlager, 1800–Heute* (Munich, 1978), 210; Serrano interview.

119. Hanne-Lore Evers to Hans, 21 October 1940, PA Evers-Frauboes; "Musikalische Feldpost," beginning of February 1942, PA Daniels; Gunter and Lissy Lust, *. . . und sie drehen sich immer noch!* (Menden, 1984), 3; Jung interview.

120. Serrano interview; *Meldungen aus dem Reich,* vol. 6, 2849, 2105; ibid., vol. 8, 3011; minutes of broadcast planning meetings of 24 November 1941 and 24 September 1942, BA, R 55/695 and 696.

121. May to Staatssekretär, 4 November 1943, BA, R 55/125; RKK file card Serrano, BDC, RKK Serrano; Serrano interview.

122. Leander, *Es war,* 210–13, 216, 220–23; *Frankfurter Allgemeine Zeitung,* 14 August 1989.

123. Andersen sang with Heinz Wehner's jazz band in Oslo in July 1942 before the Belgian jazz orchestra of John Witjes became her regular band in 1943 (Conrad, *Wehner,* 71–72; Magnus-Andersen, *Lale Andersen,* 162).

124. Lale Andersen, *Leben mit einem Lied,* 5th ed. (Munich, 1981), 162–63; Magnus-Andersen, *Lale Andersen,* 9, 14, 33, 48, 101; Liebermann testimony, 13 October 1946; Lale Andersen, "Stellungnahme," 7 October 1946; Andersen, "Story of Life," [1946], BDC, RKK Andersen.

125. Hinkel to Goebbels, 8 November 1941, BA, R 55/1254; minutes of broadcast planning meeting of 2 December 1941, BA, R 55/695; Magnus-Andersen, *Lale Andersen,* 167–68.

126. Personal file Lale Andersen (1942–43), BDC, RKK Andersen; minutes of broadcast planning meeting of 16 September 1942, BA, R 55/696; Magnus-Andersen, *Lale Andersen,* 169, 177–80, 189, 192, 195–98.

127. Minutes of broadcast planning meeting of 5 May 1943, BA, R 55/696; May to Staatssekretär, 4 November 1943, BA, R 55/125; personal file Andersen (1943), BDC, RKK Andersen; Magnus-Andersen, *Lale Andersen,* 201–21.

128. Vogel and Viera interviews; Wolfgang Borchert, *Das Gesamtwerk* (Hamburg, 1949), 256–57.

129. Künneke, *Sing,* 66–78.

130. Friedländer-Reimann interview; Friedländer-Reimann to author, 27 January 1989; protocol of compensation suit, Friedländer-Reimann vs. Federal Republic of Germany, Frankfurt am Main, 22 June 1973, PA Friedländer-Reimann; BDC, MF Wackerbarth; RMK to Gestapo Hamburg, 19 June 1944; Gestapo Hamburg to RMK president, 5 July 1944, BDC, RMK Heinz-Wilhelm Sandberg.

131. *Amtliche Mitteilungen der Reichskulturkammer,* 15 October 1943, BA, RD 33/2-2;

corr. regarding Kreuder (April–December 1943), BA, R 55/126; Hinkel to Tiessler, 4 May 1944, BDC, RMK Kreuder; Klagemann and Brocksieper interviews.

132. As was his popular ditty, "In the bathtub, I am the captain," which extolled the kind of individualism frowned on by the Nazis.

133. *Skizzen,* August–September 1937, 18; ibid., October 1939, 17; Lange, *Jazz in Deutschland,* 80; Künneke, *Sing,* 47; Horst J. P. Bergmeier and Rainer Lotz, *Billy Bartholomew: Bio-Discography* (Menden, 1985), 50; interviews with Zimmerle, Brocksieper, and Molkenbur-Schönfelder.

134. Igelhoff corr. (1942–44) BA, R 55/556 and 696; Igelhoff corr. (1944–45) BA, RKK Igelhoff.

135. Friedländer-Reimann interview (quotation); Friedländer-Reimann to author, 27 January 1989; personal file Heinz-Wilhelm Sandberg (1944), BDC, RMK Sandberg.

136. Memorandum Rückert, 20 September 1943, BA, R 56I/34; interviews with Molkenbur-Schönfelder, Haentzschel, and Dobschinski.

137. According to Midow to RMK president, 14 September 1943, BDC, RMK Karl Hohenberger.

138. Personal file Karl Hohenberger, BDC, RMK Karl Hohenberger; Molkenbur-Schönfelder and Haentzschel interviews.

139. Wallmeyer to RMK Berlin, 20 February 1940, BDC, RMK Karl Hohenberger.

140. Bessunger to author, 1 August 1989 and 10 January 1990 (quotation).

141. Pabst, "Nazi-'Kultur,' " 138.

142. Madlung-Shelton interview; transcript of Madlung-Shelton interview for "Swing under the Swastika" (see n. 37); concentration camp letter by Inga Madlung to "Ihr Lieben," May 1943, PA Ackerman.

143. Madlung-Shelton interview; transcript of Madlung-Shelton interview for "Swing under the Swastika" (see n. 37); Nielsen-Rönn interview.

144. Thorsten Müller, "Synopsis aus 'Veränderungsberichte (Zu- und Abgänge) des Polizeigefängnisses Fuhlsbüttel' für die Zeit vom 2.1.1941 bis zum 7. Mai 1943," PA Scheel; Scheel interview.

145. Panagopoulos interview.

146. Hirschfeld interview; Neuengamme commandant to Betty Hirschfeld, 3 February 1945, PA Hirschfeld.

147. Rainer Pohl, " 'Das gesunde Volksempfinden ist gegen Dad und Jo': Zur Verfolgung der Hamburger 'Swing-Jugend' im Zweiten Weltkrieg," in *Verachtet—verfolgt—vernichtet: Zu den "vergessenen" Opfern des NS-Regimes* (Hamburg, 1986), 43. As a British citizen, Kaki Georgiadis in January 1943 was sent from Fuhlsbüttel concentration camp to various internment camps where he survived the war (Harry [Georgiadis] Stephens, "Swing Threatens Third Reich," unpublished ms., Beccles [Suffolk], 1988, 119–49).

148. SS-Reichssicherheitshauptamt to Kümmerlein, 6 September 1944, BA, R 22/1191.

149. Interviews with Vogel, Engel, and Scheel; Scheel to author, 7 April 1988, and in private conversation, Mississauga, 10 April 1991.

150. Müller interview; transcript of Müller interview for "Swing under the Swastika" (see n. 37); Thorsten Müller, "Ich war ein Widerstand," in Richard Löwenthal and Patrik von zur Mühlen, eds., *Widerstand und Verweigerung in Deutschland, 1933 bis 1945* (Berlin and Bonn, 1982), 202–10; Christian Petry, *Studenten aufs Schafott: Die Weisse Rose und ihr Scheitern* (Munich, 1968); Angela Bottin, "Hans Leipelt, 23, cand. mort.," *Deutsches Allgemeines Sonntagsblatt,* 27 January 1985, 14.

151. Ursel Hochmuth and Gertrud Meyer, *Streiflichter aus dem Hamburger Widerstand, 1933–1945: Berichte und Dokumente* (Frankfurt am Main, 1969), 387–421; Angela

Bottin and Hendrik van den Bussche, "Opposition und Widerstand," in Hendrik van den Bussche, ed., *Medizinische Wissenschaft im "Dritten Reich": Kontinuität, Anpassung und Opposition an der Hamburger Medizinischen Fakultät* (Berlin and Hamburg, 1989), 405.

152. Reinhardt as quoted in Müller interview.

153. Ibid.; Müller, "Ich war"; Hochmuth and Meyer, *Streiflichter*, 413–21.

154. Ian Kershaw, *Popular Opinion and Political Dissent in the Third Reich: Bavaria, 1933–1945* (Oxford, 1983), 279–372; Michael H. Kater, *The Nazi Party: A Social Profile of Members and Leaders, 1919–1945* (Cambridge, Mass., 1983), 116–38, 213–33; Gerhard Rempel, *Hitler's Children: The Hitler Youth and the SS* (Chapel Hill and London, 1989).

155. Wunderlich interview (quotation); *Walter *1927 †1945 an der Ostfront: Leben und Lebensbedingungen eines Frankfurter Jungen im III. Reich*, Cornelia Rühlig and Jürgen Steen, eds. (Frankfurt am Main, 1983), 116–45; Koleczek interview; Schörken, *Luftwaffenhelfer*, 112, 155–56, 160, 179–80, 199, 212–14; Klaus Granzow, *Tagebuch eine Hitlerjungen, 1943–1945* (Bremen, 1965), 85–86, 111; Kempowski, *Tadellöser*, 340–44, 351, 355, 360–61, 395–400, 406–15; Muth, "Wir," 209.

156. Daniels interview.

157. Zimmerle interview. On the Wehrmacht's severe inner disciplinarian measures at this time, see Omer Bartov, *Hitler's Army: Soldiers, Nazis, and War in the Third Reich* (New York and Oxford, 1991), 96–101.

158. "Fragebogen" Berendt, 20 April 1943, BDC, RKK Berendt; Berendt interview.

159. Frommann to Michaelis, 2 September 1943, PA Michaelis (quotation); Michaelis interview. For a flattering picture of occupied Paris for purposes of Goebbels's propaganda, see Franz Rodens, "Paris 1943: Eindrücke dieses Sommers," *Reich*, 1 August 1943.

160. See *Rundfunkarchiv* 16 (October–December 1943), 207–8; ibid. 17 (April–September 1944), 67.

161. Boas interview; transcript of Boas interview for "Swing under the Swastika" (see n. 37).

162. Interviews with Freichel, Jung, Mangelsdorff, Bohländer, and Blüthner; transcript of Merkel interview for "Swing under the Swastika" (see n. 37); Hans Otto Jung's liner notes for *Swing under the Nazis* (1986), Harlequin HQ 2051, and the selections on that record (1942–44); photograph in Michael H. Kater, "Forbidden Fruit? Jazz in the Third Reich," *American Historical Review* 94 (1989), 40.

163. Mangelsdorff interview.

164. [Hans Otto Jung], "Teddy Wilson," [1943], PA Jung; interviews with Freichel, Jung, and Mangelsdorff; transcript of Lippmann interview for "Swing under the Swastika" (see n. 37); Richard W. Fogg, "Jazz under the Nazis," in *Down Beat Music '66: 11th Yearbook* (Chicago, 1966), 98.

165. See Horst Lippmann, "Die Bilanz," "Jazz-Club News," 30 September 1945, PA Jung.

166. Berk and Bohländer interviews.

167. Jung as quoted in *Stars and Stripes*, 8 May 1985; Jung interview.

168. Pick and Blüthner interviews.

169. Blüthner interview. Blüthner regularly got together with the Swede Folke Johnson and the Belgian "Coco" Collignon, as well as Pick (Blüthner, "Geschichte des Hot-Club Berlin," 14 October 1947, PA Blüthner). Former Woody Herman trombonist Mike Zwerin's "bitchy" (his own term) characterization of Blüthner as innocuous is

not only unkind, but, for lack of proper research, inaccurate and, whatever else the merits of this book may be, is yet another indicator of the overall superficiality that characterizes this impressionistic history of swing in Nazi Germany (*La Tristesse*, 43).

170. Pick interview; Blüthner interview (quotation); "Jazz-Mitteilungen," [1942–43], PA Schulz-Köhn.

171. Blüthner and Schulz-Köhn interviews; Schulz-Köhn to author, 20 July 1987.

172. Schulz-Köhn as interviewed in *That's Jazz*, 336, 339; Schulz-Köhn interview; Schulz-Köhn to author, 8 January 1989. The various details Zwerin gives about Schulz-Köhn, including his activities in France (*La Tristesse*, 31–42), are partially distorted, as are many facts in the book (such as "all jazz musicians [in Germany] were German Jews," 41), and were corrected, for my benefit, by Schulz-Köhn himself (letter of 20 July 1987), and in my interviews with his Berlin and Frankfurt friends. See the photograph in this book, showing Schulz-Köhn outside a Paris club near the Place Pigalle.

173. Schulz-Köhn interview; Schulz-Köhn as interviewed in *That's Jazz*, 340–41; notes regarding talk at Radio Nîmes, [June 1943]; Jean Vuloudjiou (?) to Schulz-Köhn, 19 July 1959, both docs. PA Schulz-Köhn.

174. The exact date of the conversation cannot be determined any more. According to Bohländer, it took place in March 1943, after the fall of Stalingrad. Jung thinks it was closer to the end of 1943 (Jung and Bohländer interviews; Jung to author, [December 1987]; Schulz-Köhn to author, 3 July 1987 and 8 January 1989).

175. Schulz-Köhn interview (quotations); *Stars and Stripes*, 4 March 1945. See also Collie Small, "100,000 Nazi Clowns on the Zany Front," *Saturday Evening Post*, 21 April 1945, 18–19, 89–91.

176. Schulz-Köhn interview; Schulz-Köhn as interviewed in *That's Jazz*, 341; Marshall W. Stearns, *The Story of Jazz* (New York, 1957), 285.

Epilogue

1. Evers-Frauboes to author, [16 July 1988].

2. "Jazz-Club News," October–November 1945, PA Jung.

3. Teddy Stauffer, *Forever Is a Hell of a Long Time: An Autobiography* (Chicago, 1976), 298.

4. Transcript of Madlung-Shelton interview for British video series, "Swing under the Swastika," Yorkshire Television, London, 1988.

Primary Sources

Archival and Oral Documents

BA	Bundesarchiv Koblenz
	NS 19/neu, 219
	R 22/1176, 1177, 1191
	R 55/125, 126, 129, 200, 242/1, 532, 556, 557, 559, 695, 696, 1254
	R 56I/27, 34, 37, 41, 82, 83, 84, 85, 92, 93
	R 59I/90
	R 78/192, 622, 694, 902, 909, 913, 1000a, 1162
	RD 33/2-1
	RD 33/2-2
BDC	Berlin Document Center
	Library, Rundfunk 62
	MF
	Research
	RFK
	RKK
	RMK
	RSK
	SS
	various personal files
DIA	BBC Data Inquiry Service Archive, London
	AEF Programs as Broadcast
	BEF Programs as Broadcast
	[British] Forces Programs as Broadcast
Goethe Institute, Toronto	Broadcast series "Jazz in Germany: A Survey of Hot Dance, Swing and Traditional Jazz in Germany, 1924 to Present," produced for and broadcast on KALW FM, San Francisco, by Dave Radlauer and Ray Taubert, n.d.

IfZ	Institut für Zeitgeschichte München
	Ma 667/5484201–02
NHSA	Niedersächsisches Hauptstaatsarchiv Hannover
	Hann. 122a, X, I, 79
SAB	Staatsarchiv Bremen
	4, 65, II E 3a 1.1
	4, 65, II A 9a 13
SAH	Staatsarchiv Hamburg
	Amtsgericht Hamburg, Abtlg. Vormundschaftswesen, 115
	XI, R 1886, 1653 Rönn
	Jugendbehörde I, 343 c
	Oberschulbehörde VI, 2 F VIII a 2/3/1
	Oberschulbehörde VI, 2 F VIII a 2/3/2
	Oberschulbehörde VI, 2 F VIII a 2/40/1
SAM	Staatsarchiv München
	NSDAP/31

Correspondence

Becke, Herbert, Düsseldorf (Germany)
Bessunger, Hanns-Joachim [H. John], Hampton Bays, N.Y. (United States)
Blüthner, Hans, Hemsbach (Germany)
Conrad, Gerhard, Menden (Germany)
Daniels, Werner, Düsseldorf (Germany)
Eisenman, Henryk [Henry], Toronto (Canada)
Friedländer-Reimann, Margot, Berlin (Germany)
Hipp, Jutta, Sunnyside, N.Y. (United States)
Jung, Dr. Hans Otto, Rüdesheim/Rhein (Germany)
Korseck, Dr. Hilde, Berlin (Germany)
Lotz, Dr. Rainer E., Bonn (Germany)
Michaelis, Kurt, Dreieich (Germany)
Molkenbur-Schönfelder, Gertie, Lindau/Bodensee (Germany)
Moser, Max, Rolandia (Brazil)
Petrushka, Shabtai, Jerusalem (Israel)
Pointon, Michael, London (United Kingdom)
Reynolds, Professor Clark, Charleston, S.C. (United States)
Scheel, Hans-Joachim, Mississauga (Canada)
Schulz-Köhn, Professor Dr. Dietrich, Erftstadt (Germany)
Stephens, Harry, Beccles, Suffolk (United Kingdom)
Susat, Jürgen W., Hamburg (Germany)

Private Archives

Ackerman, Roy, London (United Kingdom)
Adam, Lutz, Berlin (Germany)
Becke, Herbert, Düsseldorf (Germany)
Blüthner, Hans, Hemsbach (Germany)
Brocksieper, Freddie, Munich (Germany)
Daniels, Werner, Düsseldorf (Germany)

Evers-Frauboes, Hanne-Lore, Hamburg (Germany)
Friedländer-Reimann, Margot, Berlin (Germany)
Geisel, Eike, Berlin (Germany)
Hirschfeld, Hans, Hamburg (Germany)
Jung, Dr. Hans Otto, Rüdesheim/Rhein (Germany)
Korseck, Dr. Hilde, Berlin (Germany)
Lotz, Dr. Rainer E., Bonn (Germany)
Meyer, Friedrich, Munich (Germany)
Michaelis, Kurt, Dreieich (Germany)
Molkenbur-Schönfelder, Gertie, Lindau/Bodensee (Germany)
Petrushka, Shabtai, Jerusalem (Israel)
Pointon, Michael, London (United Kingdom)
Scheel, Hans-Joachim, Mississauga (Canada)
Schulz-Köhn, Professor Dr. Dietrich, Erftstadt (Germany)
Zacharias, Helmut, Munich (Germany) and Ascona (Switzerland)
Zimmerle, Dieter, Stuttgart (Germany)

Recorded Interviews

Angeli, Primo, Munich, in Munich (Germany), 3 June 1988
Berendt, Professor Joachim Ernst, Baden-Baden, in Kampen/Sylt (Germany), 15 June
    1988
Berk, Willi, Frankfurt am Main, in Rüdesheim/Rhein (Germany), 26 June 1988
Blüthner, Hans, Hemsbach, in Hemsbach (Germany), 5 June 1987
Boas, Günter, Cappenberg, in Cappenberg (Germany), 22 June 1988
Boas, Leonore, Cappenberg, in Cappenberg (Germany), 22 June 1988
Bohländer, Carlo, Frankfurt am Main, in Frankfurt am Main (Germany), 7 June 1987
Brocksieper, Freddie, Munich, in Munich (Germany), 25–29 and 31 May 1987
Daniels, Werner, Düsseldorf, in Badenweiler (Germany), 29 June 1988
Dobschinski, Walter, Berlin, in Berlin (Germany), 9 May 1987
Engel, Hans, Mamaroneck, N.Y., in Mamaroneck (United States), 5 March 1988
Evers-Frauboes, Hanne-Lore, Hamburg, in Hamburg (Germany), 18 June 1988
Freichel, Louis, Frankfurt am Main, in Rüdesheim/Rhein (Germany), 26 June 1988
Friedländer-Reimann, Margot, Berlin, in Berlin (Germany), 22 May 1989
Haentzschel, Georg, Cologne, in Cologne (Germany), 1 October 1988
Hartwig, Hajo [Harald], New York, in New York (United States), 12 April 1988
Hielscher, Margot, Munich, in Munich (Germany), 4 June 1988
Hirschfeld, Hans, Hamburg, in Hamburg (Germany), 19 June 1988
Jung, Dr. Hans Otto, Rüdesheim/Rhein, in Rüdesheim/Rhein (Germany), 5 June 1987
    and 27 June 1988, and in Toronto (Canada), 23 January 1988
Klagemann, Hans, Munich, in Munich (Germany), 24 May 1987
Koleczek, Herbert, Rüdesheim/Rhein, in Rüdesheim/Rhein (Germany), 25 June 1988
Korseck, Dr. Hilde, Berlin, in Berlin (Germany), 27 May 1988
Lehn, Erwin, Stuttgart, in Stuttgart (Germany), 23 June 1986
Madlung-Shelton, Inga, London, in London (United Kingdom), 9 May 1988
Mangelsdorff, Emil, Frankfurt am Main, in Munich (Germany), 30 May 1987
Meyer, Friedrich, Munich, in Munich (Germany), 4 June 1988
Michaelis, Kurt, Dreieich, in Dreieich (Germany), 23 June 1988
Molkenbur-Schönfelder, Gertie, Lindau/Bodensee, in Lindau/Bodensee (Germany), 2
    June 1988

Müller, Thorsten, Hamburg, in Hamburg (Germany), 13 and 16 June 1988

Nielsen-Rönn, Ursula, Hamburg, in Hamburg (Germany), 20 June 1988

Panagopoulos, Andreas, Hamburg, in Hamburg (Germany), 16 June 1988

Pick, Gerd Peter, Toronto, in Toronto (Canada), 10 July 1987

Scheel, Hans-Joachim, Mississauga, in Mississauga (Canada), 29 March 1988

Schulz-Köhn, Professor Dr. Dietrich (Erftstadt), in Baden-Baden (Germany), 4 and 5
    September 1986

Schulz-Reichel, Fritz, Berlin, in Berlin (Germany), 1 May 1987

Schumann, Coco, Berlin, in Berlin (Germany), 18 May 1988

Serrano, Rosita, Hohenroda, in Hohenroda (Germany), 17 June 1988

Tabor, Charly, Munich, in Munich (Germany), 28 May 1987

Viera, Professor Joe, Munich, in Munich (Germany), 16 June 1986 and 31 May 1987

Vogel, Robert, Hamburg, in Hamburg (Germany), 21 June 1988

Wunderlich, Werner, Baden-Baden, in Baden-Baden (Germany), 5 September 1986

Zacharias, Helmut, Munich and Ascona, in Ascona (Switzerland), 1 July 1988

Zimmerle, Dieter, Stuttgart, in Stuttgart (Germany), 24 June 1986

Index

0